EDUCATING CLERGY

EDUCATING CLERGY

Teaching Practices and Pastoral Imagination

Charles R. Foster

Lisa E. Dahill

Lawrence A. Golemon

Barbara Wang Tolentino

o

Foreword by
Lee S. Shulman

Introduction by
William M. Sullivan

CARNEGIE Y CENTENNIAL
1905 — 2005

JOSSEY-BASS
A Wiley Imprint
www.josseybass.com

Published by Jossey-Bass
A Wiley Imprint
989 Market Street, San Francisco, CA 94103-1741   www.josseybass.com

Jossey-Bass books and products are available through most bookstores. To contact Jossey-Bass directly call our Customer Care Department within the U.S. at 800-956-7739, outside the U.S. at 317-572-3986, or fax 317-572-4002.

Jossey-Bass also publishes its books in a variety of electronic formats. Some content that appears in print may not be available in electronic books.

Library of Congress Cataloging-in-Publication Data
Educating clergy : teaching practices and pastoral imagination /
    Charles R. Foster ... [et al.] ; foreword by Lee S. Shulman ; intro-
duction by William M. Sullivan. — 1st ed.
       p. cm.
    Includes bibliographical references and index.
    ISBN 0-7879-7744-6 (alk. paper)
    1. Theology—Study and teaching. 2. Clergy—Training of. 3. Pas-
toral theology.   I. Foster, Charles R., 1937-   .
    BV4020.E38 2005
    230'.071'1—dc22   2005024316

Printed in the United States of America
FIRST EDITION
HB Printing   10 9 8 7 6 5 4 3 2 1

CONTENTS

PART FOUR

The Preparation for the Professions Series

The Preparation for the Professions Series reports the results of The Carnegie Foundation for the Advancement of Teaching's Preparation for the Professions Program, a comparative study of professional education in medicine, nursing, law, engineering, and the preparation of the clergy.

Forthcoming:
Educating Engineers
Educating Lawyers
Educating Nurses
Educating Physicians

FOREWORD

"YOU'RE STUDYING THE EDUCATION OF CLERGY?" The question is asked in an incredulous tone. It never fails. Whenever I am invited to describe the research activities of the Carnegie Foundation, I always recite our decade-long program of studies on the education of professionals. As I go down the list, my companions nod politely as I intone the name of each profession: lawyers, engineers, teachers, clergy . . . The nod suddenly becomes a sharply focused act of attention: "You're studying the education of clergy?" Somehow, while waiting for me to list physicians, nurses, accountants, and the other usual suspects, the inclusion of clergy jolts my listeners into a rapt state of interest. Their response combines equal parts fascination and disbelief.

Why does the inclusion of ministers, priests, and rabbis among the learned professions so regularly elicit a strong reaction? Why is the preparation of the spiritual leaders of our churches and synagogues so intriguing? It's pretty clear that although ministers, priests, and rabbis certainly fall into the category of "professional" in our society, they are also perceived as a very different kind of professional. Yes, their calling does require extended academic preparation, normally at the graduate level. Nevertheless, it is clearly a "calling" in ways that we do not normally ascribe to law, engineering, or radiology. Moreover, unlike the other professions, I get a sense that the education of clergy is expected be more veiled, more mysterious, than the preparation of other professionals.

Perhaps the surprise also reflects some general doubt over whether it is proper to consider clergy to be professionals at all. A professional is someone who provides service for a fee. We entrust our health, our welfare, our system of justice, and the structural integrity of our office towers to professionals. We trust them to perform responsibly, and in return we pay them generously. But our rabbis, priests, and pastors are "called" to their vocations in a very special way. To them we entrust our very souls. How can we compare our souls, our destinies, and our salvation to our bridges, contracts, and gall bladders?

A number of years ago, long before I joined the Carnegie Foundation, I was visiting the Jewish Theological Seminary in New York as a member of one of their educational advisory boards. I was a yeshiva student for several years during my adolescence, and there had been a time when I had seriously considered studying at JTS. I knew a number of the faculty members rather well. As I sat eating lunch with Ismar Schorsch, then provost of the institution, he asked for some advice. Rabbi Schorsch, an eminent historian who would soon become chancellor of the seminary, made an observation much like this one:

> Rabbinical students at JTS spend most of their five or six years of study pretty much the way many centuries of past rabbis have: immersed in learning Talmud, the legal codes, the Bible and its many commentaries, midrash, Hebrew, Aramaic, history, theology, and the like. Relatively speaking, far less time is devoted to homiletics, liturgy, and pastoral care, much less supervised practical experience. When they complete those studies, they are ordained as rabbis. Most then go out and become congregational leaders all over the country. Within a year or two, I begin hearing back from them. They complain that we didn't teach them what they really needed for their work. What they really needed was an MBA, a master's degree in counseling, and perhaps a few electives in reading architectural drawings and negotiating with contractors. Did we really need to spend so much time on Talmud? I try to explain that, had they not become through study of the "holy vessels" of the tradition, their congregants would not have considered them entitled to play those other roles. How does a professional school prepare its students both for the roles they must play and for the jobs they must perform?

I've subsequently told that story many times because it seems to exemplify one of the essential dilemmas of all preparation for the professions. How does a professional school prepare its students both for the specific skills needed to perform the functions they must enact, while also preparing them to become the kinds of human beings—morally, experientially, intellectually—to whom others are ready to entrust the performance of those functions? The skills of blessing a newborn child in the synagogue or of conducting the Eucharist ceremonies in a church are not technically complex. Consoling a mourning family or speaking out critically about the moral failings of political leaders are activities regularly pursued by therapists and journalists. But what kind of person, educated in which ways and formed under what circumstances, is *entitled* to offer those blessings or perform that ritual or offer consolation or social criticism in the name of God? As Rabbi Schorsch observed, the special role of a pastor is embodied in his or her very being, in the sense that they have been formed—by their education and their calling—into "holy vessels" in the Jewish tradition, whose development and accomplishments entitle them to play their very special spiritual role. If the education of clergy is a proper example of professional education, and I argue that it is, then the experience of theological education is one from which we will have much to learn.

Why is The Carnegie Foundation for the Advancement of Teaching studying the education of clergy? Since 1908, the Foundation has been investigating the character and quality of professional education in America. When Henry Pritchett, the first president of the Foundation, invited Abraham Flexner to lead a study of medical education, he initiated nearly a century of inquiry into the academic preparation of those professionals whose services are highly valued in our society. From medicine to teaching, and from engineering to law and architecture, the Carnegie Foundation became famous for its studies of education in the professions. But never in its century-long history had it included among those professions the education of clergy. When, in 1998, we began the present ten-year program of comparative research on the education of professionals, with special attention to the processes of teaching, learning, assessment, and curriculum, we chose from the very beginning to include theological education among those professions.

Our first partner in these studies of professional education was the Atlantic Philanthropies. At the beginning of this work, they were still operating anonymously, and we were not permitted to acknowledge their role as a partner. They have since changed that policy, and it is a great pleasure to acknowledge their contribution to this effort. As we prepared to address the specific challenge of clergy education, we approached the Lilly Endowment and its long-time program officer, Craig Dykstra, with the proposal that they too join us in this initiative. I still remember vividly the first meeting with Dr. Dykstra, in which he expressed enthusiasm for the work and offered us the concept of "pastoral imagination" that has animated this inquiry from the very beginning.

At the heart of this volume is the authors' claim that there are four signature pedagogies of theological education: pedagogies of interpretation, pedagogies of formation, pedagogies of contextualization, and pedagogies of performance. Thus, the teachers of clergy must instruct their students in the disciplined analysis of sacred texts; in the formation of their pastoral identities, dispositions, and values; in the understanding of the complex social, political, personal, and congregational conditions that surround them; and in the skills of preacher, counselor, liturgist, and leader through which they exercise their pastoral, priestly, and rabbinical responsibilities.

These four pedagogies are not limited to the education of clergy, however. They are powerful instances of the kinds of teaching needed in every profession. Every profession rests on a body of text, whether philosophical, scientific, mathematical, or literary. Every profession expects that those who master those texts also are formed into women and men of integrity who can be trusted to use their knowledge and skill in the responsible service of others. Every profession expects its members to serve society by understanding critically the nature of the society it is called upon to serve, and to be more than slavish responders to the demands of their clients. And every profession rests on a body of skilled practice without which neither theory nor character is sufficient. Thus pedagogies of interpretation, formation, contextualization, and performance will reappear in our future studies of other professions, often under different names, but predictably with similar functions. To be a professional requires understanding, character, and practical skill that can be employed with sensitivity to the conditions and contexts within which one works. This is no small challenge.

When we visited Howard University's Divinity School during the site-visit portion of this project, we met a number of remarkable faculty members and students. Among the faculty members, two—Henry Ferry and Evans Crawford—left me with lovely lessons with which I conclude this Foreword.

Professor Henry Ferry has taught church history at Howard for many years. During a faculty focus group at the end of our visit, we asked the faculty members to discuss their general perspectives on teaching their subjects to seminary students. Professor Ferry volunteered that he always opened his class on church history by introducing his students to the "Four H's," which he felt would be useful to them, not only in the study of history, but in their careers as pastors more generally. The first H is honesty, the intellectual attitude with which they must always approach the study of history, even when it becomes awkward or inconvenient. The second H is humility, the growing recognition of the unavoidable limitations of their understanding and other capacities. The third H is humor. The combined impact of honesty and humility can be quite daunting and even depressing unless one can develop the ability to step back and see the humor in one's situation and circumstances. The final H is hope. Just in case the aggregate impact of honesty, humility, and humor turns into

despair, these necessary virtues must always be tempered by hope, the special feelings that faith and commitment can engender.

I trust that the research reported in this volume reflects those four
virtues. It honestly and straightforwardly recounts what we learned in our
extensive inquiries into seminary education. Some of those accounts are
laudatory, some critical, and many exploratory and filled with questions
and wonder. The report also repeatedly acknowledges its own limitations,
the limits within which any single study can aspire to offer a critical appreciation and analysis of the education of clergy across so many denominations and circumstances. There is humor in these accounts, though
more often a sense of irony in descriptions of the difficult conditions under
which today's clergy and their educators typically labor. Finally, there is
an abiding sense of hope, of professions as callings and of pastors as
agents of change and community leaders on whose shoulders our society
lays serious burdens and expectations.

Dr. Evans Crawford is the legendary Professor of Preaching at Howard,
as much a legend as a preacher himself and a teacher of homiletics. He
characterizes homiletics as creating connections between the careful study
and inspired appreciation of the sacred texts with the responsibility to
engage in prophetic ministry—the critical appraisal of the social, political, and communal conditions that surround one's congregation and its
members—in a theologically authentic manner. This conjunction of the
analytic, the prophetic, and the theological embodied in a highly skilled
performance of preaching is remarkably reminiscent of our earliest discussions with Craig Dykstra of the complex interactions among the features of pastoral imagination.

As I read the superb accounts and analyses of our studies of theological education in *Educating Clergy*, I was moved to express my appreciation for the impressive work captured in this volume. I was reminded of
the preaching evaluation scale that Evans Crawford describes in his book
The Hum, an introduction to the call and response style of preaching in
the black church. Crawford describes a five-point rating scale for evaluating student sermons, which itself employs the responses that churchgo-
ers might offer to sermons of increasing quality, from the least competent
to the most fully realized:

1. "Help 'em Lord"
2. "Well. . ."
3. "That's all right"
4. "Amen!"
5. "Glory Hallelujah"

Crawford observes that every preacher hopes to develop the homiletic gift of moving the congregation from "Help 'em Lord" to "Amen" and "Glory Hallelujah" because every preacher strives to awaken in others "a sense of wonder and Thanksgiving."

To this volume, the first of our studies of professional education to be published, and to its authors Chuck Foster, Lisa Dahill, Larry Golemon, and Barbara Tolentino, I call out both "Amen" and Glory Hallelujah." I believe that this work speaks both to theological educators and to the much larger community of educators in the professions and the liberal arts who are committed to teach their students to profess their under-standings, their skills, and their hearts with responsibility and integrity.

Stanford, California   LEE S. SHULMAN
September 2005

ACKNOWLEDGMENTS

ALTHOUGH THE AUTHORS take full responsibility for this report, this study of clergy education has been a collaborative effort from the beginning. The project originated in conversations among Lee Shulman, William Sullivan, Anne Colby, Thomas Ehrlich, and John Barcroft at The Carnegie Foundation for the Advancement of Teaching, as a part of the Program for the Preparation of the Professions directed by Sullivan and Colby. Their deliberations expanded to include other members of the Foundation staff—Rose Asera, Sheri Sheppard, Judith Wegner, and Johanna Wilson—and consultants concerned specifically with the educational preparation of clergy: Barbara Wheeler (Auburn Theological Seminary), Daniel Aleshire (Association of Theological Schools), Craig Dykstra (Lilly Endowment, Inc.), Daniel Gordis (Mandel Foundation), David Kelsey (Yale Divinity School), Jeremiah McCarthy (St. John's Seminary), Joseph P. Daoust (Jesuit School of Theology), Arnold Eisen (Stanford University), Dennis Tierney (California Commission on Teacher Credentialing), Jeffrey Solomon (Harvard University), and Wendy Rosov (then a doctoral student at Stanford University). They encouraged the development of a grant proposal to request funding for the study. The study itself was made possible by the sponsorship of the Carnegie Foundation with funding from the Lilly Endowment, Inc., and Atlantic Philanthropies.

The pattern of collaborative consultation initiated in the planning of the project was continued with an advisory committee that included Norman Cohen (Hebrew Union College), Arthur Holder (Graduate Theological Union), Willie Jennings (Duke University Divinity School), Diane Kennedy (then with Aquinas Institute of Theology and now with Dominican University), Daisy Machado (Brite Divinity School), Richard Mouw (Fuller Theological Seminary), Kevin O'Neil (Washington Theological Seminary), Wendy Rosov (Berman Center for Research and Evaluation in Jewish Education), Jack Seymour (Garrett-Evangelical Theological Seminary), and Edward Wimberly (Interdenominational Theological Seminary). Meeting twice during the study, the members of this group critiqued research protocols, explored findings, and reviewed early drafts of the report.

Members of the Carnegie Foundation staff contributed to the project in major ways—as resource persons for our questions; consultants to our efforts to construct survey instruments, organize data, and use the Web; and participants in brown-bag lunches at which we reported on research in progress. William Sullivan and Anne Colby, as directors of the Preparation for the Professions Program, provided steady guidance. Lloyd Bond, Anne Colby, Mary Huber, Pat Hutchings, Lee Shulman, William Sullivan, and Pam Grossman (a faculty member at Stanford University and director of a related Carnegie research project) joined the research team on site visits, adding insights to our observations from many academic disciplines. Richard Gale was a primary consultant on performance practices. Central to the whole enterprise were Lindsay Turner and Megan Mills, who supervised the records and managed the arrangements associated with the study. In addition, Mary Moore and Michael Peterson of the Graduate Theological Union library staff at the San Francisco Theological Seminary provided invaluable assistance in making books and other resources available to us.

Many people provided important consultation during the course of the project, notably Craig Dykstra and John Wimmer of the Lilly Endowment; Barbara Wheeler and Sharon Miller of Auburn Theological Seminary; Dan Aleshire of the Association of Theological Schools; Katarina Schuth of The Saint Paul Seminary School of Divinity, University of St. Thomas; and members of the Advisory Committee of the Wabash Center for Teaching and Learning in Theology and Religion—Lucinda Huffaker, Paul Myhre, Tom Pearson, William Placher, Mark Schwehn, Serene Jones, Diane Kennedy, and Willie Jennings. An international perspective was brought to the discussion of our research findings during a seminar sponsored by Carnegie and hosted by John Rowett, Warden of Rhodes House, Oxford University. Participants included Paul Fiddes, Harry Judge, Jonathan Magonet, Stephen Orchard, Timothy Radcliffe, John Rowett, Friedrich Schweitzer, Jane Shaw, and Michael Shire. We received helpful comments and questions when we reported on the progress of the study to sessions in the 2001, 2003, and 2004 meetings of the Association of Professors and Researchers of Religious Education, the 2002 Rabbinic Conference on Education, and the 2004 annual meeting of the Association of Theological Schools.

Almost everyone we have mentioned read some portion of the manuscript in progress. Their comments have been especially helpful as we attempted to bring focus to the massive amounts of data we collected. Gay Clyburn, director of communications and information for Carnegie, has been a constant guide as we began to move the book toward publication. Ellen Wert edited the full manuscript. Through her sensitivity to the purposes of the project and ability to bring coherence to our writing, she became a full partner in the project.

Nowhere, however, did we experience the collaborative character of this project more fully than in the enthusiastic participation of seminary executive officers, seminary faculty, program directors, students, and alumni and alumnae from each school involved in the project. We experienced openness and candor from both survey respondents and the members of the seminary communities we visited. We were, in every instance, greeted with hospitality and generosity. We engaged in robust and thoughtful discussions. We observed terrific teaching. The commitment of each of the participating seminaries to the effective preparation of clergy has been a continuing inspiration. The insight and wisdom of those we interviewed and observed have deepened and expanded our inquiry.

This report of our study, in other words, is the culmination of the effort of many people over an extended period of time. We are deeply grateful to all of them.

ABOUT THE AUTHORS

CHARLES R. FOSTER, director of the Carnegie Foundation's study of clergy education, is professor of religion and education emeritus at Emory University's Candler School of Theology where he also served as associate dean of faculty development from 1997 to 1999 and interim dean during the 1999–2000 academic year. He is an ordained United Methodist minister. His publications include *Embracing Diversity: Leadership in Multicultural Congregations* (1997) and *We Are the Church Together: Cultural Diversity in Congregational Life* (1996). Foster earned his M.Div. from Union Theological Seminary in New York and his Ed.D. from Teachers College-Columbia University.

LISA E. DAHILL, ordained in the Evangelical Lutheran Church in America, was a research scholar with the Carnegie Foundation from 2001 to 2005 and is now assistant professor of Worship and Christian Spirituality at Trinity Lutheran Seminary in Columbus, Ohio. She received her M.Div. from the Lutheran School of Theology at Chicago in 1990, served parishes in northeast Iowa, and earned a Ph.D. in christian spirituality from the Graduate Theological Union in Berkeley in 2001.

LAWRENCE A. GOLEMON participated in the Carnegie Foundation's study of clergy education as a research consultant. He is an instructor in philosophy, religion, and ethics at Dominican University in San Rafael, California, and directs the Sacred Visions and the Social Good program at Dominican and the Graduate Theological Union. He has taught at the Union Theological Seminary in the Philippines and, as an ordained Presbyterian minister, has served urban congregations in Minnesota, Georgia, and the California Bay Area. Golemon received his M.Div. and S.T.M. degrees from Yale Divinity School and a Ph.D. from Emory University.

BARBARA WANG TOLENTINO participated in the Carnegie Foundation's study of the education of clergy as research assistant. Prior to studies at

Stanford University, where she received an M.A. in religious studies and a Ph.D. in educational psychology, she designed and managed training programs in the aerospace and computer industries. She is a Roman Catholic who has been involved in parish ministry and has taught in Catholic elementary and high schools.

WILLIAM M. SULLIVAN works in the Carnegie Foundation's Preparation for the Professions Program and directs the Cross Professions Seminar. He is formulating a research design for the comparative aspects of the studies, drawing out common themes and identifying distinct practices in professional education. He is also a member of the Initiatives in Liberal Education team. The author of *Work and Integrity: The Crisis and Promise of Professionalism in America* (2005) and a coauthor of *Habits of the Heart: Individualism and Commitment in American Life* (1996), Sullivan has examined the link between formal training and practical reflection in effective education. Prior to coming to Carnegie, Sullivan was a philosophy professor at La Salle University. He earned a Ph.D. in philosophy at Fordham University.

LEE S. SHULMAN, the Carnegie Foundation's president since 1997, sets the Foundation's intellectual direction and works closely with senior scholars on initiatives. He was the Charles E. Ducommun Professor of Education at Stanford University, where he taught for eighteen years. Prior to that, he was a professor of educational psychology and medical education and founding codirector of the Institute for Research on Teaching at Michigan State University. He is a former president of the American Educational Research Association and past president of the National Academy of Education. He received his Ph.D. from the University of Chicago.

EDUCATING CLERGY

INTRODUCTION
William M. Sullivan

THIS IS A TIMELY MOMENT to introduce *Educating Clergy*. It has never been more evident that public as well as private life in America is powerfully shaped by traditions of faith commitments and religious observance. This study was born out of the conviction that the organized clergy plays a central, though unofficial, role in many aspects of national life. Through their pastoral and teaching functions, clergy of all religious traditions share characteristic and important tasks. They help individuals and communities interpret and respond to the events of their individual and family lives. But clergy also shape the ways in which individuals and groups make sense of the larger events of our common life. This study provides a searching examination of how religious leadership by pastors, priests, and rabbis is prepared and trained for these challenging times.

Educating Clergy is the outcome of a research project that began in early 2001 with conversations between officers of The Carnegie Foundation for the Advancement of Teaching and the Lilly Endowment, Inc. Under the presidency of Lee Shulman, Carnegie had embarked on a series of comparative studies of the education for various professions. Through the leadership of the vice president for religion, Craig Dykstra, the Endowment had for some time been sponsoring research into how religion, and especially religious leadership, functions across the spectrum of American life. Both institutions were—and still are—committed to the notion that a better understanding of how clergy are prepared is vital to American society. A collaborative exploration of the academic training of future clergy in academically accredited institutions was a natural point of convergence. Schools educating clergy go by many names—divinity schools, theological schools, schools of religion, and seminaries, among others. Since *seminary* is often used when referring to all of them,[1] this term will refer to the academically accredited institutions represented in this study.

To address the Lilly Endowment's concern with the quality of religious leadership, the study situates its particular questions about the education of future clergy within the broad question of how changing conditions and student demographics are affecting seminary experience. To address the Carnegie Foundation's emphasis on teaching and learning in higher education, the research examines how the academic setting influences training in seminaries and university divinity schools. Further, to ensure clear focus, the two funders agreed to confine the study to religious groups that prepare their clergy in accredited academic programs. This meant restricting the range of religious leadership training under study. However, the variation among religious traditions represented in the study remains quite broad, encompassing the preparation of Roman Catholic and mainline Protestant, as well as many evangelical Protestant and both Reform and Conservative Jewish clergy.

The Clergy Education Study in Context: Preparation for the Professions

For the Carnegie Foundation, this study is part of a larger project: the Preparation for the Professions Program. This program of comparative research seeks to discover what is common among the many forms of professional education, while also exploring the distinctive approaches to teaching and learning that mark specific professional domains. Through this program, Carnegie has also been investigating the preparation of lawyers, engineers, teachers and academics, and nurses and physicians.

Within this comparative perspective, the clergy represents a unique case. Although the clergy has ranked high among the most venerable of the traditional "learned professions"—law, medicine, and divinity—by the late twentieth century the status of the clergy as a profession had ceased to be obvious to many. One of the most important findings of this study is how much attention seminaries give to the question of what it means for the clergy to be, or not to be, a profession like others. The ongoing effort to articulate what clergy practice is about is itself an important aspect of education for the clergy. Through this study, the Carnegie Foundation hopes to contribute to clergy educators' ongoing effort to identify and articulate their distinctive purposes and practices to students, to religious communities, to the academy, and to the general public.

A Distinctive Profession, a Distinctive Education: Interpreting God

During the 1960s, a growing consensus about the nature and role of the modern professional threatened to remove the ministry from its traditional position among the learned professions. For example, the major theorist of the professions in those years, the social thinker Talcott Parsons (1968), defined the professions by their exercise of "cognitive rationality," using the analogy of technological progress through scientific investigation. Parsons suggested that a "cognitive complex" was the heart of the research university, which he conceived as the key engine of social progress. As a model, Parsons held up medicine's marriage of university-based research to professional practice and education through the application of research to practice in the teaching hospital. Parsons posited that scientific knowledge required the complement of the "moral evaluative complex," which lay outside the realm of measurable truth.

In contrast, clergy appeared embarrassingly nontechnical. Priests, ministers, and rabbis have special knowledge and expertise, but little of it can be claimed to be scientific in origin or technological in its application. All this meant that the clergy could not be viewed as professionals in the new, modern sense. They lacked specific technical competence. At a time of intensifying specialization in the academy, the education of clergy continued to rely heavily on a general liberal arts tradition. As practitioners, clergy felt entitled to address the whole of life. Although they were indeed the distant ancestors of the modern professions, for Parsons and others they remained, like artists and literary intellectuals, outside the inner circle of science-based cognitive rationality (1968; Parsons and Platt, 1973, pp. 103, 113).

Despite the religious origins of American higher education—Harvard and Yale were both established for the purpose of preparing a learned clergy—seminaries and divinity schools fit somewhat awkwardly into the late-twentieth-century academy. Within professional education, the university's embrace of "cognitive rationality" pushed toward the near-equation of detached analytical reasoning with professional competence. This orientation is manifest in the commonplace belief that professionals should function as strategic problem solvers whose value-neutral knowledge and technique can be employed in the service of any number of alternative purposes. This vision of a purely technical professionalism tended to relegate to the background questions about public responsibility and the meaning of professional work. It also placed a significant burden of proof on clergy to demonstrate expertise on the technical-scientific model.

During the great postwar expansion of higher education, many leaders in American higher education believed that history was moving toward an increasingly secular future. The expected (and sometimes desired) result was to be the marginalization of the role and status of organized religion, in particular once-dominant Protestant Christianity. However, as so often happens, the future has not turned out as expected. The surprising persistence of religious—often specifically Christian—consciousness and practice in contemporary American life, even in the secular research university, has posed with new urgency the question of the status of normative knowledge.[2]

The preparation of religious professionals according to educational models originating in the research university sets up a powerful tension between the university's predominant model of knowledge and religious knowledge. The "cognitive rationality" that Parsons posited is a way of thinking that has been developed by the sciences in an attempt to purify human observation of the world, eliminating from it individual bias and distortion. The scientific demand that things be measured, and that only measurable things be considered knowable, derives from this aim at impartial, universal truth. For the modern academy, knowledge of this kind and the disciplined pursuit of such knowledge through methodical research have become much-valued ends in themselves. These assumptions are the cultural bedrock on which the institutions of disciplinary specialization and much academic prestige rest.

For prospective clergy, this academic culture presents profound challenges of a cognitive as well as a practical kind. Both Jewish and Christian religious educators must make sense of standing within traditions of thought that antedate the cognitive revolution of modern science and that, moreover, assert alternative understandings of reality. Biblical religion is focused on claims about transcendent reality in the form of language about God. A significant part of every seminary student's intellectual task is to come to grips with the meaning God will have for his or her own life as well as for his or her future professional career. Clergy must interpret God, or at least the "God language" of their traditions, to the laity in private or public need.

These issues are vital intellectual questions for seminaries, but they also have profound practical consequences. Unlike the abstract and theoretic formulations of the modern sciences, religious understanding is deeply and inescapably connected to identity and meaning. It carries import for how one understands one's life, including powerful implications of a normative kind for how one ought to live. In many of its traditional forms, religious knowledge has argued that one can understand reality only by having the right stance toward it: that existential attunement, or grace, is a condition as well as result of knowledge. That is, the question of God, although deeply cognitive, cannot be approached on the model of empirical science. Like knowledge of art or deep cultural understanding, it benefits from critical reflection and experiential exploration. But it demands a stance different from that required by science. It requires engagement as well as critical distance. And in this stance, engagement leads.

Other professional schools face a similar if less well recognized challenge. Whatever the knowledge base of the field, professional schools are finally about educating future practitioners for their professional domain. Although they need not confront the question of ultimate meaning that the idea of God forces on clergy education, they still must promote their students' engagement with the normative identities and purposes that define the professional lives of lawyers, teachers, physicians, or engineers. They, too, must go beyond the distanced stance of scientific analysis and detached skill into the complex world of engaged practice.

The Three Apprenticeships of Professional Education

This inescapably normative dimension of professional education is a reminder that professional training has its historical roots in apprenticeship. Learning as an apprentice typically meant exposure to the full dimensions of professional life—not only the intricacies of esoteric knowledge and peculiar skills but also the values and outlook shared by the members of the profession. Around the turn of the last century, as professional training of physicians, lawyers, and clergy moved into the university, this complex of knowledge, skill, and ethos began to be differentiated into three increasingly separated dimensions: cognitive, practical, and normative.

And so professional schools are hybrid institutions. They are part of the tradition of cognitive rationality at which the academy excels. They are also part of the world of practice, emphasizing the craft know-how that marks expert practitioners of the domain. And they operate with the inescapably normative knowledge contained in the identity of being a particular kind of professional.

From the students' point of view, entrance into the professional school is still the beginning of apprenticeship, but one with three dimensions that are largely separate. Professional education is a cognitive or intellectual apprenticeship, a practical apprenticeship of skill, and an apprenticeship of identity formation. The academic setting, however, clearly tilts the balance toward the cognitive. Because professionals require facility in deploying abstract, analytic representations—that is, symbolic analysis—school-like settings are very good environments for learning. At the same time, however, professionals must also be able to integrate, or reintegrate, this kind of knowledge with practice, with everyday life. But students learn the skills of integration and reintegration mostly by living transmission—through a pedagogy of modeling and coaching. For seminaries, as for all professional schools, it is this reintegration of the separated parts that provides the great challenge.

The problem is well illustrated in engineering schools. There, the university's values inform the curriculum—the courses in engineering science or physical analysis that make up the preponderance of all programs for entry into the field. There, students are taught how the world works as understood by contemporary physical science. However, like all the professions, engineering is ultimately about *doing*—exercising practical judgment under conditions of uncertainty. The apprenticeship of practice teaches students how to work in the world. They learn about this in several curricular areas, but chiefly in laboratory courses—in which they grapple with the fact that actual situations may not behave precisely as described in theory—and in design studios. In these settings, students begin to understand the fuller dimensions of solving problems in engineering, in which economic, social, environmental, and esthetic considerations have a place, often confusingly juxtaposed to purely physical requirements.

Besides learning how the world works, and how to work in it, future engineers also confront the question of how to *be* in the world: the apprenticeship of professional identity. Today, this is often understood as the realm of ethics, which is correct in the older, expansive sense of ethics as the investigation of how best to live. Yet in many curricula, when one compares the amount of attention given to the area of ethics or professional identity with the amount of attention given to the physical world and problem solving (through courses in engineering science, the labs, or even design courses), ethics and professional identity remain curiously unaddressed, or only haphazardly addressed—often because the question of how to *be* in the world is beyond the competence of the field alone to answer. Yet engineers must answer the question in practice just as must everyone else. Furthermore, because of their peculiar knowledge and special skills, the attitudes and decisions of engineers often have effects on others and the larger environment. The formation of professional identity—the normative apprenticeship—was traditionally handled through the on-the-job training that most engineers received from the industrial corporations that employed them. Today, however, perceptive analysts of the engineering world have begun to ask if this training is sufficient in the face of recent economic and technological changes that are placing more initiative and responsibility in the hands of engineers as inventors, managers, and entrepreneurs.[3]

In contrast, the knowledge at the basis of clergy practice—religious knowledge—is directly concerned with how to *be* in the world, for religious knowledge is concerned with the significance of life in the most profound sense. However, like many other professional schools, seminaries heavily emphasize learning that takes place in the classroom. Because students typically study at some remove from the actual practice of clergy life, much of the teaching and learning in seminaries has an unmistakable academic cast that emphasizes cognitive mastery of concepts and knowledge. Future clergy do a good deal of their preparation learning in classrooms, reading and studying texts and being assessed through written examinations, usually in the form of essay questions. Still, as this volume shows in detail, educators of clergy generally work hard and creatively at linking this cognitive or intellectual apprenticeship with the demands of future clergy practice.

Seminaries also use the pedagogies of practice—the second apprenticeship—in which students learn by engaging in the actual activities of clergy practice. Simulations, case studies, field placements, and clinical pastoral education are common in today's seminaries, and they are discussed in the chapters of Part Three of this volume. At the outset it is important to recognize that the pedagogies of the apprenticeship of practice are not devoid of cognitive or theoretical content. This kind of teaching and learning brings knowledge and concepts to bear as illumination and guides to professional practice. Because the professional work of clergy is always tied to situations of human interaction and often of dialogue, the skills developed in the apprenticeship of practice—such as the capacity to listen effectively or to find the religiously significant features in the lives of congregants and their problems, or the ability to render an insight derived from religious tradition or theological argument as a practical, usable counsel—are the essential completion and complement of the cognitive capacities developed in the intellectual apprenticeship.

It is a truism that we become what we habitually do. Learning by doing therefore forms a person's dispositions, in that such learning unavoidably weaves relationships with others similarly engaged and so encourages loyalty to a group of fellow practitioners. More aware of this now, perhaps, than in the past, seminaries across the religious spectrum have been giving increasing attention to the integration of their students' knowledge and professional skills in a stable personal synthesis. This attention to the normative apprenticeship—of professional identity—takes several forms in different institutions. Some seminaries have developed programs that attend to individual development. Through formal systems of counseling and peer activity, seminaries seek to provide guidance to students in integrating the various facets of their seminary experience toward the very specific end of forming a ministerial, a priestly, or a rabbinic identity. Other seminaries pursue the goals of the normative apprenticeship in a less direct and often a more communal manner. In these institutions, the emphasis is often on shared activities outside the formal curriculum. Worship is prominent among these activities. As this volume describes, however, creating common practices of identity formation beyond the classroom or required field placement is often difficult. Commuter students and the denominationally mixed populations of many seminaries make collective formation experiences difficult.

But perhaps more so than in the cognitive and practical apprenticeships, it is in their approaches to the normative apprenticeship that the specific religious traditions embodied in the various seminary environments become most visible and important. Practices of clergy formation, it turns out, are harder to transplant from one religious context to another than are the more standardized pedagogies typical of the cognitive and practical apprenticeships. Nevertheless, the contemporary seminary scene is conspicuous for the increasing degree of attention—and experimentation—that marks this important unifying aspect of professional preparation. It is in their serious and imaginative engagement with the formative project of the third apprenticeship—examined in depth in later chapters—that seminaries have the most to offer to other domains of professional education.

A Formative Education:
The Challenge of Normative Knowledge

Compared with the education in other professions, normative knowledge and the apprenticeship of professional identity—concerned with meaning, purpose, and identity—are especially prominent in the professional preparation of clergy. Unlike engineers, architects, or physicians, clergy do not wield technological skills that enable them to alter the physical conditions of life. Instead, the clergy are caregivers and guides to meaning—working, like jurists, to discern the ethical import of their traditions.

The clergy's area of expertise lies not in physical or information systems, but in the world of social practices structured by shared meanings, purposes, and loyalties. These social networks form the distinctive ecology of human life and are the matrix of individual identity and purpose. The practices of pastors, rabbis, and priests are embedded in specific communities of religious meaning and practice. A major aspect of their professional role is to enable persons to find guidance and strength for living, through involvement with their religious communities. They mediate the resources of their respective religious traditions for the needs of contemporary life. The clergy's larger, public function arises from the inevitable impact these activities have on the larger social networks of meaning and connection that both influence and are influenced by the religious groups and purposes the clergy serve.

Normative knowledge, even when it is systematically organized, shares with practical know-how a key feature that sets both off from the analytical thinking typical of cognitive rationality. Analysis has been the golden key that opens the path of scientific advancement. Analytic thinking disengages the thinker from the everyday contexts of meaning in order to take up the position of a distanced, skeptical observer, testing possible explanations of events by rigorous trial. Practical knowledge, on the other hand, requires engagement as a condition for knowing. Practical knowledge is always learned in a hands-on manner, sometimes literally so in the case of engineers, nurses, and physicians. The normative knowledge needed for grasping the significance of activities and viewpoints requires a similar engagement: being inside the situation, not looking at it from a distance.

Within the context of engaged, normative knowledge, intellectual analysis gains a particular kind of significance. As pastoral leaders and guides to meaning, the clergy are by necessity deeply immersed in the world of everyday life. More precisely, they work to relate the world of everyday life to the transcendent purposes embodied in their religious heritage. This professional location demands a distinctive life of the mind. Educators of clergy have long known that normative knowledge has a vital cognitive aspect. As we have seen, the meaning of God for their professional practice becomes an inescapable issue for every clergyperson. And effective engagement with congregants is impossible without the ability to interpret situations effectively. Clergy are asked to make sense of complex situations in light of the commitments and values that define their identity and that of the religious tradition for which they stand. For many of these traditions, this identity is carried in classic texts, defining rituals, and customs.

A purely theoretical knowledge of these matters, although important, is rarely enough to enable rabbis, priests, or ministers to carry out their functions. They are routinely called on to cast light on those practical or "existential" matters, often personal but frequently also public, that purely technical knowledge cannot address. For this work, the classical humanities become essential resources for making contemporary, practical sense of their religious heritage. Just as ethical and political theorizing were understood in the classical tradition primarily as aids to practical reasoning and decision making, Christian theology, too, was primarily a means for guiding practice. The complex craft of Talmudic interpretation as practiced by the rabbis had as its immediate aim perspective on the tasks of living before the divine. The old adage, "faith seeking understanding," meant that religious knowledge began in engagement with certain ways of being and acting; the thinkers' task was to understand these as aspects of a larger, meaningful order of life.

In a comparative perspective, this use of the classic techniques of the humanities to bring normative knowledge to bear on practice situations gives professional education of the clergy its distinctive pedagogical ethos. At the center of this pedagogy is the idea of formation: the recognition that teaching and learning are about much more than transferring facts or even cognitive tools. Learning in the formative sense is a process by which the student becomes a certain kind of thinking, feeling, and acting being.

Such formative processes are expected to be at the heart of all forms of professional education. However, under the influence of the technical model of the professional, they are usually attended to only sporadically, and practices of professional formation are rarely explicitly recognized and named as such. Although seminaries have not escaped the power of the technical model of professionalism, the intellectual core of their teaching has been a concern with the significance and practical implications of the interpretation of texts, customary practices, and experience. This focus has kept the idea of formative education alive, whereas in other forms of professional education it has often simply been forgotten.

The Significance of Clergy Education for the Professions and the Academy

As a model, this kind of pedagogy holds significance for other forms of professional training, as well as for the academy as a whole, not least in the troubled area of liberal education. The conventional view of professionals as value-neutral problem solvers has come under increasing strain. Consider the situations that confront professionals—situations once thought marginal to well-organized domains of problem-solving technique that are now becoming increasingly common. As physicians and nurses routinely confront so-called lifestyle diseases—obesity, addictions, cancer, strokes—rather than infectious biological agents, gradually these professions are coming to realize that the professional must take into account how individuals, groups, or whole societies lead their lives. Understanding of social and cultural—even moral and religious—context, then, is becoming essential knowledge, and the ability to understand a particular patient or situation within such contexts is crucial to successful intervention.

For professionals to deal with problems such as these, they will have to replace the distanced stance of the technical expert with the more engaged role of the civic professional. That requires a more conscious involvement in the social networks of meaning and connection in people's lives. It also requires the explicit assumption of responsibility for the public purposes of the profession. Without this transformation of identity, their efforts will continue to misfire or fail. Normative knowledge, in other words, must again become an important part of the knowledge base of all professionals. And since this kind of knowledge is so closely linked to practical skills, on the one hand, and deeply formed ways of perceiving and relating, on the other, developing more effective professionals for our time requires reshaping professional preparation to incorporate the development of these skills and outlook—what in seminaries is called *formation*.[4]

The recognition of the formative dimension of education is also profoundly important for the liberal arts and liberal education. In the face of ubiquitous demands that education "pay off" in career and economic terms—that, above all, it should be "useful"—advocates of the venerable traditions of liberal education have usually been torn between two incompatible approaches. One is the idea of liberal education as the imparting of some basic cultural literacy, based on content thought indispensable to being an educated person in our time. The other rallying point has been the notion of inquiry—especially resonant among those in the scientific fields who have paid attention to these matters—or the notion of critical thinking. Here the emphasis has been on form rather than content. Advocates of this direction have seized on the observable effects of liberal education: for many of its graduates, it seems clear that it inculcates versatility of mind and intellectual strength. These qualities are useful indeed, but they rarely come in neutral, generic form.

Attention to the formative purpose of education suggests an alternative approach, one that might go forward between the horns of the familiar dilemma of content versus form. In today's undergraduate education, the development of service learning and education for citizenship show interesting structural parallels to the educational vision of clergy preparation. Educating for citizenship—a goal standard in the mission statements of virtually every type of American college or university—is clearly a matter of normative knowledge. To be effective, it must provide a functional equivalent of the practical apprenticeship in professional education. But it is, therefore, clearly concerned with something like the apprenticeship of professional identity, the formation of dispositions and character as well as ways of thinking.[5]

Like the engagement with religious tradition in seminary education, the civic purpose of higher education provides an imaginative context in which teaching and learning can assign significance to a wide variety of kinds of knowledge and disciplines of thinking: the natural and social sciences as well as the humanities. This context allows for the strengths of both the inquiry and cultural literacy programs without requiring a fundamental choice between them. These are among the positive spillover effects of an approach to liberal education that takes formation seriously. If the experience of seminaries should contribute to this retrieval of one of liberal learning's oldest motifs, that will be simply the returning of a favor. It was the humanistic education of another time that provided many of the critical cognitive tools as well as practical dispositions toward learning that enable education of the clergy to proceed today.

Exploring the education of clergy has opened new questions for those who undertook this study. These questions reach deep into the seminaries, but they also extend beyond them, into the wider worlds of Jewish and Christian religious communities, of professional preparation, higher education, and the fabric of American democracy itself.

The Clergy Education Study

This study began with an overarching question: *How do seminaries prepare students for their roles and responsibilities as clergy?*

This question focused attention on those places and practices, from classes to field education to community worship to programs of spiritual and vocational direction, through which seminaries intend to help students integrate or, as one survey respondent put it, "fit together" the various elements of their educational experience in preparation for the daily practices of clergy work.

Seminary educators, of course, prepare their students for clergy roles and responsibilities primarily through classroom pedagogies and communal pedagogies that are embedded in seminary worship, field education, governance, and community life. How do those pedagogies function? How do seminary educators think about their work? How do the traditions and contexts of each institution support or constrain educators in their work? Moreover, how do seminaries cultivate the capacity to link the pedagogical goals for student learning with the cognitive, practical, and normative apprenticeships in all forms of professional education? In short, how do seminaries cultivate what Dykstra calls the *pastoral imagination*?

Building on Dykstra's term, the study identified this capacity as the *pastoral, priestly, or rabbinic imagination*—a distinctive way of seeing and thinking that permeates and shapes clergy practice (Dykstra, 2001, pp. 2–3). This led us to the overarching question guiding our research: *How do seminary educators foster among their students a pastoral, priestly, or rabbinic imagination that integrates knowledge and skill, moral integrity, and religious commitment in the roles, relationships, and responsibilities they will be assuming in clergy practice?*

Reframing the question in this way focused attention on how seminary educators both introduce students to the wisdom and practices of their religious traditions and engage them in the constructive appropriation of that wisdom and those practices in preparing for the issues and challenges of doing ministry in situations that are always new, in circumstances that are ever changing.

This question established the framework for more specific research questions. The first was prompted by comments of seminary graduates who recalled teachers who did an "excellent job," remembered receiving a "solid education," and who became more explicit when they described their appreciation for the congruence between the assumptions about clergy practice they encountered in the seminary and the realities of their own clergy practice. Thus, their comments led us to ask *What classroom and communal pedagogies do seminary educators employ as they seek to foster in their students a pastoral, priestly, or rabbinic imagination?*

This capacity for envisioning and constructing events for student learning is implied, for example, in the words of a professor of homiletics who expects that students in his class will "build upon their homiletical skills, establish good habits of exegesis and biblical interpretation, and discover the power of language for creating transformative sermons." Terms like *building upon, good habits,* and linguistic *power* convey implicit expectations for dispositions, habits, skills, knowledge, and communicative competencies embedded in images of clergy practice influencing this seminary educator's decisions about what and how to teach. That led us to wonder how faculty members draw their students into their expectations, encourage them to embrace those expectations, and then assess their effectiveness as practitioners of those expectations.

Despite the common influence of the standards and procedures of academic accrediting agencies on the purposes and procedures of all seminary education, the study encountered a variety of assumptions and expectations about what clergy preparation entails. Classroom teaching strategies of lecture, discussion, and role play often look the same—whether in Jewish or

Catholic, mainstream or evangelical Protestant seminaries—but they seem to function differently.

For example, one expects to encounter different understandings of theological concepts such as theodicy, soteriology, and eschatology[6] among schools associated with the various religious traditions. But would one find a greater confluence of expectations around epistemological and pedagogical assumptions related to such concepts as integrative learning, critical thinking, and practices of interpreting texts?

Seminaries prepare clergy to be religious leaders in a wide array of Jewish and Christian denominational traditions. But they also perpetuate assumptions about educating clergy that can be traced back to the monastery, the yeshiva, the academic centers at Cambridge and Oxford in the seventeenth century, the University of Berlin and the normal schools for teacher training in the nineteenth century, and to the various approaches to clergy apprenticeship in all religious traditions. Any effort to understand how clergy are educated today requires understanding the influence of those historical precedents on the relationship of the mission, culture, and teaching practices of the faculty in any school. These reflections led to the study's second specific question: *How do the various historic traditions of clergy education perpetuated in seminaries' missions and institutional cultures influence the classroom and communal pedagogies and students' experience?*

Because the clergy education study was conducted within the larger project of the Preparation for the Professions Program, the study included the following third and fourth specific questions, concerning clergy education in the context of professional education: *Does clergy education have a "signature" classroom pedagogy, distinctive to it among the professions? How does clergy education emphasize and integrate the cognitive, practical, and normative apprenticeships of professional education?*

Taken together, these four questions informed an expansive research plan, described more fully in the appendix. To carry out this agenda, the Carnegie Foundation selected Charles Foster, formerly professor of religion and education and interim dean of Candler School of Theology at Emory University, to direct the project. Dr. Foster assembled the research team: Lisa Dahill, a Ph.D. in religion and a Lutheran pastor; Larry Golemon, also a Ph.D. in religion and a Presbyterian minister; and Barbara Tolentino, a Ph.D. in education from Stanford University.

The team was augmented by senior staff of the Carnegie Foundation. Psychologist Anne Colby and philosopher William Sullivan codirect the Preparation for the Professions Program and participated actively in all phases of the study. Lee Shulman, president of the foundation, was also an active participant, joining in visits to seminaries. In addition, the Carnegie Foundation's vice president, Pat Hutchings, and senior scholars Mary Huber and Lloyd Bond took part, as did Pamela Grossman, professor of education at Stanford. Lindsay Turner and Megan Mills provided administrative support.

This research team conducted a comprehensive review of the literature on Jewish and Christian clergy education; created survey instruments and conducted a survey of faculty, students, and alumni and alumnae from a cross section of eighteen Jewish and Christian seminaries; interviewed faculty, students, and administrators; observed classes; participated in the life of the community at ten of the eighteen seminaries; and contributed questions to a survey sent to half of all United States and Canadian seminary educators by the Center for the Study of Theological Education, Auburn Theological Seminary.

Central to the research method was a series of interviews, classroom observations, and focus group conversations with four faculty members from each of the schools visited. These faculty members had been identified by their deans as reflective about their practice as teachers and respected by colleagues as teachers.

The aim of this study has been to understand the pedagogical resources that educators of clergy draw on in their efforts to maintain the relationship between theory and practice, intellect and commitment. Their example and experience provide insight not only into their own endeavors but for other forms of professional education as well. If this study succeeds in making the achievements, as well as the challenges, faced in educating clergy more widely understood and appreciated, it will have fulfilled one of its best aspirations.

NOTES

1. The comparative dimension of the study limited our attention to educational institutions committed to upholding standards associated with formal academic accreditation. An even broader study needs to be conducted to account for the education of Jewish and Christian clergy in yeshiva, monastery, and congregation, as well as the education of clergy in other religious traditions such as Buddhism, Hinduism, and Islam. During the course of the study we did attempt to trace sources to the various designations for the accredited institutions that educate Jewish and Christian clergy. Results of this effort may be found in a paper entitled "The Puzzle That Is Clergy Education" on the Carnegie Foundation Web site: www.carnegiefoundation.org.

2. For example, see the papers collected in Sterk, 2002.

3. Rosalind Williams has provided a provocative discussion of this question (Williams, 2002).

4. See Sullivan, 2005.

5. See The Carnegie Foundation for the Advancement of Teaching's study of undergraduate programs of civic education (Colby, Ehrlich, Beaumont, and Stephens, 2003).

6. Theodicy addresses the presence of evil in light of God's goodness and justice; soteriology is concerned with views of salvation and resulting patterns of religious life; and eschatology is the study of the future course of history, including the end times, under the promises and providence of God.

PART ONE

SEMINARY EDUCATION

AN OVERVIEW

IN *OPEN SECRETS* (2001) RICHARD LISCHER, who teaches at the Divinity School of Duke University, recalls his first parish assignment in the 1960s. He had completed his seminary and doctoral studies and was being sent to a congregation in an economically depressed, rural community in the Midwest. As he describes the transition from school to congregation, he illustrates the challenge of linking the knowledge and skills of professional education with the judgments of professional practice: "When you pull up to your first church, it's a moment of truth, like the first glimpse of a spouse in an arranged marriage. It had been twelve years since I'd blurted out my secret at the family dinner table: 'I'm going to be a pastor. What do you think of that?'" (p. 108).

The first glimpse was not promising. Lischer sat in his car looking at the church that would be his first pastoral assignment, feeling first a "flop" in his stomach, then a "crushing sense of disappointment." He could not even open the car door to explore the grounds of the church, because to have done so "would have been an admission . . . that the assignment had been acceptable." "I wasn't so put off by the physical appearance of the church," he remembers, "as I was by its obvious irrelevance." Lischer and his seminary friends had "reveled in the social and religious ferment of the 1960s." They had read Harvey Cox's best seller, *The Secular City* (1970), and envisioned a ministry liberating the secular world of the city from "religious superstition." The reality of this little country brick church with its "broken cross and flourishing graveyard" seemed far removed from the challenges of ministry in the city (pp. 8–10).

As he tells the story of coming to terms with his calling in that community, Lischer conveys both regret and judgment about the adequacy of his preparation to be the pastor of that congregation in that community: "The endless years of our education had opened a breach between the naïve religious faith with which my classmates and I had entered the System and the even more naïve secular faith with which we exited it. Without fully realizing it, some of us were quietly canceling the terms of our call. My friends and I accepted assignments like the Cana church because eight years of theological education had rendered us uncertain of our identity and, like our professors, unemployable in the real world" (p. 40).

More than thirty years later, a priest responding to our survey of seminary graduates said that although she felt "well prepared . . . for Sunday mornings—liturgy, preaching, education," and for specific tasks of "counseling and pastoral care," the "weekly work" of "supervising and working with staff, parish administration and leadership, working with volunteers, parish record-keeping and archives, leading/working with vestries and other committees, delegating responsibilities, parish finances, stewardship of our own time and resources" had not been effectively "integrated into the priestly role." The "[s]eminary, including field education, did not give me any sense of what parish ministry is like during the week and how it all fits together." "The biggest challenge of parish ministry," she concluded, "is fitting all this together without going nuts and still having some kind of life (including sleep!)."

Other respondents reported that their seminary education had prepared them for their work: "I was very pleased with my education . . . I felt I was being trained for ministry"; "I cherished my time in seminary . . . it fed me and feeds me still"; "I received a solid education that provided the groundwork for practical application in the rabbinate"; "I feel that the professors and administration did an excellent job of providing me with knowledge and skills that have enhanced my ability to be a minister in my faith tradition."

None of these comments reveal, by themselves, why Lischer's seminary education did not prepare him to expect what he encountered in that rural congregation, what was missing from the priest's education, or, in contrast, what had contributed to other seminary graduates' sense that they had been prepared for their roles and responsibilities as pastors, priests, and rabbis.

Indeed, our curiosity about this lack of information suggested that we start this volume by considering the professional work of clergy and the key issues for seminary educators as they prepare their students for clergy work, which we do in Chapter One. There, along with the public character of clergy work, we introduce themes to be considered in subsequent chapters: the pastoral, priestly, rabbinic imagination; teaching practices designed to cultivate a pastoral, priestly, or rabbinic imagination; the pedagogical imagination shaping the teaching practices of seminary educators; and the alignment (or misalignment) of seminary educators' teaching practices with the mission and culture of their seminaries. In Chapter Two, we look at the diverse influences on seminary educators as they approach what we found to be a common goal among them: cultivating in their students a pastoral, priestly, or rabbinic imagination for clergy work.

EDUCATING CLERGY

A DISTINCTIVE CHALLENGE

CLERGY WORK HAS A DISTINCTIVELY PUBLIC CHARACTER, and clergy fill a particular professional role in American life. Clergy may spend considerable time in the solitude of their studies and work primarily in the contexts of specific religious traditions, but clergy practice consistently occurs at the intersections of personal and collective, religious and secular public experience.

For example, recalling his installation as pastor in that rural congregation, Lischer writes that in this ritual event, "The church had decreed that henceforth I would be spiritual guide, public teacher, and beloved sage to people whose lives and work I couldn't possibly understand. With a stroke of his wand, God—or the bishop—had just made me an expert in troubled marriages, alcoholism, teen sex, and farm subsidies" (2001, pp. 49–50).

With his installation, the congregation and community expected him to engage a wide range of personal and public issues through traditional clergy roles of preaching, teaching, caregiving, counseling, and organizing. Even in the most apparently private of interactions, as between pastor and hospital patient, he would be drawn into the increasingly public realms of family, medical staff, congregation, and community. This insight was the catalyst to the eventual transformation of Lischer's pastoral imagination.

The New Rabbi (2002), Stephen Fried's story of Har Zion Temple's search for a new leader, also illustrates this point. The power of the public presence and influence of Rabbi Gerald Wolpe's thirty-year tenure as that Philadelphia congregation's rabbi could not be avoided at any point in the temple's quest. As a public religious figure, his leadership of that congregation had established a standard for measuring any potential successor. He was a "brilliant orator and politician" who had originally been hired to hold a conflict-ridden synagogue together as it moved from its older and changing neighborhood in Philadelphia to a new site and new building on Philadelphia's suburban "Main Line." He was remembered for exceptional teaching, liturgical leadership, and congregational administration—each requiring public presence and presentation. He had "helped the synagogue, and American Judaism, reinvent itself in the new 'postwar era'—the one after Vietnam, the Yom Kippur War in Israel, and the civil rights and sexual revolutions in America"—movements that had challenged the very core of American Conservative Jewish identity and tradition. Fried adds that in his later years Wolpe "became best known" for the way he publicly shared the personal "pain and medical dilemmas" associated with the long recovery of his wife from a debilitating stroke, "expressing and evoking emotion in a place where reason and power had traditionally held sway" (2002, pp. 4–5).

Lischer's and Fried's stories illustrate two interrelated facts of clergy work: clergy practice occurs in public, and clergy practice engages its participants in practices of public service. Even when clergy seem primarily involved in efforts to maintain and renew the vitality of the congregations they serve, they fill roles in public assemblies that authorize their service for a wide range of public issues and concerns. They preside over religious rituals that make public significant personal transitions in life, from birth to death, and they intensify the sense of being connected with others in times of public celebration, crisis, and mourning. In the United States especially, clergy have also articulated visions of social good that have been catalysts to the organization of voluntary associations and the promotion of public policies directed to the betterment of society.

Clergy have been major proponents of the different moral perspectives at stake in what J. D. Hunter and others have recently called the "culture wars" over the family, media, education, law, and politics (1990, p. 50–51). Clergy are, at the same time, primary agents of the contemporary movements of religious fundamentalism around the world that on the one hand threaten civil liberties and on the other pose difficult questions about the relationship of religious traditions to the intellectual traditions of the Enlightenment. Many clergy are prominent and popular media personalities attracting significant segments of the population to their radio and television broadcasts and to massive public gatherings. Recent government proposals for faith-based initiatives to handle important public services would not only alter traditional views about the separation of church and state in the nation, they would also draw clergy even more visibly into roles of public leadership.

Since the practice of clergy occurs at the intersection of religious and public life, it requires an education that enhances what Mary Fulkerson, also of Duke University's Divinity School, has called a "social imagination." For seminary educators, this means helping students not only to learn "how the world works" so they can do more than theorize about the social and political world, but also to see themselves as religious leaders involved in "the action in the world."[1] From this perspective, clergy education involves more than teaching students a particular way of thinking; it requires that those ways of thinking be linked constructively with ways of being and doing. In this linking we can see in clergy education the necessary interdependence of the cognitive, practical, and normative apprenticeships of professional education.

A Pastoral, Priestly, or Rabbinic Imagination

It follows, then, that a primary task of seminary education is cultivating the pastoral, priestly, or rabbinic imagination necessary for clergy to embrace this multifaceted and public work. Dykstra, perhaps more than anyone else, has thought about the shape and function of the pastoral imagination. He describes meeting wonderful ministers who exhibited a kind of "internal gyroscope and a distinctive kind of intelligence" that he calls pastoral imagination. By this term he means "a way of seeing into and interpreting the world" that, in turn, "shapes everything a pastor thinks and does" (2001, pp. 2–3, 15). Dykstra clearly does not place the full responsibility for cultivating such a complete pastoral, rabbinic, or priestly persona on the shoulders of seminaries. Just as lawyers develop a way of thinking—a "legal mind"—through years of experience, so too, he notes, does practicing their profession over time develop in clergy a particular way of thinking (2001, pp. 2–3, 15).

Seminaries, however, are the primary settings for the intentional, disciplined, and sustained cultivation of the imaginative capacity for engaging in complex and rich professional practice. Dykstra notes that this capacity involves knowing "how to interpret Scripture and tradition in contemporary life," developing "an accurate sense of what makes human beings tick," possessing "a complex understanding of how congregations and other institutions actually work," and having both "a clear awareness" and an "analytical understanding of the world that the church exists to serve." "Undergirding" all this, he continues, is "a clarity of mind about what it means to worship God in spirit and in truth" and an awareness of how all these elements of clergy work "together with real integrity" (2001, pp. 2–3, 15).

Dykstra's description of pastoral imagination offers several clues to the formative and transformative power possible in seminary education. Seminary educators seek to form dispositions and the intuitive knowledge, or *habitus*, of a given religious or intellectual tradition in students. They intend for students to embody and equip the transformation of these traditions, as inherited "rules" are changed into "strategies" of new engagement to address new situations and circumstances (2001, pp. 2, 15). This is what Aristotle calls the transformative nature of *praxis*; John Dewey, the *reconstructive* nature of practical knowledge; and Pierre Bourdieu, the *strategies* of enacting a social practice. Throughout our interviews and observations we noticed that clergy education, however traditional, involves these transformative moments and goals.

Clergy educators innovate or adapt by drawing on the resources of inherited religious and academic traditions to convey or model for students' pastoral, priestly, or rabbinic imaginations. The result of their efforts is often transformative. In our study, students often spoke of moments in their learning as *awakening to* or *discovering* new meanings in sacred texts, alternative strategies for the conduct of some clergy practice, or new dimensions to their calling and vocation.

Clergy practice is itself a transformative art, reinvesting inherited traditions with new meanings and strategies in response to changing circumstances and shifting contexts. From this perspective, the pastoral, priestly, or rabbinic imagination requires not only capacities for engaging, integrating, and adapting learning, but also what might be called new forms of religious production. Both Protestant evangelical clergy who interpret a Scripture passage to authorize a new outreach program and Catholic priests who present the gospel in the language and cultural forms of a new immigrant population are participating in transformative practices that produce new forms of ministry.

How, then, do seminary educators think about the relationship between *what* and *how* they teach and the pastoral, priestly, or rabbinic imaginations that they seek to cultivate through their teaching? Certainly, some seminary educators teach their students as if they all will become scholars with the knowledge and skills needed to participate in the academic world of publishing and teaching. These educators emphasize the cognitive or intellectual apprenticeship of professional education. Similarly, some faculty members are primarily concerned with developing practical competencies in students for their future work as clergy. They emphasize an apprenticeship of practice or skill. However, when we asked seminary deans to identify members of their faculties who are both respected by their colleagues for their teaching and reflective about their teaching, we discovered more complex teaching practices and emphases. These seminary educators value scholarly competence and professional skill, but their intentions for student learning emphasize developing capacities for integrating various dimensions of the educational experience, what we have been calling *pastoral imagination.*

In the survey responses of nearly one hundred and thirty seminary teachers from eighteen different schools, we found clues to the pastoral imagination these seminary educators intend to cultivate. We asked them to consider a course that they "taught recently and enjoyed teaching." Rachel Adler, at Hebrew Union College, for example, teaches a course called "Constructing Theologies of Pain and Suffering." (Citations such as this one come from alumni or alumnae, student, or faculty responses to questions we posed on survey instruments developed for this study.) In this course, she intends to help her students read "some difficult classical texts richly and complexly; to pay attention to the process and methodology of different theologies; to develop an authentic, rigorous theological language for experiences to which we tend to respond either with silent terror or sloppy clichés; to address pain and suffering as specific to gendered persons embedded in specific families, communities, and cultures rather than universalizing; and to evaluate prayers and ceremonies, traditional and new, which deal with pain, suffering and loss in the light of the theological standards we are developing."

She concludes her list by writing, "You could say I want my students to be rooted in Jewish tradition, to learn to appreciate and begin to construct theologies that have integrity and don't marginalize the specific embodied, encultured people who are suffering" by focusing "the discussion exclusively on God." For Adler, these expectations for the rabbinical imagination also mean that she seeks to help "students face their own fears and learn courage."

Mary Schertz of Associated Mennonite Biblical Seminary observed that a course she teaches, "Reading Greek: the Synoptic Gospels," is "one of the two most important classes at our seminary for developing pastors who have a strong sense of what the biblical text is (and is not) and a properly chastened sense of their own power and authority as an interpreter of the text." These intentions for cultivating a pastoral imagination involve helping students learn both "a method and an attitude toward biblical studies that will nourish them and their congregations." In "Alternative Religions in America," taught by Donald Huber, professor of church history at Trinity Lutheran Seminary, we found similar attention to the interdependence of cognitive, normative, and practical goals in the process of developing a pastoral imagination that transcends denominational particularity. Huber encourages students "to listen empathetically to the religious viewpoints of others," to have the sensitivity and skill "to discuss 'strange' religious points of views with their parishioners," and to develop the ability to "teach about these groups on the basis of real knowledge of them." At St. John's Seminary in Camarillo, California, Paul Ford brings to "Sacramental Theology" yet another way of looking at the role of course work in cultivating students' ability to "understand the implications of the part of the ordination rite in which they are told: 'Accept from the holy people of God the gifts to be offered to him: Know what you are doing, and imitate the mystery you celebrate; model your life on the mystery of the Lord's cross.'"

Common to each of these seminary educators is the expectation that students will, through their courses, integrate various cognitive, relational, spiritual, and professional understandings and skills. These clergy educators know that for students, developing the capacity to integrate skills and concepts in this way involves increasing depth and breadth of understanding, expanding their ability to see connections among things typically hidden from view and to recognize the relevance of the subject to their lives and work, and learning to attend simultaneously to the multiple and often competing tasks integral to the work of clergy—tasks that originate in texts, traditions, ideologies, practices, congregations, and larger publics. Clergy educators thus approach teaching by considering each individual learner's growth as both a person and a religious leader.

Indeed, the complexity of these educators' expectations for student learning, as reflected in their goal statements, was chiefly responsible for shifting our attention from the strategic skills that seminary educators employ while teaching to the ways in which they imagine the teaching and learning enterprise. We discovered that we were exploring the movement from the *images of clergy* that informed the pedagogical imaginations of seminary educators to their *practices of fostering,* or cultivating, the priestly, pastoral, and rabbinic imaginations of their students for their future work as clergy.

The goals of these seminary educators also reveal attempts to cultivate among their students pastoral, priestly, and rabbinic imaginations that encompass concerns and values traditionally associated with the cognitive, practical, and normative apprenticeships that William Sullivan has identified as common to all forms of professional education.[2] Clergy educators give attention to the *cognitive apprenticeship,* for example, in their quests to nurture their students' ability to read "difficult classical texts richly and complexly," to have "a strong sense of what the biblical text is (and is not)," and to understand "the implications of the ordination rite."

Their attention to the *skill apprenticeship* concerned with the excellence of "knowing-how" is evident in Adler's desire that students have the ability to "evaluate prayers and ceremonies . . . which deal with pain, suffering and loss in the light of the theological standards we are developing" and Huber's hope that students will be able to teach the religious viewpoints of others with sensitivity and skill. Their goal—to foster the knowledge integral to clergy identity—is the objective of the *normative apprenticeship*. This is evident in Schertz's desire that her students develop both a "method and an attitude toward biblical studies that will nourish them and their congregations" and in Huber's intention that his students will be able to "listen empathetically" and discuss sensitively and skillfully the religious viewpoints of others to members of their congregations.

Teaching Practices in Cultivating a Pastoral, Priestly, or Rabbinic Imagination

In the seminary setting, teachers engage students—clergy novitiates—in the interactions of teaching and learning with the intention of helping them acquire and develop perspectives, dispositions, and habits—ways of thinking and doing integral to roles of professional leadership in religious communities and public life. The category of pedagogy writ large, however, encompasses topics for investigation ranging from institutional ethos to student readiness, teaching styles to learning theories, curriculum design to lesson planning and assessment. Since it would be impossible to explore all of these topics, we chose to focus our attention on teaching practices—those complex and sustained pedagogical interactions involving strategies and methods to facilitate increasingly proficient participation in the community of the practice.

We focused on teaching practices as a way to explore how seminaries prepare clergy for their professional roles and responsibilities for several reasons. In a survey of articles published over the last ten years in *Theological Education,* the journal of the Association of Theological Schools, we saw a shift of emphasis paralleled in the literature on education in general.[3] Discussions have moved from broader analyses of educational aims and purposes to explorations of clergy identity, the relevance of modes of thinking associated with the Enlightenment, the influence of institutional ethos on student learning, and the methods and strategies used in teaching. The attempts of seminary educators to account, in their teaching, for the increasing diversity in student backgrounds and educational experience and the changing expectations for religious leadership in Jewish and Christian congregations have intensified their interest in the dynamics of teaching and learning. So has the challenge to teachers to account for the "explosion of knowledge" in their decisions about what and how they teach.

We also focused on the notion of teaching practice because we wanted to resist the general tendency in the educational literature and other discussions of education to reduce teaching to technique. Technical notions of teaching, although important, do not adequately explain the significance, influence, or variety of approaches to cultivating a rabbinical, priestly, or pastoral imagination that we observed among seminary educators participating in this study.

The notion of *practice* has recently received considerable attention,[4] especially among seminary educators. Dykstra and Dorothy Bass, for example, have argued that a practice consists of "a sustained, cooperative pattern of human activity that is big enough, rich enough, and complex enough to address some fundamental feature of human existence" (2002, p. 22). From this perspective, teaching is that human activity addressing the need in human communities to transmit and renew the knowledge and skills, perspectives and sensibilities to each new generation to ensure their futures.

This means, as Alasdair MacIntyre argues, that practices such as teaching are more than instrumental activities (1984, p. 175).[5] The patterns in their activities originated in the earliest responses of humans to their environment and circumstances to ensure biological and communal survival through successive generations.[6] As practices are learned by each new generation of participants in these community practices, they move from being celebrations of discovery to being increasingly taken for granted—to becoming the ways that the members of a given community do something. Eventually, practices are so ingrained in habits and dispositions that not only are they extended over time and through generations, but also, as they are tested by new conditions and circumstances, ideas and procedures, they are renewed and even transformed. They become the structures of expertise and the resources for improvisation in meeting new and unexpected challenges. From this perspective, practices are, as Lave and Wenger have argued, the fundamental processes by which we learn and become who we are (1991, pp. 52–54). They are inherently pedagogical.

The activity of a practice, Wenger has also observed, "connotes" something we do—as in teaching (1998, p. 38). In a teaching practice the patterned activity of that "doing" consists of *methods* as optional and instrumental activities organized into coherent and complex teaching *strategies* to engage students in the intentions of a teacher (and implicitly in the intentions of the community of the practice) for their learning. The methods a teacher can use are limited only by the teacher's imagination, skill, and experience. For example, one seminary educator, pushing beyond traditional methods of lecture and discussion, observed that "We do a lot of 'hands-on' or creative learning experiences, like visiting a service of another faith, or conducting 'on the street interviews' . . . or rethinking how ordinary objects can be used to communicate a specific concept or faith supposition or truth. We also review for tests by playing all kinds of games."

Another seminary educator's description of a course illustrates how a variety of methods might be linked into a strategy to establish a rhythmic structure for student learning across an academic term:

> Lecture made up the first 4–5 sessions of the course and included case studies of the methodology I use in presenting the Talmudic tales as examples for the students. I also provided them with a library tour and resources list for finding Talmudic stories by subject matter. For a period of 2 sessions after this, students did research toward their presentations. This included study of Talmudic stories with study partners or in small groups. Students also met with me for a "trial run" of their class presentations and to discuss effective teaching strategies for them. This gave me the opportunity to discover what engaged the students, how they thought about their material, and what they felt about it. It also gave me a chance to raise questions about both the intellectual and theological/spiritual nature of the story and the presenter.

The pedagogical function of a teaching strategy such as this one is at least twofold: to gather students into the teacher's vision of possibilities for student knowing and doing in the subject and to engage students in disciplines culminating in the appropriation of that knowledge and those skills. The social function of a teaching strategy like this one emphasizes the commitment of the seminary community to the continuing vitality and relevance of the academic discipline of the course for the future of the seminary's religious tradition.

Students enter a teacher's practice through the practice's methods and strategies. Students participate in a teacher's practice as apprentices to a master craftsperson. As the teacher invites the students into the rhythmic structure of the practice, the students subordinate themselves to the requirements of the rules, standards of excellence, and roles encountered in its methods and strategies. As they rehearse the knowledge and skills toward which the practice is directed, they are gradually drawn into the deeper structures of its ways of thinking, dispositions, and habits. Over time, the knowledge and skills required to participate in the practice become increasingly familiar, even comfortable and often unconscious, enhancing (but also sometimes hindering) the continuing openness of students to learning.

Compelling features toward learning in a practice—especially in a teaching practice—are the "internal goods" that MacIntyre (1984, pp. 189–90) describes as giving rise to and filling the practice with meaning and purpose. For MacIntyre, the internal goods of a practice are evident in, first, the "excellence" identified with the performance of a practice—in the instance described above, in the extent and depth of the engagement of students in studying Talmud, compelling the students into ever deeper encounters with the text and its methods of study—and, second, the "excellence" of the goods appropriated in the course of the practice—in other words, the goods are evident through not only expanding knowledge and growing expertise but also an accompanying sense of accomplishment and appreciation of their value.

MacIntyre identifies a second internal good as "a certain kind of life" associated with the increasing claim of the competencies acquired while engaging in the practice on the ways we think, relate to others, and work at tasks. For seminary educators, this kind of life has to do with the increasing ability of students to identify the knowledge, skills, dispositions, and habits integral to the teaching practice in which they are participating with their future roles and responsibilities as priests, rabbis, or pastors—when, as in the above instance, students can envision themselves not only as students but as preachers and teachers of Talmudic texts in rabbinic practice.

In this way, the internal goods of a teaching practice intensify the relationship of students to the communities of the practice—initially, in the above instance, to the immediate community of students studying Talmud, and over time with the communities of Talmudic scholarship and rabbinic practice. Jerome Bruner borrowed the image of "distributed intelligence" to underscore the socializing dynamics in this view of a practice: "The gist of the idea is that it is a grave error to locate intelligence in a single head." Rather, it has to do with being part of specific communities "in whose extended intelligence" we share:[7] the community that forms in the classroom or other educational activity as well as the communities of the seminary, academic disciplines, religious traditions, and public life that have a stake in what is learned and how. Each of these communities brings normative expectations to what and how students shall learn.

Dykstra and Bass identify implications of this insight for a teaching practice in seminary education when they note that "Christian practices contain within them normative understandings of what God wills for us and for the whole creation and of what God expects of us in response to God's call to be faithful. Christian practices are thus congruent with the necessity of human existence, as such, as seen from a Christian perspective on human flourishing" (2002, p. 22). Christians in different denominational traditions will argue about particular ways of articulating what those normative understandings are, but they share a common relationship to the Christ event in the course of human history.

In other words, Christian, Jewish, Buddhist, or Muslim communities— or American, Brazilian, or Chinese communities, or professional societies of doctors, lawyers, or chemists, or disciplinary guilds of theologians, practical theologians, or historians—are defined, in part, by their relationship to a trajectory of normative meanings associated with real and mythic events in the past central to their collective identities and activities in the present. These communal norms not only establish boundaries for human knowing and doing in the communities in which teachers engage the learning of students, but they are also repositories of possibility and sources of constructive critique in their interactions with each other.

Pedagogical Imagination in Seminary Educator Teaching Practices

The *pedagogical imagination* of seminary educators significantly shapes their teaching practices. Through the exercise of their pedagogical imaginations, seminary educators envision pedagogical events to draw students into "existence possibilities" for their future clergy practice in the interplay of disciplinary and professional knowledge, skills, habits, and dispositions. The exercise of the pedagogical imagination involves teachers, at a minimum, in making decisions about (1) what to teach from all that could be taught; (2) how to engage students in what they intend for them to learn; (3) how to assess the extent to which students learn what was intended; and (4) how to negotiate their sense of obligation to the expectations of students, to traditions of knowledge, and to the religious communities that will be receiving them as clergy and leaders in ministry.

Although few seminary educators in the study used the language of apprenticeship to describe their teaching, we increasingly encountered the relational patterns of apprenticeship in their teaching practices. Over and over again, we heard them describe how they envision introducing students to some confluence of the traditions of knowledge and ways of knowing identified with their academic disciplines and religious communities and the traditions of practice associated with religious leadership.

They seemed intent on creating pedagogical environments that blend the values of cognitive, skill, and identity-formation integral to the three apprenticeships of professional education. They want students to develop a relationship with the subject while at the same time becoming agents of that subject through their professional roles in academic and religious communities.

Although seminary educators set goals to facilitate these intentions, their expectations for student learning cannot always be reduced to these goals. In her discussion of teaching and religious imagination, Maria Harris suggests why this may be the case. "With reference to [teacher] intention," she writes, "the role of imagination is critical" (1987, p. 67). We saw clues to the working of this teacher or pedagogical imagination in the intentions of some seminary educators to engage students in their own practice to the end they might "discover" in it "a rigorous demand" or possibility of "excellence." That demand, Harris continues, in Kierkegaard's words, is an "existence possibility" impelling students to join their teachers in choosing how to relate to the subject of their interaction with each other.

The exercise of the pedagogical imagination in the teaching practices of seminary educators becomes more visible in educational theorist Maxine Greene's description of what teachers do. "Teaching is purposeful action," she notes. Yet "it cannot function automatically or according to a set of predetermined rules" because it occurs in always-new situations and constantly changing circumstances. Teachers engage students in the repetition of complex, yet coherent, pedagogical strategies through which they expect, in Greene's terms, "to bring about certain changes in students' outlooks," to "enable them to perform in particular ways, to do particular tasks, to impose increasingly complex orders upon their worlds" (1973, pp. 69–70). From this perspective, the intent of teaching is purposeful and orderly, not random or idiosyncratic. Among seminary educators it originates in expectations for clergy practice deeply rooted in particular religious, cultural, and academic traditions and is influenced by expectations, standards, and norms in those traditions for the excellence of their efforts.

Although seminary educators typically assume their students come to their classes with some facility in the knowledge and skills for professional practice in their religious traditions, what students actually know and can do typically varies widely. Yet the habits and dispositions, knowledge and skills they do bring influence their ability to enter into and engage the various subjects of their learning. In class, they may encounter new ways of thinking and doing that challenge some and reinforce for others their prior knowledge, beliefs, and methods of study.

Students are novitiates or neophytes engaged in developing new perspectives, skills, and habits that may lead them to new understandings and competencies. As students participate in a seminary educator's teaching practice, no matter the particular intention of the practice, they move through a series of increasingly complex tasks, each typically requiring the recapitulation and repetition of prior tasks in the quest for increasingly confident competence. This learning process toward increasingly complex understandings integral to processes of professional reasoning may include several interdependent steps;[8] for example:

o Becoming familiar with the vocabulary, rhythms, methods, and genres of a given course of study.

o Developing skills to recognize tensions, questions, issues, and interpretive problems in the subject of study. This information typically requires students to rehearse over and over again what they know and can do until it begins to shape their perceptions, influence their dispositions, and take root in habits integral to the subject of their study, thereby linking knowledge, skill, and character.

o Developing the facility to identify and follow the structure, design, or argument of the subject of their learning to the point that they become increasingly aware of and invested in new issues, questions, possibilities, and competencies for their learning.

o Developing interpretive frameworks through which they may approach, make sense of, and use the subject of their learning—a process that typically requires them to review, rehearse, reappropriate, and refashion knowledge and skills developed in the repetition of each of the previous steps in this learning process.

o Developing the ability to compare and contrast what they have learned with alternative interpretive frameworks; in other words, to engage what they know through the eyes of others, providing them with the confidence and competence to critique or reconstruct what they know and can do or to construct something new. Again, moving into this stage of understanding typically takes students back through the prior steps.

A Signature Pedagogical Framework

In trying to understand the shape of the pedagogical imagination of seminary educators, and in looking closely at what might be called the "deep structures" of their teaching practice, we wondered if clergy education has a *signature pedagogy* that would be as distinctive as the Socratic dialogue in the analysis of legal cases in law schools or the mathematical analysis of structures in engineering schools.

Lee Shulman (forthcoming) has observed that signature pedagogies function as "windows" into "what counts most significantly as the essence of a profession's work." He illustrates this point by pointing to the objective conditions of diagnosis and treatment in medical practice "centered on an individual patient in a hospital bed." In explicating what he means by signature pedagogy, Shulman notes it includes four dimensions. It consists of strategies and methods that create a "surface structure" for the interaction of teachers and students. It also has a "deep structure" connecting the "concreteness of practice with the more conceptual, social or ideological aspects of the profession's essential character." It contains a "tacit structure" that includes the attitudes, values, and dispositions "modeled by the instructor and other students regarding professional practice." A signature pedagogy may also be distinguished by "what is missing"—what is not taught and what methods and strategies are not employed.

When we began the clergy study, we expected that pedagogies emphasizing the interpretation of texts and the critical reflection on clergy practice might be signature pedagogies, revealing what counts most in the education of clergy. However, as we observed the interactions of teaching and learning in seminary classrooms, we encountered too many variations even in these two approaches to be able to conclude that they or any other pedagogy dominated the pedagogical imaginations of seminary educators. At the same time, across the spectrum of the Jewish and Christian seminaries we observed four shared intentions for student learning, originating in clergy practice and embedded in a variety of pedagogies. Together they seemed to reflect what these seminary educators view as counting most in preparing students for clergy practice:

o Developing in students the facility for *interpreting* texts, situations, and relationships

o Nurturing dispositions and habits integral to the spiritual and vocational *formation* of clergy

o Heightening student consciousness of the content and agency of historical and contemporary *contexts*

o Cultivating student *performance* in clergy roles and ways of thinking

Each pedagogical intention had the potential of being expressed through a signature pedagogy. We discovered, however, that we could not anticipate how seminary educators with similar intentions for student learning would weave a variety of teaching methods into strategies for teaching. No teaching methods shared the surface structure of a signature pedagogy.

We gradually recognized that differences we observed in the teaching practices of seminary educators could be traced to varying religious and cultural assumptions about clergy practice embedded in the culture and mission of each seminary. Thus, the deep structures of their teaching practices vary. As the educators model values, attitudes, and dispositions embedded in those assumptions about clergy practice, the tacit structures of their pedagogies also differ. Something else was at work.

That something, we gradually realized, had to do with the persistence of these intentions for student learning in the variety of teaching practices we observed. We gradually recognized that together they formed a *signature pedagogical framework*. The interdependence of these intentions in the pedagogical imaginations of seminary educators influences their decisions about what and how to teach. Over time, and with much repetition, seminary educators develop distinctive approaches to the interplay of these four intentions in their pedagogical interactions with students. Those approaches, which students can often describe with considerable clarity, are the *teaching practices* that became the subject of this study.

Aligning Teaching Practices with the Mission and Culture of the Seminary

Descriptions of teaching practices, however, do not fully explain how seminary educators help prepare students for their future work as rabbis, priests, and pastors. Two phases of our research reinforced our awareness of this issue. In our review of the history of the education of clergy and the many studies of clergy education conducted over the past century, we were challenged to account for widely varied and deeply rooted historical assumptions about clergy work that continue to influence the intentions of contemporary seminary educators for the learning of their students. Understanding these traditions helped distinguish teaching practices in one seminary from those in another.

We were also fascinated by the diversity in the institutional cultures we experienced from one campus visit to the next: in the lines of authority among administration, faculty, and students; the patterns of relationship among faculty, between faculty and students, and between schools and their religious and public constituencies; the role of worship, student involvement in campus governance, and service to the community beyond the seminary; connections with sponsoring religious institutions and other academic entities; the design of the curriculum; and the relationship between course and field work.

The issue of the influence of school mission and culture on faculty teaching practices came into focus as we pondered, in each school we visited, the forces and structures that supported or discouraged teacher intentions for student learning. We had discovered in each school some students who had effectively pulled together and integrated the disparate strands of their education—from across the curriculum and in relating their academic work to spiritual growth and to professional skills integral to the daily work of clergy. We heard these reports in schools where lecture pedagogies dominated and in schools where students engaged predominantly in active learning pedagogies. We heard similar reports in schools where students experienced few overt connections between field education and class work and in other schools where the structures of field education and classroom were interwoven throughout their seminary experience. We heard these reports in schools where community worship and governance were tightly coordinated and in schools where they seemed almost incidental activities for many students (and often for faculty).

In a study of communities of practice, Wenger suggests that one may account for the coalescence of forces supporting or resisting faculty intentions for student learning by recognizing the presence of "three modes of belonging" (1998, pp. 173–4). Wenger calls the first mode the belonging that emerges from "active involvement in mutual processes of negotiation of meaning." This is the mutuality of influence in a teaching practice that occurs for students simply by participating in a small discussion group during a class session or by sharing the challenges and rhythms of an academic course and its assignments together. The second form of belonging at work in the teaching practices of clergy educators is rooted in the imaginative capacity to expand "the scope of reality and identity" in one's social world by producing new "images" and generating new relations that become "constitutive of the self" and one's participation in the community. In a pastoral, priestly, or rabbinic imagination, this is the capacity to see in a biblical text the form of a sermon, or in the depths of a fractured relationship, clues to reconciliation; to hear in an ancient prayer the voices of those who have prayed it through the centuries; in the act of a child's, generosity a vision for the stewardship of the earth. A third form of belonging in the teaching practices of clergy educators "bridges time and space" to align one's engagement in an educational activity with the "energies, actions, and practices" of something larger. In the context of seminary education, the dynamics of teaching and learning take place in and are influenced by their relationship to the "larger enterprises" of the school's mission and culture, the religious traditions that look to the school for future religious leadership, and the public realm in which those religious traditions negotiate their futures.

In a study of "good work," Howard Gardner, Mihaly Csikszentmihalyi, and William Damon use the notion of alignment to describe the coalescence of forces that support and sustain the sense that one's work, or practice, is indeed good (2001, p. 1). Although they do not use the language of belonging, they observe that good work involves more than professional skill or being thoughtful about one's responsibilities and the implications of one's work." Good work involves acting responsibly on one's personal goals in relation to "family, friends, peers and colleagues; the mission or sense of [one's] calling; the institutions with which [one] is affiliated; and lastly, the wider world"—the people we know, as well as "those who will come afterwards, and in the grandest sense, to the planet or to God." From these perspectives, work is more likely to be experienced as good both by the worker and others in the collaborative activity of the work itself, in the recognition of its imaginative possibilities, and when the worker senses alignment among all the possible relationships that impinge upon the work.

During our study, the notions of alignment and its opposite, misalignment, helped us think about how the various forces in the seminary setting contribute to or hinder the individual and collective intentions of a faculty for the integration of student learning experience in professional practice. They shed light on those aspects of a seminary education that augment and reinforce or hamper and diminish the individual and collective intentions of seminary educators for the learning of students.

The quest for alignment may be found in faculty attempts to limit or align those forces that may help in that effort by articulating academic, personal, and doctrinal or spiritual criteria for new faculty appointments, as well as academic and ethical standards for student admission; by requiring psychological tests and statements of motivation and interest in student applications; and by establishing sequences of learning in the curriculum. Some forces are much more difficult to control or manage—the relationship of student and faculty interest in a subject; the complementariness of assumptions across a faculty about the role of the classes they individually teach in the curriculum; the congruence of faculty teaching and student learning styles; the relationship of course work, worship, governance, and field education; and the confluence of academic, denominational, and cultural expectations for religious leaders.

We did not have the time or resources to investigate, as part of the study, the full range of these influences on the interaction of teachers and students in seminary teaching practices. However, throughout this volume we have attempted more generally to account for ways to assess the extent to which the alignment or misalignment of the institutional culture and mission of a school either augments and reinforces or hampers and diminishes the intent in faculty teaching practices for student learning.

In the next chapter we look closely at the diverse practices and many influences on practice that we found in the seminaries we studied. From that point, we move to an in-depth description of the pedagogies, both classroom and communal, that together prepare students for their work as clergy.

ENDNOTES

1. Quoted by Boyle (2004), p. 2.

2. This observation, described in the introduction to this study, is amplified in Sullivan (2005).

3. This movement in general education is reflected in the recent outpouring of books examining the general dynamics of teaching and learning. Some recent titles include Atkinson and Claxton (2000), Ayers (2004), Banner Jr. and Cannon (1997), Bess (2000), Ropers-Huilman (1998), and Vella (1994).

4. The defining work of Alasdair MacIntyre (1984) has significantly influenced these discussions. See, for example, Dykstra (1991), Kelsey (1992), Chopp (1995), Volf and Bass (2002), Farley (2003), Dykstra and Bass (1998), and Graham (1996).

   An important related contribution to the literature on practices among Jewish scholars is the work of Wendy Rosov (2001).

   Philosopher Paul Fairfield (2000) puts McIntyre into conversation with Heidegger, Gadamer, and Dewey in his discussion of practices.

   David T. Hansen probes, through the concept of tradition, the persisting character of practice in teaching in *Exploring the Moral Heart of Teaching: Toward a Teacher's Creed* (2001)—certainly one of the more provocative recent discussions on teaching in the life of the community.

   Michel de Certeau (1984) describes a practice as "a way of making"— "insinuated into and concealed within devices whose mode of usage they constitute, and thus lacking their own ideologies or institutions—conform to certain rules." Those "rules" thereby constitute a certain pervasive "logic." This view of practice leads de Certeau to argue that popular culture consists of "arts of making" (p. xv).

The topic of practices equally engages the imagination of social scientists and theorists. See, for example, Bell (1992), Argyris and Schön (1974), Bourdieu (1998 and 1990), Lave and Wenger (1991), Wenger's major study (1998), and Wenger, McDermott, and Snyder (2002).

5. See also Fairfield (2000), pp. 8–9.

6. Hall (1959): "I was led to my conclusion by the realization that there is no break between the present, in which man acts as a culture-producing animal, and the past, when there were no men and no cultures. There is an unbroken continuity between the far past and the present, for culture is bio-basic—rooted in biological activities" (p. 44).

Fairfield has observed that "Practices thus conceived encompass both primarily cognitive and pragmatic forms of activity including language use, hermeneutic dialogue, education, the arts, games, competitive sports, commerce, law, politics, community service, medicine, friendship, romantic love, family life, science, and scholarship" (2000, p. 9). He, for some strange reason, omitted religion.

7. In a chapter entitled "Knowing as Doing" in *The Culture of Education,* Jerome Bruner begins to explore the deeply historical and social processes of learning to know, which we are describing as our participation in social practices (1996, p. 154).

8. The schema that follows draws on Kieran Egan's study (1997) of the development of understanding. His attention was directed to the changing capacities in humans for understanding in the movement from young childhood into young adulthood. His description of the process of developing understanding, however, also seems appropriate to the experience of adults moving from ignorance to knowledge in their encounter with new bodies of knowledge or skill sets. It is in this latter sense that we suggest this schema as a way to think about the experience of students as they move through the seminary curriculum.

2

COMMON PROFESSION, DIVERSE PRACTICES

DAVID KELSEY OBSERVED, "The most obvious characteristic of the world of theological schools is the enormous diversity among its citizens" (1992, pp. 17–18). His attention was drawn to differences among the "deepest theological commitments" and the variety of "historical and sociocultural" factors influencing the decisions of Protestant theological school faculty about their educational mission—a conclusion also relevant to a discussion of the different traditions in Jewish and Catholic seminary education.

We, too, were impressed by the diversity across the spectrum of Jewish and Christian seminaries we visited, but the diversity that dominated our attention centered on the teaching practices of the faculty in those seminaries. From a distance, the teaching practices look remarkably alike from discipline to discipline, from seminary to seminary. Indeed, they do not seem all that different from teaching practices in related fields and disciplines. Up close, however—indeed, inside institutions educating clergy—their range and diversity become remarkable. Those differences may be traced in part to the range of theological and sociocultural traditions to be found among Jewish and Christian seminaries. (In Chapters Seven and Eight we describe something of the influence of those traditions.)

The diversity of teaching practices we found in the seminaries may also be traced to variations in the way clergy educators negotiate a range of social, pedagogical, and historical influences and how they view the relationship of the cognitive, practical, and formative apprenticeship.

This negotiation is part of what we are calling *pedagogical imagination.* Clergy educators view and relate to their diverse contexts in quite different ways, both when thinking about what and how to teach and while in the middle of the activity of teaching. In those moments, we see the exercise of their pedagogical imaginations. As we have already discussed, by pedagogical imagination we mean the capacity of a teacher to envision the construction of a pedagogical event by drawing on the interplay of disciplinary and professional knowledge and skills to fulfill his or her intentions for the learning of a particular group of students in a given place and at a designated time.

Minimally, pedagogical imagination involves making decisions about what to teach from all that could be taught; how to engage students; how to assess the extent to which students learn what was intended; how to negotiate one's sense of obligation to the students' expectations, traditions of knowledge, and the religious communities that will be receiving them as clergy and leaders in ministry; and how to respond and adapt to new situations and challenges while teaching. Those decisions require, as art educator Peter Abbs has argued, keeping "open a creative connection with the best of the cultural past" and taking "its collective energy forward" in quests, on the one hand, to reclaim the numinous, wisdom, and spiritual in teaching and on the other, to reduce threats to their continuing vitality posed by the "twin powers of eclectic consumerism and electronic technology" (2003, pp. 2–3).[1] We discovered among clergy educators many who share both his preference for teaching that is "challenging, subverting, transforming, and healing" and his resistance to the reduction of teaching to technique.

A Shared Goal

Differences in the exercise of the pedagogical imaginations of seminary educators may be seen in the intentions of several Bible teachers for the learning of their students. When Adriane Leveen, from Hebrew Union College, for example, described a course she teaches, she told us she wanted students "to be familiar with each of the Five Books of Moses"— the "specific themes and content as well as how the Five in their entirety work together to establish the basis of Jewish thought and belief." She then added that through this course she intends for students to develop "skills in reading and translating biblical Hebrew and in learning how to interpret biblical texts in a disciplined fashion."

James Schatzmann, at Southwestern Baptist Theological Seminary, told us that his "hope and prayer" is that through his teaching, students "will become equipped to interpret and apply Scripture wisely and sensitively."

He described for us an introductory course he enjoys teaching, in which students move systematically from an exploration of the "need for hermeneutics" to a discussion "of the Bible in terms of its major component parts and its canonical status" while "comparing and contrasting various views of biblical inspiration." The course includes as well an examination of the "historical development of the major contemporary approaches to hermeneutics" and an opportunity to apply "the principles of the grammatical-historical-theological-practical approach to hermeneutics by writing an exegetical paper," all with the expectation that students will integrate "balanced hermeneutical principles into the contexts of life and ministry."

After teaching an introductory course on Old Testament Exegesis for several semesters, Patricia Tull, from Louisville Presbyterian Theological Seminary, realized she needed to focus on skills. "I was attempting to teach them to be text critics," she observed, reflecting on changes she had made in the course, "but they are not ever going to do that. They do need to be aware of text criticism and able to evaluate textual notes. So I came up with the analogy that we were doing 'cake mix' textual criticism. We aren't cooking from scratch. We are cooking from the ingredients that textual critics have given us. We are making choices, however, among them. I want students to enter the world of the text, dwell there for a while and wrestle with it." Because "each student is different," she added, she hopes they will "revel" in the "skills that are easy for them," even as they are "introduced to skills that won't be so easy for them."

Dianne Bergant, from Catholic Theological Union, teaches from yet another perspective: "I try to get students to see that what we are doing in class—that is, handing down and re-interpreting our religious tradition from our own social locations—is just what our religious ancestors have always done." "My goal in this [introductory Old Testament] course is to give my students the intellectual tools they need to read and interpret scripture. I try to get them to understand that everybody interprets what they read or hear from their own social location." The starting point of her teaching is to help students become aware of the "diversity of situations that condition" their own readings and interpretations.

Jim Butler described a shift in the way he teaches his Old Testament introductory course, a shift that many other seminary educators had also made. "When I started teaching [at Fuller Theological Seminary], I was very focused on making sure that students had an opportunity to look at issues [of authorship and the like]—the kind of things you study in graduate school. . . . I have become more comfortable over time letting them read about those things and attending [in class] mostly to those things that create problems for them as evangelical students." This means focusing attention on "the multiple perspectives and mutually contradictory passages in the biblical text we are studying and letting the text itself challenge their assumptions." He now spends more time on what he calls his "bottom line issues—that is, talking about how would you use this in the life of the church. Who gravitates towards this literature and who would reject it?"

These seminary educators would seem to have much in common. They, like most of their colleagues, graduated from prominent doctoral programs. They write books, publish articles in scholarly journals, and participate in academic professional societies. They are deeply committed to critical methodologies for studying the texts and contexts for ministry that, in turn, inform their expectations for student learning. In this regard, most carry into their teaching the *wissenschaft* values of rationality and objectivity generally associated with the academic study of religion.

Their comments also make clear that they all have in common the task of preparing students for leadership of religious communities in the traditions of Judaism and Christianity. They participate in practices of teaching that originated in and give form to the future of the educational and religious traditions in and through which they teach. As Robert McAfee Brown notes, Christian communities—and, we would argue, Jewish communities as well—have a special relationship to certain historic and symbolic events in the past (1974, pp. 28ff). Each lives into the future with a profound memory or deep historical consciousness of that event. Something happened. Stories are told to explain and recall what happened. As time goes on, people begin to link meanings associated with those events to new situations and changing circumstances, to develop, share, negotiate, critique, and reconstruct their interpretations. Rituals are created to rehearse and intensify memories of those events. Certain dispositions, sensibilities, habits, and practices become associated with the rehearsal of those memories and participation in those rituals. People within those communities assume responsibility for handing on the stories and their interpretations—to guarantee they will not be forgotten, for nurturing the sensibilities, dispositions, and habits integral to the identity of the community, and for rehearsing the practices associated with those stories to ensure their continuing relevance. Communities, in turn, assume responsibility for training people to continue the traditions of telling and interpreting the stories and rehearsing the practices to extend their vitality and relevance into the future.

Teaching in seminaries is informed by this common goal of developing leaders responsible for maintaining and renewing—and sometimes transforming—the intent of their religious traditions for new situations and circumstances. The depth of the commitment of seminary educators to this task became evident to us as we compared faculty responses to a survey question about the most important change they hoped might take place for or in their students through their teaching. The overwhelming majority of faculty respondents explicitly described their goals for teaching and student learning, in terms that mingled cognitive and affective, disciplinary and professional, academic and religious expectations.

For example, a Scripture teacher hoped his or her students might displace "interpretive pride" with "interpretive humility" by becoming "open to surprise," "by being taken aback, to being 'disarranged' by texts they thought they controlled"; as well as to becoming "open to comfort from texts they thought were only hostile to them"; not "to fear the Bible," but to be "lovers . . . with all the possibility that image entails for quarreling, mystery, intimacy, and gift-giving."

Others anticipated the possibility that students might discover, through their teaching, ways of thinking about and relating to the work of their ministries. "I hope," wrote one respondent, "my students will come to see themselves as practical theologians engaging critically, constructively, and lovingly the practice of ministry." Another made a similar point, expressing a desire for "my students" to see "their Judaism as a praxis that is nourished by Torah study and prayer rather than as a body of data or a repertoire of teachings for them to apply to other people. I hope they learn to keep a conversation going between the tradition, its texts and values, and the world they live in, the new problems it presents and the new wonders it reveals to us. Their job is to live out that conversation with integrity and to help others learn to do the same." These seminary educators teach so their students might become professionally competent in the various roles and responsibilities associated with the professional work of the clergy. They share the desire, as expressed by one survey respondent, for students to have an experience of "ministerial formation that integrates theological vision and wise pastoral practice with a whole sense of Christian identity and vocation," or, as expressed by another, "[I hope] that students will come to see that loving God with the mind is not an alternative to loving God with the heart, but is essential to the final integrity of the latter." They also teach to develop in their students the capacity to envision strategic responses from the dialogue of religious tradition and contemporary knowledge and the ability to address challenges to the futures of the religious communities they serve.

Influences on Teaching Practices

We discovered that seminary educators are sensitive to a range of influences on their decisions about what to teach and how. Their response to these influences—as individuals and as members of a faculty—typically leads to quite different approaches to the dynamics of teaching and learning. We found five influences in the context of the seminary to be particularly powerful:[2]

- Campus setting
- Classroom setting
- Competing academic traditions
- Curricular function
- Student expectations and experience

Campus Setting

Perhaps sensitivity to Jewish and Christian messages through the ages about the nature and activity of God in the physical environment has contributed to our heightened consciousness of the influence of the environment on the interactions of teaching and learning among seminary teachers and students. Certainly, the relatively small scale of every seminary campus within the universe of higher education offered us ample opportunities to witness where and how students move through the campus, places they identify as having intensified meaning, and classrooms faculty enjoy or dislike as teaching spaces. One can, with relative ease, obtain a sense of the whole even in a school as large as Fuller Theological Seminary, with its more than 4,300 students.

When Patricia Tull meets her class at Louisville Presbyterian Theological Seminary, for example, they gather in the recital hall of Garden Court, a mansion located on the grounds of a large estate in an exclusive neighborhood of the city, a short distance from the campus of Southern Baptist Theological Seminary. Massive trees on spacious grounds with landscaped gardens provide a parklike setting for the campus, which includes Garden Court, a comparatively new cluster of stone buildings housing classrooms, offices, and chapel, and, across a ravine, a student apartment complex. A large, relatively new conference center physically extends the school's academic mission beyond its degree programs by drawing the community to the campus. The campus setting seems far removed from the rural and central city neighborhoods from which some students come—and to which many faculty and students go to fulfill classroom assignments and field placements designed to engage them constructively and prophetically with the city's legacies of racism and classism.

We encountered a quite different environment for teaching and learning in New York, as we were admitted by security guards—a beefed-up force after the September 11, 2001, attacks and the destruction of the World Trade Center towers—to the imposing complex of buildings that make up the Jewish Theological Seminary in Morningside Heights. The seminary is located down the street from Columbia University and surrounded in part by Union Theological Seminary, Teachers College–Columbia University, and Manhattan School of Music. Seminary education occurs here in the midst of a cacophony of messages about scholarship and learning, observance and tradition, the holy and the secular, safety and danger, leadership and practice—all punctuated by the rumble of the subways emerging from a nearby underground tunnel. Yet a month later, while walking under the massive trees of the Fuller Theological Seminary campus in Pasadena, California, we were reminded of the tranquility of the courtyard at the Jewish Theological Seminary and the Louisville gardens—all places providing for conversation removed from the frantic pace of busy streets and urban life.

As we moved from campus to campus, we found ourselves pondering overt and implicit values and commitments in the teaching of faculty associated with the location of a school. For example, what relationship might exist between the affluence of the school's neighborhood and the attention many Louisville faculty give to analyzing racist and unjust social systems? What influence does the racial, cultural, and religious diversity of the Los Angeles area have on Fuller faculty and student efforts to mediate the worlds of fundamentalist and mainline Protestant churches and the cultures they represent? In what ways do the values and rigor of the research universities of Columbia, Chicago, and Yale shape the faculty expectations of student knowledge and academic performance at Jewish Theological Seminary, Catholic Theological Union, and Yale Divinity School? Trinity Lutheran Seminary, with its German Lutheran heritage, is very aware of the predominantly Jewish neighborhood in which it is located; the seminary commissioned a large and striking memorial to Holocaust victims, visible to all who pass by. We wondered in what other ways the encounter of German heritage and Jewish community might shape the educational experience of Trinity students.

These questions were heightened for us during our visit to Howard University School of Divinity in Washington, D.C. In words similar to those articulated in the mission statements of every school we visited, the Howard faculty explicitly seeks to "prepare students to provide competent professional leadership in religious and secular institutions," with a distinctive commitment to "urban Black Communities."[3] Teachers meet their students on the campus of a former Franciscan college in a building displaying large sculptures of Franciscan spirituality on its external walls and housing, inside, an extensive collection of iconic images of Ethiopian Christianity; they meet in the nation's only African American research university, located in the nation's capital and thereby in the crosscurrents of city, national, and global policy debates.

The setting, in other words, provides a catalyst for a curricular commitment to teach to an espoused mission of "prophetic ministry" guided by a "passion for justice and freedom" and a "relentless search for truth." It did not surprise us, then, to hear a student say that a Howard graduate is "supposed to be able to fight the good fight, to take up the social issues, and be the activist, to take on the battles for the poor . . . I won't say to be militant, but to be the Jesse Jackson, the Martin Luther King, to hold up the banner of justice and faithfulness." He was not only reflecting the public mission of the school, he was articulating a view of expectations for his professional practice embedded in the iconic images and reinforced by the school's involvement in the life of the city and nation.

After a rather extensive discussion of the challenge Yale faculty experience teaching in religiously diverse classes in the divinity school of one of the premier research universities of the nation, one student suggested an image of the Yale graduate congruent with the image of a major Ivy League research institution: "If there's a shared vision . . . it's that . . . professors here teach you to ask big questions . . . good questions. By good questions, I mean creative questions, questions that excite the imagination, questions that challenge the individual and the society, questions that turn traditional readings of say, the Bible or theology on their head. . . . I think that's the one thing that unites both the academics and the religious."

We heard a still different perspective on the relationship of setting and educational experience when another student told us that the liturgy "is the heart of the campus" at Church Divinity School of the Pacific. We had some sense of what this statement might mean when we discovered that although the chapel sits on the edge of the campus, the daily routines of class, faculty, and student community life revolve around fifteen liturgies in that chapel each week. At each campus we visited we were similarly impressed with the extent to which the pedagogical interactions of faculty and students had been influenced by their physical and cultural setting.

Classroom Setting

Classrooms similarly enhance or obstruct faculty intentions for their teaching and student learning. Classrooms in theological schools vary significantly. The superb acoustics of the recital hall where Tull meets her introductory class on the Old Testament reinforce the aesthetic experience of singing songs in Hebrew in three-part harmony. In contrast, Butler, teaching in a school with a large commuting student body, feels constrained by the space in which he teaches. A wide and comparatively shallow classroom with desk chairs arranged on narrow tiers limits his ability to involve students in small group learning. Bergant and her colleagues teach their larger classes in three technologically "smart" classrooms carved out of the ballroom of the former hotel that anchors the Catholic Theological Union campus, but the lack of alternative spaces means they must meet some of their small classes and discussion groups around tables in the cafeteria. For Tull, Butler, Bergant, and many other seminary educators we met, the rooms—and, indeed, the larger physical environment of the school—where they teach also become resources or hindrances to their intentions for student interaction with their teaching.

Competing Academic Traditions: Paideia and Wissenschaft

Differences in the approaches of faculty to their teaching may be traced in part, as well, to how faculty individually and collectively negotiate what Edward Eggleston (1959 [1900]) once called the "controlling traditions" of a culture or community and its assumptions about the role or mission it has in the larger world. In academic settings, these controlling traditions may be traced back to different visions of the academic enterprise. The consequences of the negotiations of a faculty over the influence of these traditions are significant. They are expressed in mission statements and articulated in curriculum policies. They shape academic values and standards. They influence the habits and dispositions of graduates in professional practice.

In *Between Athens and Berlin*, Kelsey (1993) argues that one of the most influential of these "controlling traditions" in Protestant seminary education may be found in extensively shared commitments to the contrasting values of *paideia* and *wissenschaft*, the first originating in Greek philosophy and the second in the individualism and objective rationality associated with the Enlightenment.[4] Kelsey argued, however, that the values located in the authority of the tradition (*paideia*) and in the capacity for critical distance in scholarship and teaching (*wissenschaft*) "sit together very uneasily." Indeed, he concluded, they can only lead to "various sorts of negotiated truces" between their "incommensurate sets of criteria of excellence" (p. 92). The result is that among Christian seminaries, some will reflect more clearly the values of one or the other in their programs and policies. Yet as we heard seminary educators describe what they do when they teach across the spectrum of schools participating in this study, we heard most of them embrace (albeit to quite different effects) the necessary interdependence of these two traditions in their teaching.

This observation first became evident to us while visiting the Jewish Theological Seminary. Although the communal and traditional pedagogies of the synagogue and yeshiva (which share many of the communal values of the traditions of *paideia*) provide the historical backdrop for the establishment of this seminary, its founders embraced fully the rationality of *wissenschaft* scholarship that had revolutionized rabbinical education in Berlin in the early nineteenth century.[5] Frequently we heard members of the faculty say that the ultimate expression of being a rabbi is as one who studies. That was true prior to the Enlightenment and before the Jewish Theological Seminary was founded, and it continues to be true today.

Contemporary methodologies of studying texts in Jewish Theological Seminary courses have been transformed by post-Enlightenment commitments to objectivity and rationality, but the notion of obedience to Torah through disciplined study, deeply rooted in the traditions of the yeshiva preceding the Enlightenment, persists today. Scholarship is at the heart of rabbinical identity; rabbinical identity is grounded in the capacities for solid scholarship. The pedagogy of that scholarship within the tensive relationship of "Berlin" rationality and "yeshiva" communality draws both together in *havrutah* or structured dialogical study. In that relational practice, students engage in ways of learning that join ancient rabbinic dialogue and contemporary scholarly methods.

A biblical scholar in a university theological school affirmed a similar vision of the complementariness of *paideia* and *wissenschaft* when he said that through his teaching he hoped students would discover how to "combine loyalty and criticism, devotion and creativity." Butler makes a similar claim when he says he does not want students "to have one part of their brain that works critically and then another part that works devotionally." In pedagogical terms, this means that in his quest to expand and deepen both their understanding of the Bible and their faith, he has increasingly focused student attention on issues in which the critical study of Scripture collides with shared scriptural pieties. The pedagogical task is critical and objective; the learning agenda is communal and even devotional. Tull, who teaches students typically identified as more liberal than those at Fuller, has a similar intention. She wants them to be "interpreters of Scripture in a world of interpretation with others. This means that I want them not merely to be parrots of other people's views nor merely naïve readers of Scripture." Rather, she hopes they will become "active contributors to the ongoing conversation about Scripture—that they may come into their own as critically aware, theologically engaged empathic readers."

In one sense, these teachers of Old Testament or Hebrew Bible have negotiated the relationship of *paideia* and *wissenschaft* in their teaching by focusing, often unconsciously, on their students rather than on the organization or function of the seminary curriculum. Butler, for example, is sensitive to those places where the biblical text poses questions for the faith of his students. Bergant directs student attention to questions that emerge from a growing consciousness of the multiple contexts influencing their reading of any given text, with special attention to the tensions students will encounter between the authority of church tradition and local culture. Differences in the attention they give to the values of *wissenschaft* and *paideia* in their teaching may be attributed in part to their different perceptions of student perspective and experience and in part to different expectations for what they want students to be able to do when they study biblical texts. In this regard, these seminary educators also model a way to view their leadership of biblical studies in the congregations they will eventually be serving.

Curricular Function

In *The Educational Imagination* (1985), Elliot Eisner argues that every school has three curricula. The explicit curriculum is articulated in mission statements, courses of study, and syllabi. The implicit curriculum is found in the rituals and organizational structures, values and assumptions, and patterns of relationship and authority that make up the culture of a school. The null curriculum encompasses "the options students are not afforded, the perspectives they may never know about, much less be able to use, the concepts and skills" that do not become a part of their intellectual or professional repertoire (p. 107). The distinctive ways in which these curricula are configured to extend the mission and reflect the values of a seminary culture also contribute to the diversity of seminary teaching practices.

Eisner's insight about the influence of the curriculum was illustrated for us as Bible teachers described the function of their introductory courses in the explicit curriculum of their respective schools. When Tull, Bergant, and Schatzmann meet students in their introductory courses, they assume that this will be, for most, their first exposure to Bible study in graduate professional education—indeed, for many, the first since Sunday school. Their courses function as a foundation for and catalyst to advanced work in the field. At Fuller, where students are required to take three courses surveying the whole of the Old Testament literature (any one of which can be taken first), Butler must design his course with the expectation that this will be the first experience with the subject for some students and the third for others. He must figure out a way to introduce some students to the field of study while building on prior knowledge of the field for others. Leveen, in contrast, assumes students have a working knowledge of Hebrew language when planning to teach.

These basic curricular decisions point to a range of philosophical assumptions about the nature and function of the explicit curriculum in a school's mission. Daniel Tanner and Laurel Tanner have identified at least seven different views among curriculum theorists alone and then proceed to suggest an eighth (1995, pp. 87–9).[6] The seminary educators we observed, however, seemed to engage these theories not so much as different ways of thinking about curriculum but as different perspectives on the curricular task. Tull, Bergant, and Schatzmann, for example, reflect the emphases of one theory when they seek through their introductory courses to draw students into the "cumulative tradition of organized knowledge" in Scripture studies embedded in the tasks and responsibilities of clergy practice. At the same time they also view the courses they teach as an integral part of an "instructional plan" or "course of study"—another view of curriculum—to advance student learning. Some of the seminary educators we met understood their teaching, either positively or negatively, in Pierre Bourdieu's (Bourdieu and Passeron, 1977 [1990]) terms, as cultural reproduction, whereas others understood it as the "reconstruction of knowledge and experience"—two additional theoretical perspectives.

In any configuration of these theories, the courses that seminary educators teach contribute to some curricular function. At Fuller, for example, introductory courses are designed to familiarize students with the sweep of the biblical story—often called a "survey"—and an exposure to interpretive problems that story raises, with the expectation that they will, in Butler's words, "expand" (and, presumably, "deepen") their faith and knowledge, whether as academics or ministers. A similar course at Yale has a different curricular function. Yale biblical faculty immediately introduce students to the methods and practices for interpreting biblical texts, with the expectation that through this effort they will not only become familiar with their content but also become competent enough to continue the practice of interpretation in academic and ministry settings.

Jewish Theological Seminary, Louisville Presbyterian Theological Seminary, and Trinity Lutheran Seminary faculty take yet another approach. Biblical courses require a basic working knowledge of the original languages. This makes it possible from the outset to draw students into translation exercises that facilitate, over time, their increasing ability to closely and critically read biblical texts in Greek or Hebrew.

At Trinity, we saw a different view of the explicit curriculum as a template for the establishment and maintenance of learning community. The summer course in Greek introduces most students to the language and the life of the seminary. The formal teaching of Greek is embedded in a comprehensive strategy for building a learning cohort that includes student involvement in planning for worship and fellowship activities. Collaborative learning is emphasized in learning Greek and also in planning worship and fellowship activities. Decisions of Trinity faculty members about what and how to teach in subsequent courses are similarly informed by widely shared commitments among the faculty about the value of mutuality among the participants in a community of teaching and learning. Faculty members engage in predominantly transmissive pedagogies for introductory courses to Bible, theology, and church history to provide a common vocabulary for subsequent work. But they also meet informally with small groups made up of first, second, and final year students to explore in collaborative fashion their progress through the seminary curriculum. Some faculty members, moreover, self-consciously choose to shift how they teach advanced courses, to facilitate student collaboration in the exploration of biblical and theological themes, questions, and issues arising directly from ministry experience in field education and their intern year in a pastoral setting.

Faculty teaching practices are also influenced by assumptions about the curricular location of responsibility for student learning. Some faculties—both intentionally and unintentionally—locate that responsibility with the individual student. This is the case especially in large schools or schools with a high student-to-faculty ratio or a large commuting student population. If students want to probe an issue from class in greater depth or talk about a difficulty they are having in class, they are typically invited to meet the instructor during office hours. Students talked, for example, about Butler's availability after class, while walking across campus, or during office hours. In reality, however, comparatively few seek him out. The curricular assumption that students are responsible for their own learning does not require a faculty member to be particularly familiar with the learning goals and struggles of individual students. Nor does it establish expectations for highly interactive and collaborative learning environments. Indeed, in this situation many students indicate that the more traditional lecture with question-and-answer strategies works quite well for them.

The placement of a course in the curriculum also reveals explicit faculty decisions and, often, implicit faculty assumptions about the value and function of any given course in the education of their students. Is the course required, an option that fills a requirement, or an elective? Does it occur in the first semester or the last? Do colleagues in other disciplines explicitly build on the knowledge and skills developed in any given course, or does each tend to stand alone? Is a given course designed to provide the knowledge and skills for students to pass school or ordination exams? Is the course introductory or advanced? Does it assume prerequisite knowledge and skills, or is it open and available to anyone enrolled in one of the school's degree programs? Is it designed primarily for students preparing for clergy work or for an academic career? Is it linked to the research agenda of a faculty member? Whether acknowledged or not, these and other questions influence faculty decisions about what course to teach, and how to teach any given course.

The curriculum embedded in a course of study, however, is not the only explicit curriculum some seminary students encounter. In most Protestant seminaries, students work through parallel and, in some instances, competing programs of learning and preparation for ordination. At Louisville, for example, denominational ordination exams occur during the academic year. Tull and her colleagues support students in their quest for ordination by "pointing out what they should learn for the exams." The school provides staff services to help students prepare for the exams. During our visit, faculty members in a class we were visiting noted that two students were absent because they were preparing for their exams. Although the faculty has been arguing with the denomination to move the exams out of the academic year, in the meantime each of these accommodations infringes on traditional patterns of faculty time and attention and the distribution of school resources.

With students from more than one hundred denominations, Fuller makes provision for supplemental curricular offerings and experiences for students seeking to meet their various denominational academic requirements. Most Protestant seminaries approach the relationship of academic and ordination expectations within this spectrum. A common pattern involves providing specific courses to meet denominational requirements around issues of doctrine, history, and polity. Sometimes these courses exist only as a service to the denomination; in other schools they function as an integral component in the curriculum. Many students preparing for ordination in these schools also work on a set of parallel assignments to clarify their call to and fitness for ministry, and to make evident to church officials that they are intellectually, spiritually, and professionally ready to assume roles of ministry within that particular denomination. When the aggregate of students preparing for ordination in any one denomination is large enough, the values and standards for ordination in that denomination become a significant component in the school's implicit curriculum.

Their experience contrasts with the situation for students in Jewish seminaries in which the faculty decides who is fit for ordination and ordains them, or for Roman Catholic, Orthodox Christian, Anglican, and Evangelical Lutheran students in denominational seminaries in which their steps toward ordination are typically interwoven with the course of study established by the faculty.

The implicit curriculum is embedded in other structures as well. Among the most pervasive are processes for what Catholics and others call *spiritual formation* or what evangelical Protestants often call *discipling*. In schools as different as St. John's Seminary and Southwestern Baptist Theological Seminary, some of these programs are required but function outside their academic and field education structures. Many of the goals of the implicit curriculum in seminary education are articulated as dispositions, habits, and disciplines. They are espoused in mission statements, focused on in orientation programs for new students, described in student and faculty handbooks, and embedded strategically in programs, rituals, and relationships integral to the culture of the school. They become visible in shared expectations and standards for faculty and student participation and performance in worship life, in school governance, in transitional ritual events, even in patterns of greeting and interaction among members of the seminary community that tend to spill over into the conduct of a school's academic life.

We have already noted, for example, how Butler participates in the Fuller cultural affirmation of the personal piety of students, faculty, and staff by teaching in a way that will not "disrupt the faith of students" but instead "stretch it." Bergant, as a member of a seminary community that honors cultural diversity and encourages the mutuality of cultural encounter, not only embraces the academic traditions of biblical textual criticism, but also seeks to heighten student awareness to the interplay of their historical and social locations with that of the texts they are reading so they might affirm their "received tradition as Roman Catholics . . . with a critical stance toward the implication of that tradition for life today."

Most graduates of Howard, as a quite different example, assume that their education, like the ministries they anticipate, will be couched in the traditions and practices of the black church and African American culture. As Kortright Davis, professor of theology, observed, this means, among other things, that Howard students "must know how to think on their feet"—they must be comfortable with the distinctive oral traditions of black church preaching and other sites of public presentation. In other words, the perspectives that Butler, Bergant, and Davis bring to teaching their students how to read the Bible involve deeply rooted assumptions about the religious life and the interpretation of Scripture in the cultures of their respective schools.

When comparing faculty teaching practices, we also became aware of a null curriculum in each class and each school. Bible educators in schools that do not require the biblical languages are limited in the extent to which they can introduce students to the complexities and subtleties of the original languages in translation. Teachers who do not have the expertise or feel comfortable teaching students to sing or chant the Psalms will not likely introduce students to that aesthetic experience. Teachers who emphasize either critical analyses or devotional study of sacred texts will not introduce students to the power of their interdependence. Teachers, of course, must make decisions about what to include in a course and how to engage students with their intentions for their learning. The time they have, the experience students bring to the class, and the resources available all affect what they can and cannot do. Some of their decisions are conscious and others are unconscious. Whatever decisions they do make inevitably highlight some possibilities for learning and exclude others.

Student Expectations and Experience

The increasing diversity of students in programs of clergy education has significantly challenged the ethos and mission of seminary education during the past forty years.[7] Seminary educators are fully aware of the trends and their implications; for example:

○ Relatively recent decisions by Reform and Conservative Jews and many Protestant denominations to ordain women have been accompanied by dramatic increases in the number of women students and women faculty in clergy education programs. Expansion of lay ministry options has similarly brought many women into some Roman Catholic seminaries. Enrollment of women in the Association of Theological Schools, for example, increased 234 percent between 1977 and 2002.

○ A parallel increase in the numbers of historically marginalized students attending theological schools has been one of the more obvious consequences of the civil rights movement—from 4 percent of the total in 1977 to 21 percent in 2002. Especially in Catholic seminaries, these figures include significant numbers of recent immigrants from Asia, Africa, and Central and South America.

○ With expanding college educational opportunities and the volatility of the workplace, increasing numbers of older students have been enrolling in seminaries. Reports from the Association of Theological Schools indicate, for example, that theological students tend to be older than students in law or medicine, are more evenly distributed across the adult age span, and possess a wider range of educational and professional experience.

○ In some schools, these differences are compounded by the diversity of religious traditions represented in both student body and faculty. As noted above, Fuller reports a student community drawn from more than one hundred different Christian denominations; Yale students identified with thirty-nine denominations, with several reporting no religious affiliation. Even a denominational school like Candler lists thirty-six denominations represented among its student body, and North Park Theological Seminary publicizes that its student community comes from "many denominations." Students at St. Vladimir's Orthodox Theological Seminary represent a range of national and ethnic Christian Orthodox traditions. Students at Jewish Theological Seminary identify with various movements in contemporary Judaism.

Jane Shaw, dean of the Chapel of New College at Oxford University and a consultant to both this project and the Lexington Seminar,[8] has suggested that a consciousness of the importance of attending to student diversity may be endemic to American clergy education. She was most intrigued by the contrasts between an English system that finances the full education of students approved for ministry study and an American system that relies heavily on student tuition. This dependency on tuition, she suggests, intensifies competition in recruiting students and increases attention to the retention of admitted students. Her observation may help explain, in part, why many schools in recent years have been willing to admit growing numbers of "seekers"[9] whose lack of preparatory knowledge and identification with the professional goals of the seminary curriculum clearly compound the complexity of the school's pedagogical task of professional preparation with the necessity of incorporating them into a tradition of faith or observance. Rebecca Chopp's argument (1995) about the influence on seminary culture of increasing numbers of women is pertinent here. When faculties become conscious of and begin to account for the expectations and experience of each new constituency in the student community, inherited and hegemonic patterns of teaching and learning are inevitably disrupted.

All this means that with the range of diversity to be found in most schools, no faculty member can assume any particular constellation of student background or experience from one term to the next as they prepare to teach. Greene's observation that teachers teach in situations "never twice the same" is especially true of seminary educators (1973, p. 69). When Bergant walks into the first session of a class at Catholic Theological Union, for example, she must ascertain the extent to which the students she is teaching are working toward the priestly or lay master of divinity, the master of arts, or the master of arts in pastoral studies degree programs, or no degree program; the extent to which their academic and professional backgrounds prepared them for graduate professional study of the Old Testament; the charism of the various orders that send their students to Catholic Theological Union; the countries they represent and languages they speak; and, eventually, their individual strengths and problems in learning what she seeks to teach.

The challenge for Butler is even more complex. His classes, like those of Bergant, include students in different degree programs. They bring a diversity of international, ethnic, gender, age, and educational backgrounds to the study of the Old Testament. They represent as well a vast number of Christian denominations and popular religious movements. He is also conscious of the challenges of teaching some students who have recently converted to Christianity and are entertaining possibilities of ministry while still novitiates in the journey of Christian discipleship and other students who are "burned out" from the intensity of their participation in apocalyptic religious communities. For the faculty at Jewish Theological Seminary, differences between yeshiva-educated students and those coming from university Jewish studies programs pose challenges about how to respond to the variation in their readiness to engage in the rigorous reading of texts.

These "new" and often "nontraditional" students, we discovered, were often aware of the resulting tensions these differences posed for their instructors. A middle-aged woman in her seminary's honors program makes the point. She entered divinity school after years of teaching children in a public school. Her "call to ministry" was not only unexpected, it was "just overwhelming." After making the decision to uproot her life in midcareer, she discovered that "seminary was really different from what I expected it to be." Active participation in her congregation had not prepared her for the kinds of things taught in Bible and theology classes or for the resistance she felt toward the expectations of her clinical pastoral education supervisor about how she should interact with patients in the hospital. It has been a "time of transition," she said, and the two or three years of a seminary program is "not a lot of time," she added, "to transition" from one professional and thought world to another.

But now, in her final year, she said, "I'm engaging more in the dialogue, working through some issues, because I know it's about time to go out there in the real world." Near the end of our conversation, she made several comments indicating a set of issues she brought to her experience of that school's teaching that had not been addressed. "I come from an educational background"—with experience that had been generally ignored in her seminary education. She pointed to the research she had done on "learning styles and how people learn best." She regretted that, as far as she knew, no faculty member of her seminary took into account this body of knowledge in their deliberations about how to facilitate her learning or that of her colleagues.

In an essay probing the dynamics of social class in the classroom, bell hooks poses one of the issues to be found in this woman's comment for teachers (2003, pp. 147–8). It centers on the "complex recognition of the uniqueness" of each student and the range of experience and knowledge that students together bring to a teacher's intentions for their learning. The challenge for faculty occurs in the quest "to create spaces in the classroom" where all students can be heard because they sense they are "free to speak" to the questions and issues of the day, because they know "their presence will be recognized and valued." We discovered that most clergy educators share this value, but it is one much easier to espouse than to honor.

Still another form of difference, originating in student expectations for their educational experience, deepens the challenge for faculty in making decisions about what and how to teach. Most theological schools see their educational mission as advancing theological studies generally and the theological education of clergy specifically.[10] This means they admit some students anticipating a clergy career and other students seeking an academic career. The former anticipate ordination; many of the latter look forward to doctoral studies. These different expectations become clear as they describe their educational experience. Most clergy respondents to our survey viewed those years in ways summarized by one graduate as "an incredible experience": "I really loved my time at Yale"; "I was really privileged to have attended Fuller"; "HUC was an incredible experience"; "Southwestern really challenged me to think"; "I was awakened, encouraged, liberated."

Many, however, also described an experience of the tension between these two goals. A Fuller student anticipating a ministry career, for example, told us that "I think Fuller does a wonderful job of training people going into doctoral work . . . [but] I don't think it is as helpful for training for pastoral ministry." A Candler student found the school's "efforts to accommodate all religious belief" a challenge "to my faith." A student at Yale observed that some faculty "are here to create great ministers" and others are "here to create great academics." This means that "both those students who come here to become academics and those who come here to become ministers kind of get caught in the middle. . . . It's something of a blessing and a curse." A student from Jewish Theological Seminary noted, "The academic learning at JTS is great. But it is rare for the academic learning to point towards the practical rabbinate in any way. Teachers are most effective when they take into consideration the broader context of our learning." A few students shared the sentiments of a student from an evangelical seminary who expressed "dismay" and "sorrow" over seminaries "losing their identities" in a preference for "brain growth" over "spiritual growth." Since most schools engaged in the education of clergy have an academic master's degree or have students who enroll in the master of divinity degree with the expectation that it will prepare them for doctoral work, most faculty share in some way the dilemma faced by Fuller, Candler, Southwestern, and Yale: how to meet the challenge of accommodating the relationship of student academic and professional expectations for their learning.

A faculty member from a school with a very diverse student body told us that her school was the "most homogenous place she had ever been." Her comment raised a question: to what extent do seminaries accommodate—in the institutional culture, public mission, and teaching practices—the presence of differences among students? Despite shared rhetoric about institutional inclusivity, no school we visited pedagogically embraced the full range of differences faculty encountered among its students. Rather, in each school some unifying perceptions heightened faculty attention to some differences and diminished awareness of others. Certain denominational practices or beliefs, patterns of piety, historic cultural traditions, epistemological values, educational background, or assumptions about social class, race and gender, cultural, and personal learning styles provided coherence for some students, while for others, they contributed to the experience of marginalization.

Pedagogical Imagination Illustrated: Two Cases

Teaching relies on the exercise of a teacher's imagination at every stage of designing and conducting the activities of teaching and learning. It is an art form refined over time by repetition and disciplined reflection. It leads—at least in the practice of teachers we observed—to the construction of pedagogical events encompassing all the ambiguity we have been describing but directed, nonetheless, toward specific expectations for student learning. In this section, we offer an extended description of Bergant's and Tull's teaching practices to illustrate the range and complexity of the kinds of decisions seminary educators make in the exercise of their pedagogical imaginations and also to illustrate why students experience the teaching of the same literature so differently in different academic settings.

Teaching to Attend to Social Location
Dianne Bergant, Catholic Theological Union

Bergant introduced the class session we observed with an implicit challenge to the assumptions of some students about the role of women in Catholic tradition. She began the class session with a prayer from St. Teresa, noting that it was St. Teresa's day in the calendar of saints. The prayer provided her with the opportunity to emphasize the role of a woman as "thinker and teacher in the Christian, and Roman Catholic, tradition" several times during the class session. It established a theological framework for the class ("all is passing" and "God is enough"). It also functioned as a pedagogical device "signaling" for students Bergant's intention that they learn how to combine an affirmation of their religious tradition with a critical stance toward its implications for contemporary life.

She structured the rest of the class session, dealing with the book of Genesis, to help students continue to "learn how to read" because, as she emphasized, "if you learn how to read, then you can read all other texts." To develop this capacity, she leads students through the steps of a hermeneutical practice with designated texts each week. A set of preassigned questions designed to encourage students to develop the skill of taking responsibility for their own study prepares students to move through these steps, establishing, in the repetition of the process, an increasingly familiar shape for each class session. These questions engage students in the problems they will encounter as they read assigned texts. They also remind students of the various social locations of relationships involved in their reading of a text.

Bergant begins the practice "in front of the text" with the explanation that there are many "different ways of interpreting." Those ways of interpreting are what readers of texts bring to their reading. Attention to them reminds us of our social locations. When she moves the discussion to historical questions regarding the text, Bergant engages the students in exploring the "worlds behind the text." When she shifts the discussion of a text to focus on, "say how God was depicted," then "that's the world within the text." She emphasizes that this is no linear process, for descriptions of the "world within the text" typically lead one back to questions "behind the text" about the social location of those who are, in this instance, "depicting God." Bergant brings the discussion full circle when she asks students to reflect on their discussion to ascertain "how much we have interpreted the text today" and then notes once again "that's the world in front of the text."

During the class session she mostly stands or walks about in the front of the conventionally organized rectangular room, firing questions and eliciting comments prompted by the flow of the discussion, writing student responses on the board, gesticulating strongly to emphasize a point, or gesturing affirmatively when a student raises questions or makes observations on the topic at hand. She punctuates the flow of the session with highly animated mini-lectures probing the meaning of the text through a closer look at its historical and cultural context. Often she interrupts these mini-lectures either for a question she wants the students to consider or to answer a student's request for additional information.

Teaching to Appreciate Reading the Text
Patricia Tull, Louisville Presbyterian Theological Seminary

Tull shares Bergant's desire that students become effective readers of biblical texts. But she imagines the experience of student learning in a quite different fashion. She has an advantage: each of her students enters the class with some facility in Hebrew. This means that she has a ready-made structure to pose problems for student engagement: problems emerging from the task of struggling to translate texts from the Hebrew into English. The learning goal for Tull does not center on problems of translation, but on her desire that students develop a love and appreciation for reading the text. In her class, traditional cognitive expectations become explicitly affective; she expands her teaching strategies to include not only the discursive but also the aesthetic. She uses the exercise of translation, consequently, not only as a primary mode for practicing the reading and interpretation of texts, but also to establish the basic structure for the interaction of teacher and students. She encourages students to pursue their own study through recurring assignments to bring to class translations of designated texts. Before she asks the students to share their translations with each other, however, she gathers the class into what might be called aesthetic encounters with the texts of their study—first by singing in three-part harmony a song learned in Hebrew language class the previous summer, then by listening as she reads a Psalm as opening prayer. Only then do students begin the practice of translation in small groups—another version, it might be noted, of the collaborative process that Bergant uses to encourage student participation.

After the students have worked on the translation of a text in small groups, they move back into a plenary session to explore more complex issues at stake in the work of translation. Using presentation slide software, Tull compares different ancient translations of the same text and engages students in a dialogical process to raise questions and probe issues posed by the differences among them. Every so often she pauses to poll them on whether they find one translation or another more compelling. The lack of agreement in their voting dramatizes the complexity of their task.

These class sessions are highly interactive. Bergant and Tull require student participation to keep the flow going. They work to create environments in which students will publicly risk what they know and do not know. They keep a firm grip on the direction or design of the flow of the class session, but also give mini-lectures on the spot as they respond to and elicit comments from students. Although they use familiar methods—lecture, discussion, reading, questions—they weave them together into complex and creative patterns or strategies for teacher, student, and textual interaction.

Students expressed to us great appreciation for the teaching of these two women. So did students with faculty who "lectured" in more traditional ways. At Fuller, students expressed gratitude for the way Butler illuminates the usefulness of the scholarship of interpretation in the practices of pastoral ministry. We had a sense of what they meant when we heard him explain to his class how one pastor had developed a series of sermons explicating insight from the Leviticus genealogies for contemporary church life. At Yale, students talked in similarly approving fashion about how Adela Collins modeled for them the hermeneutical enterprise in the construction and presentation of her lectures in classes on the New Testament.

The differences among these teachers of Scripture cannot be traced simply to a contrast of their teaching styles as seen in the patterns of interaction they establish between the subject of their teaching and the students they teach. The differences emerge, as well, from some confluence of perspectives and sensibilities, dispositions and habits, knowledge and values that continuously influences the teachers' work—in their preparation, while they are teaching, and when they reflect on their teaching experience to make sense of it. For students, these differences among teachers are evident in

- o The transparency of their knowledge of and relationship to the subject of their teaching

- o Their ability to discern the edges of what students know and how they learn

- o Their struggle to negotiate norms from their religious traditions and academic disciplines with the relativism of language and the contextuality of truth claims

- o The range of their expectations of seminary education in forming clergy for professional roles of public service

- o Their ability to foster the imaginative capacities of students for the professional responsibilities and roles they would be assuming as clergy

We interviewed and observed highly skilled teachers. They were almost intuitively adept at making technical pedagogical decisions on the spot to shift the focus of the conversation, to introduce new information, to pick up the pace of the session, to alter the plans for the session, to defuse distractions and refocus discussion.[11] These decisions, however, revealed more than technical proficiency and disciplinary competence. They often seemed to exemplify or model the very engagement these seminary educators seek to foster in their students. Their knowledge of the subject becomes transparent as they invite students into the realm of their own questions, to probe with them problems that evoke their own curiosity, and to share with them the excitement of learning at the edges of their own knowledge. Why else would Tull want her students to experience aesthetically with her the challenge of reading biblical texts with others, or Bergant desire that students share her commitment to contextually sensitive readings of biblical texts, or Butler want his students to discover invitations to deeper faith in the process of engaging questions posed by their reading of biblical texts?

In the chapters that follow we argue that the technical proficiency of these teachers can be described more adequately by understanding the imaginative activity of these clergy educators. The building blocks or components of a teaching practice may be obvious. They include, as we have already described, the methods the teacher chooses to use: oral reading of texts, mini-lectures, collaborative translation, presentation slides. Some, like Tull, alter the pace of the class session by the expeditious use of many methods. Butler relies on just a few. The number of methods in the teachers' toolkits or their skill in using of any given method does not seem predict the degree to which students consider them to be excellent teachers.

Each teacher chooses methods to facilitate strategies that he or she designs to direct students toward explicit learning goals. These strategic goals are tangible, concrete, and typically measurable. Strategies can be structurally simple—as when Tull asks students to translate a text (goal) by writing it out (method) to be shared in small groups (method) in class so as to refine and revise their translations together (goal) in dialogue (method) with peers. These strategies are woven together into a design for a class session that, in turn, is part of a design for the course typically articulated in a syllabus. Strategies can alter the effect of any method.[12] In one class session, Tull may give a five-minute mini-lecture to explain a term in a biblical text; another to propose an interpretation; another to compare points of view; and still another to evoke debate or argument about its meaning. The structure of each mini-lecture is the same, but its function varies depending on her goal for student learning and its place in her strategy for drawing students into her expectations for their learning. The shape of the practice not only gives meaning and direction to the methods and strategies teachers may choose to enhance student learning; it also situates their efforts in the culture and mission of the schools in which they are teaching.

Diverse Practices

Although seminary educators share the goal of preparing clergy for their professional roles and responsibilities and the academic standards of regional college and university accrediting agencies and the Association of Theological Schools for Christian seminaries, the diversity of faculty teaching practices is one of the most distinctive features of seminary education. Differences in the teaching of Bergant and Tull, in other words, are no accident. Undoubtedly influenced by their own educational experience, primary sources to their differences may also be traced to variations in the ways they negotiate a range of social, pedagogical, and historical influences in and through their teaching and the ways in which they view the relationship of the cognitive, skill, and identity formation apprenticeships in and through their teaching.

We have described this constructive effort as the work of their pedagogical imaginations. It is grounded in their assumptions about the relationship of disciplinary knowing to the knowing associated with religious leadership. It becomes visible in faculty decisions about the influence of the setting of the class and school, the relationship of historic seminary commitments to both *wissenschaft* and *paideia,* the role of an educational event in the explicit and implicit curriculum, and the background and readiness of students to enter into the dynamics of teaching and learning. It is given form in classroom and communal teaching practices through which seminary educators seek to prepare students for their future roles and responsibilities as clergy.

ENDNOTES

1. Peter Abbs (2003, pp. 2–3), a professor of art education, has an "emphatically post-Christian" view of spirituality, reflecting a deep commitment to both the animating values of western and Christian tradition and post-modernity. Abbs's discussion of the spirituality of teaching actually provides a provocative challenge to any teaching in theological schools that does not take the concerns of postmodernity seriously.

2. Other factors contributing to the diversity in the teaching practices that have been in the background of our attention to those practices include denominational traditions, accommodations to changing accreditation standards, disciplinary styles of teaching (as in Huber and Morreale, 2002), views of student capacities and learning styles (as in Magolda, 1992), and the impact of technology on teaching and learning (as in Schultze, 2002).

3. "The mission of Howard University School of Divinity, as a graduate theological and professional school, is to educate, form, and empower leaders to serve the church and the world, to celebrate the religious and cultural heritage of African Americans, the African Diaspora and Africa and to engage in the pursuit of excellence in ministry, driven by a passion for justice and freedom and a relentless search for truth."

4. Kelsey (1992) observed that Christian theological schools have held themselves accountable to "two models of excellence." The more ancient is *paideia;* the more modern is *wissenschaft.* The former is most evident in

the increasing urgency articulated by theological school faculty around issues of clergy formation. The latter may be seen in the quest for academic standards and accreditation—even to the point that all but approximately thirty of the theological schools in the United States are accredited, not only by the Association of Theological Schools, but also by regional college and university accrediting agencies. In other words, most institutions of clergy education grant degrees guided by standards associated with research universities even as they struggle to incorporate values of *paideia*. Note Kelsey's discussion of *paideia* (pp. 63–77) and *wissenschaft* (pp. 78–98).

5. It is beyond the scope of this project to explore the similarities and differences between the notions of *paideia* associated with Greek culture and Jewish notions of community originating in traditions of covenant or of being a chosen people. Our point here is that both emphasize communality and intersubjectivity in the educative process. For further insight into the Jewish perspectives, see Alexander (1997), Cohen (1997), and Holtz (1987).

6. Daniel Tanner and Laurel Tanner (1995) point out that "curriculum has been variously defined as (1) the cumulative tradition of organized knowledge, (2) the instructional plan or course of study, (3) measured instructional outcomes (technological production system), (4) cultural reproduction, (5) knowledge selection/organization from the culture, (6) modes of thoughts, and (7) guided living/planned learning environment." They propose an eighth definition: the "reconstruction of knowledge and experience that enables the learner to grow in exercising intelligent control of subsequent knowledge and experience" (pp. 87–89).

7. See Association of Theological Schools (2003), pp. 17–19. The ATS figures include students enrolled in all degree programs in theological education in accredited Christian seminaries. They do not report separately those figures for students preparing to be clergy. For an expanded discussion of the changing demographics of student enrollment in Christian theological schools, see Wheeler (2001).

8. The Lexington Seminar: Theological Teaching for the Church's Ministries is a project of the Lexington Theological Seminary funded by a grant from Lilly Endowment, Inc. The project gathers faculty members from a selected group of seminaries to explore ways to be responsive to the challenge of educating church leaders in an era of significant transformation. See Warford (2004).

9. Conversation, March 2004. A discussion of the entrepreneurial dynamics at work in the recruitment of students and the effects of those dynamics on

curriculum and teaching practice is beyond the scope of this book. The story of clergy education in the United States, however, cannot be fully understood without a discussion of the effect of these dynamics on the production of theological knowledge, recruitment, and retention of faculty and students, even school mission and organizational structure.

10. See Farley (1988); he sought to engage this issue directly by advocating for attention to the necessary interdependence of the theological education of congregation, university, and divinity school or seminary.

11. See essays by Furlong, Claxton, and Atkinson in Atkinson and Claxton (2000).

12. *Method* and *strategy* are terms typically used in discussions of pedagogy. Our use of these terms is similar to that of Michel de Certeau (1984), who contrasts tactic—what we call *method*—with strategy. Methods or tactics, he observes, do not "obey the law of place for they are not defined or identified with it." Their purpose and function depend on the intent at stake in their use. Strategies, by way of contrast, "seek to create places in conformity with abstract models" (pp. 29–30). In education we see de Certeau's meaning in teaching strategies designed to produce learning that can be assessed—even measured—against some model or expectation of the teacher.

PART TWO

CLASSROOM PEDAGOGIES IN FORMING A PASTORAL, PRIESTLY, OR RABBINIC IMAGINATION

THE COMPLEXITY OF THE CLERGY EDUCATOR'S TASK is highlighted in the comments of a graduate of one of the schools in our study. Responding to a survey question about actions taken by clergy leaders of congregations in the aftermath of the September 11, 2001, attacks on the World Trade Center and Pentagon, this clergy person wrote,

> [My] first action was to gather the community in prayer and worship. Second, I needed to prepare to preach on the issue and communicate to the congregation through newsletter about the tragedy, suffering, and place of God in this mess. Third, I needed to facilitate discussion and expression of feelings about the events with parishioners. Fourth, [as a congregation we] needed to be a place open

to the community for prayer and anything else. Fifth, we needed to
talk with the kids about the event. Sixth, we needed to be a visible witness in the community through our presence and whatever else to hope
and peace.

Several themes in these comments provide clues to the clergy practice
that seminary educators assume as they teach students preparing to
become clergy. The work of clergy is complex and multifaceted. It involves
multiple roles and responsibilities attentive to diverse human needs across
the age span of the members of a specific community of faith or observance, while at the same time being aware of similar needs among persons in the community at large. Specialized knowledge and skills are
required to gather a community in prayer and worship; to prepare and
preach sermons; to facilitate discussions of personal, theological, and ethical issues; to listen empathetically to persons experiencing crisis or
trauma; and to give oversight to the coordination of all these activities.
The capacity to imagine ways of linking resources from one's religious tradition to the human and spiritual needs and expectations of congregations
and communities is a central feature of effective clergy practice.

Connecting this with the fundamental concepts we have introduced in
the foregoing chapters, this respondent's comments provide clues to the
exercise of the pedagogical imaginations reflected in the range of pedagogical practices followed by seminary educators as they seek to prepare
their students for clergy practice. Some of their pedagogical practices focus
on *forming* in students the knowledge, skills, dispositions, and habits
needed for such activities as "gathering the community in prayer and worship," and "facilitating discussion and expression of feelings." Others seek
to prepare students to *interpret* and to *contextualize* texts, situations, and
relationships when preaching, writing newsletter articles, or talking to
children about "tragedy, suffering and the place of God in this mess." Still
others seek to prepare students to *perform* appropriately and skillfully
such leadership roles as leading a community in prayer or worship,
preaching or conducting a discussion, or writing a newsletter responsive
to standards, rituals, and rules rooted in their specific religious tradition
and adapted to local expectations.

In the next four chapters, we describe features of each of the four pedagogies in clergy education—interpretation, formation, context, and
performance—that together form a signature pedagogical framework distinctive in the teaching of seminary educators who have been identified as
particularly reflective about their practice. That pedagogical framework

is shared in classes as similar and as different as those taught by Bergant and Tull. The ways in which seminary educators configure the relationship of these four pedagogies in their teaching reflect the exercise of their own pedagogical imaginations. Over time, it begins to take on the character of a teaching practice. For this reason, in these four chapters we examine this pedagogical framework to make more visible each of its component parts. We identify distinctive features in each pedagogical emphasis. Although we make some effort along the way to illustrate the interdependence of pedagogies of interpretation, formation, contextualization, and performance in the teaching practices of clergy educators, specific attention to their interdependence is the focus of our attention in Chapter Eleven.

3

PEDAGOGIES OF
INTERPRETATION

AS CHERYL SANDERS BEGAN one of her classes in her introductory course in social ethics at the Divinity School of Howard University, she observed that in contrast to the social sciences, which bracket "judgments of right and wrong, good and bad, just and unjust in our responses and actions," judgments are "central to the study of ethics." This means, she continued, that religious communities engaged in ethical thinking need to "begin to see the importance of listening and the importance of being careful to how we listen." Her meaning would soon become clear.

The class had just finished reading Charles Marsh's *God's Long Summer* (1999), about five men and women who had either supported or resisted the civil rights movement. Discussion focused on Sam Bowers, a member of the Ku Klux Klan. "Let's say that Bowers was in jail. You were the chaplain, and he requested a conversation with you. In considering your response you have a choice. You can consider him to be totally evil or mentally ill. Is there any justice in listening to him?"

For several minutes students shared opinions about what they would do. After several comments, Sanders observed that each of the five persons profiled in Marsh's book viewed Jesus in different ways. And "how we define who Jesus is . . . affects the way we view others." She then contrasted the image of an "approving Jesus looking over people who had just taken off their KKK hoods" in the 1918 movie *Birth of a Nation* with the "dynamic and changing image of Jesus" held by Fannie Lou Hamer, the powerful civil rights leader from Mississippi, which included the possibility of seeing "Jesus in people who were not Christian."

At this point, Sanders pulled up a slide introducing H. Richard Niebuhr's schema for depicting various views of the relationship of

Christ and culture in the course of Christian history (2001 [1951]). She had two objectives for using Niebuhr's *Christ and Culture*: (1) to introduce students—most with little church history background—to the range of perspectives in the history of the church for ethical judgments, and (2) to explore how various views of the relationship of Christ and culture can lead to differing ethical responses. Through these two objectives, she wanted students to "listen" carefully to the messages of Niebuhr's *text* so they would, in turn, be able to "listen" more carefully to their interpretations of ethical situations *and* to the formulation of their ethical responses to those interpretations.

Sanders's goal of teaching students to listen as a basic skill and disposition of interpretation should not be surprising.[1] Interpreting is a basic human activity in the quest to understand another person, event, or situation. "To understand at all is to interpret," David Tracy has observed (1987, p. 9). Every time we "act, deliberate, judge, understand, or even experience . . . we are interpreting." Interpretive practices are also central to the work of Jewish and Christian clergy. The people of both religious traditions are, among other things, the people of a *book* that has functioned authoritatively, if not normatively, for them through the centuries. The interpretation of that book figures centrally in their teaching and preaching, in planning for worship and community outreach.

Interpretation in Clergy Practice

Heidi Neumark illustrates this insight as she begins to tell the story of her ministry at the Church of the Transfiguration in the lower Bronx (2003, p. 15). She has been watching the televised pictures of the collapse of the World Trade Center in New York City with her son. He turns to his LEGOs to work through his reactions to this unfolding tragedy. She finds herself "listening" to Isaiah, "that ancient correspondent from the sixth century B.C.E." who when he "looked around" saw "a traumatized community taken captive and deported to Babylon, the smoking ruins of the city still blurring their vision, and choking their souls." In this situation, Neumark thought of him as a "good companion in the wake of urban ruin." With him, she found herself listening to the anticipated reactions of people in her congregation and community: "What shall I preach? 'All flesh is grass . . . '" (Isaiah 40:11). With him, she found herself asking, "What was there to say? What difference could it make?" (2003, pp. xv–xvi). And with him in the midst of the unexplainable and incomprehensible circumstances of the moment, she realized his "story cried out to be told." In the midst of the poverty, the experiences of abuse and neglect, the personal and collective pain of her community, she discovered in Isaiah's experience words of meaning and hope for the people of her congregation.

In Neumark's reflections we may note catalysts to the interpretive practices of clergy that dominate the attention of Sanders and other seminary educators: the dialectic of a story from the past that must be told, a ritual that must be renewed, a relationship that must be reconciled, questions rising out of the depths of the human experience that must be answered, meanings that must be discovered, and bonds of fellowship that must be restored. Pedagogies that introduce students to practices of interpretation and engage them in those practices are therefore central to the mission of educating clergy. They facilitate the capacity of clergy, in and through their many different roles and responsibilities, to respond to the human and religious quest for meaning. This means that pedagogies of interpretation may be found in almost every course and educational activity in the seminary curriculum. They are distinctively shaped by the quest of seminary educators to prepare their students to engage in the practices of interpretation integral to their preaching, teaching, caring, or administration.

Elements of Interpretive Practice

Tracy has identified three "realities" in the process of interpretation and alludes to a fourth. They help clarify what seminary educators do when teaching the interpretive practices of clergy work. These realities exist, Tracy contends, in all theories of interpretation.[2] They also give form to pedagogies of interpretation. They include, in Tracy's words, "some *phenomenon* to be interpreted, *someone* interpreting that phenomenon, and some *interaction* between these first two realities" (1987, p. 10). He suggests a fourth reality when exploring the role of "the larger *conversation of the entire community* of inquirers" that both encourages dialogue among interpretive possibilities and establishes a horizon for decisions about the phenomenon to be interpreted, the interpreter, and the methods that facilitate their interaction (1986, pp. 118–20).

A closer examination of Sanders's teaching practice illustrates how these four realities also function pedagogically.

Something to be interpreted. In the session of Sanders's class that we observed, the phenomena to be interpreted were couched, for the most part, in texts—the newspaper and other media texts narrating ethical dilemmas, and biblical, theological, and ethics texts introducing students to traditions and practices of ethical interpretation. Sanders explained her purpose for each text:

○ Marsh's *God's Long Summer* reinforced student expectations that their engagement with social ethics would occur within the interpretive context of the black church and, more explicitly, the black church's relationship to the American civil rights movement.

○ Niebuhr's *Christ and Culture* expanded the horizons of that interpretive community to include traditions and resources in the larger Christian story.

○ Richard Hays's *The Moral Vision of the New Testament* grounded their expanding awareness of the resources for ethical thinking in the moral vision of the Bible—for most students, the most authoritative text for adjudicating ethical issues.

Sanders's intention that students develop the capacity to listen appreciatively to these texts requires increasingly sophisticated skills for reading: using the vocabularies and interpretive frameworks of sociology, theology, and critical studies of the Bible—all in the service of social ethics. This intention becomes evident several times during the semester, when Sanders asks students to listen, through their reading of these texts, for ethical issues they see in the daily newspaper and encounter every day in the lives of their families, congregations, and communities.

An interpreter. Those who interpret make up the second reality in pedagogies of interpretive practice. Those participating in the practice in this particular class included Sanders as teacher, individual students, and the class as a community of interpretation. Sanders and her students also brought a range of assumptions and approaches to ethical issues associated with a variety of communities of interpretation—including, at the least, their families, congregations, and denominational traditions, the black religious experience in the United States, and the shared experience of participation in the larger Christian community. They did not begin the course as blank slates; rather, they brought to the subject of their learning a set of personal and collective understandings shaped by prior experience, relationships, and formal learning that had the potential to both facilitate and hinder Sanders's intentions for their learning. An even more complex task for teachers like Sanders originates in the recognition that their students approach the subject of their learning with different learning styles, a variety of gendered and cultural experiences and perspectives, and a wide range of academic and professional background experience, knowledge, and skills.

The interaction of an interpreter with something to be interpreted. Using pedagogies of interpretation, Sanders spends most of her time engaging students in Tracy's third reality. In educational settings, the interaction of interpreter with something to be interpreted is typically structured by methods chosen to facilitate the process. In Sanders's class, these methods are influenced by her perception of student confidence with the ways of thinking she is seeking to cultivate. When students are reading Marsh, they typically discover that they bring to class interpretive perspectives on ethical issues rooted in their familiarity with the religious and cultural struggles of the black church and community for racial equality. This familiarity provides Sanders with the freedom to focus student attention on developing competency in using a set of guidelines she had prepared for the analysis and interpretation of ethical issues.

With *Christ and Culture,* the practice of reading for analyses leading to ethical understandings and judgments becomes a greater pedagogical challenge. Since most students in this course lack knowledge of the larger Christian tradition, Sanders seeks to expand the horizon for their interpretations by "plunging" them into reading Niebuhr's work because it provides a way to view "the sweep of Christian history" and a typology for thinking about ethical issues. Since its unfamiliarity makes it "difficult reading" for most of her students, she leads them through the text— almost page by page during the class session—encouraging them by "giving them some cues as to how to wade through it and to see what is important." She interrupts their reading of the text at several points to ask them to draw on their expanding knowledge of Niebuhr's typology and her guidelines of analysis to assess the ethical perspectives of the persons they encountered in their first reading. In written assignments, Sanders expects students to demonstrate increasing familiarity in using her guidelines to analyze concrete ethical problems and to interpret them with insights from the traditions of biblical and theological scholarship through their readings—initially, of Niebuhr, and by the end of the term, of Hays.

Entering the work of the interpreting community. At this stage, the function of the interpretive community becomes more explicit in pedagogical practices of interpretation. Key to this level of interpretation, Tracy has argued, is the conversation—the comparisons, critiques, and corrections—that takes place between the persons interpreting and the assumptions and knowledge they bring to their reading of the assigned texts and between their personal and collective ethical understandings and ethical judgments (1986, pp. 119–20).

Stanley Fish has argued that the strategies and meanings associated with any interpretive interaction proceed from "the interpretive community" with which the interpreter identifies (1980, p. 14). They are "in effect community property, and, insofar as they at once enable and limit the operations" of the interpreter's consciousness, they also reveal the inter-preter's identification with that community and influence, and con-sequently the interpreter's *reading* of any given text, situation, or relationship (p. 14).

In reality, this aspect of teaching interpretive practice is more complex. Our interpretive interactions are typically not confined to or constrained by the boundaries of some insular interpretive community. Rather, we live in and move through various interpretive communities—family, congre-gation, culture, nation—and in any interpretive act, the community of the event or text may well have a stronger influence than all the perspectives and practices found in the community (or communities) of the interpreter (or interpreters). An interpretive practice may appear to be simple, but it is not. Teachers typically constrain that complexity by stipulating which interpretive communities will dominate their attention while engaging the subject of their inquiry.

Sanders revealed the boundaries of attention in this class most explic-itly when she declared that "how we define who Jesus is . . . affects the way we view others." Sanders's class is a class in Christian social ethics—"Christian" not in some generic sense but from the standpoint of the per-spectives and approaches to be found in the texts she had chosen for their reading. These establish the boundary or horizon for choosing the norms and criteria for grounding their interpretations of ethical dilemmas.

In her book *Ministry at the Margins,* Sanders makes more explicit her assumptions about the horizon for her own interpretive practice. She draws criteria for making ethical judgments from the dialectic of com-paring a reading of the Bible that emphasizes God's preference for the poor and outcast with the contemporary experience of those who know oppression firsthand: "the disadvantaged position of women, children and the poor in contemporary society" (1997, pp. 11, 13, 15, 22).

This means she poses ethical issues in class and assigns ethical issues for the midterm and final paper that require students to analyze the issues with a "hermeneutic of suspicion" originating in what might be called the ethics of the marginalized. She urges them to draw on insights from their readings to make "an honest assessment of where each of us stands within the status quo." That assessment involves asking such questions as "Am I especially privileged or disadvantaged by the system?" and "How would my life circumstances change if I pursued justice in my own situation, practiced equity in my dealings with others, challenged injustice in my spheres of influence and advocated increased access and opportunities for others who have less than I do?" As students develop facility in dealing with such questions as these, they demonstrate increasing capacity for the kind of critical thinking Sanders seeks in her students: thinking centered on what bell hooks has called "the practice of freedom" that "transgresses" the social forces that limit or inhibit human liberation (1994, pp. 13–14, 20–21). Because they are participants in a predominantly black church interpretive community, Sanders intends that ethical judgments flowing from their answers to these and similar questions will lead her students to proclaim the good news of God's reign in the world and the work of implementing righteousness and justice in people's lives. From this perspective, her teaching embodies Howard's mission to prepare students for prophetic ministries in the world.

Differing Pedagogies for Interpretive Practice

As we visited other seminaries, we observed these four elements of an interpretive practice over and over in the pedagogies of faculty members. The different perspectives they bring to the interpretative practices they teach are typically influenced by the academic discipline, pedagogical culture, and religious tradition of the school. Some of the differences among their perspectives may become evident in the pages that follow as we explore how four other seminary educators employ the pedagogies of interpretation. We have already seen how reading texts from the vantage point of those on the margins of society reflects the commitment of the Howard faculty to prophetic ministry in its curriculum. The dialogical practice of interpretation in Marjorie Lehman's *Mekinah* Talmud class (a course designed to help entering students meet the academic prerequisites of the Rabbinical School), as the first of our examples, permeates the interactions of teachers and learners across the curriculum at the Jewish Theological Seminary of America. Our second example explores the influence of authoritative church teaching in the pedagogies of St. John's Seminary faculty in a course on moral theology by Richard Benson. In our final example, we see how the ability to ask questions—"good questions"—that Robert Wilson and David Bartlett seek among their students distinguishes the Yale educational experience more generally.

Interpreting as Continuous Dialogue
Marjorie Lehman, Jewish Theological Seminary

Lehman, assistant professor of Talmud and rabbinics, identified by her dean as a reflective teacher, has written about the pedagogy of teaching Talmud (2002; Lehman and Kress, 2003). We observed a class she teaches for students who have not passed the proficiency exam in Talmud required for admission into the rabbinical program.

The *Mekinah* course is a year-long immersion in Talmud studies—its language, genres, thought forms, and basic tools for study—taken by entering rabbinical students preparing for the seminary's proficiency exam. It presupposes near-fluency in written Hebrew; the capacity to work with unvocalized, unpunctuated texts; and familiarity with Aramaic.

Class sessions are designed to move students through five levels that Lehman has developed for reading and interpreting Talmudic texts. These five levels, described in a grid she has designed, impose a clear structure on the complex relationships students encounter in their engagement with the text and provide a guide into the shape of the practice of reading and interpreting the text:

1. Decoding words and sentences, including vocalization and punctuation of Hebrew and Aramaic texts.

2. Examining how various strands and voices of a text are put together into a larger whole, including identifying who is speaking at any given point.

3. Exploring the explicit or implicit logic guiding the redaction of these smaller strands into the present text. This step includes attention to technical terms in the text.

4. Exploring various interpretive strands and the concerns of those who redacted these strands into the final form of the texts—giving attention to, for example, the historical, social, cultural, and religious contexts of the rabbis who wrote them.

5. Exploring the meaning students discern in the text for themselves and for rabbinic practice in their contexts today.

Lehman seeks to ascertain students' implicit grasp of all five levels. If they do not understand each part, she insists, they will never understand how it is all pieced together so as to create meaning. As they work through these five levels, students discover that they are participating in the inherently *dialogical* character of this interpretive practice found in other texts and contexts. The page layout of the text reflects the rabbinic redactors' commitment to the engagement of multiple voices: at the center of the page is the text of the Mishnah and Gemara surrounded by a variety of commentaries on the text, from that of Rashi (which appears at the top portion of the inside margin of each page) to those of later rabbis.[3] Redactors, who intentionally preserved minority voices in the text, created these dialogues. Debate among the rabbis in the text rarely leads to clear and conclusive resolution. Thus dialogical complexity, ambiguity, paradox, and conflict make up the very structure of the text. Later commentaries added to the Talmudic page during the medieval period cite other relevant material, and cross-references to other Talmudic tractates and to biblical passages in the pages of the Talmud create a sort of proto-hypertext complexity of constantly interwoven references.

The dialogical methods of Talmud study in traditional yeshivot reflect a commitment to dialogue in the quest for meaning, moreover, as pairs of students (called *havrutah,* from the Hebrew *haver* [friend, partner]) engage in continuing debate during two hours of class time each week and outside of class through the year. Through a pedagogy of mutual clarification, conflict, and illumination they engage in dialogue not only with each other, but with all levels of the conversation going on in the text. The pedagogy of the class session brings out the many often contradictory voices present in the room: in the text, in its authors' and redactors' voices, and through those of the students, the professor, and the tradition. Lehman structures and keeps open these many levels of dialogue to help forestall premature conclusions that might shut out some voices and to give students tools for practicing these simultaneously textual and contemporary dialogues at the heart of rabbinic practice.

Lehman notes that the dialogical structure of the text and of traditional and ongoing Talmudic pedagogy shares something of the contemporary realization that "knowledge is social," not absolute or universal. This pedagogy cultivates the capacity for human interaction. Working on texts together, Lehman contends, strengthens the students' capacity for deeper connections with others outside the *beit midrash* (house of study).

At another level, "studying canonical texts like the Bible and Talmud," Lehman notes, "is part of the way we understand ourselves as Jews at Jewish Theological Seminary." This means that the study of these texts "is automatically about an engagement with God and our ancestors even if we are not actually discussing God." It is the "nature, activity, and authority" of the rabbis of the Talmud, however, "which is the subject of vigorous debate and not so much the nature of God"—unless, that is, the text is specifically about the attributes of God.

Fundamentally, Lehman wants all students to realize that in this dialogical process, the point is *not* to come to some neat conclusion, to have *meaning* all wrapped up once and for all; rather, for Lehman the point is to explore *meaning* precisely in the tension and messiness of the interrelated dialogues themselves.[4] Thus, her pedagogy, mirroring the text itself, is designed to help draw students into forms of thought more open to the complexity, paradox, and ambiguity of reality—and, not coincidentally, of rabbinic practice.

In the class session we observed, students worked through a Talmudic tractate on the feast of Sukkoth. Lehman reviewed the previous session. The students then worked together from notes prepared in advance (in their pairs) and the Talmudic texts. Lehman downloaded these Talmudic texts into a word-processing program and projected them onto a screen at the front of the class, providing a visual reference for the students. One by one, students took turns reading the text out loud, which necessarily included adding the appropriate vowels and punctuation. When necessary, Lehman assisted or corrected. As one student read, another student (in charge of the laptop) inserted relevant punctuation marks, which appeared in the text on the screen. The first student then translated the text he or she had read. Finally, the student narrated how this clause, sentence, or passage should be outlined so as to bring out its implicit structure. The student at the laptop followed along, adding line breaks, providing indentation, or highlighting technical structural terms as needed.

Each step, from punctuation to translation to outlining, gave rise to vigorous debate among class members and with Lehman. Should the clause end here or here? Is it a question or a statement? How is this term translated, in light of that earlier argument? If it means this, then what are the implications, and how does this hold up in light of later statements? What technical terms are being used and how do they structure the argument? Is a given statement offered in support of an earlier one, or as a challenge or refutation to it, or is it an entirely new line of thought? As the discussion proceeded in this way, the student working at the laptop updated the text on the screen.

These debates flowed intrinsically into a discussion of the various rabbis involved, their own contexts and issues, and the inferred or obvious intentions of the redactors in constructing the textual debate in this given way. Why does Rabbi So-and-So want to defend this or that view? Why do Rashi and other commentators take the positions they do? What is at stake for them? What sort of Judaism are they advocating at that point in history? Finally, what questions do these discussions raise for the students' own practice of Judaism, for their religious communities, and for their future practice as rabbis?

Occasionally, the students move into the fifth level of Lehman's interpretive grid, exploring the text's meaning for today. The day we observed the class, for instance, Lehman pointed to this level of interpretation when she asked the students, "Why doesn't any of this material in the text parallel the issues we all learned [about Sukkoth] in school as children?" Although the dialogical process requires students to make many interpretive judgments, up to this point the resources for making those judgments originate in the text itself. With questions like this one, the students must begin to draw on their understanding of the world in which they live and of the world of the rabbinate they envision.

Perhaps the most striking contrast between the interpretive practices in Sanders's social ethics class and in Lehman's Talmud class is evident in their sources for norms in making interpretive judgments. Whereas Sanders seeks to engage students in the analysis of ethical issues from the preferential standpoint of the biblical witness to the experience of those marginalized socially, politically, economically, and religiously in the world today, Lehman's intent is for students to develop the facility to participate in the continuing dialogue of the rabbis across the ages—a conversation that will not conclude with their own understandings. For Lehman this means, as she has written:

> I certainly want my students to confront the rabbis in their rabbinic world, to hear, understand, and respect the story told by them. However, they also need to see their ancestors as they see themselves. They need to believe that there is something about the human condition that remains the same throughout the ages and that the brilliance of the rabbis is reflected in the manner in which they are able to think about the limitations and difficulties of being Jews as well as of being human. Ultimately, my goal each semester is to find a means of connecting the world in which my students live with that of the rabbis [2002, p. 89].

This vision for her students informs her decisions to "build" what she calls "a community of learners," in which each person listens to, engages, and understands their peers, first of all, as closely as possible to "the religious contexts of the rabbis they will encounter," so as to confront them with their shared experience across time with the "people of this world and as Jews of this world"; and second, as exegetes or critical interpreters of a text that is in itself an exegetical work. In this regard she wants her "students to think like rabbinic interpreters," to ask "questions the rabbis asked and strove to answer," and to evaluate whether or not the rabbis were "passive receivers of tradition or creative transmitters." This rigorous and finely tuned pedagogical practice is made possible, in part, by the shared boundaries of the seminary as an interpretive community living into and out of the shared traditions of Talmudic study.

Interpreting as Appropriating Tradition
Richard Benson, St. John's Seminary

St. John's Seminary sits on a hilltop surrounded by orange groves in Camarillo, California. The traditions of monastic life built into its architecture, the international character of its predominantly male student community, and the graduation requirement of bilingual proficiency not only distinguish the setting and program of the seminary from those of the Jewish Theological Seminary and Howard University's Divinity School, but also highlight significant differences in their pedagogical cultures.

We had a clue to what those differences might be when Benson—a Vincentian priest, professor of moral theology, and dean of the faculty—told us he wanted students "to appropriate" church tradition so as to "make use of it in ever-changing situations" with the intent of renewing and revitalizing it. This explicitly interpretive practice became evident in the goals he articulated for a course in fundamentals of moral theology, a session of which we observed.

Since most students want "to jump to the 'what'" or subject matter of a course, he told us, "my first goal is to introduce them to the methodology of moral theology." This means trying to help students "understand how to teach Catholics to make decisions" and to "give folks . . . the credit for learning how to make moral decisions." This requires that they "need to be taught clearly what the church teaches"—Benson's second goal—and then "they should be told why the church teaches it"—his third goal for student learning.

On the day we observed his class, the students arrived before Benson. They included, he had told us, two Korean and three Vietnamese students who had been born "outside the United States" but had completed their secondary and college educations in the United States, as well as eight Hispanics, one Samoan, and two "Anglos." As Benson walked into the room, students began asking him to clarify expectations for the format of a future assignment. With much bantering back and forth, he answered them while booting up his laptop. Eventually a slide appeared: "Embracing the Dying: A Roman Catholic Moral Context." He then asked a student to pray, "but not the fifteen cycles of the Rosary this time." Laughter rippled across the room. Later, we learned that the last time this student had prayed, it had been "a very long prayer." This time, it was brief and in English—not, as was the typical practice, in the student's first language.

After the prayer, Benson complimented the class on a set of good exams. No one, however, had correctly answered the extra-credit question.

Assuming the role of a game-show host, Benson offered a set of clues as the students searched for the answer. When a student finally identified the name of the first bishop of Los Angeles, Benson observed with a wry grin that the man had also been a Vincentian.[5] He then took roll: it is required by the church to help assess student accountability. Because Benson does not like to monitor student attendance in this way, class members make a game of it by giving humorous responses in their first languages when their names are called.

At this point, he moved into the main body of the class session. "This course is a foundational course. Although some of you want to learn how to deal with moral issues that come up in ministry, the real issue has to do with 'what ought we to be as disciples'"—with "how I can be moral." In other words, he had a goal for student learning that took precedence over those he had described earlier—a goal related to their calling as Christians and to their vocation as priests. He reminded them they had already identified and explored resources for the moral life in spirituality, Scripture, natural law, and, most recently, moral theology. He then led them through a review of basic principles in Catholic moral theology that were the subject of the exam he had just returned to them.

The review had the character of a vigorous and highly charged Socratic recitation of primary principles and rules in moral theology. Benson's questions pushed students to articulate, as clearly as possible and in their own words, official church teachings about basic, but complex, doctrinal principles and practices in moral theology.[6] He asked a question and called on a student to respond. He continued to ask questions—first of one student, then another, and then another to refine, focus, and correct prior responses—until he was satisfied with the adequacy of their answers. Calling on students across the room, excluding no one, he kept the pace moving quickly, punctuated with light touches of humor that often made or reinforced a point, often challenging or affirming a student's response in the process. Students had to think quickly and express themselves articulately.

Benson's stated concern that the course should prepare students for discipleship became obvious at several points. With a trace of humor, he illustrated several moral principles and rules by identifying moral dilemmas affecting the students' own formation. This included indirect challenges to specific students whose smoking or eating habits inhibited their moral authority. Without diminishing academic rigor, he conveyed the message that the academic work of the seminary exists in service to the larger task of formation for the priesthood.

Several elements in the interpretive practice Benson teaches are readily evident. Students are, to begin with, drawn into the dynamics of learning as apprentices in the interpretive process—also part of Sanders's and Lehman's pedagogy. The practice in Benson's class involves three distinctive features: first, demonstrations of increasing personal ability to articulate understandings of authoritative premises in Catholic moral theology; second, increasing confidence and competence in using those understandings to adjudicate moral issues and dilemmas; and third, increasing confidence in recognizing the resources and boundaries for moral theological reflection in pastoral situations. Their responsibility—a fourth step in becoming interpreters—becomes explicit when they encounter ambiguities in their shared Catholic interpretive tradition in situations where they must draw on all they know to make moral judgments. In this sense, moral theology is, for Benson, a pastoral theology directed explicitly to the care of souls.

To help students begin to grasp the interdependence of these elements, Benson shifted attention to a case study of a seriously ill seventy-five-year-old man. The man and his wife had asked the doctor to halt aggressive measures to prolong his life, but the doctor did not want to do so. Benson read through the case, carefully explaining each of the medical terms in the case. He then divided the class into small groups to decide whether in their role as priests they would agree with the doctor or the family. After several minutes of lively debate, Benson called the students back into the larger group with the observation that "we must be careful to discover what the family is thinking." He first asked students to identify responses that would be typical in their own cultures. A Samoan student said, "[We] would want to bring the sick man to Honolulu or America to get more sophisticated advice." A Korean student said that out of respect for the elderly "[We] would want the aggressive measures removed so the person might die with dignity." Students from Mexico and Vietnam said they would want to take the elderly person home so the family could take care of him.

Benson then asked someone from each of the four small groups to report on the discussion. Additional differences of opinion immediately became apparent. In two groups the majority agreed with the doctor; in the other two groups, the majority agreed with the family. Each group argued for their judgments from the premise of church teachings they had been studying, but their comments also revealed the influence of both deeply rooted cultural assumptions and respect for the medical profession.

This discussion provided the backdrop for the next part of the class session, Benson's lecture on moral theological reflection in situations of death and dying. During this final section of the two-hour class, Benson used presentation slides to present an outline of the lecture and its major points.

He gave students a copy of the outline with plenty of space in a right-hand column for taking notes. Through the lecture, Benson reviewed the case in dialogue with teachings of the church. He concluded the lecture by demonstrating how the process could lead to a moral theological position that gave preference to the views of the elderly couple.

Reflecting on the class session, we found ourselves comparing the interaction of teacher and students to a post-scrimmage review. Perhaps the fact that all participants were male reinforces the image. Like a good coach, Benson complimented class members on ways they had done well on the test they had taken the previous week. He reviewed the rules of the game (the principles and rules of moral theology) by asking students to retrieve important pieces of information, asking peers to correct wrong answers, and letting members of the class know where they had made mistakes on the test on those principles and rules. Then he sent them into a practice session to use the principles and rules they had been reviewing in the analysis of a moral dilemma in priestly practice. In the plenary session that followed, he guided them through yet another recapitulation of the rules and principles, but this time in dialogue with how they had used them when working through the case study.

Benson's teaching had several distinctive features: the explicit and careful use of recitation; the dialogical interplay of personal, cultural, and Catholic sources to the interpretive process; the modeling of that process in his own moral theological reflections on the case; and the coaching he gave students as they practiced making moral judgments about the case.

In a context many would describe as constrained by well-defined and authoritative principles and doctrines, Benson's practice seemed quite open. When asked why, he located this openness in a process of *appropriating* church tradition. The boundaries for knowledge of that tradition are established by the church. Priests are not about the business of creating new knowledge as such. Rather, they must know the principles and rules of church teachings (in this case, of moral theology) well enough to interpret them faithfully in the midst of the ambiguities of the moral issues they will face in their ministries.

For Benson and others we met, priests cannot simply tell people what the church says; they must help them understand the meaning of what the church says. Appropriation, from this perspective, is not passive internalization: it involves the capacity to make judgments about the meanings of "what the church says." In this distinction, Benson illustrates once again the influence of a horizon of interpretation for *reading* to develop an appropriate and comprehensive grasp of the whole of the tradition and *critical thinking* to make sense of that tradition in new situations and for new questions and challenges.

Interpreting by Choosing "Right Methods"
Robert Wilson and David Bartlett, Yale Divinity School

The pedagogies for introducing students to the interpretive practices of clergy in "Expository Preaching," Wilson and Bartlett's course at Yale Divinity School, reflect the long history of attention to theories of interpretation among Yale University faculty generally and to the focus that Divinity School faculty give to hermeneutics throughout the school's curriculum.

Wilson and Bartlett have taught this course together seven times over the past thirteen years. They inherited the course, long a part of the Divinity School curriculum, from a colleague, now retired, whose approach to the class involved inviting different professors of Bible to lecture on a range of relevant topics. Wilson and Bartlett decided to change the character of the course by teaching it "from beginning to end, sharing responsibility for the whole life of the class" even though to do so means a regular teaching overload for Wilson. When they engage in the critical reading of biblical texts, Wilson leads class discussions of Old Testament texts and Bartlett leads class sessions on New Testament texts.

Their course, which fulfills an elective requirement in preaching, is organized to follow the lectionary or three year-long schedule of Bible readings for worship. In six segments through the semester, students participate in class sessions to engage in the critical interpretation of a designated text from the lectionary, review and critique sermons they write based on that text, and then, if they have not practiced preaching in another course, they preach their sermons to their peers. Wilson and Bartlett pace the course so that students involved in field education may use sermons they write in their congregational placements on the appropriate day in the church calendar. Students are expected to write their sermons with particular congregations in mind.

Typically, eighteen to twenty students enroll for the class. This year, however, nearly fifty students showed up for the first class session of the term—too many for the team's conventional approach to the course. Although the class included both women and men and seven or eight students with African American, Korean, or Hispanic heritage, the diversity that dominates Wilson and Bartlett's attention is religious. Episcopalians and Roman Catholics now outnumber the Congregationalists, Presbyterians, and

Methodists who once made up the majority of the student body. The most recent catalogue lists thirty-nine denominations represented among the students enrolled in the school. This means that students bring expectations for learning to preach from widely diverse worship and preaching traditions and styles.

In an effort to retain as many of their pedagogical values as possible with this particularly large class, Wilson and Bartlett divided the class into three groups. They made it quite clear they would not let the class enrollment reach this number again because "it is just very hard to have any kind of intelligent discussion" in a class that large, and the interaction they prefer to model between the two of them in the small group setting gets lost. Wilson, Bartlett, and a local pastor who had once taken the course rotated leadership among these groups for reviewing sermon manuscripts and listening to sermon presentations. Students prepare for the discussion of sermons in these small groups by reading an assigned text on crafting sermons that is not discussed in class. During the third section of the course, again in small groups, those who need to meet the school's practice preaching requirement preach their sermons.

The semester typically begins with two days of lecture. Wilson begins with a class session on "how to do exegesis for preaching." Bartlett follows up with a session on "how to move the exegesis of a text into a sermon." The sessions introduced students to the function of the practicum section of the course. We did not have the opportunity to observe this, but Bartlett describes his stance in *Between the Bible and the Church* (1999, pp. 15–16): when preachers "are in conversation with Scripture, Scripture is still the senior partner in that conversation." One is to approach a text "profoundly aware of the questions and circumstances" of the congregation to which one will preach, but "the proper way to interpret biblical narrative is not to look at the history behind the narrative, nor at the intention of a real or implied author, nor at any kind of separate subject matter, but to look at the narrative itself." The biblical text to be interpreted "provides the source and the criterion of faithful preaching." It not only establishes the horizon for the interpretation of the text, it is also the catalyst to the interpreter's imagination. This means that Wilson and Bartlett's goal for students is to prepare sermons that "grow organically out of the text in some way."

Students enter this course with at least one year of work in an introductory course on interpreting either the Old or New Testament. This allows Wilson and Bartlett to assume that all students in the class will have been introduced to the "critical tools" for interpreting biblical texts

and, consequently, will have an awareness and competency with methodologies for reading "the Bible for some purpose." Unlike Lehman, however, Wilson and Bartlett cannot assume student knowledge of Hebrew,
and unlike their peers in Presbyterian and Lutheran seminaries, they cannot assume student knowledge of either Greek or Hebrew. Proficiency in
the biblical languages is not a required part of the Yale curriculum. This
means they seek to read the English text "in an intelligent way using all
the critical material available but without getting hung up on it."

Wilson summarized their approach: "I would call it a kind of common
sense reading of scripture that focuses on simple questions like, 'What
does this text really mean?' 'Can I make sense out of this text?'" This
leads to "the next set of questions: 'how does this text address the present
situation of the community in some way or another?' Those are the two
stages. One is reading the text now, [and the other concerns] how it addresses a particular set of issues we might want to talk about." The text
establishes the boundaries or horizon for the work of this interpretive
practice. The challenge for Wilson and Bartlett as they lead students
through the interpretation is to help students engage the text in ways that
expand and deepen their view of the text; indeed, to open it up so as to
begin to think about ways in which it might shape a sermon.

The class met in a very large room. In the center of the room, tables
had been arranged to form a large rectangle, which in turn was surrounded by another rectangle of tables and chairs. Wilson, Bartlett, and
the assisting pastor were seated at one end of the inner table. Some fifteen
students sat around this table; the rest of the students at tables around it
and on a row of chairs up against three walls of the room. Despite the size
of the class, and in a fashion similar to Lehman's, Wilson and Bartlett
used questions to establish the structure for the exegetical class session.
But these questions had a different focus from Lehman's.

Wilson began this session's discussion of Psalm 51 with a few introductory remarks about "where the psalm falls in the lectionary." And then
he asked the first of a series of questions that would guide the class
through the entire psalm. "Where does the text start and end?" Eventually a student suggested it begins "before the first verse." Wilson agreed.
"The Hebrew text includes the heading in the verses but no English text
does. This means the verse numbers are off—by two verses. So what is the
source of the title?"

This last question led into a discussion of the work of editors, the concerns that might motivate their decisions about shaping the text in particular ways, and the significance of their concern for the work of the

preacher. In this instance, Wilson pointed out, the issue for the editor is the incident recounted in 2 Samuel about David and Bathsheba. The concern is David's sin, but the focus of the psalm is God's reaction of forgiveness.

He read the Samuel text and set up a dialogue between the psalm and this story, contrasting perspectives and assumptions informing each text. This set the stage for the task of working through each of the verses in the psalm. In Socratic style, Wilson asked questions that might tease out an expanding understanding of the text under consideration. "What puzzles you about this text or what questions does it raise for you?" What, he asked, does it suggest about "how we should think about sin?" "About the nature of God's forgiveness?" When students asked about the meaning of a word or verse, he turned the question back to the class.

Later, Wilson explained that after the class has worked through the text of the day, if they have time they move on to questions originating in their role as preachers: "Where do you think you might go from this particular text?" "What legitimate theological points or ethical points or practical points about living the Christian life could you make on the basis of what we now know about this text?" But in this class session, the discussion reached only to verse 13 before the end of the class hour. Wilson announced they would continue in the next session—presumably to complete the discussion of the verses of Psalm 51 and make the interpretive move toward the creation of the sermon.

The intent of this course—to equip students to do expository preaching— shapes the interpretive practice students are learning and the pedagogy of the instructors. Not only are students expected to develop increasing sophistication in reading texts for greater and deeper understanding, but they must also make judgments about how to use understandings of their reading to prepare a sermon that might speak relevantly to issues and concerns of a specific congregation. Wilson and Bartlett give explicit attention to the practice of critically interpreting texts by repeatedly working through a similar set of questions to discern their meanings. The process is a collaborative one; the instructors guide it with a set of questions they expect students to be able to replicate after they have completed the course.

In this regard, Wilson and Bartlett modeled for students an observation Wilson had made about the role of methodology in the interpretation of texts in an essay on the Book of Kings (2000). He noted that among biblical scholars, the debate over methodology had become "increasingly acrimonious and shows no signs of being resolved in the near future"— in part because scholars working with a particular text tend to "project the results of that work onto the Bible as a whole, as if the whole of scripture shared a common set of literary characteristics." Since biblical literature is not so uniform, he suggests that the debate might be more productive "if scholars were to try out different methods on different types of literature in an effort to build up a comprehensive collection of cases that would separate fruitful methods from unfruitful ones" (p. 294). So, Wilson concluded in our discussion, "I always tell students that what one has to do is pick the right method."

In this regard, the pedagogical intentions of the introductory courses on interpreting the Old and New Testaments seamlessly flow into this course. The process in each is the same: "learning how to ask questions that will yield" in this course either a sermon or a theological point "that organically grows out of a particular text." Although Wilson and Bartlett expect that students will learn more explicitly to make the connections between the interpretive practices of their classroom to the lived dynamics of congregational life in practical theology courses and field education, they also assume that the interpretive practices of this course are pastoral practices and will, in fact, shape student approaches to the interpretive tasks of pastoral leadership.

A Common Goal: Critical Thinking as Interpretive Practice

Although pedagogies of interpretation vary significantly, clergy educators widely share the view that practices of interpretation require that students develop the ability to *think critically*. We saw this view in every aspect of our study: classroom observation, interviews, and the surveys.

For example, when the participants in the Auburn 2003 faculty survey[7] were asked to identify their primary intention for student learning, 41 percent of the respondents identified *the capacity for critical thinking* as their most important pedagogical concern. Another 36 percent identified the closely allied intention for the *integration of material* as the primary focus of their teaching. We discovered in our interviews, however, that many seminary educators view critical thinking as a primary aspect of the *integration* they seek in student learning. This suggests that the desire to facilitate *critical thinking* or *critical reflection* dominates their pedagogical imaginations.

When asked to define what they mean by *critical thinking*, most describe what we have been calling practices of interpretation—in Sanders's words, the capacities for *reading* and *analyzing* texts, situations, and relationships. As so defined, the goal of critical thinking is *understanding*, which Sanders and her colleagues across the spectrum of clergy education view as *making sense* of the text, situation, event, or relationship under discussion. What seminary educators look for as *understanding*, however, varies. This means that significant differences also exist among the pedagogies of interpretation through which seminary educators engage students in the quest for understanding.

This should not be surprising. As Tracy observed, interpretations vary depending on who is doing the interpreting, the relationship of the interpreter to the subject of interpretation, and the particular community or group in which the interpretive activity is taking place (1987, pp. 9–10). Less visible are the criteria in pedagogies of interpretation that establish the boundaries or horizon for making interpretations.

Sanders, for example, argued that the adequacy of student practices of ethical reflection originated in their views of Jesus. She did not have just any view of Jesus in mind. She gave preference to views honoring the experience and perspectives of marginalized and oppressed peoples; views shaped in turn by the experience of the black church in the United States and informed by the history of theological thinking about Jesus. In establishing this horizon for the analysis of ethical issues, she illustrates Dykstra and Bass's argument that if a practice is to be Christian, the frame of reference for understanding the practice is a theological one (2002, p. 21). This means, among other things, that she approaches practices of interpretation with a deeper and more complex frame of reference than would be possible if she limited student attention to methodologies of interpretation. She shares the conviction of liberation theologians that the standpoint or social location of the interpreter influences the perspective and the relevance of any interpretive practice.

Her methods of reflection reinforce this commitment. She draws on resources from theology, ethics, and the social sciences to shape a practice requiring a consciousness of the larger Christian tradition in relation to the experience of oppressed and marginalized peoples. In a pedagogical environment that combines the rigors of Harvard, where Sanders received her doctorate, with the call-and-response patterns of black church worship, students, for the most part unconsciously, become increasingly familiar not only with sources for ethical reflection in the Christian tradition but also with modes of analysis originating in the work of Aristotle, Aquinas, and Marx.

Students encounter a variation on Sanders's approach to interpretive practices in Benson's class on moral theology. Despite commonalities in the subject matter of these two courses, Benson's pedagogy reveals different assumptions about the shape of the interpretive practice he intends for the learning of his students. The official teachings of the Roman Catholic Church on moral theology establish the interpretive horizon for his students' learning. He shares Sanders's conviction that one's relationship to

God is a precondition to the interpretive practice, but the view of God forming the interpretive horizon for his own expectations of student learning has been predominantly influenced by the theological and spiritual traditions of the Roman Catholic Church rather than by traditions reflecting collective experiences of oppression and injustice. As a teacher of moral theology in that interpretive tradition, he has a fourfold aim for his students: that they

- ○ Appropriate a working knowledge of those teachings
- ○ Develop enough proficiency to recognize their ambiguities
- ○ Struggle to make sense of the concrete and lived moral or ethical issues encountered in pastoral settings
- ○ Make appropriate pastoral judgments to address and engage those issues

This means that Benson draws students into a practice of negotiating the authority and truths of church tradition while exercising implicitly the values of rational objectivity associated with Enlightenment epistemologies in critical reflection on moral questions or issues.

Lehman's students also encounter the tension between the authority of tradition and reason in her class on the Talmud. But the notion of tradition as a religious horizon is quite different from that in Benson's class. It is not codified in doctrines and principles, notions of truth, or even necessarily in the symbol "God." Rather, it exists in and through the dialogical practice done through the centuries of interpreting the text, which in turn gives form and purpose to the interpreting community in which the practice is embedded. The practice centers on a struggle for understanding originating in the conviction that truths can never be fully or adequately articulated. Although Lehman and Benson both assume that reason functions to open up and make more accessible the resources of tradition, Benson assumes, in contrast to Lehman, that truth is amenable to textual or doctrinal codification. Hence the interpretive struggle for Benson focuses on the quest to discern truth faithfully to its intent, whereas for Lehman the interpretive struggle originates in the dialogical structure of the Talmudic text and continues as students enter the debate about its meanings.

Wilson and Bartlett reminded us that Yale Divinity School's mission statement describes seminary education as an exercise in the "love of God." The intellectual exercise of that "love" exists in a different kind of tension from that in the teaching of Sanders, Lehman, and Benson. It involves negotiating values among Christians from many traditions, a few students from other religious traditions, a few students who identify with no religious tradition, and the more general university commitment to modes of rational inquiry as the dominant horizon for any interpretive activity. In Wilson and Bartlett's course on expository preaching, that horizon is more explicitly Christian than it is in their introductory courses on the interpretation of Old and New Testaments. Students produce sermons to be preached, for the most part, in Christian congregations. Attention to the task of interpreting Scripture in this class centers primarily on methodologies of literary and historical criticism also found in other text-based courses across the university.

It is in the writing of a sermon—with guidance from a common text on crafting a sermon—that students are expected to give attention to criteria for interpretation from their own Christian traditions in the move from the critical interpretation of the text to the interpretation, in the sermon, of understandings gleaned from their study of the text. So on any given day the instructors and students may be reading sermons attentive both to the standards of methodological objectivity valued by the university and to the theological perspectives and preaching traditions of the various congregations for which they were written.

The Complexity of Teaching Critical Thinking in Clergy Education

These reflections on the teaching practices of these clergy educators suggest to us that the dynamics of teaching critical thinking in clergy education may be more complex than is usually taken to be the case. Stephen Brookfield (1987), in an important study of critical reflection that has been read by many seminary educators and used in many faculty workshops on teaching and learning, has argued that educators teaching for critical reflection need to employ teaching strategies designed to help students identify and challenge the assumptions they bring to the study of any given text, situation, event, or relationship, as well as the contextual influences that inform their thinking about the issues and ideas related to the subject of their study, to the end that they will begin to explore and imagine new ways of thinking and acting (p. 15). The concluding step in the process involves the development of a disposition of "reflective skepticism" toward our human proclivity to perpetuate "fixed belief systems, habitual behaviors, and entrenched social structures" and to seek ultimate solutions or final answers (p. 9). We met no seminary educators who would generally disagree with the values in this view of critical thinking, but our reflections on the teaching practices of clergy educators indicate that Brookfield's categories need refining to reflect more adequately what clergy educators actually do.

In the first place, clergy educators are especially attentive to the dynamic character of the interpretive horizon that functions as both source and boundary for the criteria and norms used in an act of interpretation. We have already seen how tradition as a religious horizon is open, porous, contradictory, and ambiguous and thereby invites—indeed, compels— each of these seminary educators and their students as future rabbis, priests, or pastors to interpret. Even more important, each assumes— despite very different assumptions about the role and authority of tradition as a religious horizon—that an expanding consciousness of that horizon confronts the interpreter with new questions requiring new, refined, and even alternative interpretations. They also assume that the kinds of questions arising from this encounter reinforce the assumptions and values that inform the practice in the first place. This means Benson, for example, will emphasize questions that make more accessible church teachings and Lehman, in contrast, will reinforce questions that refine, sharpen, and intensify debate.

Second, clergy educators take into account in distinctive ways views of time that influence their perception of the horizon of the practice. Indeed, all interpretive practice requires a time dimension, but approaching an interpretive practice with a consciousness of a religious horizon makes time meaningful in a distinctive way. Wilson and Bartlett, for example, make explicit in their teaching the progression of past, present, and future as three distinct but interdependent moments of cognitive activity. The exercise of interpreting a text together involves critical capacities for discerning and assessing meanings hidden from consciousness in the text. The sermon seeks to glean from that study—an exercise of imagination— possibilities for the future revealed in the study of a text written in the past for living in the present. In their classroom one has a clear sense of the historical situation of the text *and* of the interpreter reading the text.

In contrast, Lehman, although recognizing the importance of "studying the Talmud as a reflection of the past," will eventually draw students into a practice that can blur the relationship among past, present, and future. As partners in dialogue, students of the ancient rabbis shifted back and forth between memory as retrieval to memory as dialogue; from reason as critical evaluation to reason as imaginative engagement with voices past, present, and future. For Benson, the critical assessment of the present must necessarily begin with an adequate retrieval of the official memory of the church articulated in doctrines and principles and embodied in rules and rituals that in turn provide resources for the imaginative apprehension of a viable future for critical reflection on present experience. On the one hand, Sanders's class seems to follow the pedagogical pattern we observed in Wilson and Bartlett's class, but in the black church tradition there is a notion of time similar to that in Lehman's class. The relationship of past, present, and future is less linear. One walks with, even behind, the mothers and fathers of the tradition when engaging an ethical issue or question. This suggests that a consciousness of the operative meaning of time can reveal, in any understanding produced by processes of critical thinking, deeply rooted assumptions.

Third, critical thinking for clergy educators involves an apparent dichotomy between critical skepticism and passionate engagement among these seminary educators with the subject of their teaching—especially at the point of drawing students into the critical thinking directed to understanding the subject of their teaching. This commitment was reflected in two interdependent teaching strategies for facilitating the encounter of students with a designated subject for their learning. The first involves *modeling* for students the practice they intend for them to learn—that is, making transparent the claim of the interpretive practice in their own approach to and relationship with the subject of their study. It is this transparency that students ascribe—in the words of a Howard student— to teachers who "walk the talk." In the first two sessions of the semester Wilson and Bartlett, for example, spelled out the elements and tasks integral to the practice they would be rehearsing throughout the course of the semester. In each class session that followed they led students through the process of that practice, repeating over and over again a distinctive set of questions emerging from their own engagement with biblical texts to guide students in their reading. These questions focused first on reading the text to apprehend what it might be saying and second on proposing meanings pertinent to the task of writing a sermon with a specific congregation in mind. In this process, Wilson and Bartlett both exemplify and reveal, in their engagement with biblical texts, their intentions for student learning. Through the repetition of this practice, they expect that with time students will begin to internalize those and related questions for reading biblical texts and preparing sermons long after the conclusion of their seminary career.

This was not a new practice for these students. They had already been immersed in its perspectives and approaches in their introductory classes in Old and New Testament. But it was not yet a practice that many engaged in with confident competence. So Wilson and Bartlett not only modeled the practice, in each class session they *coached* the class as a whole toward the perceptions, sensitivities, dispositions, and habits associated with the critical reading of biblical texts, then coached individual students as they moved those interpretations into sermonic forms. The most explicit moments of the coaching of individual progress in the practice occurred through words of encouragement, questions that requested further engagement with a given text or thought, and the feedback on and assessment of sermons.

Benson, perhaps more than the others, most explicitly embraced the more traditional role of coach—creating exercises for the rehearsal of a body of knowledge or a practice of moral theological discernment, cheering student progress, giving students direct feedback in the course of the class session as well as during designated times of assessment in the academic term, diagnosing barriers to their learning and proposing strategies for working through them, and presenting new ways of thinking and resources for tackling the challenges posed by the course before giving them a case or assignment through which they might enter into the practice of interpreting. In similar ways, Sanders structures each reading and writing assignment to reinforce the interpretive practice students experience in class. As we have already noted, Lehman teaches by inviting, challenging, questioning, and giving resources to students as they become increasingly confident with the various tasks of reading and interpreting Talmudic texts as well as with the role and authority of being a participant in the interpretive dialogue of Talmudic study. The emphasis on modeling and coaching in teaching interpretive practices illustrates one way in which seminary educators engage students in the cognitive apprenticeship of professional education. In this instance, students learn interpretive practices by being gathered into practices of interpretation.

Our fourth point is that for most clergy educators the end of critical thinking is not reflective skepticism; it is to move students through reflective skepticism to service, praxis, or some action responsive to the influence or claim of the religious horizon on the interpretive practice. All professional education involves the interplay of reflective skepticism and service or praxis, but what is distinctive in clergy education is the knowledge that the religious horizon poses existential and unavoidable demands on the interpreter.[8] For example, while Lehman recognizes the value of rational objectivity about the subject of one's study or the ability to distance oneself from the subject of inquiry in a stance of continuing reflective skepticism, she also hopes her students will become passionately engaged in the dialogue with each other and the commentaries of the ancient rabbis. Sanders and Benson intend that student ethical and moral judgments will reflect not only the disinterest of objective observation and critical distance, but also a deepening sense of identification with and commitment to black church and Roman Catholic traditions of ethical and moral thinking. Wilson and Bartlett are not interested in student sermons abstracted from the messiness, contradictions, and hopes of living congregations. The quest for objectivity typically associated with critical thinking that opens up the resources of an interpretive community for analysis and critique is chastened by a corresponding quest for a deepening commitment to the relationships and practices of the interpretive community. This commitment both informs their thinking on the one hand and is the context of their professional practice on the other.

As we have already noted, this means Lehman intends for her students to discover they are participants in an ongoing conversation with rabbis across the centuries, and to bring those conversations to life in the experience of congregations. Benson, in contrast, assumes his students will be interpreters of an authoritative tradition in situations and circumstances never twice the same. Bartlett and Wilson assume students will discover that the questions they bring to any biblical text will be challenged and refined as they are themselves interrogated by questions emerging from the texts they read in relation to the congregations for which they will be writing sermons. Sanders, from still another perspective, assumes that a more expansive understanding of church teachings through the ages may both enhance students' wariness of the potential, in any ethical judgment, for perpetuating historic patterns of injustice and oppression and deepen their identification with Jesus' work of justice and reconciliation in specific acts of prophetic ministry. Despite these differences, embedded in these different intentions for student learning is the common concern that their students will develop the critical capacities for thoughtful interpretations of sacred texts and traditions in contemporary situations.

Interpetive Pedagogies in a Signature Pedagogical Framework

Pedagogies of interpretation are prominently featured in the teaching practices of seminary educators. They share a common structure: they focus the attention of students as interpreters on their interaction with some text, relationship, or situation to be interpreted to deepen, expand, or transform the trajectory of understandings and meanings of the communities of interpretation to which they belong. They share a common purpose: they draw students into the quests of the communities of faith or observance with which they identify for understandings at the edges of human knowing and meanings in the midst of the ambiguity and complexity of human experience—quests that dominate the attention of clergy in such professional activities as preaching, teaching, and caregiving in moments of human crisis and tragedy. The pedagogies of interpretation of seminary educators, however, are also distinguished by the diversity of their perspectives and practices. In this regard, they reflect the myriad of variations that exist in the interactions of different interpreters with the same object of interpretation, and even in the same interpretive community. How many more variations of understanding and meaning are possible when one considers the diversity of perspectives and histories of interpretation to be found across the spectrum of Jewish and Christian religious traditions on almost any text, situation, or event? In this study, we had a glimpse of that variety as we observed the influence of the experience of the poor and marginalized in the interpretive pedagogy of Sanders, the rabbis through the ages engaging Lehman and her students, and the official teachings of Catholic tradition in Benson's teaching.

Pedagogies of interpretation also figure prominently in what we identified as the signature pedagogical framework shaping the teaching practices of seminary educators. Even as Sanders, Lehman, Benson, Wilson, and Bartlett draw students into cognitive activities centered on the interpretation of texts, they are cultivating in them ways of thinking at the center of their perception of clergy being and doing. In other words, they are cultivating in their students ways of thinking associated with their assumptions about the professional identity and roles of clergy, expanding their consciousness to the influence of historic and contemporary contexts on the interpretive task, and preparing them through a variety of assignments for the performance of their interpretive skills in a variety of public settings. In these educators' pedagogical goals, we may begin not only to discern the distinctive shape of the teaching practices of a Sanders, Lehman, Benson, Wilson, or Bartlett, but also to identify how they engage students in the interplay of the cognitive, skill, and identity formation goals they have for their learning as future clergy.

ENDNOTES

1. Academic religious educators have for some time explored patterns of pedagogies of interpretation. See, for example, Lee (1971), Little (1983), Moore (1991), Osmer (1990), and Seymour and Wehrheim (1982).

2. One of the intriguing ironies of our study is the gap between the contentious debates over theories of interpretation in scholarly discourse and the lack of attention among many seminary educators to the interpretive

practices in their pedagogies. Students are often introduced to issues integral to these debates, as we saw most explicitly in Bergant's concern that students be able to discern the social locations of both writers and readers of texts. Many seminary educators, however, typically seem to engage their students in interpretive practices without much more than a passing reference to the content or method of their practice.

3. The Mishnah is the earliest layer of systematic deliberation on Jewish law. Developed over centuries of oral debate beginning well before the Common Era, it was eventually compiled and redacted into written form around 200 c.e. and forms the core of the Talmud. The Gemara is the earliest layer of commentary on the Mishnah and is interwoven with the Mishnah at the heart of the pages of Talmudic text. These two textual layers require student proficiency in both Hebrew and Aramaic, and they contain a variety of often competing rabbinic views on the topics under debate. Rabbi Scholomo Yitzchaki, or Rashi (1040–1105 c.e.), is often identified as the greatest of medieval writers of commentary.

4. This commitment may be contrasted with the later medieval Codes that attempted to synthesize and harmonize into a system of laws all that was left intentionally open-ended in the Talmud—a commitment that also emphasized the centrality of ambiguity and intrinsic relationality in Talmudic scholars' conceptions of reality.

5. The Congregation of the Mission is typically called the Vincentians, after its founder, St. Vincent de Paul.

6. For example, Benson spent considerable time working through the elements of the "principle of double effect." This principle, often associated with the work of Thomas Aquinas, suggests guidelines to determine ways to assess what is morally permissible in actions directed toward a good end even though one knows that the action will also bring about bad effects. In this discussion, students identified the classical formulations of conditions for making judgments in these situations.

7. A general report of this survey may be found in Wheeler, Miller, and Schuth (2005). Not all the data relevant to this study have been included in this report.

8. Peter Hodgson underscores, in rather elegant fashion, the significance for clergy educators of a religious horizon:

[I]t appears to me, the way beyond absolutism and relativism may be found, if it is to be found at all, through engagement in some form of transformative, emancipatory praxis. Faced with a physical menace, an ethical dilemma, or an intellectual impasse, the determination to act can often have a salutary, clarifying, releasing effect. One moves ahead only by moving ahead, and often it is only in the motion that one discovers capabilities and directions. Logical contradictions may become more "soluble" under concrete conditions of praxis. One must have the courage to act upon convictions, to take the risk of a venture into the unknown—not foolishly, of course, but wisely, responsibly. The lack of objective certainty with respect to the horizon and consequences of an action, and the recognition that every act is ineluctably conditioned by, and relative to, specific circumstances of time and place, must not of itself be allowed to have an immobilizing effect since there simply is no human action on any other terms [1989, p. 41].

4

PEDAGOGIES OF
FORMATION

A DISTINGUISHING FEATURE of professional education is the emphasis
on forming in students the dispositions, habits, knowledge, and skills that
cohere in professional identity and practice, commitments and integrity. The
pedagogies that clergy educators use toward this purpose—formation[1]—
originate in the deepest intentions for professional service: for doctors and
nurses, healing; for lawyers, social order and justice; for teachers, learning; and for clergy, engaging the mystery of human existence.

Among Jews and Christians, the possibility for the human encounter
with that mystery has often been described as participation in the creative
and redemptive activity of God, and it is symbolized in notions of salvation, redemption, *tikkun* (the healing of the earth), or *shalom* (the harmony intended in creation). Cultivating student participation in the
creative activity of God expands the attention of clergy educators: to foster the pastoral imagination, they not only advance but also embody religious knowledge; not only develop professional competency in their
students but also nurture authenticity and integrity of faith or observance
in religious leadership. In our study, we observed pedagogies that engage
students in practicing the presence of God, holiness, and religious leadership precisely at the intersection of pastoral, priestly, or rabbinic knowledge and skill with religious commitment and professional integrity.

Pedagogies to cultivate this interdependent spiritual and professional
formation have often been located outside the seminary classroom. They
are often found in the worship life of the seminary community, in prayer
groups and devotional disciplines, in the governance of the life of the seminary community, in organized activities responsive to human needs both
in and beyond the seminary, and in the supervision of field education and

clinical pastoral education.[2] (We explore some of these communal peda-gogies of formation in Chapters Nine and Ten.) However, we learned in this study that clergy educators also engage students in pedagogies of for-mation in the classroom. Many student respondents spoke of them as they expressed appreciation for teachers who foster *in their classes* dispositions and habits that explicitly integrate religious knowledge, clergy identity, and character. Through interviews and classroom observation, we became familiar with classroom pedagogies that clergy educators use to explore and foster the interplay of academic, spiritual, and professional practices.

Pedagogies of Formation and the Rabbinic, Priestly, and Pastoral Imagination

Pedagogies of formation shape the rabbinic, priestly, or pastoral imagi-nation in distinctive ways. They foster the professional identity and integrity that functions as a lens or framework through which students view and appropriate the knowledge and skills associated with the work of the profession. In clergy education, the religious dimensions of the hu-man experience are given precedence in the content and structure of these pedagogies. We use the term *religious* to account for the human impulse toward some ultimate concern or meaning (to follow Tillich). It refers to the symbols, relationships, rituals, and formulations of belief and prac-tice that give that impulse particularity in historical traditions and com-munities and give impetus in seminaries to the education of leaders to extend and renew their meanings and practices. For Christians and Jews, the notion of *spirituality* has become an increasingly important way of talking about the appropriation of the religious in its particularity as spir-itual formation. (In Chapter Nine, we focus attention on communal ped-agogies in the practices of spiritual formation.)

Pedagogical Challenges to Formation

The challenge of forming the religious identity and vocation, the spiritual dispositions and habits, of students in the contemporary seminary is dif-ficult. Faculty in most seminaries report their students come from an array of religious backgrounds and have widely varying experiences with clergy roles and responsibilities. Some students have had a lifelong immersion in a tradition; for them, the tradition's roles and relationships, prayer forms and metaphors, texts and rituals are second nature. Some students are re-cent converts whose academic knowledge and religious background are often limited to a significant religious experience. Others are seekers who wander through the curriculum like tourists in a holy site. Some students are attracted to the phenomenon of religion but resistant and sometimes even hostile to the disciplines of religious practice. Still others have an interest in religion or theology that is purely intellectual or academic.

In discussing their roles in cultivating—in an academic setting—the distinctively religious dimensions of clergy leadership, seminary educators often spoke of the need to address three pedagogical challenges. First, however formed or unformed students may appear to be in their religious traditions, they have been, at the same time, quite well formed by other personal, cultural, and spiritual forces. Students enter seminary deeply rooted in family traditions and local or regional subcultures. They have been influenced by the values of advertising and popular culture. And they have internalized (and in some instances appropriated) prevailing views of race, gender, social and economic class, and religious diversity. The clergy educators noted that, compounding this challenge, students may resist or subvert those faculty intentions for their spiritual and professional formation that challenge their beliefs and traditions.

The second pedagogical challenge, clergy educators noted, is the task of helping many students grow out of the naïve, precritical, sentimental, or quasi-fundamentalist piety with which they enter seminary and into what nineteenth-century German Protestant theologian Friedrich Schleiermacher called a "pietism of a higher order," or what philosopher of religion Paul Ricoeur called a "second naïvete." This challenge surfaced in our conversations with faculty and in their responses to our survey questions. For example, one Catholic seminary educator, in words that echo Ricouer's, expressed the hope that students would "move from being people of naïve, unquestioning belief to become people of critical faith." One Jewish seminary educator would like students to "become aware of the diversity and complexity of the tradition" and discover "there are rarely simple answers," so that if "they find themselves saying 'Judaism believes' or 'Judaism says,'" they will recognize "they are probably at least partially wrong." An evangelical seminary educator made a similar point: "I hope students will understand their own experience is not the norm against which they should gauge all other people's faith. I want their worlds to be expanded—to see that they have just a glimpse of faith—that the Kingdom is larger than they have experienced—that they will never know it all."

The third pedagogical challenge for many seminary educators originates in the tension they experience between helping ground students deeply enough in a religious tradition for it to be truly "formative" in the face of conflicting cultural and societal values, and at the same time wanting them to remain open enough to engage truths in other religious traditions. Despite this widely shared goal, the *degree* of openness seen as desirable in approaching the beliefs and practices of "others" varies widely from tradition to tradition and from school to school. In some seminaries, faculty members engage students in formative pedagogies "internal" to a given religious tradition as a prerequisite to their encounters with people whose beliefs and practices are different; in others, faculty guide students in practices of openness and radical humility toward any or all who are "other" as primary aspects of their personal, spiritual, and professional formation.

Pedagogy of Formation: Three Approaches

As we interviewed and observed Jewish and Christian clergy educators dealing with these challenges, we noted three pedagogical strategies that contribute to the formation of the pastoral, priestly, and rabbinic imagination; these strategies are intended to lead the student to practice the presence of God, practice holiness, and practice religious leadership.

Practicing the presence of God. A Bible teacher indicated pedagogical possibilities for this practice: "Through engagement with the biblical material, I hope students will have an encounter with the mystery of God and the mysteries of faith that provide a way of living and serving faithfully and reflectively all their life long." Another teacher, more cautious about the way the term *God* has been used in Jewish and Christian history, articulates this practice as living with humility in the face of mystery.

This pedagogy centers on *awakening* students to the presence of God, the holy, the realm of mystery that transcends human consciousness in texts or reality itself. As we will see in the following section, for Marianne Meye Thompson of Fuller Theological Seminary, this task does not end with an awareness of God, the holy, or mystery. It culminates in a transformation of consciousness—of seeing and making sense of things from the perspective of the wholly other symbolized as God, the holy, or mystery. The perspective of the self in this effort is recentered. It establishes an alternative angle of vision to that of one's prior view of self, other, and community. This means that for Thompson, a course on the New Testament holds up a mirror to the human condition so that students might not only see themselves to be truly at the mercy of that wholly other power but also discover, in this new perspective, resources in that other for reordering their priorities and practices—to see things, as Greene has observed, "as if they could be otherwise" (1995, p. 19).

From this perspective the pastoral, priestly, or rabbinic imagination does not treat the world or religious tradition as predefined and given;

rather, it draws on personal and communal encounters with God or the holy (past and present) as condition and impetus to envisioning, constructing, or transforming that which has been received to address new challenges and changing circumstances.

Practicing holiness. This pedagogy is implied variously in the words of faculty members as learning to "love Jesus more," "to see their Judaism as a praxis . . . nourished by Torah study and prayer," or "to live on every word and gesture, taste, touch, smell, sound, and sight of the liturgies they celebrate with people." In various ways, seminary educators seek to nurture dispositions and habits that embody religious commitments integral to clergy identity. Pedagogies for practicing holiness typically build on pedagogies awakening consciousness to the presence of God—but not necessarily so.

For Albert Rossi of St. Vladimir's Orthodox Theological Seminary, they clearly do. In his class, Rossi uses a teaching strategy that emphasizes the cultivation of religious dispositions and habits for religious leadership through the dialectic of devotional readings and class reflections on the meaning and experience of being religious—in this instance, in relation to a hypothetical question from a teenager. Through the practice of these dispositions and habits, students take on a way of being that is distinctive to the Christian Orthodox religious tradition. Over time, the pedagogical intent is that they will eventually embody the values of that religious tradition to give it form in how they speak and relate, think and act. The attention is to the character of the clergy—to the congruence of devotion and belief, to mind and heart.

Practicing religious leadership. Clergy educators describe this approach variously as "serving as God's partners on earth," interpreting and applying "Scripture wisely and sensitively," bearing "the tradition" as "agents of God in the lives of others," and conveying "excitement about the relevance of doctrine in addressing (through preaching) the real needs and questions of hearers."

Pedagogies for practicing religious leadership enact those dispositions and habits in specific responsibilities and roles associated with clergy practice. They are directed to forming skills, but even more to forming patterns of leadership in which the theories clergy espouse are congruent with the theories embedded in the dispositions and habits that shape how they negotiate the interplay between institutional processes and the people who participate in them.[3] As described later in this chapter, Mary Hughes of Trinity Lutheran Seminary leads her students into this practice by focusing attention on the kinds of judgments that are integral to leading ministries of education. These judgments occur in the interplay between the vision for those ministries that is articulated in the theologies of Christian education they are developing and the discernment of its realization through available curriculum resources and programmatic structures.

In each of these pedagogies, clergy educators seek to teach in ways that embed the knowledge and skills of a seminary education in the religious commitment and integrity of clergy practice. In the pages that follow, we first explore distinctive features of each of these pedagogies. At the conclusion of the chapter, we discuss ways in which pedagogies of formation engage students in the cognitive, practical, and professional apprenticeships of clergy education.

Practicing the Presence of God
Marianne Meye Thompson, Fuller Theological Seminary

Thompson is a professor of New Testament at Fuller Theological Seminary. When asked how she envisions herself as a teacher, she said she sees herself primarily as a "pastor, not a parish pastor" but rather as one for whom the "presentation of ideas and their application is pastoral from the outset." In contrast to her early years of teaching, when she was primarily teaching students "biblical content," she now "realizes that above all else one is always teaching oneself. You are the lesson students see. You can't teach truth, especially spiritual truth that you yourself don't know."

Thompson explained the difference by recalling that she used to teach students about such things as the recurring use of the word "immediately" in the Gospel of Mark. "What use is it?" she asked. Now when teaching this New Testament book her aim is to show that "we are ultimately at the mercy of God." For instance, when reading the passage beginning with Mark 4:10 about how Jesus teaches in parables, she rhetorically asks students, "Where does this leave us?" Then she answers her own question: "Precisely at the mercy of God." She pointed out how this difficult passage highlights the Gospel writer's core concern. It involves a radical trust in God—a trust that God *will* open our eyes and ears to hear, understand, and be saved. Seen in this light, she traces the Markan concern with opening eyes through the Gospel, from the "tearing open" of the heavens at Jesus' baptism, to the "tearing of the temple curtain at his death and the opening of the tomb at his resurrection," interspersed with stories in which, through his healing, Jesus opens the eyes and ears of people. In contrast, she added, "the eyes of the disciples are never opened"—and that insight leaves hanging the question, "Will Jesus open their eyes too?

Or ours?" Thompson observed that this type of teaching contrasts with her descriptions of "eighteen typical Markan characteristics" more representative of her early years of teaching. Now she is primarily interested in the ways in which the Gospel "presents Jesus" and what the "meaning of discipleship to this Jesus is like. Who is God? What is God doing in the world? How does this particular text reveal this about God?"

We observed the final class session of Thompson's introductory New Testament course on the Gospels. With eighty students, her predominant mode of teaching may be described as a form of interactive lecture. Using a cordless mike so as to be heard throughout the large classroom, she began the class session with prayer. She then distributed an outline to orient students to the session's content. She intended to review and reinforce key themes and ideas from the semester—some of which may appear on the final exam. She worked her way through this outline methodically, using presentation slides to show pictures and other visuals throughout the session while peppering her verbal comments with personal anecdotes and examples from film, novels, sermons, and, especially, hymns. She lectured briskly and at times humorously. Students, mostly young men but also one older woman, asked occasional questions, which she answered respectfully, although a student trying to challenge her at one point did not win the debate.

The two-hour lecture encompassed everything from rather extensive archaeological evidence—both textual and contextual (pictures of ruins and the like)—concerning the origins of the Gospels, through synopses of each Gospel writer's and Paul's overarching visions of what "Gospel" meant for them, to the question, "What [then] is the Gospel?"—that is, what is it for us today? Here she presented a compelling picture of a communally experienced and world-encompassing Good News, challenging all the while the predominant individualistic bias in the faith of many students. She illustrated the necessary connection between biblical texts and preaching in real-life pastoral service by presenting several amusingly appalling sermons she had found on the Internet as examples of how *not* to interpret the Gospels. This provided a sobering reminder to the students that people *will* be paying attention to what they say, and what they say had better reflect the Gospels in pointing, above all, to Jesus Christ and his power to heal and save: "If you remember nothing else from this course, nothing at all, please remember this!" were her final words of the term.

In our follow-up interview, Thompson described what at first sounded like a very different pedagogy in a seminar she taught twice several years ago. In this advanced class, with fifteen handpicked students, she created an experience with students that led them through progressively deeper encounters with God by means of a dialectical encounter with biblical texts through critical reflection (that is, the historical and literary interpretation of texts) *and* personal and communal prayer. She recalls the class as probably her most memorable: "I've never had such a group of students!" The seminar began with "positive" biblical texts of divine presence and love but gradually moved into more and more "difficult" texts in which God is portrayed as arbitrary, cruel, or absent. She described the profound shifts the class repeatedly experienced when students' critical study of these texts, often frustrating and painful, gave way in class to *prayer* to God about or with the texts. Over the course of the quarter, the students led devotions on these texts, creating very moving presentations (including, in one case, a stunning series of woodblock drawings) reflecting their experiences with the texts, one another, and God in the class.

In the seminar, which met twice a week, Thompson spent one class period (Tuesday) each week in exegetical study—study that, as the texts presented more and more difficult or ambivalent images of God, elicited increasing frustration among the students. These were advanced students. They had already completed courses like Thompson's introductory course described above. In that class, prayer had established an explicitly religious framework for the "academic" work to follow. As Thompson teaches that introductory course, it is also a pastoral practice—the presentation of her own encounter with the mystery of the biblical text and her experience of its possibilities for the church and world. Most students in the introductory course did not yet recognize that through her teaching Thompson was drawing them into the interpretive study of Scripture as a devotional practice; that they were learning a technical vocabulary for encountering the mystery beyond the limits of their existing knowledge or experience. The advanced seminar built on these assumptions, but despite their prior academic experience, students were still apparently shocked by some of the bewildering and alienating images of God *within* the texts. That was their Tuesday experience. As Thompson reports it, "I remember one time you could just feel the tension in the room. It was just awful in terms of the anxiety."

On Thursdays, however, the class engaged in shared prayer, using these same texts. Thompson reports on the difference that activity made: not pushing aside the new, frightening dimensions of the divine in order to withdraw back to a safer, comforting, familiar God, but somehow moving into these new images of God on a different level—the difference of speaking in the second person "to" this God rather than only in the third person, "about" God. Thompson concluded our conversation by rhetorically asking, "Did God change?" and then answered her own question:

"No. But it sure changed the way we felt about the problem." She found it interesting that the students were much more willing to address the problem of the sovereignty of God in prayer than in the abstract analysis of texts. "The abstract sovereign God is a [much more] scary God."

In this class, the reciprocity of pedagogies of analysis and prayer established a structure for a deeper engagement with the intentions of each. Other seminary educators similarly intend for their students to experience something of the interdependence of the academic and the religious through their teaching. A university divinity school professor, for example, expressed the desire that his students would develop a "deepening knowledge, experiential and reflective, of the love of God out of which they will have the resources they need for ministry and an ongoing practice of prayer." One of Thompson's colleagues expressed a similar hope for his students: that "through an engagement with the biblical material" they would encounter "the mystery of God and the mysteries of faith that provide a way of living and serving faithfully and reflectively all their life long."

In her ethnographic study of spiritual formation in a Jewish seminary in the United States, Wendy Rosov quotes a seminary administrator and philosophy professor who makes a similar claim: "I have this plaque that was given to me: 'Shiviti hashem li'negdi tamid' [literally, "I set the Lord before me always"]. "I think that is the most important line in the bible. It means that wherever you are and whatever you are doing, that's a chance to encounter God and be with God. . . . I'd like to find a way to cultivate that in students" (2001, p. 102).

Rosov continues, "This notion of cultivating an awareness of God, of nurturing the development of a disposition that is open to and primed for an experiential encounter with God is . . . ultimately what spiritual formation was about" for the Jewish faculty and administrators she interviewed. Rosov's language in this sentence—"cultivating an awareness of God . . . a disposition open to and primed for an experiential encounter with God"—prompts seminary educators like Thompson to teach not only to the deep longings that many students bring to their seminary studies, but to their future roles as the religious leaders of congregations.

While many seminary educators include pedagogies that practice the presence of God in their teaching, for others, the language of prayer—and even of God—is not adequate to the quest for spiritual and professional formation. We are cautioned, for example, to remember that for many Jews, as one faculty participant in the study reminded us, "the nature of Jewish spirituality is such that it does not always reflect itself in a prayer mode. Study of the sacred text is in itself a religious obligation." A Christian professor, commenting on a question we asked about the exercise of prayer in the classroom, observed that it "makes no room for disciplines of meditative reflection," which this person "practices regularly, often with particular students or class in mind." Another Christian professor who has "been thinking a lot about spiritual formation in relation to pedagogy," notes that although "pedagogy is a deeply spiritual thing for me I cannot say that having an insight in class reveals God's presence to me." Yet, most seminary educators we interviewed shared the sense that in some way an expanding consciousness of the mystery that is symbolized by most Jews and Christians as God is a critical dimension in the formation of students as priests, rabbis, or pastors. Practicing the presence of God facilitates students' access to that "holy ground" of which the scriptures and texts in both Jewish and Christian traditions speak. This practice is, for most, the primary catalyst to and resource for the pastoral, priestly, or rabbinic imagination.

Seminary educators draw on a variety of pedagogical methods and strategies to facilitate the practice of the presence of God, mystery, or transcendence. The most common involve some form of prayer or meditation. We discovered in the Auburn 2003 faculty survey that 67 percent of the respondents agreed that it is "important to open or close class sessions with some form of prayer or meditation." For some, the daily liturgies of the whole seminary community establish the religious context for the interplay of their teaching and student learning. For others, leading the class in prayer (or asking a student to do so), marking times of "centering silence," singing hymns, reading poetry, or using guided meditation flows seamlessly into the class session. Only 11 percent of participants in this study strongly disagreed with this practice of using devotional or meditative activities in class. Representative of this group would be the seminary educator who said, "I do not assume that my students, by virtue of signing on for my classes, have designated me as their spiritual leader. Thus, I do not lead students in prayer or other devotional activities. In my opinion, the authority they grant to me as a teacher should not be confused with the spiritual authority one might grant a priest or pastor." For seminary educators like this one, practices of vocational and spiritual formation belong elsewhere in the seminary experience.

Pedagogies practicing the presence of God, however, are not limited to modes of prayer. In Thompson's teaching she witnessed to the religious significance and meaning of biblical texts through the use of rigorous literary and historical methods of textual criticism. She engaged students in exegetical exercises to help them discover how those texts point to Jesus. What distinguishes these pedagogies is not so much the method or strategy as the dispositions conveyed through them during class and in her interactions with students, colleagues, and others more generally. Of primary importance in Thompson's teaching is the disposition of *transparency*. This was Thompson's insight when she realized she was teaching herself—but not in the sense that she was to be the object of student learning. Rather, through her particular imaginative apprehension of the presence of God as a New Testament scholar, students could see possibilities for their own relationship to that presence. Just as professors teaching "toward" mastery of subject matter consider the modes of their research and scholarly conversation as models of excellence in teaching, so, too, seminary professors like Thompson give form to their teaching practices with habits and dispositions they seek to cultivate in their students. They attempt to model, in other words, possibilities for the relationship with God or mystery or transcendence as believer, observant, or devout that they encourage among their students.

Practicing Holiness
Albert Rossi, St. Vladimir's Orthodox Theological Seminary

Perhaps it should be no surprise that seminary students consider the transparency of a teacher's commitment as one of the most formative influences in their own preparation to be clergy. In the teaching they most remember, students report catching a glimpse, through their professor's teaching, not only of "exciting subject matter, but of living Torah, living Truth"; "not only knowledge about God but knowledge and love *of* God"; not only an encounter with the professor's "wisdom of the tradition . . . [but through him] also the realness of the Divine." This observation leads us to a second and closely related pedagogical practice integral to forming clergy identity, spirituality, and practice—one that we have called the *practice of holiness*. We received a glimpse into its possibilities while visiting St. Vladimir's Orthodox Theological Seminary in Crestwood, New York, where we visited Rossi's class.

Rossi is a clinical psychologist who had taught for years at Pace University in New York before joining the St. Vladimir faculty. Like most of his students, Rossi is a convert to the Orthodox faith; in his case, from Roman Catholicism. When we met him, he expressed his appreciation for the question we had asked faculty participants in the survey regarding an image or metaphor of themselves as teachers. He describes at length his image of a nursing mother learning to "let down" her milk (something he had learned from his wife when their children were infants). It conveyed to him the experience of letting the Holy Spirit "down," through him, to his students through his teaching. We later saw something of what he meant while observing a class he was teaching.

The class session we observed is part of a two-year course in theological reflection that runs concurrently with the two years of field education required of all students. During their second or "middler" year the students are involved in pastoral activities in a local hospital, prison, clinic, or social service agency. In their third or senior year they work in a local Orthodox parish. Although students do not receive grades for the course, they can either pass or fail it. The class meets every other Thursday evening. Because of the somewhat unusual place of this course in the seminary curriculum, Rossi sees this class and his role in it as different from other courses he teaches. He builds the course exclusively on respect and vulnerability rather than on the implicit power to grade. He describes this model of nongraded teaching as a form of "eldership," an image central to his Orthodox sense of respectful spiritual authority.

After an opening prayer and some reflective exercises of review, Rossi turned to the topic of the previous few class sessions: "What does it mean to put the mind in the heart in prayer?" He suggested a role-play exercise: "Let's pretend we are a high school class, and have someone volunteer to come up here to the podium and answer this question for the high school students: 'What does it mean to put the mind in the heart?'" After a long silence, Rossi called on a student who came forward, took his place at the podium, and then, speaking in his role, said, "Stop worrying about it. Worrying keeps you in your head. Just *pray*, and keep on praying. And, God willing, it will happen." Rossi commended him and asked if anyone would like to answer in a different way. Another student came forward and said: "I don't know *what* it is but I know *how* to do it. Just stand quietly, breathe gently, and imagine you are standing at the top of a bluff above a lake, in your swimming trunks." A couple of people in the class snickered, to which he responded, "I'm serious. Imagine you're in your swimming trunks looking down at the water, and then you dive in, or else slowly you let yourself down by a rope ladder, and descend piece by piece, hand by hand, down into your heart." Another student followed him: "In beginning composition class you are taught to develop your own writing voice. Here I think it's about developing your own true prayer voice, your own true humble voice, and to learn to distinguish that from all the other voices within."

Next, Rossi described how, along these lines, a certain passage from the devotional readings of the past two weeks had stayed with him (the class was praying together through an anthology of Orthodox spiritual writings he had given out earlier in the year). He had been planning to mention this passage in this class session, but then received an e-mail from the only woman in the class—indeed, in the whole Master of Divinity program—who, to his amazement, described her reaction to the same passage. He found her reflections so moving he had invited her to share them with the class. She came forward to the podium and described her reaction to this passage that compares one's human will to a "rotten thread" that is always breaking. She recalled how one day during the previous week, while walking between the chapel and the dorm, she was reflecting on how human hunger for God is described in the text as a "longing in my heart." Then, she reported, "suddenly it happened: this hunger sucked my mind down into my heart. This hunger is stronger than my will—where does it come from?" It comes from a "deep essential need for God." How does one stay there? "I must keep my neediness, weakness, sinfulness before me." As the text says, she explained, "'Keep your mind in hell and despair not.'" She continued, "I don't like this neediness, this hunger—parts of me rebel and want to be self-sufficient. I can't put my mind in my heart by my own will but only by this inner hunger, which can be very painful, an encounter with my limits."

After her reflection, Rossi then spoke of the importance of learning to put one's mind in one's heart as not only the center of Christian Orthodox spirituality but also crucial to ministry as the condition of being simultaneously active with others and aware of the holy presence of God. He quoted Jean Vanier of L'Arche community in Canada as saying, "We are the poor." Rossi elaborated: "Jesus came to save the *poor,* not to save those who serve the poor. So we *are* the poor—or else we're in deep trouble!" The prayer experience of learning to descend into our own "hungers" or "limits" is just such an encounter with personal poverty that is at the heart of ministry. This means, among other things, that the priest or minister is not to be "above" others, "serving" them, but "to be *with* them in their poverty *and ours.*" It involves the formation of a distinctive habitus aligned with the deepest values and priorities of the religious tradition.[4]

Wendy Rosov has explored an image well known in Jewish circles in describing the character of this habitus: rabbis are meant to be *klei kodesh* (holy vessels) (2001, pp. 94ff). Although every form of professional education is concerned with nurturing the character and ethics of students who will be assuming professional practice, to frame the relationship of professional identity and integrity as cultivating *klei kodesh* is unique to the education of clergy. The term, derived from the term for the ritual vessels used in temple worship, describes the rabbi as one whose very being, whose entire personhood, is meant to embody the presence and reality of

God for others. Rosov quotes William Lebeau of the Jewish Theological Seminary who notes that "Rabbis . . . are instruments for transmitting the sacredness of the Jewish tradition through contact with others, rather than 'holy people' set aside from others. *Klei kodesh* are endowed with attributes enabling them to transform that which comes into contact with them" (p. 95). These attributes reflect the relationship and interplay of religious commitment and professional integrity. The implications are several. Since rabbis, priests, and pastors embody, and thereby model, their religious traditions for and with others, it truly matters how they speak and act.

Rossi addressed this issue in speaking to his class. It matters, Rossi emphasized, that one's prayers are congruent with one's relationships with others. This was a theme we often heard during the study. It matters that clergy treat their own bodies and needs with respect. It matters how they speak of God or the mystery beyond human comprehension, sacred texts, and rites; how they describe and enact their own "posture" relative to their tradition's highest values; how their voices may shift—either into a somehow truer or more artificial-seeming register—when they pray in public, preach, or teach. It matters what local and national policies they support, how they preach about racism, whether their own way of life manifests concern for the earth, how they treat family members and neighbors.

Parker Palmer (1998) makes a similar point about the effects of teaching in general. "Good teaching," he argues, "cannot be reduced to technique; good teaching comes from the identity and integrity of the teacher" (p. 10). His descriptions of these two dimensions of the teacher are relevant here. By *identity* he means "an evolving nexus where all the forces that constitute my life converge in the mystery of the self." Identity is not static, but a "moving intersection of the inner and outer forces that make me who I am" (p. 13). Integrity has to do with the "wholeness" he finds as these various forces form and reform the "pattern of my life" (p. 13). In words reminiscent of Rossi's, Palmer reflects on the capacity of teachers for cultivating the "connectedness" of student identity and integrity by weaving complex webs linking themselves, their subjects, and their students in ways that their students can, in turn, learn to use to weave a world for themselves (pp. 14–16).

Teachers will use many different methods and strategies to weave that web. For example, in the class session we observed, Rossi wove an educational experience for students to cultivate sensibilities and skills integral to a disposition for mediating the relationship of adolescents to the mystery of life. The strands of that pedagogical moment included the field education experience of students with young people. A common devotional reading provided a common reference and practice for everyone in the class. Through role-playing, students practiced speaking from their religious tradition to a question originating in the religious quests of adolescents. He commended each of their efforts and then put their responses into a theological framework that reinforced the disposition he was encouraging through the role exercise. He had been in communication with the members of the class through e-mail during the week. In similar fashion, Thompson combines lecture, prayer, question and answer, the use of presentation slides, exams, textual analysis, and struggle into a learning experience for her students.

Modeling the practice of holiness. But the connections among teacher, subject of inquiry, and students woven by these and other teachers we met are made not so much by their methods "but in their hearts—meaning *heart* in its ancient sense, as the place where intellect and emotion and spirit and will converge in the human self" (Palmer, 1998, pp. 10–11). We are back to Thompson's insight about teaching "oneself."

When the seminary students in our study described teachers who had significantly influenced their preparation for ministry, they often commented on the interdependence of teacher identity and the integrity of their teaching practice at the juncture of their relationship to the subject of their teaching and the students they were teaching. One wrote, for example, that an influential teacher was "more of an old-school 'yeshiva rabbi' as opposed to a modern academician. The amount of personal investment he had in the material elevated the coursework to something much more significant than 'the study of' particular religious phenomena." Another student describes the "faith, knowledge, and enthusiasm" of another teacher as "contagious. He truly is a light that spreads to others, a fire that ignites the flame of learning in others." A student at St. Vladimir's, talking about a colleague of Rossi's, observed that he "has a manner about him that I found engaging." He "truly believes his faith and lives his faith, and that helped me in the course. It helps in receiving information . . . when you can just *see* someone truly living his faith, it adds a push of reality to it. I see it in his mannerisms, the way he interacts with people, his gentleness and caring of people and understanding."

For these students, pedagogies of formation have much to do with how teachers model the practices of holiness they seek to teach. In their comments, the students reveal that in clergy education the underlying telos, or ultimate purpose or end, of the profession is at stake. If Jewish and Christian clergy lead religious communities toward transformations of alignment with images of God, or with capacities for justice and compassion emerging from the deepest convictions in those traditions, then it matters how clergy model or embody these values as a central dimension of their ministries.

The implications for seminary educators become evident in several pedagogical assumptions in Lebeau's and Rosov's descriptions of the image of *klei kodesh*. First, pedagogies of formation reveal the transforming power of the teacher's relation to God or to the mystery that is the subject of religious inquiry. This suggests that faculty attention to cultivating practices of holiness that complement their continuing quest to deepen the mastery of the subject of their teaching is an important dimension in their own formation as clergy educators.

Second, the embodiment of this transforming power can also feel transforming to those who come into the teacher's presence, as if in some small or large way they themselves are being moved by a glimpse of God or the realm of mystery. In these moments, what we are here calling *embodiment* is the impetus to and expression of the *transparency* we described earlier—for what is being glimpsed in such moments is not finally (or only) the actual person, but is in fact the goodness, beauty, justice, love, mystery, or living reality that is the object of the teacher's own attention. As a Bible professor quoted in Rosov's dissertation (2001) puts it, becoming *klei kodesh* means "that you become living Torah in the broad sense" (p. 97). Or, as a professor at the Catholic Theological Union observed, it occurs as her students "realize they [too] are bearers of the tradition and agents of God in the lives of others." These professors engage students in practicing Torah, in bearing witness to truths they teach, as they gather them into the rehearsal of beliefs, actions, and values associated with authentic faithfulness or observance. Over time, they too may acquire the gestures, habits, and inflections that give evidence of an ever-deepening immersion into the languages and practices of faith and observance that construct and renew their traditions.

A third implication may be seen in Rossi's response to student participation in the role play he had constructed for them, to practice talking to teenagers about a disposition integral to the spirituality of their religious tradition. In commending their efforts, he encouraged them to probe increasingly deeper and more complex possibilities for their responses. In this regard, pedagogies practicing holiness are more concerned with fostering the character of the habitus of the religious tradition than in replicating its rules.

A fourth implication for the teaching of clergy educators follows: all teaching is in some way formative—or deformative. Teachers, including seminary educators, cannot choose whether or not their teaching practices will be formative. However, attention to their own practices of holiness, in whatever form they take, heightens their attention to dangers in their power to form and influence student learning. The dangers are many, ranging from the hypocrisy of embodying something that is not authentic to the unintentional modeling of confusing messages about the value or significance of the subject of their teaching in professional practice, to the tendency among some teachers to seek out students who, for the most part unconsciously and uncritically, will emulate their perspectives or take up their research or teaching agenda in their own work.

Seminary educators engage students in pedagogies of formation not only to cultivate dispositions and habits of the heart that contribute to the integrity of clergy identity. They are also concerned with developing students' capacity for religious leadership to extend these practices of formation beyond the seminary into the communities where they will be the agents of the religious dimensions of life. This pedagogical concern may be seen in the teaching practice of Mary Hughes at Trinity Lutheran Seminary.

Practicing Religious Leadership
Mary Hughes, Trinity Lutheran Seminary

When we arrived in her classroom at Trinity Lutheran Seminary, Hughes was already setting up two overhead projectors. The desk chairs, she explained, were typically arranged in a circle, but she had opened it at one end to make room for the projector. Hughes had told us earlier that the class included twelve clergy candidates and three lay students; eight of the students were women and seven were men. As students arrived, they randomly distributed themselves around the room. They seemed expectant; the atmosphere was quiet but congenial.

During their middler, or second, year of seminary, students take this required introductory course, "The Ministry of Educating," as well as companion courses in pastoral care and preaching. Through the seminary's ministry in context program, all three courses are coordinated with parish responsibilities. The course is divided into two sections taught at the same time by Hughes and her colleague Diane Hymans. They do much of their planning together and often exchange teaching responsibilities. Hughes says she has probably "taught the course thirty-five times." Through the years, her goals for student learning have emphasized their gaining the ability to "articulate a theory of Christian education," which includes dealing with curriculum and the nature of learning; increasing their ability as teachers; and developing a view of Christian education across the "wide span of the congregation." Her expectations for student learning, however, have changed over time. She used to be "much more formal and academic." She required the students to read "a wide variety of books." Now she is more interested in having them think about how they might "summarize" a presentation "to a Christian education committee," or communicate a theory informing their work in a "letter to the congregation." In words remarkably reminiscent of Rossi's, she says that no matter what assignment she gives them, she wants them to "to have it in their heart" when they articulate it. The presentation must, in some way, have integrity—revealing some congruence of theological knowledge and religious commitment in clergy practice.

Hughes began the class session by noting troubles facing two absent students—one whose wife had had a premature baby the night before, another whose husband was anxiously preparing for back surgery that evening. Most students seemed to know about one or both of these circumstances, and some added further information. The point seemed to be, in a sense, less about giving information than about acknowledging concern and care for members of the class and community. It also meant that the class began on a serious, even somber note. Hughes then asked a student to pray, for which he seemed to have prepared (later she told us she rarely asks for a volunteer on the spot). The prayer reinforced concern for the two students whom Hughes had mentioned.

Hughes then directed the students' attention to the handouts she had distributed before the class began. The activities of the day, she warned students, would be "messy" as they moved back and forth among the curriculum resources she had brought for them to review and critique, but the learning goal for their time together was to understand the many considerations that need to be taken into account when making decisions about the resources to be used in educational ministries. She started by going through a sheet listing "myths about curriculum," noting, for instance, that curriculum is often thought to be a solution to problems of teaching and learning. "People often say, 'If only we had the right curriculum, all would be well.' But that is never true." Curriculum, she told students, is simply one piece of an educational program.

It was clear during this segment and throughout the class that Hughes had in mind a number of points she wanted students to recognize as being important. She did not hesitate to articulate and emphasize them in explicitly didactic ways. She solicited students' views throughout and used them to illustrate or "get to" key points, but she had determined these points in advance; this is not a class in which student interests direct the flow of conversation or in which "meaning" is constructed by the group.

Hughes's use of space reinforced this dynamic. She moved around in the entire inside circle, almost always moving and talking at the same time, often crossing the room to stand directly in front of a student as she called on him or her, and sometimes perching on the table in ways that slowed down the pace and focused attention on a single point or exchange for a longer period. For example, twice she moved to a spot in the circle where the only Baptist student in the class (also the only African American) was sitting. Hughes used the experience of this student, evoked in a short exchange, to make a larger point about the differences between curricula that are fully consistent with Lutheran theology and those that are not (for instance, around baptism and when it occurs). At the same time, Hughes was careful to say (with what seemed like an effort to include this Baptist student) that the issue was not whether a particular curriculum was good or bad, but whether the curriculum and the theological commitments of the congregation or denomination were aligned or consistent. Indeed, she pointed out, it is possible that one might choose to use materials from a different faith tradition if that consistency could be maintained or used to highlight contrasts of perspective.

Hughes dedicated the majority of class time to the analysis of teaching plans and resources found in two different sets of curricular materials, one published by the Evangelical Lutheran Church of America press, Augsburg Fortress, and the other from a nondenominational Christian publisher. Hughes instructed students to work in groups of two and three to look closely at these two teaching plans to determine how they were similar and different, and which would function better in their congregational settings. The driving questions for their investigation were "How does theology shape curriculum, and how does theology guide the decisions we make about curriculum?" The groups began working right away, and seemed focused on the task. The discussions were not noisy, but they seemed intense. Later, with the full group assembled, she asked the students to "tell me about the two pieces." Students jumped in immediately, characterizing their perceptions of the two sets of resources and pointing to the theological issues they dealt with. It was clear that one point that Hughes wanted the students to "get" was that nuances matter: the two lesson plans they had reviewed were quite similar, so students had to examine the materials closely (a skill they presumably learn in classes focused on textual exegesis) to note the differences. And they seemed to be quite good at this.

One segment of discussion, for instance, was about how the two sets of materials treated the concept of sin. The lesson here shifted to a "meta level," becoming a chance to articulate the Lutheran view of sin—not so much as individual disobedience but as a shared condition of estrangement from God. Later in the session, Hughes noted that when working with congregation members involved in Sunday school leadership, the pastor has a chance to reinforce fundamental theological concepts that parishioners otherwise might not know or know only vaguely.

Hughes allowed the discussion of the curricular materials to go on for about fifteen minutes, with lots of give and take with students but, as before, with her insertion of important punch lines. Finally, in what might be described as the climax of the class, Hughes paused to ask the question the entire class session had been leading toward: "What's the point? Why are we doing this? What have we been doing and why?"

Answers started out at a more or less literal level: "We've been examining curriculum." But Hughes then moved to the larger point: "What is your role, as the person who is theologically trained, in selecting curriculum?" She concluded the discussion with a short lecture about the responsibility that the students will have in selecting appropriate curriculum: "You can't use knee-jerk methods or criteria. Many curricula—not just those from Lutheran publishers—are worth looking at and perhaps using. Your unique role is in understanding the theological implications of your choices. Whatever you do, do it with your eyes wide open." Hughes then observed that everyone brings biases or touchstones to the selection of curriculum. She revealed to the students her own: how baptism and prayer are treated. "You will have others," she told students, "but the important thing is to know what they are." Hughes concluded the class by making her point, described above, about the opportunities pastors have for reinforcing the theological concepts.

In Hughes's class, we see in action a pedagogy directed to developing among students clarity about their role as teachers or educators as leaders of congregations. In that pedagogy we may also identify pedagogies directed more generally to the formation of religious leadership in other roles of the clergy—preacher, teacher, counselor, administrator, community organizer, evangelist—integral to their religious tradition's vision of ministry, priesthood, or rabbinate.

We have already seen some of these pedagogies in Thompson's and Rossi's classes. Thompson, for example, constructed a course whose overarching structure rests on a vision of religious leadership that includes the capacity to experience and engage particular (often "difficult") scriptural texts as *simultaneously* the subject of critical analysis *and* Word of God. She seeks to prepare students for forms of ministry in which head and heart are profoundly linked—or, as she herself puts it of her teaching as a whole, "I try to get them to see that we are trying to 'form their hearts

intellectually and their heads spiritually.' I try to mix the metaphors."
Rossi intentionally tries to model priestly leadership embodied in the
Orthodox Christian notion of "eldership"—a practice of holiness based
on respect and mutual companionship rather than on the authority to
grant grades. He also helps students discover connections between the
spiritual resources of their tradition and their emerging priestly identities
by inviting them to practice teaching a central dimension of Orthodox
spirituality—in this class session, by discussing ways to pray with the
mind descending into the heart. Rossi provides ways for students to practice forms of religious leadership rooted simultaneously in their personal
spiritual experience and in their shared tradition: in the prayer text class,
whose members read together each day; in the writing exercises given in
each class session; in brief practice sessions in class; and in the in-depth
reflections he invites students to give.

Hughes also employs pedagogies practicing the presence of God—most
explicitly in the prayer that begins each class session—and practicing holiness, especially through teaching strategies designed to facilitate the development of a community of teaching and learning.[5] Her pedagogical
practice, however, emphasizes the perspectives and skills integral to her
expectations for the religious leadership of congregations—the ministry
of education in particular.

We noted at least three emphases in Hughes's pedagogy. The first is
Hughes's quest to create in the class a learning community—gathered in
prayer, bound together through a mutuality of concern, engaged in an
explicitly religious enterprise of collaborative theological inquiry focused
on issues in the leadership of the educational ministries of congregations.
The character of that learning environment and the relationship of persons who participate in it are important to Hughes because they nurture
in students expectations for the learning communities they will be fostering when they themselves will be teaching, both during the same term, in
the seminary's ministry in context program, and later, in their internships
and ministries.

Hughes's second emphasis is her overarching concern that students
develop a theory of Christian education—in other words, that they articulate a *vision*, grounded in their religious tradition, for determining a
course of action in clergy practice. Her third emphasis is closely related
to the second; we saw evidence of it when she engaged students in the collaborative exercise of *discernment* to ascertain the presence or absence of
that vision in the events of ministry—in this instance, in developing criteria for choosing resources for teaching and learning in the congregational
setting.[6] In this enterprise, Hughes facilitates opportunities for students

to practice exercising judgments at the intersection of church tradition and congregational life, Lutheran theology and Lutheran piety, clergy and lay roles in the congregation's educational ministry.

Vision and discernment: cultivating a pastoral imagination. Hughes's use of the interplay of vision and discernment moves beyond developing in students the ability, as leaders of religious communities, to solve problems. It cultivates a way of knowing that emphasizes what Dykstra has called "a strenuous effort of moral imagination" into encounters with the mystery of reality known "only through a glass darkly and never exhaustively" (1981, pp. 34–36). For Jews and Christians, this way of knowing originates in and has been renewed through the ages in the responses of people to the stories of God. It shapes their expectations as religious leaders, initially by facilitating their participation in the shared task of religious communities of living toward or into the vision embedded in those stories. Through their participation, they may increasingly identify with its significant events. They begin to bear its burdens and hopes. They begin to view themselves as agents of its future. This is the intent behind Hughes's quest that students develop a theory of Christian education. It is more than an intellectual exercise: it is the formulation of their relationship to the stories of God as they have been told in their denominational traditions.[7]

This way of knowing then gives form to their leadership as the students begin to articulate and give expression to possibilities they can envision from their tradition's story for the future of a congregation or religious community. This is an act of discernment (Foster, 1989). It points, as Charles Wood has observed (1985, pp. 67-8), to "particular things or situations in their particularity." It highlights an "appreciation of differences" as in the contrasts discovered during an exercise to compare the perspectives of two publishers of curriculum resources in Hughes's class. It "discriminates" rather than synthesizes to facilitate the capacity for making choices among alternatives. This is the disposition and skill Hughes is nurturing as she engages her students in an exercise to develop their ability to make judgments about the adequacy and relevance of curriculum resources for a congregation's educational ministry. This is a highly nuanced activity, one to which the students at Trinity have been introduced through courses in Bible, theology, and church history, but it is now directed to a specific clergy responsibility in the leadership of a congregation. It takes time to cultivate because, as Wood has also observed, one must be "*disposed* to discern" (p. 75). Among other things, clergy educators must test, often challenge, and sometimes correct students' "pre-understandings," which are often naïve, sentimental, and superficial. They

must guide students in acknowledging their limited understandings—
sometimes in unlearning them, sometimes by expanding or transforming
them. They must recognize the limits of students' skills to refine and develop them. Distinctive to clergy education—in comparison with other
forms of professional education—is the necessity of learning to make judgments in reference to some understanding of the presence or leading of
God or the dynamics at work in the mystery of human experience in a
given situation.

Nurturing capacities for discernment, while engaging students at the
edges of their understandings and the limits of their skills, is an especially
crucial role in professional education. Lee Shulman has made the point:

> When student-professionals move out to the fields of practice, they find
> inevitably that nothing quite fits the prototypes. The responsibility of
> the developing professional is not simply to apply what he or she has
> learned to practice, but to transform, to adapt, to merge and synthe-
> size, to criticize, and to invent in order to move from the theoretical
> knowledge of the academy to the kind of practical clinical knowledge
> needed to engage in the professional work. One of the reasons judg-
> ment is such an essential component of clinical work is that theoreti-
> cal knowledge is generally knowledge of what is true universally. It is
> knowledge of regularities and of patterns. It is an invaluable simplifi-
> cation of a world whose many variations would be far too burden-
> some to store in memory with all their detail and individuality. Yet
> the world of practice is beset by just those particularities, born of the
> workings of chance. To put it in Aristotelian terms, theories are about
> *essence,* practice is about *accident,* and the only way to get from there
> to here is via the exercise of *judgment* [2004, pp. 553–54].

From this perspective, developing capacities for discernment in professional judgments cannot be taught in rote fashion. Hughes took note of
the multiple sites of potential *accident* in clergy practice when describing
for us the many ways in which her students will actually be engaged in
the educational leadership of the congregations they will be serving. Those
unexpected and typically unanticipated catalysts to clergy practice may
occur, she told us, when giving attention to the many individual and communal processes of becoming Christian in a congregation—"in the schools
of the church, the vacation Bible school and Sunday school" and other
educational activities, in "committee meetings, the church council, the
church's newsletter," and in relation to "what the building looks like," or
"how they interact with parents who want their children baptized." This
suggests that for seminary educators to recognize the unexpected dynam-

ics of religious leadership, they must nurture their own (and their students') imaginative capacity to envision in the unexpected incidents of practice possibilities for "intentionally helping people grow in faith [all life long] through study, through reflection upon their experience."

Since no seminary educator could prepare students for the number or variation of these educational settings, moments, or roles, fostering the religious leadership of clergy typically shifts the role of the teacher from instructor to mentor or supervisor. This role takes time and focused attention, competency and improvisation. When reflecting on her own efforts to develop this imaginative and improvisational capacity in students, Hughes explained how she assumes this mentoring role both in and outside the classroom setting:

> When students give some work to me or when they're in class and say
> or do something, I try to take it from that point and help move them a
> little bit further by saying: "Here's what I appreciate about what you
> said and here might be the next step, or here might be a question to
> consider."
>
> I make a note of some things that are really of interest to me. . . . If
> I see something that's really problematic, I'll point that out. I'll call
> attention to something [that] is just plain off-base . . . theologically for
> their particular denomination, or if it is personally inappropriate. But
> many times, by encouraging something they're doing right, and
> proposing the next step, they're kind of self-correcting and they gradually move toward improvement or better understanding.

At another point in our conversation, she mentioned that she also helps students who have difficulty "putting it all together" by giving them "rich feedback" both in person and on their written work, sometimes requesting they rewrite their work, "sometimes even suggesting wording . . . to put their ideas into a more focused form." What motivates all this effort? The bottom line is that she wants them to give effective leadership to the educational ministry of congregations, not only "to do it well," but through their leadership to "serve God faithfully," with "joy and excitement." She hopes that "what we do in this class contributes to that."

Formation Pedagogies in a Signature Pedagogical Framework

The attention given to pedagogies of formation by seminary educators may be one of the most distinctive features to be found in the education of clergy. The pedagogical challenge these pedagogies address for seminary educators is the expectation of religious communities (and the larger public) that clergy should embody in practice the values and commitments they espouse; to reveal in their character their own engagement with God or the relationship they have with the mystery beyond the edges of human knowing and experience. In this regard pedagogies of formation distinctively influence how seminary educators configure the elements of the signature pedagogical framework of clergy education to account for the mutuality of the cognitive, practical, and professional apprenticeships in educating clergy. This emphasis undoubtedly originates in the attention given in pedagogies of formation to the interdependence of mind, body, and heart in clergy knowing, doing, and being. The contribution of pedagogies of formation to their interdependence may be seen in the ways these seminary educators have assumed responsibility for mentoring students in the mutuality of the cognitive, skill, and identity formation apprenticeships in clergy education.

In the courses we observed, for example, Thompson and Hughes use a body of information students are expected to know to provide the basic structure and establish the general objectives for the course. The institutional rationale for their courses would seem to emphasize the values of the cognitive apprenticeship. Class sessions draw students into those values predominantly through pedagogies of interpretation similar to those we described in the previous chapter. Students do not successfully complete these courses if they do not demonstrate some predetermined grasp of that body of information. In his field education seminar, Rossi shifts the focus of the cognitive apprenticeship from the appropriation of a body of knowledge to the integration of that knowledge in practices of the profession.

These three clergy educators, however, are also concerned with the competency or effectiveness of their students. Hence they focus attention on the development of skills associated with clergy practice: learning to read sacred texts requisite to preaching, teaching, and other functions of ministry (in Thompson's introductory course) to the exegetical skills (worked on each Tuesday in her advanced seminar); from developing a theological rationale for a ministry of education to developing plans and conducting teaching events(in Hughes's class); from participating in the disciplines of prayer to practicing ways of talking with teenagers about the deepest dimensions of the religious life (in Rossi's class). A prominent theme in the cultivation of these skills centers on the contextual relevance of their efforts.

Learning these skills, however, is neither incidental nor the primary focus of their teaching; rather, Thompson, Rossi, and Hughes all have in mind some expectations for the kind of religious leaders their students will become. In this regard, the attention of these three seminary educators to the future performance of their students in their professional roles is directed to concerns associated with the apprenticeship of identity formation. That performance is shaped by the character of their own engagement with the deepest meanings and obligations discovered through their study. Rossi teaches, for example, toward the possibility that his students will learn "to take their minds down into their hearts" and in the process take on the meanings and practices of Christian Orthodox spirituality in and through their priesthood. Thompson wants her students to meet Jesus in the texts they are studying, to discover themselves living into the mercy of God, because their responsibility as they preach and teach is to be present to those encounters for the people in their congregations. In a similar, but distinctive way, Hughes expects her students not only to know Lutheran theology (or that of their own denomination) but also to reflect and reveal its meanings for congregations through their decisions in the most basic of their roles and responsibilities as religious leaders. Pedagogies of formation, in other words, figure centrally in the commitment of these seminary educators to the mutuality of knowledge and spirituality, identity and integrity in the professional formation of clergy.

ENDNOTES

1. The term *formation* has a range of meanings in different contexts. Typically, Roman Catholic schools use the term to encompass the entire program of priestly development. Thus they speak of *academic, pastoral, spiritual,* and *human formation* as the four key elements of their programs. Most non-Catholic seminaries use the language of formation to intend only the latter two of these elements, though they rarely speak explicitly of *human formation.* They usually speak of formation in ways that center in spirituality, but are understood expansively rather than narrowly. Thus non-Catholic seminaries may use the language of (spiritual) formation to include broadly what Catholic seminaries address separately as *human formation.* Sometimes, non-Catholic seminaries speak of *pastoral formation,* or the formation of pastoral or rabbinic identity as well. The language of *academic formation,* however, is rarely if ever used outside the Catholic context. In this chapter we are looking at classroom practices that especially focus on the identity and integrity of clergy—that gather up the broader notions in Catholic theological education but with primary attention to the interplay of pastoral and human formation.

   Let us also note that in our research interviews, as well as in literature on the subject, almost no one—even in Catholic communities who use this terminology most frequently—is truly satisfied with formation language.

Objections typically come in three main forms. People variously object to (1) the metaphorical implications of people as lumps of clay, passive and more or less infinitely malleable, plastic to the will or power of some superior shaping force; (2) the unvoiced assumption that those who are responsible for "forming" in the seminary are faculty or administrators (or spiritual directors and other program leaders in the area of spirituality), raising questions thereby about competency and training, hierarchies of relationship, and potential abuses of power; (3) the implication sometimes heard within the language of spiritual formation that a preordained pattern or "form" exists to which the most diverse human sensibilities and vocations and personalities must somehow be "conformed."

2. An explicit exception to this claim is the recent proposal by Virginia Samuel Cetuk (1998), who argues that all aspects of the seminary experience should be viewed by students as a journey of spiritual formation.

3. Cf. Argyris and Schön (1974).

4. We are not wishing to suggest a strict linearity in this process, as if experience necessarily comes first and embodiment second; for of course the practice of forms of prayer, worship, service, devotion, observance, and so on, over time—their embodiment, if you will, in a person's and community's very flesh and being—is itself a primary means by which these persons and communities are invited into new and ongoing experience of the divine.

5. Note that Hughes teaches in a school in which the rhythms of liturgy establish one of the structures for the flow of the academic calendar; also that at Trinity issues of a student's call and religious commitment are addressed in a variety of ways through the interplay of school and denominational programs and processes.

6. Wood (1985) explores the relationship of vision and discernment in the academic study of theology. Although our concern centers on the professional education of Jewish and Christian clergy, his discussion has influenced our thinking.

7. For one elaboration of this theme, see Groome (1980).

5

PEDAGOGIES OF
CONTEXTUALIZATION

WHEN WE ASKED SEMINARY EDUCATORS to tell us about a course they especially enjoyed teaching, many identified one in which they sought to help students understand the context of a text, historical event, or religious practice; engage in some process of contextual analysis; or explore possibilities and strategies for social or systemic change. This attention to context is most immediately evident in the titles of courses they described for us: "Images of Christ in World Christianity," "Religion and the American Way," "The Rabbi and the Hospital," "Urban Church Ministry," "Global Urbanization and Mission," "Liturgy and Culture."

Seminary educators attend to context for good reason. Jewish and Christian clergy are responsible in great part for the continuing vitality and relevance of their particular religious traditions in a wide variety of congregational and other institutional and social settings. Those settings exist, however, amid the fractures of modernity: at a time when communication technologies and demographic mobility intensify the blurring of the boundaries of ethnic, cultural, religious, and national identities; and in a world in which patterns of injustice and oppression not only persist but find new and often more pernicious forms. Such forces as these disrupt long-held assumptions about the perdurability of communities and their traditions.

We observed seminary educators who teach, in other words, with an increasing awareness of the permeability and fragility of the communities their students will be serving as rabbis, pastors, and priests. In their view, central to the mission of seminary education are teaching practices that heighten student awareness to the dynamic character of the content and agency of contexts. At the same time, they seek to develop in their students the sensibilities and skills to contextualize core values and practices from their religious traditions—sometimes in the new and changing landscapes of their ministries, at other times in quests to transform oppressive or discriminating structures and relationships inherited from the past. To achieve these goals, clergy educators use *pedagogies of contextualization.*

Pedagogies of contextualization are the third of the four pedagogy categories that make up the signature pedagogical framework of the Jewish and Christian seminary educators we observed. In this framework, pedagogies of contextualization complement pedagogies of interpretation by helping students become aware of the influence of contexts on religious meanings and in religious practices. They also ground pedagogies of formation in the interplay of historical and contemporary contextual influences on the identity and practices of the leadership of religious communities. Indeed, throughout the study we noted the particular interdependence of interpretive, formative, and contextual pedagogies in the teaching practices of a significant number of seminary educators. They approach the education of clergy assuming that meaning and identity are always contextual, that content is hidden unless contexts become accessible to critique and open to transformation.

A Rising Interest in Context

Robert V. Moss has traced this interest in *context* in Protestant theological education back to H. Richard Niebuhr, Daniel Day Williams, and James Gustafson, who, in the 1950s, argued that "theological education" must be seen "in the context of the church and its mission in the world" (1957). This view of context is apparent in the seminaries we visited as part of our study:

- o In the curriculum of Trinity Lutheran Seminary, first- and second-year students participate in a program called "Ministry in Context." In this program, students begin to develop capacities for *reading* congregations as "living human documents" (a practice deliberately appropriated from clinical pastoral education) with the intellectual rigor typically associated with the reading of literary texts in the classroom.

- o Howard University School of Divinity expands attention to the *world* as context in a course called "Ministry and Contextualization." In this course, students probe biblical, historical, and theological sources for ministries in their social and cultural contexts while at the same time developing "methodological concepts pertinent to understanding ministry in a pluralistic world."

○ Many seminary educators, in a variety of seminary classrooms, share the commitment of Bergant (see Chapter Two) to expanding the contextual consciousness of students in her classes. They attribute this commitment to the influence of their own social locations on their thinking even as they explore the influence of the historical, social, and religious contexts on the object of their study.

For these seminary educators, contexts, as settings of human interaction, have *content*. Contexts consist of patterns of relationship and social structures, historical trajectories and local particularities, status and power configurations, values and commitments, and dispositions and habits that intrigue contemporary social analysts. They include, as John Gumperz has observed, *events* as "stretches of interaction bounded in time and space" filled with resources, people, cultural patterns, local wisdom, and situational dynamics embedded in *activities* in which the interactions of people are constantly changing (1992, p. 44). Bernard Meland has described contexts as structures of experience. They possess "an organic inheritance" that for the successive generations participating in them may well exceed their perception of their "depth and range" (1972, pp. 98–99). Although we may typically be unaware of much of a context's content, its elements can, like those of a text, be teased out into the open to be *read*. The intent of such reading is increasing consciousness: "wide-awakeness" is the term Greene (1978) uses to indicate the capacity to see into what is usually taken for granted.

Just as pertinent pedagogically, contexts also have *agency*. An emphasis on contextual agency originates in the recognition that just as the structure and placement of words in a paragraph influence the meaning of a sentence, contexts of human activity also influence and shape what we think, how we perceive, and why we act as we do. The Candler School of Theology's *Contextual Education Handbook* illustrates the point in describing assumptions that inform the program. "Christian identity as a basis for ministry" is shaped by the embodiment of "practices . . . embedded in diverse institutional, social, and cultural contexts." Robert Schreiter, a theologian at the Catholic Theological Union who has spent much of his career exploring the issue of context, suggests this is an increasingly shared assumption. He has noted that while theologians through the centuries have not changed their views about the purposes of theological reflection, today they pay more attention to how contextual circumstances shape the messages they seek to communicate (1985, p. 1).

Schreiter identified three catalysts to this growing interest among Christian theologians and clergy regarding the content and agency of contexts, and they are relevant to our discussion of the teaching practices of Jewish and Christian seminary educators. The first catalyst may be traced to the *"new questions"* (Schreiter's italics) that religious leaders are being asked, "questions for which there [are] no ready traditional answers" (p. 2). As a Christian theologian in a seminary sponsored by missionary orders of the Catholic Church, with students from around the world, he is particularly attentive to challenges faced by Christian missionaries and missiologists seeking to interpret the Christian message in new and unfamiliar cultural settings. Schreiter notes that they find themselves ask-ing questions for which they had no ready answers: How does one celebrate the Eucharist in a society with no tradition of bread or wine? How does one celebrate baptism in cultures that view the pouring of water on one's head as a curse? How is someone from a democratic society to under-stand the relation of church and state in a repressive governmental regime?

More generally, Jewish and Christian leaders have also been encountering new questions originating in the responses of people to the influence of contemporary movements in science, technology, economics, and politics on their world views and religious practices; in the distribution of economic resources and political power; in the hegemonic patterns perpetuating patterns of racism, sexism, classism, and other "isms" in social, political, economic, religious, and cultural institutions:

> How are the people of religious traditions that value *gathered* congregational practices or religious observance, for example, to view the possibilities and problems for their common life in *virtual community*?
>
> How are notions of justice identified with redressing the needs of the poor, deeply rooted in Jewish and Christian traditions, to be understood in relation to the competitive and acquisitive values of a global consumer culture?
>
> How are religious peoples to address the power dynamics at work in the interdependence of local and global contexts?[1]
>
> What is the role of tradition in communities increasingly influenced by the rational and technical objectivity of modernity?

Beneath these questions is another, closely related: how are the people of historic religious traditions to draw on the past in circumstances for which there are no precedents? In asking this last question, Christian theologian Douglas John Hall had in mind the totally new challenge of thinking theologically "under the threat of nuclear annihilation" (1991, p. 38). For Jewish educators Seymour Fox, Israel Scheffler, and Daniel Marom, a similar question emerged from the persisting challenges of the Holocaust to the orientation of the internal life of Western Jewry (2003, p. 6).

The consequence, Schreiter suggests, is that "theologies once thought to have a universal, and even enduring or perennial character" often now are seen as being "regional expressions of certain cultures" (1985, p. 3). "*Old answers*" he concludes, do not adequately address these "*new questions.*" Although Schreiter's attention was again drawn to challenges faced by missionaries from cultures in the northern and western hemispheres seeking to communicate the Christian gospel to people in cultures with different world views and practices, his insight has broader significance. Not only have the dominant perspectives in Jewish and Christian traditions been challenged by minorities, women, and the poor, but a consciousness of historical and social pluralism following the Enlightenment has given rise to questions for people from all religious traditions about the adequacy of overarching philosophical or theological systems. Discoveries in the natural sciences have increasingly challenged the adequacy of historic formulations of primary doctrines and practices. Many students of theology and religion increasingly find themselves dissatisfied with universalizing ideas or methods in their study.

Again, Hall envisions in these situations that every context holds its own distinctive problematic, requiring religious leaders to ponder the continuity of their traditions in their contextual particularity. Hence there is now a range of religious and secular readings of Torah in contemporary Jewish circles; the development of black, feminist, womanist, *mujerista, minjung,* global, and ecological theologies among Christians; and a host of ethical perspectives—medical, legal, feminist, and the like—to address issues that clergy face along with their colleagues in other professions.

Schrieter makes one more point. New, contextually sensitive theologies no longer tried "to apply a received theology to a local context," but instead "began with an examination of the context itself." In doing so they gave *priority to the present* (1985, p. 4).

This emphasis on the present is evident in the teaching practices of many seminary educators. For example, beginning with the context itself is the intent of Trinity Lutheran faculty members when they help students learn how to *read* the congregation and its history as context for pastoral leadership. More generally, seminary educators have been encouraged to emphasize the present by women and students of color, who have both challenged teaching tactics that minimized or ignored their questions and perspectives and promoted pedagogies to engage students in analyzing the power dynamics in any social process. For seminary educators, teaching for contextual consciousness is a first step in teaching contextually relevant practices.

Three Pedagogies of Contextualization

In this chapter, we explore three pedagogies—perhaps distinctive to clergy education—that contextualize student learning. Although definitions vary for this relatively new word, *contextualization,* it commonly refers to the task of making explicit the socially situated nature of all knowledge and practice.[2] In the education of clergy, pedagogies of contextualization emphasize that clergy practice is itself socially situated: each sermon, each ritual, and each professional action both is influenced by and shapes a particular congregation in a given neighborhood in a specific cultural setting. The first seeks to develop in students a *consciousness of context*—its content and agency. Seminary educators articulate this intention for student learning in a variety of ways: to help students understand the "historical and cultural context within which the Old Testament was produced" and "the ways that educational structures, teaching relationships, and processes of learning give shape to personal and communal experience," or to help them learn how to "think contextually" about the "theological task."

A second pedagogy focuses attention on developing in students the ability to *participate constructively in the encounter of contexts.* This is a primary intention of faculty seeking to heighten student attention to the dynamics of cultural or religious pluralism. In one course, a seminary educator, for example, seeks to prepare students "to become adept interpreters of the cultures of the broader world in which they find themselves and the evangelical community as well as to help them understand the complex interaction of those communities and its effects upon their own thinking."

A third pedagogy of context engages students in processes of social and systemic change in what might be called the *transformation of contexts.* Survey respondents described pedagogies for the transformation of contexts in courses seeking to help students become "attuned to their own culture, bias, ministry style and background as they do social analysis" in their ministries or develop increasing awareness of "the politics of biblical interpretation" while learning, at the same time, to exegete texts from a feminist, womanist, or mujerista perspective, for "a concrete communal setting." In the following sections, we observe these pedagogies in the classrooms of three clergy educators.

A Pedagogy of Contextual Consciousness
Shaul Magid, Jewish Theological Seminary

When we visited Jewish Theological Seminary, Magid, associate professor of Jewish thought and chair of the department of Jewish philosophy,[3] was teaching a course that seeks to foster in students a consciousness of Conservative Jewish identity shaped by two incommensurate contexts: modernity and tradition. The embrace of modernity, Magid argues, is a distinctive challenge for religious communities whose identities are grounded in the transmission of tradition: the receiving, passing on, and renewing of deeply embedded and inherited shared patterns of thought and action. The tension in this effort, specifically between the relativity of norms in modernity and the significance of what we have been calling the *interpretive horizons* in religious traditions, permeates the daily routines of the rabbi, especially in roles of teaching and preaching. These tensions are equally real, we contend, for Christian clergy.

The specific pedagogical challenge Magid sets for himself is to "enlarge the canon" of the seminary's rabbinical student education beyond "the nineteenth- and twentieth-century modern liberal Jewish thinkers or Christian thinkers." To accomplish this task, he introduces the students "to an alternative canon of texts written in the modern period," from "a kind of extreme, fundamentalist, ultra-Orthodox perspective." Conservative rabbinical students, he told us, rarely encounter these writers.

Magid's learning agenda for the course centers on how to begin to engage the tension between the "pluralist" self of modernity and what he describes as the "universal" self associated with traditional notions of identity. Although Magid does not assume students will adopt the perspectives of these writers, he wants them to discover the sophisticated ways the authors both deal with contemporary problems and reveal, in the process, "real fissures in the Conservative movement." They need to engage these alternative voices, he told us, because they cannot develop a viable "theological vision" for contemporary Conservative Jewish life and clergy practice unless they are able to respond constructively to these "alternative visions" of their tradition in the context of modernity.

Magid uses several approaches throughout the course. He first introduces students to the literature on modernity—to heighten their awareness of the content of modernity as the context for contemporary Conservative Judaism. Next, he has students engage a series of fundamentalist responses to modernity, raising such questions as "What does it mean to be Zionist?" He then has students explore how traditional societies view authority as a way to critique modernity's devotion to autonomy. Finally, he explores with students what "ultra-Orthodox thinkers understand the purpose of the study of Torah" to be as a way to help them think about what the goal of study is in their own movement.

On the day we observed a session of this class, Magid commented on the pride the Jewish Theological Seminary has taken in its approach to negotiating the relationship of modernity and tradition over the years. The problem, he continued, is that the assumptions and forms of thought integral to modernity have increasingly been taken for granted. He then reiterated the rationale for the seminar: to make explicit those shared and often hidden assumptions by exploring the character of modernity through texts written by scholars of modernity who assume that modernity and tradition are incompatible. In the process, he challenged the adequacy of pedagogical efforts to address issues of personal and cultural identity through practices of social analysis alone. Instead, he concluded, one must draw on resources, often deeply hidden, in Jewish tradition.

Magid identified two goals for the class session: (1) to discover whether or not the texts he had assigned have anything to "say to us," and (2) to explore whether Conservative Judaism's unexamined view of modernity needs to be reassessed in light of views held in Orthodox Judaism. At several points during the class, Magid focused the discussion on issues and practices around which the tension is particularly lively. A commitment to "compromise," he suggested, is one example. To make his point, he observed that for Conservative Jews, the notion of "original sin is an act of compromise." Since compromise ameliorates difference, it "is precisely what modernity values." One of the Orthodox critics of modernity the class had been reading contrasted compromise with *conviction*—that is, a disposition choosing one perspective over another. The act of choosing, for this writer, was the higher value even if it meant choosing secularism.

Magid explained that the reading for the day's class is rooted in the Hasidic tradition. It emphasizes the centrality of devotion in Orthodox Judaism that challenges, among other things, Conservative Jewish efforts to teach courses *about* Judaism. What purposes do these courses serve: "history, information, or skills?" Magid asked. To teach devotion rather than Judaism suggests an alternative model of teaching—one that "values universalism"—a way of seeing the specific in relation to the whole rather than the "particularism" of a specific religious tradition or the objectivity emphasized in the analytical study of religious traditions.

Before Magid could continue, members of the class jumped into the conversation. One student (who, as time went by, increasingly articulated his appreciation for the Orthodox perspective of the text they were discussing) reinforced Magid's point. He observed that the Orthodox quest for truth "focused attention on the universal, whereas in more liberal settings the focus of attention is on truths." Another student immediately disagreed, arguing that "while the Orthodox perspective may be more universal, with their argument that only Jews have the truth, they are also particularist." Soon every student had entered the conversation. The debate continued, often with great intensity.

Magid took control of the discussion for a few minutes (something he did four or five times during the two hours) to ask such questions as, "What is the goal of the Conservative project? Is it passionate worship? To keep Jews Jewish?" In this instance, he answered his own question. "It focuses more on the latter. There is no sense of universalism in the project. There is no infrastructure in Conservative Judaism to maintain universalistic goals." The students were clearly not intimidated by the force of Magid's argument or by the strength of his voice. One student immediately "resisted" this conclusion. "We are trying to convince people there is something distinctive about being Jewish." Magid challenged him to identify that "thing" and then noted for Orthodox Jews it is summed up in the statement "God commands." This brought the class back to the earlier discussion of the dynamics of universality to be found in human responses of devotion and obedience.

With twenty-five minutes left in the class session, Magid again pulled the discussion back to the text. He noted that the author's view of teaching or study contrasts with the Conservative Jewish assumption that studying Judaism is similar to the study of anything else—that is, to create a sense of objectivity about the subject of inquiry. "This," he continued, "is the cornerstone of teaching at the Jewish Theological Seminary." But it is not the author's view. He returned to an earlier statement. "It is passion. So, how does one teach passion?" The contrast, he suggested, may be seen in Orthodox efforts to immerse oneself in the "logic of the text" rather than in seeing "what's on the page," to enter the mind of the writer rather than to use the tools of literary or historical analysis. The latter approach, he argued, is not conducive to absorption in the spiritual exercise that exists in the text's logic. In the Talmud, by way of contrast, he concluded, spirituality is in the construction of the text.

We had reached the end of this two-hour class session. Magid dismissed the class with an announcement of the reading to be done for the next session. It felt as if the discussion had ended in the middle of a paragraph.

Magid had told us previously that in some class sessions he and the students work through a text line by line. In other class sessions, he encourages free-flowing conversation and intense debate. At first glance, the structure and teaching methods of the session were not much different from those in other seminar sessions we observed: shared reading of a common text (sometimes outside of class and sometimes during the session), introductory comments to set a framework for the discussion to follow, general discussion moderated by the professor or designated student leader, and a summary presentation or discussion. Magid introduced students to unfamiliar texts in the larger Jewish tradition and to the tasks of reading fundamentalist Orthodox Jewish texts to better understand Conservative Judaism. Magid rehearsed these tasks in two ways: by persistently asking how the text illumined the "Conservative project" and with the two writing assignments for the seminar.

However, the structure of the practice of teaching and learning in this seminar is actually more complex. In our conversations with Magid, he repeatedly emphasized the need for Conservative rabbinical students to become aware of the unexamined assumptions of their religious tradition and practice. He wants them to engage the texts he chooses so they might become increasingly conscious of the challenges of being a Conservative Jew—of becoming rabbis in a tradition that embraces the context of tradition *and* modernity. Magid illuminates the struggle of living in the midst of that context by exploring Conservative Jewish assumptions about modernity along with Orthodox critiques of modernity. For Magid, any rabbi's lack of consciousness of the tensions between the contexts of tradition and modernity is a serious professional problem. The seminary, he contends, graduates too many students who are incapable of thinking through the philosophical and theological issues these tensions create or of leading congregations that are struggling with them.

As we observed Magid in the interplay of these implicit interpretive and formative pedagogical goals, we saw that he adroitly assumed several pedagogical roles. He *presented* the theoretical framework for the course in the syllabus and in the continuing rehearsal of basic assumptions informing the course. He structured the class session so students could rehearse or *practice* the dialogical encounter between Conservative assumptions and expectations from challenging Orthodox perspectives. This practice took the form of collaborative debate and argument—a strategy for the dialectical struggle for meaning and authority highly valued by Conservative Jewish educators. We had reached that point in the semester when students were no longer intimidated (if they had ever been) by Magid's professorial authority, so that his role was often reduced to that of one of the participants in the debate of ideas. There was a difference, however. From time to time, he interrupted the discussion to guide or *coach* students in this practice by urging them back to a more careful reading of the text, or by asking new questions that reinvigorated their struggle to make sense of contextually incompatible ideas and values. The practice was not brought to a conclusion, but was clearly to be resumed in the next class session or more informally in the hall or cafeteria.

Most pedagogies of contextual consciousness in seminary education are employed to heighten student awareness of the contexts that have shaped sacred texts and their interpretations over time; given rise to traditions, rituals, or practices that continue to have meaning and power for contemporary religious communities; or influenced the course of events in the heritage of those same religious communities. Faculty describe these contextual goals in many ways: "I want my students to learn about Paul's life and times," or "to develop an appreciation for the effect the New Testament has had upon the life of the church and culture," or to "interpret contemporary issues in the religious sphere in light of their historical roots." The intent is to help students see ancient texts, events, and traditions in their own context; to extricate their original meanings from the layers of meaning that have accrued to them over the centuries.

In this course, Magid engages in a similar task but he does not focus, as do his colleagues in Talmud and Bible courses, on discovering contexts in the past so much as he is interested in helping students discover features with which they are not familiar in their present context. All these seminary educators seek, however, to deepen student awareness of the influence of context on meaning and practice to the end they might think more rigorously about their own thinking. For Magid, that desire focuses on helping students discover distinctive features of their Conservative Jewish identity and heritage that are often hidden in the tradition's accommodation to values and perspectives identified with modernity. He wants them to be prepared to engage in a more "authentic speaking" in their preaching and teaching in congregations struggling to negotiate practices of observance with taken-for-granted notions of modernity.

In this regard, Magid, and other seminary educators seeking to cultivate in students an increasing consciousness of the contexts that shape their lives, share at least one aspect of Paulo Freire's pedagogies of "conscientization."[4] These educators assume students are "empowered subjects," capable of achieving "a deepening awareness of the social realities which shape their lives," and discovering "capacities to recreate" themselves" (Elenes, 2003, p. 199). This "recurrent, regenerating process of human interaction" has an emancipatory character, clarifying "hidden dimensions" of their experience in the world (Gore, 2003, p. 333).

When Magid describes his intentions for student learning in his course, he privileges the quest for a modern Conservative Jewish identity liberated from unconscious participation in ways of thinking, perceiving, and doing associated with modernity. The intent is not so much to liberate them *from* the influence of modernity as it is to provide resources for reconstructing their response to modernity from inside the traditions of Judaism. Other seminary educators teaching for contextual consciousness have similar intentions for student learning. They describe their hopes for students' learning as developing "contextual awareness"—that is, becoming increasingly aware of the contextual *content* of a text or setting in which they find themselves—so they might be more attuned to their own cultural and religious biases and the effects of those biases in their ministry, whether in congregations or elsewhere.

Still other seminary educators extended the goal of developing in students a contextual consciousness to include the task of preparing them to mediate *the encounter of* contexts. We observed a seminary educator in a class at Catholic Theological Union engaging students in this contextual pedagogy.

A Pedagogy of Contextual Encounter
Thomas Nairn, Catholic Theological Union

At first glance, the pedagogy embedded in Nairn's syllabus for a course in medical ethics appears to be the traditional one in academic professional education: a pedagogy to move students from theory to practice. Indeed, Nairn's course description, with its three goals for student learning, clearly articulates a goal of moving students from theory to practice: (1) "a general understanding of the issues and concepts and tools of biomedical morality," (2) "an appropriation of the Catholic tradition and its usefulness for contemporary medical ethical questions," and (3) "a general ability to minister to those facing medical ethical decisions." Nairn's list of required texts, schedule of topics, and assigned readings conveys the same purpose.

However, a phone conversation prior to our class visit left us with a much different perception. Nairn said that when he began teaching the course, it was "very theoretical." He developed "nice deductive conclusions that may or may not have worked in practice." After some hospital clinical experience, his views of medical ethics issues became "grayer than they used to be" and he began to use "real case studies" in his classes. Three other catalysts contributed to new directions for his teaching practice: (1) changes in the church meant students need to know what the church has said and is saying "so they can know why they agree or disagree" with what it says; (2) recent changes in the Vatican's approach (it has become "more hesitant") to making some pronouncements about medical ethics have shifted more responsibility for those decisions to the people who must make them; and (3) changes in the educational experience and age of students and the increasing numbers of women attending Catholic Theological Union bring to the course students with new expectations. With further reflection, Nairn identified "3 R's" as the general goals guiding his decisions about what and how to teach: "react, retrieve, and reconstruct." Nairn has taken great care in choosing these three words.

REACT. Nairn expects students to be increasingly engaged by and act on issues and questions that are emerging from and, in turn, shaping the contexts of their ministries. This practice of engagement—of seeing and hearing into the contextual dynamics of an ethical issue—establishes the framework for "reacting." He invites students to develop skills for *reacting* by focusing their attention on identifying "the facts of the case" they are investigating.

The task involves more than recognizing new ethical issues linked to the rapid changes in medical technology. The diversity of students in every Catholic Theological Union class (something he relies on pedagogically) makes this a complex task. At least half the students in the class we visited were from many different countries. Perhaps as many as two-thirds of the members of the class were preparing for ministries in one of the school's more than thirty-five sponsoring religious orders, with their different charisms, traditions, and cultures. Among this group, most anticipate ordination. Approximately a third of the class were preparing for lay ministries—some in local parishes, others in hospital chaplaincies or educational ministries. With this diversity of contextual experience in mind, Nairn urges students to discern the facts of the case from their particular cultural, national, gendered, and theological perspectives. Nairn deliberately encourages a consciousness of this diversity by inviting students to articulate the varying perspectives they have on what the facts of the case might be.

For example, in the case analysis we observed, some students (primarily from societies with sophisticated technologies) identified the facts of the case we were analyzing as having a medical basis; others (mostly, but not all, from developing societies) located them in a spiritual disorder. These contrasting readings of the facts of the case culminated in a diverse list of ethical issues in the case. Beneath the articulation of each of these issues, Nairn pointed out, could be found layers of different cultural, technological, and religious commitments and perspectives.

Nairn designs this cross-cultural encounter to ask students if they have their "facts right." The notion of *right,* students rather quickly discover— and then have reinforced repeatedly through the semester—has as much to do with the relationship of their reading of the facts and circumstances *they* bring to the case as with their *reading* of the facts and circumstances of those *involved* in the case. The contextual practice of *reacting* that Nairn is teaching, in other words, centers on simultaneously expanding student consciousness of their own contexts in dialogue with their deepening consciousness of the contexts of those involved in the case—and later in the ministry situations they encounter.

RETRIEVE. Nairn's pedagogy engages students, as well, in *retrieving* the Catholic tradition for assessing the facts they have identified. And if students cross-register from neighboring Hyde Park seminaries, he encourages them to seek sources relevant to the case from their own denominational traditions—an invitation that further expands the variety of perspectives in class discussion. By asking them to retrieve resources from their religious traditions, Nairn seeks to deepen in students their identification with those traditions.

Nairn guides the task with a question: "What is the Christian vision that informs the ways we view the facts of the case?" With this question in mind, Nairn's students work their way through official church documents on medical ethics, paying attention not only to the specific guidance they give, but also to the vision for the church and humanity that informs each document. They discover, in the process, that official church documents are also limited resources for making ethical decisions or even for understanding the church's position. Additional readings are necessary to illuminate both changes in church thought and policy over the years, and the diversity of cultural and social perspectives and practices—over time and in the present—on specific medical ethics issues. During this class session, for example, students discovered, among other things, that in contrast to current Catholic ecclesiastical policy, from the fifteenth century until the 1890s the church had approved the possibility of some sorts of abortion for women whose lives were endangered.

This process of retrieval requires critical skills honed through practice with interpretation. For Nairn this process of retrieval is achieved most effectively through the tools of "mutually critical correlation." He had learned this method of textual analysis in graduate school from his theology professor, David Tracy, who in turn had been influenced by the work of Paul Tillich. Nairn expands its original intent in class sessions by putting into dialogue church policy with multiple cultural perspectives for insight into given ethical issues. Nairn reinforces this patterned critical *retrieval* in the way he grades assignments. Students who choose to write a homily, for example, must demonstrate the use of scriptural texts in helping congregants deal with an issue. Homilies that simply append a Scripture text automatically receive lower grades. In similar fashion, students also receive a lower grade when they only "*apply* theory to practice" in analyzing a case.

RECONSTRUCT Nairn understands that answers to medical ethics issues are typically "obsolete every six months." New technologies, new discoveries, and the vast differences in cultural perspectives on health and healing that clergy typically encounter mean they can rarely approach ethical issues with ready answers. Hence, Nairn asks students to ponder this question: "What does ethics have to say to the interaction of the facts of the case or situation with the Christian vision?" Ethical decisions from this perspective require respect for religious tradition in relation to the knowledge of medical science and the facts of the case, rooted in its cultural context.

As we observed a class session, we saw how Nairn's "3 R's" influence his decisions about what and how he teaches. He began the class with a brief prayer and an overview of the session. After introducing a case for analysis, he divided the students into small groups composed to reflect the diversity of the class. He asked each group to identify the facts in the case. The facts they identified reflected the diversity of their cultural and social perspectives. Nairn then used a general discussion of their lists of facts to establish a framework for a series of brief lectures on how to read disparate facts on their own terms and in relation to church teachings relevant to the case. In a final step, Nairn drew the class into a conversation about the range of facts the students had identified and relevant church teachings to delineate ethical responses that would be both consistent with church teachings and contextually relevant. Nairn told us that students rehearse this "practice in medical ethics" in each class session. Written assignments throughout the semester provide opportunities in another medium for additional practice.

During a conversation after class, Nairn created an image for us of "the world" as the larger context in which his teaching occurs, illuminating something of the meaning and urgency of this pedagogical practice. As

Nairn explained, the world in which ministry takes place is made up of innumerable tensions: between conservative and liberal, male and female, hierarchical authority and personal authority, high- and low-tech cultures, technology and spirituality, sin and grace, creation and destruction, and so on. Most of us try to resolve these tensions, he suggested, by swinging to one side of the tension or the other. For Nairn, that is not a viable ethical (or theological) response. The only place to "live" or "do ethics," he wrote, in words that reminded us of Palmer's description of the space of teaching and learning (1998, pp. 73–74), is in "the center of the tension."[5] The result is evident in Nairn's efforts to guide students through a strategy for ethical thinking about medical issues that both respects and critiques cultural experience and church policies, affirms and challenges the resources of technology, and sees value in and also questions the usefulness of both high- and low-tech cultures. In describing this strategy, Nairn noted that the first class sessions during a semester often include moments of "contained conflict" as students encounter and begin to engage differences in their experiences, opinions, and cultural perspectives. But as the semester unfolds they begin to listen into their differences—not necessarily to appropriate them, but to discover their meanings and to appreciate their significance for each other. Nairn experiences deep satisfaction when students reach this point of "working from the center" of those differences. He hopes they will carry this practice (which is reinforced in other parts of the Catholic Theological Union curriculum) into their ministries, initially in the Catholic Theological Union's field education program and later in congregations, schools, and other church agencies.

Nairn, we discovered, is far from alone in the attention he gives to teaching to enhance student facility for religious leadership in the cross-contextual encounters of a pluralistic and mobile society. These contextual practices are central to the mission of the Catholic Theological Union and permeate the teaching practices of his colleagues. Throughout the study, we found a similar emphasis in goals for student learning. Some faculty members described their desire that students become, in the words of one respondent, "aware of their social locations" while at the same time developing a "global perspective of reading the New Testament"; another respondent voiced a desire that students become "rooted in Jewish tradition," while learning "to appreciate" and "construct theologies that have integrity and that don't marginalize the specific embodied, encultured people who are suffering." Another seminary educator teaches so that students might become "a bridge between the languages and cultures" of students in the school and in their places of ministry. From different vantage points, one seminary educator hopes to help students develop "increased awareness of the politics of biblical interpretation," and another to help students "think of Christianity as a 2000 year developing story, seen through changing paradigms of thought." Each of these clergy educators seeks to foster among their students both an awareness and an appreciation for diversity in the human experience and change in communities over time.

In Christian seminaries, pedagogies for contextual encounter are often most evident in courses designed to help students explore ways to communicate the Christian message to people in cultures where it is not familiar. This concern was the original impetus to Schreiter's inquiry into the dynamics of ministry activity in missionary settings. Ethicist John Stott ponders the challenge: "How can I, who was born and brought up in one culture, take truth out of the Bible which was addressed to people in a second culture, and communicate it to people who belong to a third culture, without either falsifying the message or rendering it unintelligible?" (1980, p. viii).

This concern lies at the heart of a course, "Christian Apologetics," that William Dyrness teaches at Fuller Theological Seminary. In this class, he seeks to prepare students to share the Christian gospel with people for whom it is not familiar and in places where it is unknown. This challenge is deepened by Dyrness's desire to help students avoid in their own practice the imperialism of past missionary activity.

Thus, in a lecture we observed, he proposed that sharing the Christian gospel with these goals in mind involves at least five steps:

1. Entering into the life of a community by engaging in all manner of generous and supportive activities to earn the trust of community members

2. Being alert to the potential in episodes that create a real need for consolation and support as teachable moments

3. Knowing biblical texts well enough to be able to readily identify selections that may be read together to convey comfort and insight

4. Sitting and reading biblical texts together to show connections between the words of Scripture and the painful situations in which they find themselves;

5. Being prepared to build from the particulars of this particular conjunction of experience and text to the larger context of faith and belief

Dyrness further reminded students this pedagogical process takes time. It involves developing sufficient familiarity with the context of an "other" to enter it on the "other's" terms, while at the same time learning to read and share Scripture through the lens of the personal and cultural experience of that same "other," to the end that the "other" might discover the transforming power of the Gospel in his or her own context. Those who teach or evangelize, however, are not unchanged. They too learn, in the process, to "see" the Gospel afresh from inside the perspective of those they have been teaching or evangelizing.

As we reflected on our observation of Nairn's teaching and our discussions with other seminary educators who engage students in pedagogies of contextual encounter, we identified that they may be distinguished in several ways: they nurture the capacity for empathic consciousness, facilitate mutual understanding, and foster dialogical reciprocity.

NURTURING THE CAPACITY FOR EMPATHIC CONSCIOUSNESS. In pedagogies of contextual encounter, teachers seek to develop in students an appreciation of the other on the other's terms. In some theological circles, this capacity is described as the ability to "cross cultures." As the *Handbook* guiding the field education program at St. John's Seminary makes the case, "if we know who we are, we are not threatened by others; if we accept who we are, we accept others; if you don't know who you are, the dominant culture will define you." This capacity for contextual self-knowledge, however, is the corollary of "getting to know the other in their otherness," which similarly requires learning how to allow others "to define themselves" and how to approach them in their diversity with "respect and reverence."

FACILITATING MUTUAL UNDERSTANDING. Pedagogies of contextual encounter also have as a goal facilitating a mutuality of understanding across the many facets of our human differences. This requires minimizing the distortion that typically occurs in any act of communication. The intent in pedagogies of contextual encounter, as Ira Shor and Paulo Freire have written, is that "the object to be known is *not* an exclusive possession of *one* of the subjects doing the knowing" (1987, p. 99). The focus of teaching is not on teachers (or missionaries or evangelists) giving "knowledge to students in a gracious gesture." Instead, the object to be known mediates the worlds of all those involved in the teaching and learning interaction as they bring their perspectives into conversation with each other. This is a primary feature of Nairn's pedagogy. He places a medical ethics case figuratively on the table at the center of the small group that "meets around it and through it for mutual inquiry." Each member of the group speaks to the case from the perspective of her or his own context, but each is also simultaneously pulled out of the relatively safe environment of his or her context to meet others on the common ground of the case. That students often experience this common ground as tension is not a problem for Nairn. Rather, it provides the impetus to deeper ethical reflection and the mutuality of continued learning.

FOSTERING DIALOGICAL RECIPROCITY. Pedagogies of contextual encounter also foster the dialogical reciprocity of appreciative and critical inquiry. Sharon Welch provides a way to think about this intention in teaching practice (1991, p. 88). She contrasts the communal ethics of MacIntyre and Stanley Hauerwas, based on the "prerequisite" of "cohesive community with a shared set of principles, norms, and mores," with an "ethic" that combines the "pluralism" of the human community with "social responsibility." An ethic grounded in cohesive communities lacks "the means," she argues, "to criticize constitutive forms of injustice, forms of exclusion and limitation central to the operation of a given social system" (pp. 86–87). (Welch's examples of such forms include the institutions of slavery and the oppression of women in ancient Athens.) An ethic that takes seriously the contextuality of human experience shifts the pedagogical focus to the interaction of perspectives and experience of all who have a stake in the issue.

In Nairn's class, that encounter occurs as students enter into dialogue or conversation with each "other." The goal is not consensus but the interplay of mutual appreciation and mutual critique. This goal shifts the power dynamics in the pedagogical interaction. Welch draws on the work of Anthony Giddens to make this point: in our gestures of recognizing "the other," we may also discover the promise of a solidarity that does not deny our differences (Welch, 1991, p. 95). This relational possibility emerges in Nairn's class as students grant each other "sufficient respect to listen to their ideas . . . to be challenged by them" and discover, in the process, that their lives are "so intertwined" as to be accountable to each other (p. 95). For Nairn, this practice of contextualization emphasizes the development of a *habitus* for continued learning at the intersections of the diversity in the human community.

Pedagogies for Contextual Transformation
Scott C. Williamson and Amy Plantinga Pauw,
Louisville Presbyterian Theological Seminary

In a class session at Louisville Presbyterian Theological Seminary, we observed two seminary educators engaged in a pedagogy that moves beyond a quest for the mutuality of respect in the encounter of contexts to challenge contextual practices and structures that perpetuate patterns of dominance or oppression. They seek, in other words, to set in motion, through their teaching, changes of consciousness integral to changes in social systems and structures. The course we observed was entitled "Womanist and Feminist Ethics" and taught by Williamson, an African American ethicist, and Pauw, a European American theologian.

Taking advantage of the seminary's support for team teaching, Williamson and Pauw decided to offer this advanced course to introduce students to resources produced by nineteenth-century black and white women that are relevant to contemporary ethical reflection and action. In this course they hope students may become alert to the dangers of placing their perceptions and expectations on others and at the same time develop capacities for listening to others to the point that they can let their "own emotional responses be tempered and broadened by hearing [one] another."

Although Williamson and Pauw's intentions for student learning sound similar to Nairn's, they have something else in mind. Those intentions became increasingly evident when they described an introductory session for the course we would be observing. It had begun as "an impromptu assignment." They had given each person in class the name of a nineteenth-century woman. "In the next class session they were supposed to go around the circle and in a second or two identify these women." When the exercise concluded, Pauw noted that "the room was full of these nineteenth-century voices." The discussion turned to how these "lost voices . . . continue to trouble and disturb us, and to stir outrage in us." Members of the class then began to explore why they felt outraged and to ponder why "we continue to struggle with their issues." Pauw and Williamson recalled the class session as being both "emotionally fraught" and "intellectually engaged." The teachers were, however, as Williamson concluded, "well on their way" to engaging students in what we are describing as a pedagogical practice of contextual transformation.

Students taking the course had previously completed a two-semester course sequence of introductory theology and history that functions in the seminary's curriculum as the introduction to the major theological doctrines of the church. The course we observed is one of several electives through which students may meet an advanced requirement in either theology or ethics. Twenty-five or so students had enrolled for the course during the semester we visited the campus. There were two African American women, six European American men, and one Filipino man; the rest were European American women. The group sat around a set of tables arranged in a large rectangle: the instructors sat side by side at the front of the room, and the students sat along the other three sides.

Although the instructors told us students typically begin class sessions with a prepared meditation related to the subject of the day, Pauw assumed that responsibility in this session by reading an excerpt from an essay by C. Eric Lincoln about driving through the swamplands of South Carolina and hearing the voices of men and women who had died either as captives on the voyage from Africa or as slaves in the swamps. She concluded the reading with the observation that Lincoln could "transcend time and space to participate in the suffering of people long past." He exemplified a disposition embedded in the expectations of the instructors for student learning in this course: that is, the capacity for listening to oppressed voices in the nineteenth century so "that we might more clearly hear our own voices" in the human struggle over power and place.

During a conversation after class, Williamson expressed his delight that the "students were getting it." When we asked what he meant, he answered that after only five sessions, members of the class had, with little overt coaching, begun to move through the three phases of thinking he and Pauw were trying to cultivate: (1) historical dialogue, (2) ethical and theological analysis, and (3) critical reflection and action. The terms Williamson used to describe the students' progress, however, only hinted at the teachers' intentions for student experience and learning.

Williamson, who had responsibility for guiding the group's discussion the day we visited the class, initiated the *historical dialogue* by reviewing topics to be addressed during the session: to make visible patterns of racism in the suffrage movement, to probe the meaning of emancipation for black women, and to explore historical sources for a contemporary womanist theology of suffering. Referring students to their reading for the day, from Angela Davis's *Women, Race, and Class,* he asked them to identify sources of the tension over voting rights in the nineteenth-century women's suffrage movement. One by one, students around the table identified thoughts and concerns of black and white women from that century whose work anticipated themes in contemporary womanist and feminist writings and strategies. Attention was drawn to racist practices among white suffragettes.

Williamson shifted the focus of the students' comments by asking members of the class to ponder why Shawn Copeland, author of an essay in Emilie Townes's *A Troubling in My Soul: Womanist Perspectives on Evil and Suffering,* might ask if the voices of the black women they were reading were authentic. With this question, students began to contrast the experience of black women portrayed in an essay written by Frederick Douglass (who spoke "for them") and essays from black women from the same historical period (who wrote "from their own experience"). In the discussion that followed, Pauw and Williamson guided the students' attention away from the dominant voices of black men and white women to the relatively invisible words and experience of African American women.

At this point assumptions informing the course became increasingly explicit. This historical dialogue with nineteenth-century women drew on resources from a specific theological context as a framework for analyzing their experience. In this class session, for example, Williamson introduced the second "phase" in the way of thinking they were cultivating, *ethical and theological analysis,* by asking students why it was important for Copeland to develop a theological definition of suffering *before* she explored the meaning of suffering in the experience of nineteenth-century African American women.

In the conversation that followed, students noted that Copeland needed to make a distinction between "suffering that has no value and suffering that is redemptive" if suffering is to be the "lens through which we might look at the values of the experience of people who had suffered." Williamson illustrated the contextual influences on Copeland's definition by analyzing the text of the spiritual "Wade in the Water." "Why would you wade in the water that God is going to trouble?" he asked rhetorically. "Not because it is a peaceful place, but because it is the right place to be—because healing, freedom is the result of being there." Suffering, in other words, is a significant source for resistance and a way of affirming the experience of "black women carrying the cross of Christ." Pedagogically, this meant, for these students, that the experience of black women suffering atrocities of slavery, racism, and sexism established the theological framework and provided theological resources for contemporary ethical reflection integral to their own liberation from oppressive and marginalizing forces. Williamson and Pauw's goals for student learning at this point had moved beyond the quest for understanding to a change or transformation of consciousness.

Williamson and Pauw moved the students to the third phase in developing a way of ethical thinking responsive to voices on the margins. Williamson asked students to listen to their own experience of this nineteenth-century heritage through a womanist theology of suffering. Williamson again led the discussion into this phase of *critical reflection and action* by asking students how the writings of these women illuminated how they themselves might be caught in contemporary practices of racism. In the conversation that followed, students variously confessed to racist attitudes and behaviors, described their unintended involvement both as victims and perpetrators of racist social patterns, expressed anger about the systemic character of racism in which women generally (and they particularly) participated, and shared thoughts and ideas for personal, religious, and social transformation. Although we did not hear the language of reconciliation during the class session, much of the interaction among students emphasized the capacity of hearing each other out of the experience of the other, toward some reconciling action with each other and the groups (by race, culture, gender, social class, and the like) they represented. For Williamson and Pauw, not only is this pedagogical phase necessary to any personal or cultural transformation liberating people from racism and sexism, it also shifts the focus of the class. The students move from the transformation of consciousness to a transformation of their relationships with each other, with the school in which they were studying, and, inevitably, with the institutions in which they either are or will be engaged in ministry.

Williamson and Pauw organized the class session as a practice session in "ways of thinking" that honor and, indeed, give precedence to those who have experienced oppression and marginalization. The catalyst to the practice was a set of readings by nineteenth-century black and white women in dialogue with texts by contemporary womanist writers Copeland and Davis. That dialogue was initiated and sustained by questions guiding the discussion. In a rather informal Socratic style, and with additional comments from Pauw, Williamson initiated, probed, pulled, encouraged, supported, and tested student comments. On other days, they noted, Pauw takes on this role. In their classes, sitting side by side, collaborating in planning, and with an occasional reinforcing word, they *model* possibilities for empowered male and female, black and white conversation that turned upside down deeply rooted conventions in the history of those relationships.

The students may have been "getting it," as Williamson claimed, but clearly this was so because the instructors attentively coached them through the elements of the analysis they were practicing. The students' comments ranged from reporting information from their reading, to sharing stories from their own experience to illustrate a point in the discussion, to confessing their complicity in structures of racism and sexism, to challenging signs of that complicity in their own comments. The discussion was punctuated by laughter and expressions of frustration and pain. The instructors, however, maintained a firm control on the process. They returned to the guiding questions when the discussion began to wander, identified historical precedents in personal experience, and summarized major themes again and again in the discussion. Indeed, our experience with one student underscored our observation. During the class session, all but one of the students spoke. Later in the day, that student told us this was one of the most important classes she had taken while at the seminary.

We identified at least three distinctive features in Williamson and Pauw's pedagogy for contextual transformation. The first is highlighted in Schreiter's observation that the multiplicity, variability, and interpenetrability of contexts means that we must approach any definition of context provisionally. In pedagogies of contextualization this involves, as Scheffler has noted, *stipulating frames of meaning and methods of analysis* for specific situations and sets of circumstance. Williamson and Pauw, for example, explicitly stipulated both content and method for the study of theology and ethics in this course from inside the context of the experience of nineteenth-century black and white women and through the contextual experience of racism and sexism. In so doing, they created an alternative and circumscribed pedagogical environment in the seminary's academic program.

A second feature of this pedagogy of contextual transformation involves the *retrieval of deeply rooted and often hidden or repressed communal memories* that may provide an expanded or alternative vision to current experience and resources to challenge forces that inhibit or limit student experience. From this perspective, Williamson and Pauw introduced students to the suppressed voices of black slave women regarding the liberative activity of God, to challenge equally hidden but operative theological and ethical assumptions that perpetuate gender and racial discrimination and oppression in the church and nation. This task typically confronts students with the necessity of making decisions about what to do with their new information and of developing new ways of thinking about how they see themselves in the seminary and their religious communities.

Greene coined a term that suggests a third strategic emphasis in their pedagogy: to *demystify* the status quo, the taken-for-granted, the unexamined and assumed by helping students become alert to the presence of the hidden curriculum in their larger educational experience (1978, pp. 54ff). This effort also leads to alternative perspectives and practices. Williamson and Pauw drew their students into this pedagogical practice by highlighting the authority of the heretofore mostly suppressed voices of nineteenth-century black and white women to reveal persistent and, for the most part, hidden patterns of racism, sexism, and classism among themselves and in contemporary theological and ethical thought. These strategies of demystification typically stir up the power dynamics at work in the classroom. Students struggled during this class session, not only with their continuing participation in historic structures of racism, sexism, and classism, but also with the persistence of these structures in their relationships with each other.

During this week of the semester, however, Williamson and Pauw had begun to see a difference in their interactions. Within the safety of a fairly tightly prescribed conversational process, the dynamics of the interactions in this classroom context were being transformed. Students had begun to read assigned texts as sources for an alternative ethic to that which typically governed their relationships with each other. Through such a transformation of contextual consciousness among their students, Williamson and Pauw envision the possibility that their students will embrace this alternative ethic in addressing the structures of racism, sexism, and classism they encounter in the contexts of their future ministries.

A Final Observation on Pedagogies of Contextual Transformation

We were intrigued throughout our study to discover that despite the familiarity of many seminary educators with such postmodern theorists as Pierre Bourdieu, Michel Foucault, Jacques Derrida, and Marion Iris Young, and the significant contributions that many seminary educators have made to discussions of postmodernity in religious theory and practice, we met few among them who were familiar with the corresponding theoretical work on "critical pedagogy."[6] From another perspective, we did not discover any visible remnants of earlier movements for social change influencing the conduct of seminary courses and field education: the anticommunist crusades in a few Catholic seminaries in the 1930s and evangelical seminaries during the 1950s, the worker-priest movement that influenced the education of priests in some Catholic seminaries during the 1960s, or Saul Alinsky's community organizing movement in Protestant seminaries during the 1960s and 1970s.[7] In other words, we did not meet any seminary educators in these schools whose teaching practices explicitly engaged students in activities focused on *the systemic and social transformation of institutions or systems.*

Of all the seminary educators we observed, Williamson and Pauw most nearly reflect the perspectives of pedagogies of systemic and structural change in their teaching, particularly when they introduce students to the writings of womanist and feminist theologians—many of whom have been major participants in the academic discussions of critical theory. The primary focus of contextual transformation for Williamson and Pauw in this class, however, is to equip students with the knowledge, skills, and sensibilities for critical reflection and action in the classroom to take up the challenge of transforming the structures of racism, oppression, or marginalization they encounter beyond the classroom in their churches and communities. Survey respondents who espoused values associated with critical pedagogies similarly seemed to embed them primarily in pedagogical practices for *reconciling* relationships in the academic setting rather than *transforming* the institutional cultures and systemic structures and processes of the academy or religious communities.

In Magid's intentions for student learning we may discern a clue to why a commitment to reconciliation may predominate in the contextual pedagogies of seminary educators. Seminary educators participate in religious traditions that rely on living communities for continued vitality and relevance. In the contemporary situation, those communities experience considerable stress from the rapidity of change, the expansion of knowledge, and the blurring of community boundaries in the dynamics of contemporary pluralism. Communities are composed of relationships that are shaped by events and circumstances—events and circumstances that are in the distant past. Perhaps, then, we should not be surprised by the focus of seminary educators on practices in the classroom to sustain and renew those historic relationships and to serve as a model for the students' eventual leadership of congregations. Their students will be giving leadership to religious communities at a time in the history of humankind when the magnitude of global systems and the volatility of contemporary institutions make the challenge of facilitating the continuity of religious traditions and their liberative transformation seem formidable.

Contextual Pedagogies in a Signature Pedagogical Framework

Pedagogies of contextualization figure prominently in the teaching practices of seminary educators. Their impetus originates in the concern of seminary educators that the ministries of their students should be, on the one hand, faithful to truths embedded in their sacred texts and religious traditions, and on the other hand, relevant to the contemporary experience of the religious communities they will be serving. As one dimension of the signature pedagogical framework in clergy education, pedagogies of contextualization also contribute to the distinctive shape of the teaching practices of seminary educators. We have seen something of the range of their influence in the teaching practices of Magid, Nairn, Williamson, and Pauw. In distinctive ways, these educators each emphasized the importance of appropriating a body of information, developing a way of thinking, and cultivating a manner of being that accounts for the dynamics of historic and contemporary contexts in the performance of any clergy practice.

For example, Magid engaged students in an academic exercise—the analysis of the contextual influence of modernity on Conservative Judaism—as a "trial run" for the discussions they would be having as rabbis leading congregations struggling with what it means to be both Jewish and modern. Nairn similarly insisted that students identify facts in a medical ethics case as an academic exercise to sharpen the skills of seeing those facts from the vantage point of different personal and cultural perspectives and making ethical judgments that respect the wisdom of their religious traditions. The movement among pedagogies of interpretation, formation, and performance is also evident in the attention to context in Williamson and Pauw's teaching: they drew students into the practice of identifying theoretical assumptions in the experience of oppressed and enslaved women as an integral step in analyzing the experience and meaning of their suffering and identifying implications for engaging the power dynamics in the ethical issues of their own ministries.

In this interplay of interpretive, formative, contextual, and performance pedagogies, these seminary educators, like those we have described in prior chapters, have developed teaching practices that merge, in students' experience, features associated with the cognitive, skill, and identity formation apprenticeships in clergy education. Each seeks to shape and, in some instances, transform how students envision themselves as priests, rabbis, or pastors. Attention to the intersection of a cognitive and identity apprenticeship permeates the practice of dialogue in Magid's class. It is evident in the way Nairn shifts his students' perspective from personal experience to the tensions in the human experience as the place for addressing ethical issues. And it is evident in Williamson and Pauw's practice of asking for ethical reflection from the standpoint of the marginalized. In these efforts, these seminary educators are not only expanding the knowledge of students; they are also shaping habits of mind, dispositions, and sensibilities for the students' future leadership as pastors, priests, and rabbis contextually responsive to the traditions and experience of the religious communities they will be serving.

ENDNOTES

1. Christian theological educators have given much attention to the global context of theological education and to ministry. The topic recurs in

numerous issues of *Theological Education* in discussions of the purposes of theological education and the content of the curriculum. See for example, Volume XXIII (Autumn 1986) 1 on "Global Challenges and Perspectives in Theological Education," Volume XXIX (Spring 1993) 2 on "Globalization and the Classic Theological Disciplines," and Volume XXX (Autumn 1993) 1 on "Globalization and the Practical Theological Disciplines."

2. David Hesselgrave and Edward Rommen (1989, pp. 28–29), trace the concept of "contextualization" in the Christian theological world back to the publication *Ministry in Context: The Third Mandate Programme of the Theological Education Fund (1970–77)*—a project of the International Missionary Council and, after its merger with the World Council of Churches, of its Division of World Mission and Evangelism. It referred to a concern that the education of clergy, especially in what was then called "Third World" nations, be equipped to address "(a) the widespread crisis of faith, (b) the issues of social justice and human development, (c) the dialectic between local cultural and religious situations and a universal technological civilization" (*Ministry in Context,* 1972, 17–18). Hesselgrave and Rommen go on to note that "To its originators it involved not only a new point of departure but also a new approach to theologizing and consequently, to theological education: namely, praxis or involvement in the struggle for justice within the existential situation in which men and women find themselves today."

3. Following our visit to Jewish Theological Seminary, Professor Magid accepted an appointment as associate professor of religious studies at Indiana University.

4. Near the end of his career, Paulo Freire wrote that "I like to be human because in my unfinishedness I know that I am conditioned. Yet conscious of such conditioning, I know that I can go beyond it, which is the essential difference between conditioned and determined existence. The difference between the unfinished that does not know anything of such a condition, and the unfinished who socio-historically has arrived at the point of becoming conscious of the condition and unfinishedness" sets the stage for "the construction of my presence in the world" (1998, p. 54). Central to his life work was a pedagogical quest to help others similarly become conscious of the conditions of their worlds so they might engage in that constructive task. He called that constructive process in educational settings "conscientization." His original concern centered on the lack of conscious- ness about the political and economic conditions limiting the ability of

Brazilian peasants to construct their own lives. In the United States, however, appropriations of his quest for contextual consciousness have had more to do with those conditions that inhibit or marginalize the full realization of personal and corporate selfhood.

5. Palmer (1998, pp. 73–4) expands on the notion of teaching from the center of the tension of opposites in a discussion of the paradoxes of pedagogical design in teaching. In all teaching he suggests the space of teaching and learning should be "bounded and open," be "hospitable and 'charged,'" invite the "voice of the individual and the group," honor the "little" stories of students and the "big" stories of the disciplines and tradition, support "solitude and surround it with the resources of community," and welcome "silence and speech."

6. For overviews of the themes in the writings on critical pedagogies, see Leistyna and Woodrum (1996), Darder, Baltodano, and Torres (2003), and Greene (1996). Among theological educators, Rebecca Chopp's study *Saving Work: Feminist Practices of Theological Education* (1995) is one of the more visible discussions of seminary teaching practices and critical theory.

7. During the 1930s, Alinsky initiated a grassroots movement in Chicago that fought for improvements in the quality of the lives of people: in low-income housing, public education, living wage jobs, the removal of toxic waste, and so on. His work continues in many cities through the Industrial Areas Foundation he founded; the work is typically supported by the religious community. During the 1970s, some seminaries provided opportunities for students to participate in activities of community organizing. In those efforts they were introduced to the pedagogy of the movement in Alinsky's *Rules for Radicals,* published in 1971.

6

PEDAGOGIES
OF PERFORMANCE

ONE OF THIS STUDY'S AUTHORS vividly remembers a moment from his own seminary experience:

> Robert Seaver was teaching a class at Union Theological Seminary to improve our public speaking and reading skills. We took turns reading scripture, reciting poetry, and delivering short homilies or addresses, and received critical appraisal for each performance from Seaver and our peers. One day, Seaver assigned an especially reticent student the task of memorizing the speech from Shakespeare's *Henry V* inciting the king's soldiers to fight the French at Harfleur (3.1.1–34). When it came this student's turn to rouse us to move "Once more unto the breach, dear friends. . .," Seaver pushed all the desks back against the wall, asked him to stand on the table at the front of the room, told the rest of us to assume roles as soldiers milling around the field, and urged him to so inspire us we would follow him enthusiastically into battle. His first attempt failed miserably. Seaver told him to try again—and then again. In that third, or perhaps fourth, time, his voice began to convey something of the force and power of Shakespeare's poetry, and we boisterously cheered him on as he shouted, "Cry 'God for Harry, England, and Saint George!'" Through similar, although less dramatic, exercises throughout the semester Seaver emphasized the need for us to pay attention to the quality of our performance in the public roles we would be assuming as clergy.

Indeed, the clergy may be among the most public of professions. Some, like evangelist Billy Graham, speak to vast audiences by way of radio and television and in large public assemblies. Others stand in the traditions of Martin Luther King Jr., Fred Rogers, Dorothy Day, Abraham Joshua Heschel, James Dobson, or Archbishop Romero, advocating visions of society that are informed by their religious traditions. Countless other clergy—women and men whose names are not well known—lead local, national, and global organizations striving to give those living on the margins of society access to programs and resources for improving health, education, and spiritual and social welfare. Many supervise or teach in elementary and secondary schools, colleges, universities, and seminaries.

A congregation is also a public—some as small as ten to fifteen people and others as large as many thousands—and whether the clergy person is leading a congregation or a larger agency that supports it, he or she will regularly preach, teach, lead worship, conduct meetings, preside over ceremonies and rituals, write books and newsletters, pray with individuals and groups, articulate theological perspectives on policy and program issues in religious and civic meetings, and mediate personal and ethical conflicts between persons and in organizations.

Pedagogies of Performance

Congregations—and the public—have high and consistent expectations for the quality and character of the clergy's public work. To prepare their students to meet these expectations, seminary educators engage students in pedagogies of performance—the fourth group in the signature pedagogical framework of seminary education. Through these *pedagogies of performance* seminary educators emphasize the interaction of academic and religious expectations for effective leadership in clergy practice.

The challenge of preparing students to be adequately proficient in meeting the variety and range of expectations for public leadership from congregations, civic communities, and religious traditions is a big one. Clergy educators *perform* pedagogically in the classroom, and more generally in the life of the school, to establish a way of thinking and being for doing, a habitus of clergy *performance,* that permeates everything their students will do professionally—from preaching, liturgical leadership, teaching, and counseling, to the leadership of neighborhood food banks and interfaith housing initiatives; from leading women's Bible study groups to directing summer youth camps; from offering deathbed prayers to conducting bar and bat mitzvah classes.

The complexity of this challenge becomes even more evident in the variety of responses of the clergy in our survey who identified what in their seminary educations had prepared them to respond as they did to the tragedy of September 11, 2001. A coordinator of liturgy and parish life told us that "The Benedictine tradition of formation, prayer and consecrative time to God [in the seminary] gave me a structure to *reach out with ritual* when words seemed inadequate." A pastor said that seminary "taught me to *have a pastoral word and presence* in a time of death and destruction." Another respondent wrote that "seminary taught me to read the sources closely and with reflection, taught me *to write,* taught me to *use myself as an instrument* through which God is present for my congregants."

None of the pastors, rabbis, or priests responding to this question explicitly used the language of performance, but in each instance the formative, contextual, or interpretive practice they describe culminates in its public exercise. Hence, the language of performance provides a useful vocabulary for describing both the public exercise of clergy roles and responsibilities and the pedagogies of seminary educators directed to cultivating proficiency in these public roles. The relationship of the performance of the teacher to the future professional performance of students may be most clearly seen in the coaching pedagogies often found in classes of liturgy, preaching, and teaching—that is, those clergy practices most explicitly like the practices of the theater from which performance language derives—but in seminary classrooms it also becomes evident in the cultivation of such basic clergy performance practices as reading and interpreting sacred texts, reflecting historically and theologically on beliefs and practices, or making ethical decisions.

We use the term *performance,* therefore, in its most obvious sense. It is a way of thinking and being revealed in the act of doing, carrying out, or putting into effect. It is a sermon delivered, a prayer offered, a meeting conducted, or a theological argument articulated. Excellent performance requires practice: a pianist critically appraises repeated efforts to improve the performance of a musical composition; a basketball player spends hours refining stance, thrust, and arch of the ball to improve a free-throw shot. All clergy roles require practice in this sense. Indeed, in practicing the performances of preaching, teaching, praying, theological reflection, exegesis, pastoral care, or administrative oversight, clergy take on the habits of thinking and dispositions of the practice.

Performance is a particularly useful lens of analysis for exploring the role of seminary educators in cultivating the professional proficiency of clergy.[1] Since performance per se is not a primary theological discourse, it does not tilt our discussion toward one particular tradition, school, or discipline. It is not confined to the analytic categories of any of the disciplines in the seminary curriculum. At the same time, it permeates the ways seminary educators talk about the evidence of student learning and readiness for clergy work, as in "most students *performed* well on their final exams," or "the quality of student preaching in chapel this semester was high."

In this chapter, we turn our attention to describing classroom pedagogies that seek, among other intentions for student learning, to cultivate capacities for clergy performance. We begin by describing the pedagogical approaches of two seminary educators who, through their teaching, foster student proficiency in performing clergy practices—one in a practicum concerned with liturgical leadership, the other in a first-semester course in church history. Through these case studies and other examples drawn from our questionnaire and site visit data, we then explore four elements of performance that give a distinctive shape to the public dimensions of clergy work.

Pedagogy of Liturgical Performance
Richard Fragomeni, Catholic Theological Union

Fragomeni, a priest of the Diocese of Albany, New York, is associate professor of liturgy and preaching at Catholic Theological Union in Chicago. As described on Fragomeni's Web site, "Central to his work is a fascination with the power of liturgy and preaching in the transformation of consciousness." In addition to full-time teaching at the seminary, Fragomeni has a heavy schedule of preaching, presiding, and leading workshops in the Archdiocese of Chicago and around the country. He also serves as rector of The Shrine of Our Lady of Pompeii in Chicago.

A member of the word and worship department of the seminary, Fragomeni teaches several courses designed to prepare students for ministries of preaching and worship: among them are "Liturgical Preaching," a foundational course in liturgical theology, and the "Worship Practicum" required of all senior students preparing for ordination as priests. In this latter course, students practice the basic skills employed in presiding at the sacramental rites of the church. To allow students an opportunity for intense practice, the seminary limits enrollment in the course to twelve students. In the class session we observed, the students ranged in age from late twenties to early forties, hailed from the United States and several other countries, and belonged to several of the religious orders that make up the seminary community. The students sat around tables formed into a square at one end of a long and narrow classroom. A rudimentary and bare plywood "altar," apparently intended for practicing liturgical performance, was at the other end of the room.

The three-hour class session began with an opening prayer reflecting themes from that day's feast (St. Teresa of Avila). A review of the class discussion from the prior week led to an extended discussion of Fragomeni's expectations for assignments, in which students work in small groups to plan and perform liturgies of initiation, marriage, or burial. Fragomeni clarified procedural expectations and modes of assessment. He then focused attention on the subject of the current class session: gestures and practices associated with the Eucharist.

Fragomeni led the discussion in Socratic fashion, moving back and forth between questions to clarify the meaning of the rubrics or directions printed in the text and performance practices of leading a congregation in a prayer central to the ritual. He stressed that each word or phrase in the text is very specific, asking the students, "How are you to use your voice? Where do you put your eyes? Where do you put your hands?" Repeatedly, Fragomeni demonstrated various options for the students— "Like this? Or this?"—and pushed them to consider carefully what each possibility might mean and reveal, theologically and liturgically.

Fragomeni described how to mark a liturgical text to best bring out its meaning for a congregation. He illustrated the process by distributing copies of a eucharistic prayer covered with his own markings for inflection and emphasis. As he worked through each line of the prayer, explaining why he marked the text as he did, Fragomeni repeatedly emphasized his expectation that students will similarly be able to provide a rationale for every vocal and physical gesture they will use in an upcoming videotaping. He asked them to turn in their marked-up versions of the eucharistic prayer they had chosen; he would evaluate both their choice of emphases and their adherence to their markings in the videotape they are preparing. For the remainder of the class period, Fragomeni continued this interactive process of probing the implications of priestly actions for each section of the Eucharistic liturgy. When rubrics in the liturgy specified specific gestures, he discussed their significance. When no gestures were identified, he pressed students to think about what they might do and why.

The class session made apparent the pedagogical significance of the videotapes, as did the magnitude of the preparation required of each student. Over the semester, each student prepares *two* videos of two eucharistic liturgies (one weekday and one full Sunday mass). Each video includes members of the student's small group in the roles of deacons or acolytes and musicians and other congregation members. The student presider must display many skills. He must demonstrate he has learned the words and appropriate movements of the basic rite and can use voice, eyes, and gestures in ways that reflect not only a sense of confident presence, but also intentional and defensible interpretive foresight. To fulfill this task, the student must choose a specific day in the liturgical calendar; select songs; prepare and preach a homily for the Sunday mass; select, mark up, and prepare to read or chant a eucharistic prayer; and be prepared to give the rationale for every conscious or unconscious detail of his performance. For instance, during a discussion of the gesture of elevating the eucharistic elements at the final doxology in the liturgy, Fragomeni concluded: "I'm going to be watching how you do this on tape, gentlemen. How you treat these elements shows, more than anything you ever say, what you really feel about transubstantiation." After Fragomeni views each video, he meets individually with the student to discuss what he heard and saw. Thus, each student has two consultations to explore his liturgical decisions, his actual performance as recorded on tape, and the deeper implications of both personal faith and priestly role, as manifested by the video.

In our follow-up conversation, Fragomeni reflected on the various roles he assumes in challenging and affirming students and his sense of accountability to them and to the church they are preparing to serve. His teaching is influenced by his recognition that when presiding in the liturgy or preaching, the priest conveys to the congregation the fullness of his relation to God. Both in class and in the video assignment, students discover the vulnerability of that relationship in a performance practice such as liturgy or preaching. Thus, at times, Fragomeni sees his role bordering on spiritual direction, as he discusses the videos with individual students, attending to what he and they see while at the same time trying to discern where to push and where a student's sense of personal shame might not yet permit comment, correction, or even praise. It is, he said, "a faith performance, their soul witnessing to their hope." This inevitably leads to conversation about how they are growing spiritually so that their preaching and presiding might continue to grow in authenticity.

Pedagogy of Cognitive Performance
Rebecca Lyman, Church Divinity School of the Pacific

Fragomeni's liturgy practicum illustrates many of the features of the "skill apprenticeship" in clergy education. He models expectations for priestly liturgical performance for his students and then coaches them into increasingly proficient performance of liturgical practice. It is less evident how seminary educators teaching courses typically identified with the "cognitive apprenticeships" of professional education similarly engage students in pedagogies of performance for clergy practice. In an introductory course in church history, however, we met students who experienced standards and guidelines not only for their performance in future classes but also for the public dimensions of their future roles as priests. These students described for us a way of thinking, cultivated in the class, that prepared them to enter into the theological discussions of the seminary and that shaped expectations for their preparation and performance as preachers and teachers. Lyman, at the Church Divinity School of the Pacific, a seminary of the Episcopal Church, teaches this course, which students take during their first semester in the seminary.

In our initial conversation, a phone interview about the syllabus of the course we would be observing, we discussed at length Lyman's experience in teaching this course over the past eighteen years, her expectations for student learning at the beginning of their seminary careers, and her approaches to engaging students with the subject of the course. She told us she inherited a love of history from her mother. When questions came up, they would "check the facts" together and her mother would often draw "parallels to how the past shaped the present, usually critically and with little nostalgia." For Lyman, the blending of this experience with the emphasis on holiness and social justice from her "Methodist preacher's kid upbringing" helps explain why "history as an intellectual and spiritual discipline is alive" for her, and why she tries to "blend excellent knowledge of the past with the hope of transformation" in the present. Having taught at Oxford as a graduate student, she adapted the "Oxford tutorial of essays and dialogue." She appreciated its emphasis on "learning through questions, assuming a diversity of perspectives," and "seeing the process as creating a peer relationship." Over the years, she has expanded and refined this "elitist" tutorial practice for use with groups of students in the classroom.

She compared the course we would be observing to a cross-country trip on a freeway. As she and students in the class work their way through the semester, they take some "exits" to focus on certain texts, figures, and events and bypass others. Along the way, she follows a consistent three-step pedagogical process through which she expects students to (1) read texts "carefully and closely" so as to "listen carefully to the author first before leaping to judgment (you might learn something even from unpalatable folks like Constantine)," (2) develop increasing facility for "understanding" those texts in their particular historical contexts, and (3) demonstrate the capacity for reflecting on the contemporary meaning and significance of these texts. Through these three steps she intends for students to develop a "broader historical 'understanding' of how culture shapes theology and practices (and therefore begin to understand how culture shapes us)"; to become increasingly proficient, in other words, in the performance of a way of thinking about history—that is, a way of participating in religious tradition. Students work their way through each of these three steps through the semester in the course as a whole, in each class session, in six reaction papers, and in an oral final exam.

For several years, Lyman had noticed that during the oral exams she conducts at the end of the semester, students would often say that something in the course had "changed their minds." This observation led her to become even more explicit in her expectation that students would develop a philosophy or theology of history. "I tell students that I am a kind of evangelist—that they have got to think historically." This means, she continued, that "I really preach openness, humility to the past" and "I quote T. S. Eliot" to make the point that historical perspective involves "the wisdom of humility" and that "humility is endless."[2] This notion has profoundly influenced her view of "the authority of the past, its human weakness shared by us and them, and our need to be part of the same process of making meaning without triumphalism." From this perspective she hopes that students will develop, through her teaching, "a critical appreciation of tradition, the ability to dialogue with that tradition," and to discover in the process that "being a teacher of wisdom is a pastoral activity." She identifies herself as "a liberal Anglican practicing historical criticism," but she tells her Catholic, Unitarian, and mainline Protestant students they are "to figure out in their essays how history fits their own identities." This involves discovering "historical criticism as a tool" for faithfully "living out/creating our identities in a multiple Christian context" and for becoming increasingly confident "about our identities" as priests and pastors, "open to the world and to different kinds of people."

"I assume we are a learning community," she observed, "engaged in mutual exploration." She feels she has an advantage among her colleagues because she teaches this class in the first semester of a student's theological education experience, when they "are often frightened, but keen." They come expecting to engage "a body of knowledge they want to know and which gives rise to questions" even though they may have some awareness this new knowledge may also lead to personal and professional pain. The ground rules for engaging this quest to know in the mutuality of students and teacher in this learning community are never spelled out, but they do shape the life of the course: questions are honored as the impetus to learning; acknowledging ignorance is both catalyst to questions and a reminder of the value of intellectual humility; knowledge is openly shared; respect permeates the interactions of teacher and students as well as student and student; being prepared for active participation in class is assumed. Lyman summarized her approach by affirmatively quoting a student who urged her to "tell us what we need to know," but to "not make us look stupid."

Several days after this initial conversation, we asked a group of students completing their last year of seminary if they had had a course or participated in some other event that had functioned for them as a rite of passage in their educational preparation for the priesthood. Eight of the nine identified Lyman's course in church history. (The ninth person had transferred from another school and had not taken the course.) When we asked why this particular course, one student said, "When people with one-dimensional notions of the church take this course, they are surprised by its actual history." Lyman's three themes ordering the readings and discussion of the course—"theology, community, and spirituality"—provide a way to think about "theological issues and historical events" encountered in other courses in the curriculum. Another student noted, "She sets a standard of excellence and expects it in turn." "Her papers are great preparation for writing sermons," said another. The guidelines for the way of thinking at the heart of Lyman's teaching practice provide a structure for thinking through an issue. The papers must be brief and to the point. And the experience replicates the anxiety of writing sermons because "they have to be turned in before the readings on which they are based are discussed in class." Someone else observed that the class is also a "great preparation for future classes" not only because it "provides background to the theological issues and historical events from later periods," but because Lyman's expectations for their participation gave them confidence to speak up in other classes they had taken in other seminaries in the consortium of schools that make up the Graduate Theological Union.

When we asked what it was about the class that led them to make these claims, they had no difficulty answering our question: Lyman expects students to read texts "critically and carefully" and to "see what is going on behind the text." "She really values struggling with the text" and affirms "our efforts to find our own voice." In these comments, we recognized the interplay of her intentions for student engagement with the interpretive, contextual, and formative practices we discussed in earlier chapters. But the students continued. Although the class includes people with different opinions "she is able to guide the conversation" through "these opinions." In fact, "she draws her points right out of students." And "people are comfortable speaking out in her class."

The oral examination that concludes the course at the end of the semester clearly had special meaning for this group. They reported approaching it with great anxiety. Yet it was, in many ways, the high point of the course. They recalled that Lyman did not expect them to be prepared to answer all the questions she could ask. Rather, they remembered that she had asked them to be prepared to address questions about two themes from the course.[3] In this culminating performance practice, most people discover in the process "they know more than they thought" and look back on the methodology of the course as a "great tool of preparation for future work." They expressed appreciation for the historical background that would inform subsequent coursework, and also for the confidence they had gained through the course in using that knowledge.

Later that same morning, we walked into a large classroom with several rows of desk chairs arranged generally in a semicircle. Twenty students were already in the room, some talking in small groups, others reading. Another fifteen or so arrived within the next few minutes. Lyman walked into the room, greeted us, and made her way through groups of students to the front of the room. Waving a sheet of paper high in one hand, she announced it was time for people to schedule their oral exams. Immediately, most of the students began to crowd around the table where she had put the sign-up sheet while two or three students waited in line to talk to her.

When the sign-up line had diminished somewhat, she walked behind the table and said, "OK, it's time to start now." She distributed a handout for the day's discussion. It included a chronology of events and people important to the formative years of Islam, between 600 and 800 C.E., on one side and a summary of key ideas to be addressed during the class session on the other. After clarifying expectations for the oral exam and distributing a list of books for the second semester course in the field to be taught by a colleague, she introduced the topic for the day.

After noting that the topic had special relevance for Christians in the wake of the September 11, 2001, attacks, Lyman invited students to share their own knowledge about Islam "because this is not the area of my primary expertise." Two or three students briefly described encounters with Islam while traveling. She then asked, "What characteristics of Islam did you note from your readings for today?" While Lyman wrote their contributions on the blackboard, students from all over the room called out features of Islam they had picked up from their assigned reading. The list summarizing their contributions grew quickly to include such things as "monotheism, religion of the book, theocracy, politics, religion without much Christology, Jesus as prophet, pilgrimage, disciplined, modesty, surrender." This extended interaction moved quickly. At times, Lyman stopped to ask a student to elaborate on or clarify a statement. For example, after one student had said that Islam was "a religion without much Christology," she pushed the student to clarify views of Jesus held by the Muslim writers they had been reading.

With this expansive list covering the board, she turned around to face the class. "What does this list remind you of? Where do you see commonalities with Christianity and Judaism?" This seemed to signal the shift of focus from the text to the context in which it had been written, the second step of Lyman's three-step approach. The discussion included some bantering back and forth between students and instructor as she picked up on students' comments ("both are monotheistic," "both are rooted in Torah and claim to be children of Abraham," "each has a vision of theocracy"), affirmed them, and either expanded on their comments or asked subsequent questions to clarify or connect their comments to earlier contributions. When Lyman developed a student response further, she typically either linked it to another word or phrase on the board or clarified its social, cultural, or intellectual context. These statements, however, rarely exceeded four or five sentences. It soon became obvious, as Lyman moved from item to item on the board, that she was developing an orderly and coherent argument about the origins and development of Islam.

At this point she turned her question around: "What impact did Islam have on eastern Christianity?" She again wrote the students' responses on the board and drew lines between ideas to illuminate similarities, differences, tensions, and struggles among the three religions "of the book," without losing focus on developing an appreciative reading of the flowering of Islamic religion and culture. She brought the conversation to a close by asking whether the discussion had helped them understand something of the sources for the contemporary notions of jihad. Students then began to make connections among the various comments and to fill out the overview of Islam that Lyman had been developing during the class session.

Lyman then moved away from the blackboard to stand in front of the table. Whether intended or not, this change signaled a transition in the character of the conversation. Instead of receiving student comments to create an argument, Lyman began facilitating, or monitoring, a fast and free-flowing conversation to ensure that everyone could respond to the question, "What does this history help us think about today?" The conversation had shifted to the third step in Lyman's pedagogical practice: to invite students to reflect on the meaning and significance of their reading. During this interchange, as many as a third of the students in the classroom responded with comments ranging from a comparison of Islamic and Christian views of the relationship of conquest and conversion to a discussion about sources for Islamic views of women. The discussion could easily have continued, but the ninety-minute class session came to an end. Lyman dismissed the class with the observation that many of the issues they had discussed would come up again when they explored the engagement of the Arabs and Franks in the next semester's course, to be taught by a colleague.

The understated artistry of the flow of the session; Lyman's ability to create a coherent "lecture" out of the observations, insights, and opinions of students; the clarity of key ideas and their relationship to each other emerging from the interaction of teacher and students; the exuberance of student engagement with the session—all impressed us. The clarity with which students recalled their experience of the class two years later provoked our curiosity. At least at first glance, it seemed that Lyman had somehow bridged, for these students, the tension that often exists between their role as students "in" an academic setting preparing "for" roles they will be assuming later in congregations and other ministry settings.

Pedagogies of Performance: Four Major Features

A cursory look at the pedagogies of Fragomeni and Lyman suggests significant differences in the assumptions they have about their teaching and the strategies and methods they use to engage student learning. A closer look at what and how they teach, however, reveals several shared features that we found in pedagogies to cultivate student performance of practices associated with the public work of clergy.

In his study of liturgical leadership, Richard McCall identified four features of performance that seem equally appropriate for a discussion of the pedagogies of performance: (1) the script of performance, (2) the performer and the audience, (3) the means or manner of performance, and (4) the *telos,* or desired end, of performance (1998, p. 135).

Script

Script focuses attention on what is to be performed. In clergy education, the script is typically a "text" to be interpreted and performed in public. It may be printed, embedded in oral tradition, expressed in some art form, or patterned in ritual. In Fragomeni's class session, the text consisted of the written and unwritten rubrics of the eucharistic liturgy. He led students through a collaborative exegesis of meanings and gestures explicitly and implicitly embedded in this text as the basic *script* of future priests' liturgical performance.

Through a composite strategy of demonstration, exhortation, instruction, and textual analysis, Fragomeni prepares students to demonstrate their ability to perform that script in a videotaped presentation. In this class, the script is given by religious tradition and is so authoritative that any deviation must be justified carefully. Practicing liturgical performance, in other words, requires the ability to perform judgments grounded in knowledge cultivated in other parts of the curriculum—especially in Scripture, doctrine, and liturgical theology classes. Fragomeni interjects questions into the exegetical exercise leading to the preparation of the video that tests the student's familiarity with the boundaries of the text, both to make clear where the text is unambiguous and to be followed, and to ascertain when its ambiguity requires judgments about the extent to which a particular interpretation or action is consistent with Catholic tradition.

In Lyman's class, the script consists of questions for historical inquiry that open up the sources in texts to reveal the trajectories of contemporary Christian religious traditions and practices. She identifies the performance practice she seeks to cultivate in her students as the capacity to "think historically." This cognitive skill and spiritual practice involves more than understanding. It requires relating to the past with "humility" to "foster openness in finding surprise in the familiar or the ability to be challenged and changed." This disposition or imaginative capacity colors the performance of the clergy practices she seeks to cultivate: it integrates (albeit in a distinctive fashion) contextual, interpretive, and formative practices integral to the work of clergy. The push toward integration in Lyman's pedagogy emerges from the sustained and patterned interplay of those questions as students begin to think historically—to see themselves as participants in the traditions of discourse about the texts they are reading.

In many classes, the script may be less apparent than it is in Fragomeni's or Lyman's classes. In worship classes in other schools, students may not be working with prescribed liturgies or set prayers. The emphasis in some homiletics classes may be on oral presentation without manuscript or notes. In some theology or history classes, students may be working with texts from several religious traditions. In pastoral care or ethics classes, the text may be a case, an ethical dilemma, or an interaction with a person or group of persons. The performance that is the object of these classes may appear to be more spontaneous and often quite personal; indeed, to use a musical analogy, improvisation might seem a more apt way to view the pedagogical intent of these performance practices. Such an approach to performance may be seen in the goals of several seminary educators we interviewed: "to get students to 'think on their feet' theologically"; "to encourage them in appropriating the Christian faith tradition in such a way that they can articulate its contents in an engaging way, and so empower others to think and act theologically"; "to foster a sense of inquiry and openness toward the world and its challenges for Christian witness and service."

One seminary educator describes this improvisational capacity as helping "students realize the limits of correct thinking (while extolling its importance) and to learn to read the tacit dimensions of human interaction, and to address *there* the issues, dilemmas, causes they might otherwise have addressed only by way of expressed opinion or adequate theory." Yet even in these more open-ended intentions for student learning, an implicit (and often very powerful) "script" still operates. Just as musical improvisation requires extensive training in technique, theory, chord progressions, and, in groups, a shared harmonic and rhythmic structure, the same is true in the improvisation of clergy practices. From the complex patterning of oral engagement between preacher and congregation and the ways of bringing the heritage of the black religious experience into the reading of Scripture in many black churches, to forms of spirit-led spontaneity in evangelical or Pentecostal congregations,[4] to ways of being present to different hospital patients and their families, or to the negotiation of conflicts between persons or groups in a congregation or community, each follows some formal or implicit script.

In each of these instances, some degree of originality is expected within the basic script. Dale Andrews, who teaches a course on preaching at Louisville Presbyterian Theological Seminary, makes the point. He noted that in the pulpit "you are not just preaching your exegetical points. You are preaching convictions within a 'meaning-making' process. And so there's a kind of marriage between your convictions and your studies, and between your personal experiences and those anticipated experiences among your hearers. The end goal is then how to construct sermons and . . . prepare for the preaching event, between those interests."

Whether clergy educators teach so that students may adhere to the authority of certain texts or must decide about the authoritative claims of any text, these textual artifacts (doctrines, formal rituals and rules, institutional structures, artistic representations in music or visual art) are expressions of the possibilities to be found in the script of clergy performance. Fragomeni, for example, teaches to prepare priests for the performance of their liturgical roles in Catholic parishes or in other gatherings of Roman Catholic Christians. Lyman teaches to prepare students to participate as clergy in the humanistic traditions of modern Christianity, especially as

they are given form in the Episcopal Church. They both teach to prepare students to perform their religious *traditions* as ways of living into
or embodying the activity of God in the present moment and place.

Tradition in this sense—whether viewed as received whole from the past,
embodied anew in the present, or creatively innovated into the future—
is the paradigmatic "script" of the clergy educator and thereby of clergy
practice or performance. This means that clergy educators teach that students might engage—indeed, participate—in the scripts of their religious
traditions as they study and pray, teach and preach, conduct worship and
extend care, guide committees and call for justice. In the exercise of these
professional practices, the script as religious tradition is constantly being
tested, interpreted, recast, and enacted. It is being *per-formed*: through
("per-") the shifting exigencies of time and context constantly being embodied ("-formed") anew. And this interplay of *per-formance* and *forming* often takes place with transforming intent.

The Performer and Audience

Our first impression of Fragomeni's teaching was his "larger than life"
presence in the teaching role, the confidence of his grasp of the subtleties
and nuances of the text that engaged the collective attention of the students
of his class, and his command of the rhythm and flow of his interactions
with them as together they worked with the text of the eucharistic liturgy.
He seemed, at times, to be the actor performing for his student audience.

Our first impression, however, quickly gave way to another.[5] Fragomeni
engages his students more as the director of a play or the choreographer of
a dance. His vision of the performative possibilities of the liturgy in sustaining and renewing Catholic religious tradition establishes expectations and boundaries for their interactions with each other during class
sessions and evokes possibilities for their eventual leadership in parish
liturgical life. In Fragomeni's classes both teacher and students are on the
"stage" of religious tradition, being introduced to and guided through a
particular script of that tradition with the expectation they will then perform that tradition on videotape in preparation for performing that tradition in congregational liturgies.

In Lyman's class our attention was also drawn first to her own pedagogical performance: from the way she established the order of the day,
to the confidence and authority with which she took student comments
and organized them into a coherent "lecture." This first impression, however, also gave way to our growing awareness that she had established a

pedagogical structure through which students were developing a perspective—one grounded in humility before the texts they were reading—and confidence in their own skills as *per*-formers of the script of religious tradition. Lyman both models that perspective and repeatedly coaches students through the three steps of her pedagogy toward confident performance of their religious traditions in other academic settings and, eventually, in their preaching and teaching.

We were intrigued by the ability of Fragomeni, Lyman, and most of the other seminary educators we observed and interviewed to motivate and sustain the interest of students in learning. They seemed wary of using methods and technologies simply because they had been touted by others for their creativity or ability to engage student attention. They viewed the availability of new computer and video technologies, for example, as one among several resources now at their disposal to facilitate their teaching. The use of video as a means for students to demonstrate their liturgical proficiency in Fragomeni's class is a typical example. What distinguishes the teaching practices of these seminary educators is their ability to craft journeys that engage student imaginations through the resources and methods relevant to the courses they are teaching. As in Fragomeni's and Lyman's classes, they both model and lead students on that journey in every class session and every assignment through ways of thinking and relating to texts and practices pertinent to the work of clergy.

The excitement of learning in classes like these emerges from the growing confidence of students in their ability to make appropriate and relevant judgments as clergy. Their growing sense of competence includes not only increasing familiarity with the knowledge and skills integral to clergy practice but also with their growing acceptance of its standards of excellence in their actions and with their increasing ability to play with its possibilities in new situations and for different circumstances.

Bourdieu suggests that a game provides a metaphor for the experience of learning in the context of a teacher's performance: "Having the feel for the game is having the game under the skin; it is to master in a practical way the future of the game; it is to have a sense of the history of the game. While the bad player is always off tempo, always too early or too late, the good player is the one who anticipates, who is ahead of the game. Why can she get ahead of the flow of the game? Because she has the immanent tendencies of the game in her body, in an incorporated state: she embodies the game" (1998, pp. 80–81).

In a teaching practice that draws students into the mutuality of cognitive, practice, and professional apprenticeships, the feel of the game is embodied in dispositions and habits manifest in their public performances. This shifts the traditional focus of attention associated with cognitive apprenticeships on the mastery of subject matter from building up bodies of information to demonstrating mastery of information-in-use. Even in schools that overtly value pedagogical practices of subject-matter mastery (such as Yale Divinity School), Wilson and Bartlett want students to see that asking questions of a biblical text inevitably leads to asking questions about opening up that text in a sermon. A similar observation may be made about Benson's teaching practice: he uses recitation pedagogical strategies to build students' confidence in their ability to use that information in a manner faithful to its intent. In each instance, the teaching practices of these seminary educators are designed to carry students from the classroom into the larger world of clergy practices.

In this sense, the usual differentiation between actor and audience gives way to varying patterns for the reciprocity of student and teacher roles. Note, for example, how the seminary educators we have been describing transpose notions of stage and audience in the seminary classroom. Although he holds on to his overarching intentions for interaction with his students, Fragomeni, like many of the clergy educators we observed, also arranges the classroom environment to facilitate student interactions with each other and to reinforce his expectations for collaborative comment and critique.

Other clergy educators (for example, Wilson and Bartlett, Williamson and Pauw) establish a "head of the table" position from which they coach a collective conversation toward some goal for their learning. Still others, like Magid, sit among students, who then take charge of the conversation. Hughes paces the floor inside the circle of students—talking sometimes to the group as a whole and sometimes to individuals in one-on-one conversations she intends the rest of the class to "overhear." Sanders, in contrast, alternates between standing next to her laptop to move slides on the screen and sitting at a table (which, in that long and narrow lecture hall, meant nearly half of the students could not see her clearly). Yet she adroitly paced their interaction during the two-hour session, from didactic instruction while students listened, to facilitating a discussion among the members of the class with each other, to moments of prophetic preaching in dialogue with student affirming feedback. In still another pattern of interaction, Lehman transformed classroom dynamics as she both led and joined students in the collaborative task of Talmudic translation and interpretation.

Although the fluidity in the various roles of performer and audience between teacher and students in these classes seems to occur for the most part unconsciously, it also anticipates a mode of interacting as clergy with laity and as communities of faith or observance and God. For seminary educators their classes become the stage for their performance of the script of these relationships embedded in religious tradition. Their students will take that performance "on stage" as preachers, teachers, counselors, evangelists. Backstage, both seminary educators in their classrooms and their students in their future roles as clergy choreograph local enactments of religious tradition in the concrete, ever-changing circumstances in which they find themselves. And both are members of the audience, too—seminary educators as learners to the teaching of their students, and students when their congregants or community leaders perform either on stage or as choreographers of some event or program. The performance of seminary educators from this perspective significantly shapes the future professional performance of their students.

Means and Manner of Performance

The means and manner of performance focus attention on *how* clergy educators pedagogically facilitate in students a growing awareness of and confidence in their proficiency as performers of religious tradition. Fragomeni, for example, engages students directly, helping them move from an awkward to a graceful performance of a ritual text or script, with the hope that, when the students are priests, through their performance the text may come to life for their congregants.

Two pedagogical tasks come into play within the broad topic of means and manner of performance. The first centers on developing proficiency or competency. The skills needed for effective liturgical leadership range from very concrete to quite general. How dress and gesture, comportment and voice inflection set up certain times and spaces as "holy" or "liminal"; which rhetorical devices or exhortatory strategies draw a given congregation or community into the deepest insights of the religious tradition without marginalizing, oppressing, or alienating its members; how one's use of touch in some cases opens intimacy with God and in other cases represents a devastating breach of professional boundaries—all these and many more are questions of the means and manner of performance. As McCall writes regarding liturgical performance,

> [T]he cues given by different liturgical gestural-styles can be seen as meta-statements about the nature of the liturgical act. Something quite different is . . . being "said" by the elaborate, highly-structured movement and "manual acts" of the medieval Solemn High Mass than is

being "said" by a celebration in which the participants try as hard as possible to use only "daily" technique in movement and gesture. The "manner" of performance, that is, constitutes a further *differentium* which must be taken into account not only in differentiating performance from non-performance and dramatic performance from liturgy, but also in accounting for the different effects of liturgies performed in different manners[6] [1998, p. 93].

The second pedagogical task involves helping students move beyond a consciousness of "knowing how" to the "smooth, unreflective mastery" identified with expertise or virtuosity in professional performance. In writing about virtuosity in the professional practice of teachers, Guy Claxton has observed that it "embodies observations, distinctions, feelings, perceptual patterns and nuances that are too fine-grain to be caught accurately in a web of words." It is given form in a phase of learning in which "hunches," "feelings," or sometimes even "guesswork" become necessary steps toward the mastery of some professional performance (2000, pp. 35–36).

Fragomeni pays close attention to both of these pedagogical issues. Because the course is geared as a practicum around questions of liturgical practice, he directs student attention to matters central to effective ritual presiding—that is, to a concern for skillfulness or competency. Where one directs one's gaze while leading a public prayer, how posture and gesture affect the perceived meaning of ritual action, how one's voice interprets a text, and how one both decides on and best conveys this interpretation in proclamation or praying—these are not afterthoughts to the "serious" study of ritual theory or liturgical history; they are the very essence of how one *enacts* the tradition's significance in concrete practice.

As Fragomeni heightens his students' consciousness to the meaning and significance of their most minute decisions, he also anticipates that they will move through the awkwardness in their performance that this consciousness inevitably creates to the ability to make appropriate decisions without consciously thinking about them. In other words, he brings to focus in the activity of preparing for liturgical leadership all that they have previously learned about worship (its history, theology, and guiding principles and its context in denominational politics and congregational culture) in relation to their own experience of worship and the totality of themselves (their bodies, voices, breath, and creativity).

Through processes of planning, rehearsing, conducting, and evaluating videos, Fragomeni introduces these future clergy to patterns of thinking in the midst of priestly practice: crafting and performing rituals faithful to the intent embedded in their rubrics, with the hope, that, by the grace of God, they will "work" in the lives of real, unpredictable human beings who often have little awareness of that intent. The students are enacting—sometimes awkwardly—the integrative, discerning, often intuitive and complex imagination at the heart of clergy practice, as that inevitably comes down to the very practical embodiment of theory and theology in concrete decisions, concrete actions, concrete performances.

For Lyman, the quest for student proficiency and competency is located in a carefully chosen strategic cluster of common teaching methods (such as lecture, reading, conversation, and tests) to facilitate increasing student familiarity with a designated body of historical information and to explore the claim of its meanings in their thinking and how they relate to those meanings. The strategic ordering of these methods of teaching distinguishes the function of each. Readings, for example, function as catalysts to the engagement of instructor and students with texts and their traditions. During class sessions, student comments drawn first from their reading and later from their experience are woven into a coherent argument ordered around a set of questions that give structure not only to class discussions but to all their written work. The argument emerging from the interaction of instructor and students in turn becomes the catalyst and framework for exploring issues integral to the argument.[7] The way of thinking that students rehearse through this teaching practice becomes increasingly familiar—even comfortable and unconscious— through repetition, thus enhancing (and perhaps hindering as well) continued student openness to learning. Their relationship to this teacher has something of the character of apprentice to master craftsman, as she models and coaches them into particular ways of perceiving, thinking, and doing related to the historical consciousness and traditional practice in the work of the Episcopal priesthood. In this regard, she reminded us of the leader of a jazz ensemble, holding in her mind a clear sense of the way the music should sound, expecting each person to be prepared to contribute, open to improvisational surprises in student comments, and all the while correcting mistakes and miscues, striving for ever higher standards of performance.

Although the clergy educators we observed engaged students in the means and manner of performing their religious traditions in a variety of ways, most employ some of the features in Fragomeni's and Lyman's teaching: careful and continuing discussion of principles and methods integral to effective performance; some form of safe, graduated and repeated "rehearsal" of skills being discussed and developed; some form of peer feedback or supervision by the seminary educator or an experienced practitioner; and the chance, in some or all of these moments in the educational activity, to engage in careful, integrative analysis of one's emerging practice in relation to coursework, interactions with congregants, and personal faith or observance.[8]

When reviewing these efforts we may again discern something of the function of pedagogies of performance in the proficiency of a practice. Fairfield makes the point: "We may speak of a practice as displaying a basic animating spirit in which practitioners become involved, which makes demands of us, and conducts us toward a condition of self-forgetful participation" (2000, p. 10). When that happens in the classroom, both teacher and student experience an alignment of self with their knowing and doing. It may not happen often, but when it does, both teacher and student may feel, when they leave the classroom or other site for teaching and learning (or when they reflect on the experience), that they have been in what Robert Inchausti has called a "golden room where honesty, subtlety, truth, and precision give form to their deepest sense of themselves" (1993, p. 162).

The Telos of Performance

Giving attention to pedagogies of performance reminds us, as well, of the influence of the conscious and unconscious intentions or goals of teachers on the interactions of teaching and learning. These intentions or goals direct a teacher's strategies toward the *telos* or ultimate ends of a teacher's pedagogy. They include not only explicit goals related to knowledge and skill, but also expectations for the pastoral imagination and the professional habits and dispositions originating in the academic disciplines, religious and academic traditions, and mission and culture of a school. When Fragomeni, for example, directs student attention to the diversity of cultural patterns in liturgical practices, he shares intentions couched in the Catholic Theological Union's mission statement "to educate effective leaders for the church whose mission is to witness Christ's good news of justice, love, and peace to people of all nations." When Lyman wants students to discover that teaching wisdom as a pastoral activity involves them in critical dialogue with their religious tradition, her intentions for their learning reflect the commitment of the school to "provide the highest quality Christian theological education environment of scholarship, reflection and worship, rooted in the Anglican tradition." These mission statements identify *internal goods* that Fragomeni,

Lyman, and their colleagues have in mind for student learning as they model and coach students into ways of thinking, doing, and being integral to the professional practices of the clergy in their religious traditions.

When McCall urges us to be mindful of the end of any dramatic, liturgical, or pedagogical act being performed, he is encouraging us to be aware of how the "ends" of a performance help determine other characteristics of the performance (1998, p. 91).[9] The implications of his insight are several. The relationship of the performer to the text and audience and of time and space will be handled differently when the ends envisioned for the performance vary. Fragomeni's detailed work in preparing students for their own video performance brings this issue to the surface: "What is your intention in using that gesture?" "What are you hoping to convey with this story in the sermon?" "What does your tone of voice here reveal about who God is for you?" The intent behind Fragomeni's questions reveals his commitment to the alignment of the script chosen or prepared for a given occasion, the means and manner of its performance, and the intended goals of the performance. The assumption at work here is that the greater the measure of such alignment, the more likely students (and later, through their leadership, the congregants they serve) will find themselves participating fully in the script—in the drama of Catholic religious tradition—focused, in this class session, in and through the eucharistic liturgy.

Lyman is similarly attentive to the relationship of the ends of her intentions to the means of her teaching practice. She organizes her teaching to invite students into the academic and spiritual disciplines of her own practice as a church historian. Students encounter practices of historical (1) perspective taking, (2) thinking and (3) self-consciousness by participating in those practices in each class session and through each assignment. Lyman structures the course so that students rehearse this integrative practice again and again to facilitate their increasing ability to discern, examine, and eventually to assess "internal goods" associated with historical thinking. The significance of that rehearsal is intensified by heightening student recognition of criteria for excellence in the practice as it begins to influence their thinking while preparing them for the culminating oral exam of the course.

For the students we met, this event functioned as a rite of passage in their education. It confirmed for them and for each other that they had acquired sufficient vocabulary and skill to participate fully in the Church Divinity School of the Pacific community in the consortium of seminaries that make up the Graduate Theological Union. It bolstered their confidence in their ability to continue the educational journey that they had begun toward ordination as priests and pastors. More specifically, it provided an opportunity to demonstrate their ability to begin to do the kind of integrative historical thinking Lyman intended for them as preachers and teachers of the wisdom of the religious tradition.

Integration in the Pedagogies of Performance

As we reflected on the teaching practices of Fragomeni, Lyman, and others we observed, we were increasingly aware of the integrative dynamics at work in pedagogies of performance. Clues to this insight may again be traced to features of performance. We have argued that religious tradition is the script for pedagogies of performance. It is also the script for pedagogies of interpretation, formation, and contextualization. Through pedagogies of performance, teachers provide ways for students to express or give form to the knowledge and skills, perspectives and attitudes acquired through their engagement with religious tradition.

The students' performance inevitably reveals the adequacy and effectiveness of their efforts to make sense of or give form to what they are learning. To what extent is their performance faithful to the internal contours and limits—the internal goods—of their religious traditions? To what extent does their performance push the edges, critique, or creatively rework their traditions? To what extent does it move back and forth between the faithful or correct adherence to an explicit script handed down through the generations and the finding of spontaneous expression in some moment of improvisation in response to some new condition or situation? In what ways does the student internalize the world view or take on the dispositions and habits of participation in the community of the tradition?

Answers to questions such as these suggest that what matters in any given pedagogical performance in the education of clergy is a student's ability not only to articulate a theological argument or interpret a biblical or Talmudic text or lead a congregation in the singing of an ancient hymn, but to do so in a way that extends the discussion of that argument or interpretation or ritual act within that student's religious tradition; not only to demonstrate the ability to conduct a wedding ceremony or teach a bible class, but to do so in a way that reveals they are participating in a tradition recognizably "Conservative" if Jewish, "Anglican" or "Baptist" if Christian, or a combination, if they are working at some confluence of two or more traditions.

When Fragomeni, for example, assesses the faithful and thoughtful use by students of the rubrics for Catholic liturgies—including their knowledge not only of the rite, but also of various principles shaping its historical development, theological significance, and symbolic/ritual efficacy—he draws heavily on criteria originating in *pedagogies of interpretation.*

As we have seen in the prior discussion of pedagogies of interpretation (see Chapter Three), they cultivate a student's ability to use methods that deepen understandings and expand meanings associated with the texts and contexts of religious tradition. Therefore, when Fragomeni insists that students mark and submit the version of the eucharistic prayer used in their videos, he is emphasizing interpretive criteria emerging from both scholarly discussions of liturgical theology and expectations of effective liturgical leadership. This confluence of interpretive and contextual categories from scholarship and liturgical practice also shows up in his evaluation of students' homilies on their videos and, more subtly, his evaluation of their verbal and gestural interpretations of the many prayers and ritual actions of the mass.

The pedagogical framework in Lyman's class reminds students over and over that any interpretation of texts involves an increasing consciousness of historical and contemporary contextual influences on how they articulate or give form to their interpretations. In a similar fashion, when Kortright Davis at Howard expects students to demonstrate the ability to "think on their feet," his attention is directed to the effectiveness of the oral performance of interpretive practices drawn from scholarly and pastoral reflections on both the black church experience and the traditions of Christian theology. When Williamson looks for "clarity of thought" in student written or oral interpretations of theological and ethical issues, he adds that "clarity of thought is not enough. Some students have philosophical capacity [but they are] still clueless." This means he is also looking for their ability to read the contexts of this interpretive activity to demonstrate, through their preaching, teaching, pastoral care, or administrative performance, that they can "discern what is really going on."

These comments suggest that these professors view their intentions for the learning of students from inside the *means and manner* of the performance they expect from them, whether as scholarship or in preaching, pastoral care, or ritual. Both performances of academic and of ministry exercises in the classroom are evaluated against norms inherent in their respective contexts: biblical exegesis coming through a sermon, for example, is evaluated differently from exegesis in a scholarly paper devoted to that task. The criteria for demonstrating exegetical excellence in a sermon are different from those for demonstrating exegetical efficacy in a scholarly paper. Even if the exegesis itself is equally sound in both cases, it will be framed and expressed or performed differently, according to purpose.

Further, as we have seen previously, in order for either the sermon or the paper to be judged excellent, some dimensions of practice must be emphasized over others: in the sermon, body language, delivery, inflection, pacing, plot, and use of silence are especially important, whereas in a research paper, methodological rigor, accuracy and breadth of citations, logic, critical depth, flow, and originality take precedence. Yet in clergy education, distinctions between the cognitive intentions embedded in the research paper and the professional and practical intentions for the sermon are not quite so neat. Hovering in the background of an exegesis assignment is the expectation that students are developing a way of thinking associated with scholarly practice for performing the homiletical interpretation of texts. In the evaluation of a sermon is the expectation that students' preaching will be grounded in the scholarship of exegesis.

The integrative function of pedagogies of performance may again be seen in the attention given by clergy educators to raising the consciousness of students to the transference of the relationship of *performer and audience* in any pastoral, priestly, or rabbinic practice. Seminary educators are challenged when a student performance is technically proficient, theologically sound, or a marvelous instance of its genre, but has little possibility of reaching, engaging, or moving the people for whom it is intended. Fragomeni addresses this challenge by intentionally heightening student awareness to the effects on people of the various elements of their own performance in liturgical practice. Evidence that students are developing that awareness occurs as they bring to their performance of particular texts or scripts of religious tradition in liturgical settings, a consciousness of the communities and cultures, the relational dynamics, backgrounds, needs, and the images of God held by the people with whom they are or will be working. This awareness, typically associated with *pedagogies of contextualization,* is manifest in the students' choices about and deployment of skills for performance.

Fragomeni encourages this increasing consciousness by probing the adequacy of articulated ideas and suggested gestures through highly contextual (mostly cultural) banter, questioning, and anecdotes. In class, his conversation revolves repeatedly around questions: "How is this gesture done in your home congregation [or culture]? What forms of eye contact would be appropriate or inappropriate for a priest to use [in your culture]?" He also gives his students the option of performing their videos in a language other than English, necessitating the presence of additional priest-evaluators who have those language and cultural skills during formal assessment conversations.

The integrative character of pedagogies of performance may also be found in the ways in which seminary educators cultivate personal authenticity or integrity *in* the performance of clergy practices—what one Howard student described as "walking the talk." This is what Lyman seeks when encouraging a stance of humility in reading and interpreting texts in both academic and ecclesial settings. This is what Fragomeni intends as he pushes students to move beyond the recitation of the *right* words or the use of the *right* gestures to make evident some personal investment, some sense of engagement with the subject of the practice they are learning. He seeks to cultivate, through the practice of the words and gestures they are using, not only deepening knowledge and increasing skill, but a disposition of transparency before God to the end that they might model the *holiness* reflected in being *klei kodesh* or holy vessels as priests in and through their ministries.

Thus, for Fragomeni—and, to varying degrees, most of the clergy educators we met—engaging students through pedagogies of performance includes paying attention to the importance of their spiritual and vocational formation for clergy practice. He assumes that the wholeness, fitness, and spiritual capaciousness, if you will, of *klei kodesh* makes a difference in the quality of the ministries of these "vessels."

Fragomeni pays close attention to matters of formation. This pedagogical emphasis occurs most vividly in his conversations with students about the videos they have produced. In these conversations, each student is invited to ponder and give voice to aspects of his own faith, doubts, and questions, to explore the personal dimensions of the raw edges in his videotaped performance, and to probe how his proclaimed words and enacted gestures mirror or conceal his actual personal engagement with Catholic tradition.

Lyman did not talk about the formative dimensions of her teaching as much as Fragomeni did, but her attention to matters of priestly formation comes into focus as her students prepare for the oral exam at the end of the semester. In the days and weeks prior to this event, they report heightened anxiety due to the fear that they may not be able to answer some question adequately. Given the lore passed along from one generation of students to the next, they fear, even more, the possibility that during this event they will discover they cannot adequately "put it together"—that is, demonstrate the integration of what they are learning with their calling—to be seen as viable candidates for continued study and the priesthood. After the event, however, those same students look back on the exam conversation as a confirmation of their academic and vocational readiness to move on with their education toward ordination or some other form of ministry.

In previous chapters we treated the pedagogies of clergy education we observed as if they were basically separate, or at least best understood in distinction from each other. In pedagogies of performance, however, it becomes evident that the teaching practices of clergy educators, as well as the practices of clergy—intuitively and spontaneously, as well as reflectively and critically—involve teacher or clergy in some configuration of interpretive, formative, contextual, and performative practices.

To write a theological essay, preach a sermon, or choose a prayer for public worship is both an academic and a ministry practice. Each of these performance practices involves teachers and their students—and later, their students as clergy with congregants—in the interpretation of sacred texts while attending to the dynamics of formation responsive to the needs of people and their sense of the presence or activity of God and to the influence of context at work in both processes of interpretation and formation. The impulse toward integration does not only occur in the classroom through faculty pedagogies of performance. It may also be found more generally in what we are calling the corporate or communal pedagogies of the school, the focus of our discussion in Chapters Seven through Ten.

Pedagogy, Performance, and Vocation

Wisdom and Play

Faculty members responding to the Auburn 2003 faculty survey reported they are well satisfied with their jobs. Seminary graduates, in turn, rank the quality of teaching highest among indicators of their satisfaction with the services and resources of their schools. Comments from faculty respondents to the survey we conducted illustrate these findings. "I enjoy teaching very much and feel that I have the spiritual gift of teaching," wrote one. "I am able to pursue courses that interest me. Our student population is remarkably diverse, which enriches the experience. The opportunity to help think through issues of significance for our tradition in this context is very rewarding." Another observing that teaching "is a calling, not a career" noted that "my life is graced even by its most mundane components." Part of the satisfaction experienced by these seminary educators comes directly from the integrative challenge of weaving, "together personal, skill specific and conceptual/theoretical/theological material." This means for one more seminary educator that "teaching is my passion. I can't imagine doing anything else that would be as personally rewarding."

Implied in each of these comments is the recognition that the experience of teaching that mediates the relationship of the cognitive, practical, and professional apprenticeships in the education of clergy may, at some point, verge on *play*.[10] As we bring this chapter to its conclusion, we use the term *play* deliberately because it highlights an important relationship between the performance practice of teachers and the present and future performance practice of their students.

At times the seminary educators we observed were clearly *on stage*. They *played* in various ways to their students as audience: when, for example, Sanders slipped for a few moments into a voice of prophetic preaching; when Fragomeni, Benson, Magid, or Thompson told a story or powerfully demonstrated the argument of a point; or when Fragomeni, Lyman, and many other seminary educators we observed highlighted some pedagogical interaction with humor. Seminary educators like Fragomeni, Wilson and Bartlett, Hughes, and Bergant also *played* with the educational experience as they carefully choreographed the flow of class engagement with the topic or issue of the day so that, as in a drama, the interaction of teacher and student moved back and forth from intensified concentration to moments of relaxation and respite.

The *script, means,* and *manner* of their teaching—that is, the knowledge, skills, concepts, values, attitudes learned over years of teaching—have increasingly been absorbed into the tissues of their being; into their minds' and hearts' own "muscle memories." Over time, the exercise of their teaching has gradually become second nature, to the point they now attend almost unconsciously to the flow and rhythm, the interior movements and ongoing subtleties of student interactions with the resources and methods of their teaching. The rules or harmonies that shape their pedagogies for mediating knowledge, developing skills, and fostering aptitudes and attitudes reflect the consummate and graceful performance and absorbed excellence we typically identify as expertise. In their *play* they model the expectation that their students will also develop—typically long after their classes have ended—patterns of expertise. To that end, clergy educators spend much of their time coaching students toward the expertise they envision for effective clergy practice.

Claxton has described this dynamic in teaching (or in clergy practice) as the "smooth, unreflective mastery of complex but familiar domains" (2000, p. 35). We often identify the thinking processes at work in those moments as intuitive. In teaching it actually reflects a habitus or totality of a way of thinking, being, and doing so familiar that teachers are able to "go through a whole lesson, adjusting or even abandoning their actions and intentions as they go, without being conscious of much reasoning, and without being able to say why or how they made the 'decisions' they did." In the theological world, this capacity has been described as a kind of practical discernment developed over time through persistent attentiveness to the knowledge and practices of a seminary educator's religious tradition and academic context. It includes the growing ability to take into account the subtlety and complexity of emerging pedagogical possibilities in ways they may or may not be able to articulate consciously.

Ultimately, the dynamics of play and discernment in teaching performance are inseparable. This is one of those points when the connections between the practices of the seminary educator and the developing practices of the student as clergy are most intensely experienced. As one seminary educator said, "When I've had a good teaching day, one in which the students and I feel transformed by the material and the experience, it feels magical." As another seminary educator wrote at the conclusion of his survey response, this kind of "teaching is difficult to attain," adding that "[g]enuine, thoughtful teaching, like research and writing, can only come from deep engagement with our fields of study and practice." This seminary educator then concluded: "Much that popularly passes for strong and creative teaching may have a rather short half-life" because it lacks "a true wisdom borne of scholarly discipline and moral growth in our sense of vocation."

In the teaching we observed, that wisdom seemed most palpable when teachers were able to engage their students in the dynamics of playing with serious things—when they modeled for students a capacity for play that in turn revealed possibilities for play in their own anticipated professional practice. This is the observation of a Jewish Theological Seminary graduate describing a professor "who was, for me, an exemplar of Jewish life, and, as such, brought that to class. It was hard for me to separate who he is and what he stands for from what he teaches." In this regard, through his teaching he witnessed to and modeled possibilities in his own practice for the interdependence of person and vocation, knowledge and skill, moral integrity and religious commitment in the future life and work of this rabbi.

ENDNOTES

1. We have chosen to employ the notion of performance even as we have recognized that it is often considered problematic when linked to the professional practice of clergy. Performance language often refers to an

act as something done for show. It is staged or scripted without intention beyond itself. It is often identified with entertainment and consequently associated with popular appeal and mass marketing. Invariably, performance language is linked to notions of evaluation or assessment. Our usage of the notion of performance is further complicated by some academics and artists who speak of all of life as "performance." They suggest that every gesture, word, or action is inherently a matter of self-presentation in the complex web that makes up the power, role, and identity dynamics in all human interaction. Each of these uses of the notion of performance has the potential to subvert the expectations rooted in tradition and embedded in religious communities for the public performance of clergy. We are cautioned by these uses of the term as we describe the teaching practices of seminary educators attentive to the public dimensions of clergy practice.

2. T. S. Eliot, "East Coker," *Four Quartets* (London: Faber and Faber, 1944). The passage she quotes includes these lines:

Do not let me hear
Of the wisdom of old men, but rather of their folly
Their fear of fear and frenzy, their fear of possession
Of belonging to another or to others or to God
The only wisdom we can hope to acquire
Is the wisdom of humility: humility is endless.

3. Later, while describing the oral exam, Lyman noted that she "doesn't simply ask questions they can answer," but instead asks students to "choose two themes" from the course they would be willing to discuss in a comprehensive fashion.

4. For a provocative look at embodied aspects of the "text" enacted in selected charismatic religious contexts, see, for instance, Percy (1999, pp. 1–29).

5. See Boal (1992, p. 89) on "spectactor" as a category that helps to expand and subvert traditional notions of "actor" and "spectator."

6. This category of the means and manner of performance also includes "the further dimension of 'time span' [as] having a definite beginning and ending, and 'place and occasion.' These terms serve further to delimit or differentiate *performed* events from *everyday* events" (Boal, 1992, p. 89).

7. We return to this point elsewhere in this volume. We were intrigued to discover, when exploring the relationship of the deep structure of a faculty member's instructional activity to the learning it elicited from students, that the same instructional strategies employed in the service of different pedagogical practices could have quite different pedagogical consequences.

Lecture, for example, can describe, interpret, evoke, synthesize, challenge, deconstruct.

8. For an engaging and reflective look at very similar processes as they operate within a related professional field—that is, of medical (specifically surgical) practice—see Gawande (2002). In particular, Gawande explores notions of "practice" and the necessity of providing graduated learning opportunities that are safe not only for the novice learner but also, obviously, for the patients (in the case of clergy, the congregants) involved.

9. In commenting on the purpose or desired end of theatrical performance, Richard Schechner writes, "[Victor] Turner locates the essential drama in conflict and conflict resolution. I locate it in *transformation*—in how people use theater as a way to experiment with, act out, and ratify change. Transformations in the theatre occur in three different places, and at three different levels: 1) in the drama, that is, in the story; 2) in the performers whose special task it is to undergo a temporary *rearrangement* of their body/mind; 3) in the audience where changes may be temporary (entertainment) or permanent (ritual)" (1988, p. 170).

10. The language of *play* here is deliberate. Indeed, a further dimension of performance expands into the notion of play in ways that subvert the performer/audience distinction altogether. This is most suggestive for clergy practice precisely at those points where reference to God radically subverts categories of actor/spectator and begins to open into mystery, liminality, and transformation—all elements of play. McCall (1998, p. 90) writes, "[Johan] Huizinga's characterization of play as 'voluntary activity,' which is 'set apart from ordinary life' underwent an expansion in Roger Caillois' *Man, Play, and Games* (1961) to include six qualities of playing, described as (1) not obligatory, (2) circumscribed in time and space, (3) undetermined, (4) materially unproductive, (5) rule-bound, and (6) concerned with an alternate reality [Caillois, 2001, p. 25]. This set of *differentia* differs from the one we have been compiling in *not* being concerned with the audience/performer dichotomy. 'Play,' in this sense, is the play in which all are involved rather than the 'spectator sport' in which one group performs for another." (Note that in the 2001 edition of Caillois' *Man, Play, and Games* these qualities appear on pp. 9ff.) See also Huizinga (1950).

PART THREE

COMMUNAL PEDAGOGIES IN FORMING A PASTORAL, PRIESTLY, OR RABBINIC IMAGINATION

THUS FAR, WE HAVE BEEN LOOKING AT how the clergy imagination is cultivated in—and through—classroom pedagogies of contextualization, formation, interpretation, and performance. These *intentional pedagogies* shape seminary educators' explicit expectations for their students' learning. However, these intentional pedagogies do not explain differences we encountered, for example, in the experiences of students in introductory courses in Old Testament at Fuller, Yale, and Louisville, where students read many of the same commentaries and use similar methods of interpretation.

Earlier we had noted that at Fuller, Butler engages students with the critical study of biblical texts to "stretch their faith"; at Yale, Wilson engages students in the quest for the "right method" to interpret a given passage; and at Louisville, Tull wants students to have, among other things, an aesthetic experience of the text. What lies behind differences like these in the teaching practices of seminary educators?

In our next four chapters, we take up this question to look beyond the classroom to the corporate or *communal* pedagogies students experience in and through the life of the schools they attend. In Chapters Seven and Eight we explore the influence of traditions of seminary education in the mission, culture, and teaching practices of clergy educators. We argue that values and perspectives embedded in these traditions permeate the articulated goals and chosen strategies of teachers as *implicit* corporate or communal pedagogies.

We were alerted to the influence of these traditions in *Being There* (Carroll, Wheeler, Aleshire, and Marler, 1997), the ethnographic account of two Protestant seminaries distinguished from each other primarily by the traditions of theological education embedded in their cultures. We discovered something similar during our visits to seminary campuses. Formal and informal practices of teaching and learning reflected a range of pedagogical traditions in seminary education that distinctively shape what and how contemporary seminary educators teach and students learn.

In making these distinctions, we are again building on Elliot Eisner's insight into the influence of the *implicit curriculum* of schools on student learning. By that term, Eisner means what a school teaches unintentionally "because of the kind of place it is" (Eisner, 1985, p. 91). His attention was drawn to the influence of teacher methods, school reward systems, school organization, building, and arrangement of classroom furniture on student learning. We have also been intrigued by how the seminary community that is the school shapes student learning.

Although the traditions of seminary education may be construed in a variety of ways, we focus attention, in chronological order of their founding, on five that have figured prominently in the course of American seminary education: among Christians, the professional freestanding seminary, the religious training school, the school of emancipation, and an Americanized European seminary tradition; and among Jews, a seminary renewing its religious tradition in relation to the modern university. We trace the trajectories of these five pedagogical traditions and explore their continuing influence on teaching and learning in contemporary American seminary education.

We also discovered during our visits that seminary faculty and administrators expend considerable time and energy in formal practices of teaching and learning outside the classroom—and often outside the structures of academic credit. In Chapters Nine and Ten we explore two of these more explicit corporate or communal pedagogies. The first is found in the cultivation of spiritual practices, primarily in worship, small groups, and patterns of spiritual direction. The second is found in programs to develop professional practice, variously called supervised ministry, field education, or contextual education. Each, we discovered, contributes significantly to seminary efforts to foster the pastoral, priestly, and rabbinic imaginations of seminary students. In Chapter Nine we turn our attention explicitly to pedagogies outside the classroom devoted to fostering corporate and individual spiritual practices. In Chapter Ten we examine several approaches taken by seminaries to the supervision of student learning in contexts of professional practice.

7

TRADITIONS OF
SEMINARY EDUCATION AND
THE PASTORAL IMAGINATION

IN THE QUEST FOR MEANING, clergy engage religious traditions in distinctive ways. Whereas professions driven by science and technology, such as medicine and engineering, constantly update and revise frameworks of knowledge, and law uses past documents as precedents for particular cases, clergy view the relationship of past, present, and future as an ongoing conversation. Ancient sacred texts of Bible and Talmud, for example, remain sources of primary codes, symbols, and narratives of meaning, even as modes of interpreting them have changed over time. Clergy practices emphasize longer views of both past and future.

This longer view of time has contributed to an ambivalent relationship with "modernity" in the clergy profession. Although other professions have fully embraced forms of reason, autonomous selfhood, and civil institutions associated with the Enlightenment, clergy—both liberal and conservative—have been more selective about which aspects of modernity they will embrace, tolerate, or resist. Throughout our study, for example, we discovered that seminary educators were typically influenced more by modern practices of thought, organization, and communication than by theoretical perspectives about the "authority" of claims of religious truth over contemporary life and knowledge. Modernity permeates the contemporary forms and expressions of Jewish and Christian religious traditions—and the education of the clergy in those traditions—but not always in ways anticipated or prescribed by a theoretical or theological stance.

In this chapter, we focus our attention on five figures whose distinctive negotiations with modernity persist in the traditions of seminary education they helped to found: Timothy Dwight, who significantly influenced the development of the professional, freestanding seminary; Emma Dryer and the Bible, or religious training, school; Daniel Payne and the schools of emancipation; John Ireland and the modern diocesan seminary; and Solomon Schechter and the rabbinical seminary. Through their stories we explore three sets of questions:

1. What is the *public mission* that predominates in each of these educational traditions? Specifically, in what ways does it serve a religious community and tradition, an academic constituency or school of thought, and the wider society or national consciousness? How do *student constituencies* marked by class, race, and gender shape the mission and ultimately the culture and pedagogies of each seminary tradition?

2. What is the tradition's *cultural ethos*? Is it marked by professional formation? Intensive text study and academics? Spiritual formation? Specialized mission work? Does the ethos stress *paideia* or *wissenschaft* in its communal practices?

3. What are its *teaching practices*? What goals, methods, and strategies for student learning are emphasized? What are the explicit, implicit, and null curricula embedded in the schools of each tradition? How are the mission and cultural ethos translated into curricular structures? What cross-curricular practices help bind them together? What emphasis is given in teaching to some balance of *paideia, wissenschaft,* and *professional skills* development?

At the end of each historical sketch, we consider the *pastoral imagination* cultivated through each seminary tradition. We ask, in particular, how each seminary tradition shapes the habitus of dispositions and world views of their clergy and the *transformative practices* that accompany them.

From this perspective, the *pastoral imagination* cultivated in these traditions of seminary education may be viewed as a form of mediation between religious tradition and the forces of modernity. Because seminary education is both formative and transformative of persons and traditions of practice, we suggest distinct types or ideals associated with the view of the mind of a pastor, priest, or rabbi in each tradition. These types serve as distinctive portraits, or models, of pastoral identity and practice within and among various traditions of Christian and Jewish schooling. As such, they influence the goals and strategies of many seminary educators as, through their teaching, they seek to cultivate in their students an imaginative capacity for professional practice.

From Apprenticeship to Schools of Piety and Intellect

Timothy Dwight and the Professional, Freestanding Seminary

Colonial America followed the English pattern of schooling for the professions of divinity and law. Colleges with a classical curriculum—from Harvard in the North to William and Mary in the South—were established to provide the educational foundations for each. Following the completion of this course of study, students entered several years of apprenticeship with a master practitioner (Fraser, 1988). Although the theological traditions of Calvinists, Baptists, and Anglicans varied, each perpetuated the English formula of college to apprenticeship in clergy education. This was the educational experience of Timothy Dwight (1752–1817), whose vision for educating Protestant clergy would eventually lead to a new form of clergy education. After graduating from Yale College in 1769, he apprenticed with his uncle, Jonathan Edwards Jr. (Wenzke, 1989, p. 27). That apprenticeship typically would have involved Dwight's reading and then writing a theological thesis on books in Edward's library, shadowing him in his weekly pastoral duties, and eventually preaching in his congregation (Woods, 1885, pp. 19–20; Miller, 1990, 54–56). Although Dwight was a successful product and later a distinguished proponent of this pattern of clergy education, as the nineteenth century dawned he saw the need for a new kind of educational institution. His vision culminated in the transition of Protestant clergy education in the United States from a post-college apprenticeship to post-baccalaureate training at a seminary.

A Classical Education and the Rhetorical Arts

Dwight came from two proud New England families. His father and paternal grandfather were attorneys and public officials. On his mother's side, Dwight was the grandson of America's most famous theologian, Jonathan Edwards, who, during the mid-1700s, had founded the "New Divinity" movement that influenced the course of American Protestant theology for the next one hundred and fifty years (Holifield, 2003). Dwight was both precocious and ambitious (Wenzke, pp. 22–53; Fitzmier, 1998, pp. 28ff). He learned to read the Bible at age four, passed the Yale entrance exams for Latin and Greek by eight, mastered Josephus and Hooke's history of Rome by ten, and entered Yale college at thirteen, the same age as did his famous grandfather.

At Yale, Dwight read the scientific works of Newton, the practical divinity of New England clergy, and the new philosophy and literary criticism from Scotland and England, with John Locke's epistemological philosophy crowning his senior-year curricular experience (Wenzke, p. 26). After securing the master's degree in 1772, he was invited to join the Yale faculty as one of four tutors. During this time of revolutionary unrest, Dwight's own teaching focused on "oratory, English grammar, composition, and the cultivation of an effective style" of speaking required of law and divinity (Wenzke, p. 38). He and the other tutors pushed the Yale Corporation to include in the curriculum the modern Scottish rhetorical studies of Lord Kames, George Campbell, and Hugh Blair (Wenzke, pp. 27ff; Fitzmier, pp. 30ff). As founders of "the first genuine American school of literary criticism," they became known as the "Connecticut Wits" (Wenzke, p. 31; cf. 87ff).

The Union of Piety and Intellect

After his father's untimely death in 1778, Dwight returned to Massachusetts to assist his family. There he started a grammar school and preached occasionally in the local church. Eventually he was called to his first pulpit in Greenfield, Massachusetts, where he preached a moderate version of his grandfather's "New Divinity," emphasizing affections and virtues. In Greenfield, he established an academy that soon rivaled the enrollment and offerings of Yale.[1] Convinced that girls were "capable of mental improvement" (Wenzke, p. 156), he boldly opened the entire course of study to them as well. In 1795, he accepted a call to the presidency of Yale, where he advocated the union of intellect and piety as the surest foundation for modern learning.

On the side of the intellect, he argued for the "Reasonableness of Christianity," in the tradition of Locke and the Scottish divines and against the French *philosophes*. He taught rhetoric, exhortation, and homiletics for future lawyers and ministers, who shared the aim "to persuade men to become good" (Fitzmier, p. 89). He strengthened the sciences and humanities by adding chairs in law, chemistry and natural history, languages and ecclesiastical history, and medicine. Dwight oversaw the establishment of a school of medicine, but his dream of a divinity school at Yale was not realized until 1823, well after his death.

On the side of piety, under Dwight's leadership Yale became a center of Protestant voluntarism and mission. Divinity, he believed, should always "affect the heart" in its intellectual and moral pursuits (Wenzke, p. 37). He developed a rhetorical form of practical divinity, combining his moderate version of Edward's theology with his love of the belles lettres. The conversionist themes in his theology and the affective style of his preaching helped fan the flames of the national revival called the "Second Great Awakening" (Wenzke, pp. 48ff; Ahlstrom, 1976, pp. 418ff). When his own political vision of "Godly federalism" for America was defeated by advocates of Jeffersonian democracy (Fitzmier, pp. 163–80), he re-envisioned the church as a voluntary society that could transform American culture. Lyman Beecher, one of his most prominent students, illustrated this vision when he argued that "A land supplied with able and faithful ministers, will of course be filled with schools, academies, libraries, colleges, and all the apparatus for the perpetuity of republican institutions" (Wenzke, p. 6). To this end, Dwight recruited hundreds of students at Yale as missionaries of this Protestant cultural vision, often through societies he had helped found, like the American Missionary Society and the American Bible Society (Fitzmier, pp. 72ff.; Wenzke, p. 49).

Andover and the Professional, Freestanding Seminary

When the Congregational Church lost state support and cultural dominance in New England, Dwight and his Calvinist allies saw the need for an independent, graduate-level seminary in the region. Dwight's close friend, the Reverend Jedediah Morse, had watched in dismay as fellow Overseers at Harvard narrowly endorsed a Unitarian, Dr. Henry Ware, for the professorship of divinity in Cambridge (Fitzmier, pp. 63ff). With Dwight's blessing, Morse approached a dissenting member of the Harvard Corporation, Dr. Eliphalet Pearson, to explore the possibility of founding an alternative divinity school in cooperation with the well-respected Phillips Academy in Andover, where Pearson was principal. Dwight and Morse were able to obtain support from both traditional and New Divinity Calvinists for the new institution. Since the school wanted its own board of visitors, it was finally agreed in 1808 to establish a freestanding institution that would be in Andover but not linked to Phillip's Academy (Woods, pp. 47ff; Miller, p. 68).

The new Andover Theological Seminary was a unique institution in American higher education in three important ways. First, it was the first freestanding graduate school in the nation, free of state finances or university resources. While Dwight petitioned the Massachusetts legislature for a charter (Fitzmier, p. 63), funds had to be raised entirely from donors. A $100,000 bequest pulled from Harvard after the Ware appointment (Woods, pp. 47ff) was supplemented with gifts totaling more than $300,000—a sum larger than Harvard's endowment. Second, the founding of the seminary effectively united different theological factions in New England. Dwight worked tirelessly to bring traditional Calvinists such as

Stuart Moses, who became the first biblical professor, and New Divinity clergy such as Leonard Woods, who became the first president, into the project. Woods even convinced anti-institutional "hyper-Calvinists"[2] such as Nathaniel Emmons to join the seminary's cause of resisting the Unitarianism of Harvard.

Third, the school was established as a post-collegiate, graduate-level program that organized modern scholarship around professional service to society. As a member of the first board of visitors, Dwight worked closely with Morse to design the organization and curriculum of the new school to reflect a broad-based, voluntary Protestant vision. The result was a formal curriculum in Bible, doctrine, history, and homiletics that stressed both intellectual formation in the best of European and American scholarship and the practice of ministerial arts. Fourth, when Dwight, as the leading Calvinist divine in New England, was invited to share a vision for the seminary at the opening convocation in the spring of 1808, he proposed lofty educational standards for the institution that continue to influence assumptions about contemporary seminary education: adequate funding, sound trustee management, an extensive library, a professional and specialized faculty, a division of theology into distinct disciplines, a three-year program to master the subjects, and a large student body (Miller, pp. 68–69).

Protestant Pedagogies of Professional Education

The first Andover professors emphasized developing the intellect with professional practice in the classroom. Woods, as president and professor of divinity, combined lecture, open discussion and debate, and the presentation of student dissertations among peers with the intent of enhancing intellectual and pastoral growth simultaneously (Woods, p. 163). The professor of Bible, Moses Stuart, immersed himself in Greek and Hebrew and German scholarship, and eventually produced one of the earliest English texts of modern biblical interpretation, the *Hermeneutics of Ernesti* (Woods, p. 160). His work established Andover as a center of modern biblical scholarship, producing quality scholars *and* ministers of the Word. In the tradition of Dwight, the second president, Ebenezer Porter, taught homiletics more "as an art rather than as a science," an approach that "depends essentially on practice" (Matthews, 1837, p. 25). The entire curriculum was designed to integrate biblical and theological scholarship into a popular, understandable, practical, and compelling message.

The professional focus of Andover's divinity curriculum heightened the need to coordinate text-based studies with oral performance. The classical, liberal arts background of the older apprenticeship model had provided an almost seamless movement from the study of classic texts to public oratory in preparing pastors for their public role as preachers. By intensifying attention to both the academic nature of text studies and the professional arts of ministerial practice, Andover faculty's pedagogical innovations exposed the gap between them. Woods changed the classic apprenticeship practice of assigning student theses to be written individually and presented for class commentary; instead, the class wrote a thesis together and submitted it to the professor for editing (Woods, pp. 161ff).

Dwight and other New Divinity leaders expanded the Puritan emphasis on preaching to include a multitude of rhetorical arts: public prayer, catechesis, pastoral conversation and discipline (Holifield, 1983, pp. 67–106). They also refined the movement from the texts of Bible, history, and doctrine to public oratory (Cunningham, 1942, pp. 38–40; Wenzke, pp. 37ff). In the homiletics course taken during the final year, for example, a student was expected to demonstrate enough facility with biblical texts to engage a threefold preaching practice: "opening" the Biblical text in its literary (and later historical) context, "dividing" the text according to its basic doctrines, and seeking its "uses" in the lives of parishioners (Hudson, 1956, p. 189). A host of new "pastoral manuals"—often patterned after Richard Baxter's classic, *The Reformed Pastor*—stressed the proper social conduct and conversational arts of ministers as they engaged in moral and spiritual counsel (Holifield, 1983, pp. 117–31). These public and predominantly oral arts of the minister required students to demonstrate their ability to tailor increasingly specialized knowledge to an expanding range of ministerial roles and situations.

The dual emphasis on classical text studies and public oratory established the pedagogical practices that mainline Protestant seminaries of the future would emphasize: interpretation and performance. As we discuss in Chapter Three, this interpretive move involves a text or phenomenon—in this case the Bible—and an audience or community of reception. In the nineteenth century, the clergy's interpretation of the Bible was increasingly marked by a technical apparatus of linguistic, philological, and historical devices that arose from the specialties of biblical and theological disciplines in the seminaries. Although the interpretive direction remains one of authoritative transmission from clergy to communities as in Puritan days, increasingly it is subjected to the test of *public persuasion* through rhetorical performance. A corresponding shift takes place from a focus on local and congregational needs to public and civic requirements for a shared national vision. With an increasingly pan-Protestant vision for the

nation, the performative practices of public oratory were crucial to the viability of Protestantism as a public discourse in rebuilding the democracy.
Historic Protestantism relied on a class of educated clergy to mine sacred
texts with new forms of learning, fashioning a contemporary, civic ideology for the new nation.

The increased emphasis on coordinating academic learning with professional practice in the Protestant seminaries left the formation of *piety*
largely to *communal pedagogies* outside the classroom. Consequently, the
seminary community became the teacher of piety: through regular chapel,
the "Wednesday Evening" religious seminars with faculty, student-led
prayer and study groups, individual counsel with faculty, and student publications and missionary societies (Woods, p. 165). This reliance on communal pedagogies, often student-led and -organized, to shape piety
became a fixed pattern of Protestant seminary education in the decades
that followed. The formal curriculum focused on academic and professional development; this informal, corporate curriculum bolstered spiritual improvement.

Public Vision and the Pastoral Imagination

Several cross-curricular practices and discourses facilitated the pedagogical movement from text-based studies to oral performance. One of the
most influential was the symbolic interpretation of Scripture inherited
from the Puritans, who had rejuvenated the ancient church practice of
identifying signs or "types" in one book of the Bible as fulfilled in those
of another and extended it to include the natural world and contemporary society (Cherry, 1980, pp. 14–65). Jonathan Winthrop, for example, described the Massachusetts Bay Colony as being, like the New
Jerusalem in the Revelation of John, a "city on a hill" bringing light to
all the nations (Ahlstrom, p. 45). Jonathan Edwards saw in natural sun-
light intrinsic harmonies and vibrations of color, a perception that allowed him to coordinate a reading of Newton's optics with the complex
harmonies of God's governance, the soul, and the cosmos (Cherry, 1980,
p. 28). Dwight, too, was skilled at symbolic exegesis of the Bible—as, for
example, when he described the American Revolution as a contemporary
"Conquest of Canaan" in its quest for freedom (Wenzke, p. 27). The
practice of symbolic interpretation, then, cultivated a theological aesthetic across the curriculum that involved an almost seamless, perceptual
extension of Biblical imagery into the natural world and contemporary
social events.

The Puritan view of a constructive, figurative imagination found modern successors in nineteenth-century Romanticism, especially in the works of Samuel Taylor Coleridge in England and Horace Bushnell in the United States. By drawing on Kant's view of the "productive imagination," Coleridge and Yale graduate Bushnell saw the imagination as the constructive force of reason that reshapes the perceived world into a unified whole by means of a guiding image (Cherry, 1980, p. 7). Bushnell first identified the problem of God's revelation as one of the "forms and figures" of language during a guest lecture at Andover in 1839 (Cherry, 1980, p. 169). Later, he developed a figurative theory of religious language that became the bedrock of modern, liberal theology in the United States (Kuklick, 1985, 165–69; Holifield, 1983, pp. 458–60).

A second cross-curricular discourse in nineteenth-century Protestant seminary education focused attention on the religious affections and the will. Jonathan Edwards revised the older Puritan practice of first explaining a text to the mind, then outlining its applications to the heart (White, 1969). He argued that effective teaching and preaching must be aimed at the unity of the heart, mind, and will in an act of true spiritual "sensation" or "apprehension" (Holifield, 1983, p. 76; Holifield, 2003, p. 110). Only then, he believed, could the bondage of our natural understanding to self-love be reoriented toward the love of Being (or God) over the love of self. In contrast to Newton's notion of causation, Edwards's contention was that human understanding is not determined by nature, but is shaped by the interest and movement of the will. Hence, the power of reasoning is "first dependent on a preceding act of the will," in the form of intellectual interest and judgment (Wenzke, p. 66). Dwight revised Edward's theology in a rationalist direction, emphasizing that humans are intellectually free to recognize true ideas as reflections of divine design (Wenzke, pp. 66ff). Only the will's moral judgment and action remain bound by selfish interest, so inspired exhortation aims to reorient the moral activity of the will to embrace the truth held by the understanding. In short, "Truth is an act, it is a virtue" (Wenzke, p. 73).

This combination of discourses on symbolic interpretation and the will contributed to a view of the pastoral imagination as *constructive and transformational*. As the world is refigured or revisioned through new symbolic readings, it can be transformed by a new orientation of the will directed to the realization of this new vision. The voluntary activism of nineteenth-century Protestantism—the establishment of Sunday schools, common schools, and colleges; the founding of new congregations; the expansion of the social visions of missionary and reform societies; and the critiques and advocacy of national expansion and industrialization—

owes much to these two features of the pastoral imagination generated by Andover and by other new seminaries that appropriated its vision for the education of Protestant clergy.

God's Army for the Working People

Emma Dryer and the Religious Training Schools

By the mid-1800s, a new religious leadership emerged in the voluntary Protestant societies springing up across the United States. After the Second Great Awakening, men and women took up, as a religious calling, the causes of temperance, popular education, and home and foreign missions, and gave leadership to the Young Men's Christian Association (YMCA), Young Women's Christian Association (YWCA), and a host of similar service institutions. After the Civil War, these mission societies found renewed purpose in rebuilding the nation and assimilating scores of new immigrants into the American dream. Often lay-led and funded, these mission organizations established a pattern of Christian leadership for women and men relatively independent of the traditional denominations and their clergy. The need for a new kind of schooling to educate the leaders of these early "para-church" movements found form in the religious training school. Emma Dryer (1835–1925) was a pioneer in the religious training school movement and was the behind-the-scenes founder of the Moody Bible Institute in Chicago.

Emma Dryer and the Precedent of the Normal School

A gifted educator, Emma Dryer honed her career at Illinois State Normal School, a flagship institution in the movement to train public school teachers. Founded in 1857, it was the second normal school in the West. Unlike the normal schools in the East, which emphasized elementary education, Illinois State Normal School provided a broad, college-level program to prepare teachers for all levels of public education. It eventually became the first state university in the West (Harper, 1939, p. 80). Under the remarkable leadership of Richard Edwards, students were exposed to a full range of subject matter, elementary to high school, and to the science and art of teaching all ages. Edwards integrated the "practice of teaching" (Edwards, 1965, p. 81) throughout the curriculum: in regular class exercises, in "mock" sessions and role plays, and in supervising a "model school," which he considered "unquestionably essential to the complete idea of a Normal School" (Edwards, p. 81). Edwards set high standards and rhetorically defended teachers as full-fledged professionals: "have we not well-defined, universally acknowledged, practically important principles as well in the Teachers' College as the College of Physicians?" (Edwards, p. 80).

In this rich and innovative environment, Dryer developed a distinguished career. After college in New York, she taught in Knoxville and then joined the Normal School faculty in 1864 as an instructor in grammar and drawing (Dobschuetz, 2001, p. 41). With a strong educational background, keen intellect, and excellent organizational skills, she soon rose to the rank of principal or "dean" of the female faculty (Getz, 1969; Day, 1936, p. 263). In this position she became one of the distinguished educators in the West, a status enhanced by her association with Edwards.[3]

From the normal school movement, Dryer developed a broad vision of what a religious training school could be. It should be *populist* and *democratic,* serving common people, not the upper classes. It must be *coeducational,* ensuring that both women and men were prepared for religious leadership. It united an array of subject matter by focusing on *pedagogical delivery.* It emphasized *practice* or *work* as an integral part of professional education, especially through a model or laboratory school. Finally, it must be an integral part of a *distinct,* but *cooperative educational network,* serving institutions like congregations and Sunday schools, and providing leadership for higher-education programs in colleges and seminaries.

Dryer's School of "Bible Work"

In 1870, a life-threatening bout with typhoid transformed both Dryer's faith and her vocation. Following an experience she attributed to divine healing, she became a devout believer in Christ's imminent return (a movement known as "premillennialism") and began looking for a new form of religious service (Daniels, 1877, p. 504; Dobschuetz). During a visit to Chicago, she witnessed the devastation of the Great Fire of 1871 and responded immediately to the crisis: "Churches, Sunday schools, day schools, were scattered. The hungry were to be fed, the naked clothed, and the sick cared for. I was accustomed to organize and conduct schools, and not all willing hearts and hands around me, could organize as quickly as I could do it. I saw clearly, that I must remain for a time and learn much while teaching and helping others" (Getz, p. 32).

After her success with the Great Fire relief work, she became the superintendent of the Women's Aid Society, the forerunner of the YWCA in Chicago. Women's Aid was an exemplar of Christian social work at the time, providing food, clothing, and health care to the working poor of

Chicago (Findlay, 1969, p. 321). But unlike her contemporary Jane Addams of Hull House, Dryer always coordinated social work with a soul-saving gospel.

In Dwight Moody, Dryer soon found a colleague for her urban ministry. When she met him in 1872, he was a young evangelist without a high school education, but with remarkable ambition and rhetorical power. A former shoe salesman, Moody applied retailing methods to the work of saving souls. He kept detailed records of contacts, public assemblies, and conversions (Brereton, 1990, pp. 52–54). At Moody's urging, Dryer moved to Chicago in 1873 to direct his Sunday school at the Northside Tabernacle and to organize the Bible Work of Chicago (Daniels, 1875, p. 188). The latter was "devoted to a program of personal evangelism among the poor, including house to house visitations, women's prayer meetings, and tract distribution" (Findlay, p. 322). At Dryer's insistence, the program uniting biblical witness and social service included "Sewing Schools" and a "Working Woman's Home," which taught job skills and social etiquette (Dorsett, 1997, p. 168; Dobschuetz, p. 46). True to her normal school training, Dryer founded a "daily morning school for children" whose families could not afford the fees of public schools (Getz, p. 59). In contrast to Dryer's coeducational vision, however, Moody insisted that she train only women so as not to compete with the seminaries: "We'd find ourselves in hot water quick, if we undertook to educate young men" (Getz, p. 32). Consequently, Bible Work programs were "extensions of the domestic sphere . . . in such fields as health care, education, and social service" (Dobschuetz, p. 47).

Despite these gender restrictions, Dryer's ministry was so successful that it laid the groundwork for Moody's Bible School. The Bible Work of Chicago branched out all over the city and established an office at the new YMCA building downtown. Dryer reported, "Our workers had their appointed districts, in which they held meetings, and visited from house to house, cooperating with the nearby churches. Workers read their reports of daily work, weekly, in the Bible-Work Room, in the YMCA building, to which all contributors and friends of the work were invited" (Getz, p. 34). Using Moody's retailing methods, Dryer kept accurate records that measured success and impressed donors.[4] Dryer finally convinced Moody to rent several buildings to house and train workers next to the Northside Tabernacle, on the present-day site of the Moody Bible College (Day, p. 262).

Eventually she also convinced him to include both men and women in the program, in line with her normal school vision (Getz, p. 32). The Reverend W. H. Daniels saw in her work the beginning of "a great school for

Christ," similar to Spurgeon's London Bible College, where students came "from the level of the people, wholly wanting in professional training, but mighty in the Scriptures" (Daniels, 1875, p. 189).

Evangelical Center of Prayer, Study, and Work

In 1879, when Dryer collapsed from exhaustion, Moody sent her to Mildmay, England—the site of a famous evangelical conference center—to recover.[5] There, she encountered a training school committed to a range of Bible and mission work, including "soup kitchens, a hospital, kitchen gardens, a circulating library . . . home nursing services, [and] a home for converted prostitutes" (Dorsett, p. 46). In this setting, Dryer's earlier belief in "Christ's imminent return" was deepened and renewed by the premillennial theology of John Darby[6] that permeated the life and work of Mildmay, her health was restored, and her vision for a strong Christian training and service institute in Chicago was reinvigorated.

Back in Chicago, Dryer laid the groundwork for the second phase of the training school in the formal lectures of the May Institute following a pattern of normal school institutes that Henry Barnard had inaugurated in Connecticut in the 1830s (Harper, p. 51). In 1882, she invited a gifted teacher and scholar, W. G. Moorehead of Xenia Seminary (Presbyterian), to share his expertise in a way local practitioners could use. Dryer viewed this short-term training course for women and men interested in religious work as a "trial session" of things to come (Getz, p. 34). Because Moody was preoccupied with tours on the East Coast and in Europe, Dryer had to raise money locally through friends such as Cyrus and Nettie McCormick, of farm-implement fame. During the next three years, the May Institutes grew from fifty students to more than one hundred. Under pressure from the McCormicks and others, Moody finally joined the fundraising efforts in 1885, challenging city leaders to raise $250,000 for a residential training school (Getz, p. 60).

By the time Moody returned to Chicago, Dryer had instituted much of her original vision in a distinctive educational institution. It was *populist* and *coeducational,* in that women and men without much schooling had the chance for ongoing study and religious work. The training was *practical* and *technique oriented,* as students learned from teachers and peer groups how to educate, organize, witness to, and serve the urban working class. The atmosphere of the training school was *devout* and *urgent.* Daily activities included Bible study, prayer, and work-reflection groups— all marked by a premillennial imperative to save as many souls as possible before Christ's return. Above all, the school was infused with the *detailed work* of each student, marked by daily visitations and outreach, regular reporting on progress, and some supervision. The formal unity of the curriculum was located in the religious work of students and group reflection upon it; informally, the communal practices of prayer and Bible study set the tone of their educational experience.

Two Kinds of Training Schools

Moody's view of the training school eventually diverged from Dryer's. The success of the May Institutes and Moody's fundraising drive brought him back to the city to lead the charge in building a residential training school. However, he reoriented the populist vision of the school from a coeducational institute to one that trained "gap-men" for ministries with the working class—something refined seminary graduates simply could not do: "I believe we have got to have gap-men—men to stand between the laity and the ministers; men who are trained to do city missions work. They have got to know the people and what we want is men who know that, and go right into the shop and talk to men. Never mind the Greek and Hebrew, give them plain English and good Scripture. I do not want you to misunderstand me, but the ministers are educated away from these classes of people" (Getz, pp. 36–37).

Although Dryer convinced Moody that the Bible Institute "will help the seminaries" by providing able assistants and specialized courses to urban clergy (Getz, p. 185), Moody set aside her "cooperative" vision for one that would compete directly with seminaries in training a new breed of religious worker, arguing that "I will have some trouble with the seminaries but if a few of my friends will stand by me it will come out all right" (Getz, p. 307).

However, although Moody saw an evangelical opportunity for expanding the appeal of his message, his donors envisioned a new social mission for the emerging Bible Institute. The 1880s were a time of industrial expansion, mass urbanization, and unrest among the working class. Cyrus McCormick Jr. faced mounting labor unrest at his farm-implements factory, culminating in the bloody Haymarket riots of the spring of 1886 (Dorsett, pp. 322ff; Pollock, 1963, p. 261). Another industrialist and donor, T. W. Harvey, wrote Moody that same year, "Either these people are to be evangelized or the leaven of communism and infidelity will assume such enormous proportions that it will break out in a reign of terror such as this country has never known" (Findlay, p. 327). In short, the large industrialists of the city wanted a Bible institute to train workers in piety, obedience, and the American work ethic. In Moody, they found someone who could deliver a message that both saved souls and preserved capital.

These two visions of the training school—one in the spirit of the normal school for building up the common people through Bible education and mission work; the other for retraining laborers away from class consciousness toward an individual, soul-saving message—simply could not coexist. The conflict between Dryer and Moody is often attributed to different power needs (Pollock, p. 270), organizational abilities (Getz, p. 38), or financial disputes (Dorsett, p. 274). But in the end what drove them apart were two incompatible visions for the new school. Moody threatened to resign from the board when a financial matter did not go his way. Nettie McCormick was incensed at this power play, and Dryer wrote to chastise Moody "for acting without respect for others" (Dorsett, p. 274). Despite compromise (Moody ran a board of trustees filled with businessmen, and Dryer ran a management board filled with women), the fissures were too deep to heal.

The bicameral organization of the school allowed Dryer to continue her vision of uniting Bible education and mission work, but only for a while. In January 1888 she began the first extended training session for women, "to give thorough instruction in the Word of God, and a practical training in the various forms of Christian work" (Getz, p. 40). The May Institute for men and women grew steadily each year until 1889, when Moody announced a full-time residential program. To better compete with the seminaries, Moody recruited the conservative scholar A. R. Torrey, who held a doctorate and had studied in Germany. As the industrialists' hold on the school grew, women were "squeezed out" of significant leadership (Dobschuetz, p. 48). When the Moody Bible Institute officially opened in the fall of 1889, Dryer was demoted to work under a new director of women's work, and by the end of the year she was asked to resign (Dorsett, p. 440 n. 10). Nettie McCormick recalled half of her $50,000 pledge to Moody and gave it instead to support Dryer's new work with the Chicago Bible Society (Dorsett). In the end, the Moody evangelicals opted for a male-dominated institution, eschewing the coeducational spirit of the normal schools.

Training School Pedagogies of Skill and Piety

Dryer's religious training schools and those that followed in its tradition used pedagogical practices with several unique features. At the heart of the movement was the use of *personal outreach and small groups* to develop piety and to minister to others. As Dryer wrote in 1870, "The ultimate object of this Bible Work is to make known salvation through Christ by reading the Bible to individuals in their homes and in small meetings collected for the study of the Scriptures" (Getz, p. 60). Weekly, Bible workers reported to peer groups about their efforts and sought advice from senior workers and teachers. School plenaries included lectures on principles of outreach and service, as well as discussions on individual student experiences, an early form of "ministry practicum." Even the social work—from sewing classes to food and clothing relief—relied on personal outreach and small groups to understand people's needs and communicate with them. Dryer's use of Mildmay method, including an emphasis on personal holiness from Methodism and the Keswick movement,[7] intensified small group work among students, especially to develop their own piety (Carpenter, 1997, pp. 8ff; Brereton, p. 22). Working and witnessing for the Lord and then reporting on that work to peer groups became the primary means of developing students' Christian character and strengthening their vocational resolve.

Another distinctive feature of training school pedagogy was the *practical orientation* of teaching and learning. The training school curriculum combined basics in "seminary-like" subjects of Bible, history, and doctrine with subjects of evangelism and outreach, such as church music, mission and evangelism, religious education, social work, health care, domestic science, and industrial arts (Brereton, p. 61). The range of subject matter was linked by a concern for "useful methods, practical application, and efficiency" (p. 62). These were the first schools for religious leaders to develop courses and departments of fieldwork (p. 114). Like the normal schools, religious training schools emphasized learning how to *deliver* a given subject over mastering disciplinary knowledge. Both the normal and the training school assumed that students would become lifelong learners and that mastery would eventually come through ongoing study in service of practice. All of this was done with a populist disdain for the abstract nature of seminary studies. Moody, for example, took pride in a school that developed "men of one book" by replacing the refined disciplines of theology, rhetoric, and history with "the reverent and prayerful study of the Word of God" (Daniels, 1875, p. 189). He boasted that sixty days in his institute was "worth more than a year's study" at any seminary (Dorsett, p. 307).

Consequently, the religious training schools laid the groundwork for *performative* and *formative* teaching practices common to fundamentalist and evangelical schools in the twentieth century. Unlike the professional orientation of Andover, the Bible and training schools emphasized *skills development* as a means for instilling *piety* among workers and recipients. Professional roles and identity were displaced by Christian character as the integrating habitus of the Bible school. The overarching goal of forming strong Christians, in whatever line of "Bible work," accounts for the wide range of vocational training common to these schools from the beginning, as they prepared missionaries, teachers, social workers, evangelists, preachers, and youth workers. Performance for the sake of piety, then, became the hallmark of evangelical seminary education.

Marketing the Gospel and the Pastoral Imagination

The theology that eventually dominated the training schools and Bible institutes was a distinctive combination of Baconian induction and premillennial eschatology. In contrast to the seminaries' historical and linguistic study of Greek and Hebrew biblical texts, the training schools combed the English Bible (King James) inductively for "factual" claims of revelation. The Bible schools wanted to educate pious, God-fearing interpreters of the text armed with a message easy to communicate and, thus, market to the masses. Dryer, for example, developed a personal method of "codifying" biblical teachings according to her views of Christ's second coming and her own doctrine of spiritual healing—views that Moody detested (Dorsett, p. 168). Moody and others latched onto the dispensational premillennialism of John Nelson Darby—a theological perspective that divided the history of the Bible into various "epochs." Each epoch was identified by a dispensation from or covenant with God, from Adam and Eve, to Noah, to Abraham, and on to Christ—culminating, however, not so much in Christ's life, death, and resurrection, but in his anticipated "second coming."

This dispensational system had enormous advantages for serving the practical and mass-marketing goals of the Bible Schools. Expectations of Christ's imminent return gave urgency to Christian evangelism and outreach. It offered a developmental, "history-like" view of the Bible that eschewed the twin evils of evolution and historical criticism espoused by modern seminaries. Perhaps more important from a pedagogical standpoint, it arranged thousands of texts and verses of the Scriptures into a storehouse of empirical "facts" that could easily be charted into stages, reproduced, and disseminated in Bible study groups (Brereton, p. 20). Students, for example, charted the dispensations for display in class or on the doors of their dorm rooms.

The view of pastoral imagination at work in the pedagogies of these training schools and Bible institutes was *urgent* and *entrepreneurial*. If God's revelation was a storehouse of facts, bearing down upon the world with cataclysmic urgency, the task was to organize the message in a sustainable form and develop creative methods to disseminate it both personally and through modes of mass communication. The minister's ongoing movement, from personal engagement with the message, to organizing and disseminating the message for each new group or population, required tireless energy and dedication. Bible training school students usually sacrificed a secure wage and home to pursue their vocations. Most lived in subsistence and insecurity, relying entirely on small donations for "start-up" ministries in the mission field (Brereton, pp. 132–38). The dual pressures of Christ's return and the viability of one's ministry allowed little time for studious reflection or questioning of a gospel message that, quite simply, must be true. Bible school students were trained as "God's army" in service of the masses, marching to save as many souls as possible from coming tribulations.

Schools of Emancipation

Daniel Payne and the African American Seminaries

A simmering national crisis led to the transformation of clergy education in African American churches. Prior to the Civil War, most black pastors had been trained through an apprenticeship system and, for the most part, without the benefits of a college education. Like white Methodist and independent Baptist congregations that initially shunned a college-trained clergy, black churches trusted on-the-job training and the guidance of the Spirit to cultivate their leaders.

A handful of white denominational seminaries—notably Oberlin in Ohio (Congregationalist), Gettysburg in Pennsylvania (Lutheran), and the Oneida Institute in New York (Presbyterian)—had been admitting and graduating a few black ministry students. White denominations had also founded two black theological institutes: the Ashmun Institute (later Lincoln University) in Pennsylvania (1854, Presbyterian), and Wilberforce University in Ohio (1856, Methodist). The African Methodist Episcopal (AME) Church established Union Seminary in Ohio (1847), which later merged with Wilberforce (Daniel, 1925, p. 19; Payne, 1873). These schools linked the education of clergy to the wider social and cultural project of uplifting the entire race through education. Wilberforce's founding charter, for example, established "a literary institution of a high order for the education of the colored people generally, and for the purpose of preparing teachers of all grades to labor in the work of educating the colored people" (Payne, 1881, p. 101). Although placing clergy education within the context of a liberal, collegiate education was not new in the United States, linking it to the social and cultural mission of racial emancipation was.

As the nation moved through the Civil War years, the prospect of freeing over four million slaves in the South (Daniel, p. 75) led many church leaders to call for a national plan of "freedmen's education" to include the training of clergy, lawyers, and doctors. The American Missionary Society (Dwight had been one of the founders) took up the challenge, and, with the assistance of funds from the Federal Freedman's Bureau, established a network of black schools ranging from schools with liberal arts instruction, such as Howard in Washington, D.C., to normal schools such as Ely (later, Simmons) in Louisville, and technical institutes such as Hampton in Virginia (Bond, 1966, pp. 28–32; Daniel, p. 76). Black denominations also built schools and seminaries throughout the region (Lincoln and Mamiya, 1990, pp. 29-30, 53, 60, 65, 89). Eventually, black and white church organizations, working with the federal government, built over four thousand black schools throughout the South. Together they educated almost one-quarter of a million freedmen over a five-year period (Bond, p. 29).

Daniel Payne: Self-Taught Student and Educator

Daniel Payne (1811–1893), African Methodist Episcopal pastor and later bishop, helped forge this new pattern of clergy education for African American emancipation. Payne was born a freedman to parents of a pious and lower middle class background in Charleston, South Carolina. His parents, both of whom Payne lost before age ten, encouraged their son's learning in the black Methodist church there. After his parents' deaths, an aunt with means continued supporting Payne's education and spiritual growth (Griffin, 1984, pp. 96ff). Although he had had only two years of formal schooling by the age of twenty, he developed proficiency in Greek, Latin, French, classical literature, English grammar and composition, the sciences, mathematics, and philosophy (Payne, 1888, pp. 21–24). His insatiable hunger and gift for learning were given direction by a distinct call from God as a young man to "educate thyself in order that thou mayest be an educator to thy people" (Griffin, p. 3).

This calling was fueled by a job interview with an Englishman who sought an educated black man to handle his affairs. He said something Payne would never forget: "Do you know what makes the difference between the master and the slave? Nothing but superior knowledge"(Griffin, p. 20). From then on, Payne sought to close the knowledge gap between the races. Payne led a successful grammar school for African American children in Charleston until slaveholders persuaded the South Carolina legislature to outlaw all forms of schooling for blacks on April Fools Day, 1835. Heartbroken, Payne urged his students to hold on to his vision for their education:

> Pupils, attend my last departing sounds;
> Ye are my hopes, and ye my mental crowns,
> My monuments of intellectual might,
> My robes of honor and my armor bright.
> Like Solomon, entreat the throne of God;
> Light shall descend in lucid columns broad,
> And all that man has learned or man can know
> In streams prolific shall your minds o'er flow [Payne, 1859, p. 33].

Shunned as an educator in the South, Payne took his vision to Gettysburg Seminary in Pennsylvania, where he forged a theological vision for the education of his people (Griffin, p. 3).

At Gettysburg he studied with the great Lutheran theologians Samuel Schmucker and Charles Krauth. Payne coupled their understanding of Christian sanctification as ongoing progress in the Christian life with a Wesleyan notion of *perfection*: "What our Lord required was that his followers should as soon as it was practicable, become full-grown Christians"(Griffin, p. 52). Unlike many Wesleyans of his day, however, Payne linked spiritual growth to formal education as the "means of grace" for reaching the state of "sanctified knowledge" (Griffin, p. 53).

Payne was about to challenge the traditional reliance of African American congregations solely on a Spirit-filled ministry. Morris Brown, the second bishop of the AME Church, persuaded Payne the denomination could use his educational vision for the training of ministers. Over the next several years, Brown cultivated Payne's leadership and defended his controversial "Epistles on the Education of the Ministry" (Griffin, p. 3), which in 1843 had almost split the denomination. Forces in the church against an educated clergy were strong. Richard Allen, founder of the AME Church and its first bishop, along with other denominational leaders, mistrusted higher education, especially if patterned after white institutions, to serve the "plain and simple gospel" because it dampened the Spirit of God (Griffin, pp. 29–30). Payne replied to their criticism with his own call to arms: "O, cheer us, then, while we labor to beautify and array [the Christian life] on to perfection [through] sacred learning" (Payne, 1972, p. 1).

Payne struggled for years against the resistance in black churches to formal education, and after his own election to the episcopacy and "with the support of a few clergy," one commentator writes, he "literally forced higher education upon his denomination" (Griffin, p. 5).

He accomplished this task by rescuing Wilberforce University, which had fallen on hard times during the war and was about to be sold by its Methodist sponsors to the State of Ohio for an asylum. In 1863, the recently elected Bishop Payne raised enough money to buy the fifty-two-acre campus. In the midst of these efforts, and on the afternoon of President Lincoln's assassination, an arsonist set fire to the main classroom and dormitory building and several cottages, destroying everything (Payne, 1888, p. 154). Payne's abilities as a fundraiser shone after this tragedy. He tapped connections in black and white abolitionist society, raised $35,000 from the Methodist Missionary Association and $25,000 from the U.S. Congress, and, over the years, gathered numerous donations on trips throughout the nation and to England. These forays into white society secured Wilberforce's future by the turn of the century.

A Vision for the Education of Black Clergy

In 1859, Payne articulated the elements of his vision for African American ministerial education in an essay on "The Christian Ministry: Its Moral and Intellectual Character." An educated clergy was essential, first of all, to overcome the "darkness, the superstition, and errors of heathenism" in slave religion (Griffin, p. 81). This meant the conditions of white oppression shaping black spirituality must also be reformed. Second, the clergy must embrace education as a means of personal Christian growth because the Holy Spirit "insists upon a proper and diligent exercise of the intellect, for the purpose of improving it, by a daily, habitual, continuous contact with the Truth" (Payne, 1972, p. 13). Growth, for Payne, fulfills God's intent for humankind, since all people were made "for thinking, investigating [and] discriminating" so that "all their studies and researches into religion, science, and philosophy" might lead to "knowledge of the truth, as it is in Christ Jesus" (Griffin, p. 82). Establishing a close tie between learning and faith was, for Payne, key to the success of black seminaries and colleges. If education was the primary means of achieving full emancipation, it could be that only in service of a divine plan.

Third, clergy education required a formation process superior to the acquisition of facts or the skills of a trade. The character of students must be shaped to conform to their new knowledge at hand. Students must have "improvable minds" (Payne, 1972, p. 14), an "unquenchable desire for useful knowledge," and a humility that is "partly intellectual and partly moral," and they must develop "correct judgment" and "application" of what is acquired (Griffin, p. 15). Payne took the classical emphasis on education as the formation of a person, or *paideia,* and spiritualized it with a Wesleyan emphasis on uniting piety and intellect in a higher state of grace. Education, like faith, was inherently teleological for Payne; it required the development of virtues to equip people to use their newfound knowledge.

Finally, clergy education would be necessary to uplift the entire race and to demonstrate the God-given equality of African and European descendants. Payne was keenly aware of the unique role of black ministers in the new social order. The minister, above all other leaders, must exemplify the new life of freedom, and empower others to reach it: "The calamitous fact that our people are entombed in ignorance and oppression forever stares us in the face; it shall be the fuel of the flames that consume us, and while we talk, and write, and pray, we shall rise above opposition and toil, cheered and inspired by . . . God whose lips have said, 'The priest's lips should keep knowledge'" (Payne, 1972, p. 1).

The minister's charge was no less than the destiny of the race. This social and political mission required, as W.E.B. DuBois would later observe, that the black minister must be a "leader, a politician, an orator, a boss, an intrigue, an idealist" marked by an "adroitness with deep-seated earnestness, of tact with consummate ability" (Daniel, p. 29).

African American Seminary Pedagogies of Emancipation

Wilberforce adapted Methodist patterns of theological education within the liberal arts to fit the demands of racial emancipation. American Methodists had established scores of colleges across the country, with more than two hundred in the Midwest alone (Miller, p. 420). As they began to value a learned clergy, Methodists merged their small, vulnerable seminaries with their larger and more stable colleges (Miller, p. 426). In these settings, the English tradition of clergy education within the college or university was revived in the United States. Theology was in constant conversation with the liberal arts. Payne and other black educators adapted this Methodist pattern to the needs of African American emancipation. Black pastors had to embody the character and race-identification required of emancipatory leaders, and they had to be trained in an array of practical skills required of the first black-owned and -operated institutions (Mamiya, 1995, p. 45).

Despite similarities with other liberal arts institutions, Wilberforce had a distinct ethos reflecting the social and cultural mission of African American emancipation. The needs of the black community required that seminary pedagogies address an array of subjects, including economics, politics, education, and cultural expression (Mamiya, p. 46). As one historian has put it, black seminaries had to prepare leaders for a church that served as the center of the African American community: as "their school, their forum, their political arena, their social club, their art gallery, their conservatory of music" (p. 46). If the black church were to serve as "lyceum and gymnasium as well as sanctum sanctorum," its leaders must have a broad range of knowledge, as well as skills in public speaking, organizing, and leadership for the entire black community (p. 46).

Unlike their counterparts in most white, freestanding Protestant seminaries, the clergy at Wilberforce were taught in the milieu of other professions committed to black advancement, such as law, teaching, and pharmacy. For example, Payne viewed a strong normal, or teacher education, department as essential "because of its great usefulness to the work of Christian education among the freedmen" (Payne, 1873, p. 10). It also meant that black clergy, unlike most of their white counterparts, were educated in a school with women. Of one hundred and fifty-three students enrolled in 1873, for example, sixty-two were female, ninety-one male. Quite practically, this coeducational ethos meant that students could find fitting spouses to enhance the development of new, black institutions— from families to churches to businesses. In the end, working alongside future teachers, pharmacists, and journalists established the pastor as a leader with and among other black professionals as all collaborated in advancing the cause of African Americans.

Payne's dual emphasis—on education as a means of grace, and on developing racial leaders—set the stage for a distinctive emphasis on *formative* and *contextual* pedagogies in most African American seminaries in the twentieth century. Forming pastors of vision and character, who embodied the hopes of an emancipated people, was crucial to the black seminary. Not only did pastors have to be exemplary Christians, but they also had to speak for the needs and aspirations of the race in all they did. Although seminary curricula were broadened to include political, economic, and eventually black cultural studies, it was the ethos of black seminaries and colleges that embodied a new context of learning and ministry, centered on racial emancipation. The seminary, like the black church, served as a new context of freedom, in opposition to the oppressive social structures around them. Religious leadership, in this new context, required new understandings and practices of racial justice. Formation for the sake of a new social context, then, became the hallmark of African American pedagogies.

Transformation and the Pastoral Imagination

Distinctive cross-curricular practices of African American seminaries provided a common focus for faculty teaching. Emancipation required the personal transformation of black leaders through self-help and character and leadership development. Tuskegee and other institutes, for example, described their mission as "character building through practical education, industrial training, and self-help" (Washington, 1905, p. 96). Pastors and other black leaders were expected to demonstrate self-reliance and success as a model and message for the entire community. Congregations and communities expected seminary graduates to have the rhetorical skills to champion the populist message that African Americans could rise above the horrific and unjust legacy of slavery to become leading citizens of the nation. By the early twentieth century, the need for new forms of leadership among "race men and women" (Mamiya, p. 45) who could speak for their people in the face of white supremacy led to new courses in the curriculum in black history and sociology.

A second cross-curricular practice was a hermeneutic that linked a mighty and just God with personal and social transformation (LaRue, 2000). Practices of study, devotion, and homiletical inspiration forged close ties between notions of God's active justice, personal transformation, and racial solidarity. Biblical studies emphasized the mighty acts of God on behalf of a chosen people, especially through motifs of protecting and guiding people through exile and deliverance. Christian doctrine emphasized God's sovereignty and providence, not unlike the high Calvinism of Princeton (Cone, 1975, pp. 35–49; Griffin, p. 62), but always in service of a people long oppressed. History studied heroes and martyrs standing up against the Babylons of the past, including post-Reconstruction America. Yet practices of devotion and piety were deeply personal and soul changing, as they brought each and every black man and woman into the orbit of this broad and powerful narrative. These hermeneutical practices were simultaneously communal and personal, historic and situational, activating and healing.

The pastoral imagination shaped by these pedagogical emphases was one of *narrative possibility*. No other seminary tradition would form a narrative pattern of Biblical interpretation that balanced the poles of racial solidarity and individual care, social justice and tender mercy, human evil and community hope. The black preacher came to embody this dramatic narrative in his or her speaking, personal counsel, and presence. Black clergy stood for their people in everything they did—especially in the public eye of the dominant white culture. The gift of oratory was a learned practice begun in seminary life, but honed on the anvil of weekly and sometimes daily preaching, even as students. On the cusp of building a new society and raising up a people, the black pastor was looked upon as an icon of hope for a new world.

Americanizing a European Tradition

John Ireland and the U.S. Catholic Seminaries

Two educational traditions dominated U.S. Roman Catholic clergy education in the mid-nineteenth century (Schuth, 1989, pp. 11–28). The first was the *diocesan free-standing seminary,* established at St. Mary's in Baltimore in 1791. Since the Council of Trent in the 1580s, diocesan priests had been required to be trained under episcopal auspices. In the American mission field, the diocesan seminary evolved into a freestanding and independent institution, with its own facilities, faculty, and local governing board. American bishops solicited leadership for these schools from the Sulpician and Vincentian orders in France (Kauffman, 1988). Proven seminary leaders, they were readily available in the anticlerical aftermath of the French Revolution. The goal of the diocesan seminary was clerical formation of the seminarian into "the interior state of the exterior mystery" of Christ's own "states" of life, moving from the state of infancy to teacher to victim-priest (White, 1989, pp. 10–11).[8] More than twenty of these diocesan schools existed by the 1840s.[9]

The other Roman Catholic seminary tradition was the *religious order house of study.* It drew on traditions from as far back as the twelfth century that intertwined spiritual formation and theological study in preparing monks, friars, or priests for non-parish, specialized (or "apostolate") ministries.[10] In these houses of study, seminarians were trained alongside laity in a college program (Schuth, 1989, p. 30). The spiritual gift and calling or charism of each order's founder; the freedom from episcopal oversight; their nonparish orientation to ministry through teaching, service to the poor, health care, or evangelism; and their independence from diocesan authority and structures distinguished them from the diocesan seminary.[11] Contemporary Roman Catholic seminaries, while extending these two traditions into the twenty-first century, have also seen many changes. The story of their development during the latter part of the nineteenth century is inextricably interwoven with the vision and work of John Ireland (1838–1918), an Irish immigrant who would become the bishop of St. Paul, Minnesota.

John Ireland: Young Immigrant and Seminarian

Ireland was born in rural Ireland. His father, a carpenter and small parcel farmer, was a harsh disciplinarian hardened by labor; his mother was devout and protective of her six children. The family joined the one and a half million Irish fleeing to America after the great famines of the late 1840s (Curran and Emmett, 1988, p. 184). By 1852, the family had migrated to St. Paul, Minnesota, where the Catholic Church was led by Joseph Cretin, a graduate of the premier French Sulpician seminary.

Bishop Cretin recruited Ireland when he was fourteen for seminary formation in France. There he joined the *petit seminaire* of Meximieux, which provided the academic and spiritual prerequisites for entrance into the *grand seminaire*. A detailed spiritual and academic regimen carefully habituated seminarians into an *esprit ecclesiastique* for the priestly life (O'Connell, 1988, pp. 45ff.; Schuth, 1989, p. 30). Students arose at 5:30 A.M., recited three Hail Marys, washed, dressed quickly, and went to morning prayers and silent meditation guided by devotional manuals. After low mass was celebrated and breakfast shared, students attended class; this was followed by community lunch and a brief time of self-examination. The curriculum focused on the classics: first in Latin—Cicero, Horace, Virgil; then in French—La Fontaine, Bossuet, Racine, and Moliere. Only the ablest students, Ireland among them, were allowed to study Greek. Other subjects in the humanities included geography, history, science, and mathematics. In the afternoon, students engaged in physical exercise or work on the grounds. Dinner was preceded by a community recitation of the rosary and followed by individual study. Students had a brief nightly prayer and self-examination; then the lights went out around 9:30 P.M.

Ireland remembered the *petite seminaire* as a place of "unalloyed happiness" (O'Connell, p. 45). His subsequent years at the *grand seminaire* run by the Marists (Society of Mary) in Montbel were less satisfying (O'Connell, pp. 56–68). Although some of the traditional theology he was taught took hold, any sense of *fraternite* with the religious brothers did not. Whether he thought the Marists' mission in the South Pacific too narrow or their efforts to wrestle autonomy from the local bishop too self-serving (O'Connell, pp. 56–57), Ireland developed a suspicion of religious orders that he took back to Minnesota, where he served the church first as priest and later as bishop.

Forging a Public Priesthood for America

Ireland may have been a scholar in his own mind, but he was an activist at heart. Through his engagement with social and cultural issues of the day, Ireland forged a vision of a "prosperous, civic-minded Catholicism" that would eventually shape his view of seminary education (Curran, p. 195). The temperance crusade provided Ireland with a national platform for his ministry and the Church (O'Connell, pp. 88–114). He successfully organized a statewide Catholic Abstinence League, traveled widely in the United States and Europe to speak out against the destruction of Christian homes and the political corruption of allied moneyed interests and liquor industry lobbies (O'Connell, p. 249), and eventually was elected to lead the national Catholic Total Abstinence Union of America.

Ireland championed land and labor rights for new, and mostly Catholic, immigrants. Ireland's answer to the urban blight of the East was to resettle immigrants in the land-rich West (O'Connell, pp. 135–61). With Bishop Spalding of St. Louis, Ireland founded local and national immigration societies, including the Catholic Colonization Bureau. As a broker of land grants given to the Western railroads, the Colonization Bureau sold lands to immigrants at a fair price; the railroads provided inexpensive transportation and supplies to create settlements on their routes, and the diocese received a free parcel of land for building a church and school in each new town. By 1880, Ireland's Colonization Bureau had made eleven land sale ventures with the railroads, and helped settle over 380,000 acres in western Minnesota, from which he received handsome commissions (Wangler, 1988, p. 68).

Ireland worked with Archbishop Gibbons of Baltimore to ally the Catholic Church with American labor unions. The rapid industrialization of American cities created poor working conditions for immigrants, which labor organizations tried to redress (O'Connell, pp. 230ff). The largest of these, the Noble and Holy Order of the Knights of Labor, was mostly Catholic in membership, and it operated in secret out of fear of owner reprisals. Pope Leo XIII had prohibited church involvement in any secret society, because he associated them with the anticlericalism of the Masons. With anxieties heightened by labor crises, such as the Chicago Haymarket riots of 1886, the American archbishops disagreed over supporting the Knights of Labor. With local persuasion and international diplomacy, Ireland and Gibbons received an "exemption" from the pope's ban for the Knights, thereby securing the Catholic Church's identification with labor in America for decades to come (O'Connell, p. 394).

Finally, Ireland forged a partnership between Catholic and public schooling in Minnesota that had repercussions even in Rome. Catholics objected to the Protestant character of American public schools, including the plain reading of the Protestant King James Bible (Lannie, 1988). After becoming archbishop of Minnesota in 1888, Ireland promoted a public-parochial school partnership in the townships of Faribault and Stillwater, and he defended the plan in an address to the National Education Association in 1890, "The State School and the Parish School— Is Union between Them Impossible?" (O'Connell, pp. 294–96). The controversy raged among the archbishops, with the "Americanists" on Ireland's side and the traditionalists pitted against him.[12] Finally, Pope Leo XIII approved Ireland's plan, greatly enhancing his prestige in the Vatican and at home. Ironically, the partnership was short-lived in Minnesota, but Ireland's reputation for public leadership in schooling had been established. Consequently, Ireland's intense public involvement with temperance, immigration, labor, and public education secured his national reputation as a public priest and bishop. He loomed larger than life over the seminarians under his care, modeling a level of ecclesial statesmanship to which they could only aspire.

The Third Council of Baltimore: A New Plan for Seminaries

When the Third Plenary Council of Baltimore convened in 1884,[13] Ireland was poised, with episcopal rank and national fame, to exert some real influence. Rome called the council to standardize clergy education, streamline relations with the bishops, and rein in the sometimes unruly American provinces (White, 1989, pp. 145–64). This goal was met, in part, through the first uniform plan for seminary organization among either Catholics or Protestants in the United States. Major seminaries would be established in each archdiocese or province, and minor or preparatory seminary programs would, ideally, be established in each diocese. The plan endorsed episcopal control over seminary training and a strong liberal arts background for the priesthood, as Ireland had hoped.

Ireland advocated for strong academic standards and a long formation period for seminarians. The six-year *minor seminary curriculum* (White, 1989, pp. 155–56) included Latin and English, basic reading in Greek, and ethnic languages (such as German) when appropriate. A liberal arts education was endorsed, to include history, geography, mathematics, natural sciences, music, and bookkeeping. The capstone was a strong foundation in church doctrine. The *major seminary curriculum* (White, 1989,

p. 157), also six years, would consist of philosophical subjects—from metaphysics to ethics—and natural sciences. Theology included dogmatic and moral theology, biblical exegesis, church history, canon law, the theory and practice of liturgy, homiletics, and ascetic theology with a spiritual director. Philosophy and theology courses, following the 1879 *Aeterni Patris* of Leo XIII, were to adhere to the writings of Thomas Aquinas as an antidote to modernity.

Founder of Schools

A strong seminary tradition existed in Minnesota before Ireland was even ordained. Benedictines, at the invitation of Bishop Cretin, established a monastery and seminary near St. Cloud in 1856, patterned after St. Vincent's in Pennsylvania (White, 1989, pp. 116–117; O'Connell, pp. 198–199). St. John's effectively trained religious and diocesan priests especially for ministries in German-speaking communities. Within a decade, St. John's became an abbey, with a national reputation for learning and spiritual formation. The Minnesota legislature bestowed degree-granting rights on the seminary in 1869, and in 1878 it was recognized by the Holy See as one of only a few pontifical faculties in the United States able to grant doctoral degrees.

Ireland's long-held prejudice against religious orders and his public debates with St. John's over temperance led him to limit the influence of the abbey and to establish his own seminary. He acquired a Catholic industrial school, in which he opened St. Thomas Aquinas Seminary in 1885 with six faculty and sixty-two students. His envisioned in St. Thomas an "American Meximieux," or *petite seminaire,* for high school and college students and seminarians. St. Thomas promised to "make the young man a scholar, in the true and full sense of the word, ready for the theological seminary, or for the schools of law and medicine, or qualified for any social position he may covet" (O'Connell, p. 205). Ireland insisted on a liberal arts education at the heart of the curriculum, and he occasionally interrupted a professor's lesson to lead a spontaneous reading of Virgil. The school produced sixty-three priests before the *grand seminaire* was built, almost ten years later.

The long-awaited dream of a Catholic University in America also came to fruition, in part, from Ireland's work. One of his friends from Colonization days, Bishop Spalding of Peoria, made the close acquaintance of a young heiress, Mary Caldwell, who pledged $300,000 for a national university. Spalding and Caldwell envisioned "An American Catholic University" that would "never be under the control of any religious order" and would always be governed by the bishops (O'Connell, p. 208). Americanists rallied around the school as the hope of Catholic youth to become "intimately conscious of the truth of their religion and of the genius of their country" (O'Connell, p. 208). Even traditionalists like Corrigan and McQuaid supported the concept, but quarreled over the proposed site of Washington, D.C. as an encroachment on the Jesuits at Georgetown. The Americanists finally won the day, due to Caldwell's insistence. Ireland's proposed name, "Catholic University of America," was adopted, and John Keane, another Americanist, was appointed the first rector. Initially, the Vatican balked at the idea of a "graduate theology program" in fledgling America, but after some revisions of the plan and a direct appeal from Cardinal Gibbons, Leo XIII approved, and it opened in 1889 (White, 1989, pp. 189–96).

The Saint Paul Seminary

Ireland was determined to establish a *grand seminaire* for his province, but securing the finances was daunting. With the crash of 1893, the fortunes of the archdiocese—and of Ireland's vast land holdings—took a nosedive. But the wealthy owner of the Great Northern Railroad, James J. Hill, whom Ireland had met through the Colonization Bureau, came to his aid. Though nominally a Methodist, Hill supported Ireland's dream, partly in devotion to his Roman Catholic wife, but more as an investment in the new pool of immigrant labor in the West. He wanted to Americanize the immigrants through an educated priesthood:

> Look at the millions of foreigners pouring into this country to whom the Roman Catholic Church represents the only authority that they either fear or respect. What will be their social views, their political action, their moral status if that single controlling force should be removed? It is not of any more importance to the Church that young men should be educated for its priesthood than it is to the State that this undigested mass of foreign material should be dealt with by those who alone have power to mould it into new shape. . . . This is as much a matter of good business as is the improvement of farm stock or the construction of a faultless railroad bed [Moynihan, 1953, pp. 243–44].

Hill contributed $250,000 for the palatial seminary grounds, and gave another $3,000,000 for an endowment (White, 1989, p. 175). Due to Ireland's own financial troubles, Hill insisted on managing every dime and detail of the construction. Meanwhile, Ireland commissioned O'Connell of the American College of Rome to recruit a first-rate European faculty—including, if possible, Alfred Loisy. Although Loisy had been dismissed from a Paris institute for his modernism, Ireland still considered him "the best biblical scholar in the Church" (Moynihan, p. 244; cf. White, 1989, p. 200).

When the seminary opened its doors in 1895, it had a promising young faculty of eight scholars (without Loisy). The curriculum covered all the foundations identified by the Third Council of Baltimore: two years of philosophical sciences, hermeneutics, and classical languages (from Hebrew to Latin), and four years of theological sciences, from dogmatics to moral theology to history to liturgics and homiletics (White, 1989, p. 239). But Ireland was intent on adding the modern sciences and literature, to create true faithful priests who were also "gentlemen" of the age (p. 212). For Ireland, a seminary education should be steeped in Catholic tradition and enlivened by contemporary knowledge:

> First, theology. Whatever else the priest takes with him into the world, if he carries not in soul and in hand the Gospel of Christ, he is not a minister of Christ. The sciences covet the aid of faith, which is a voice from the far-beyond, whereof nature is silent. Faith appeals to the sciences for confirmation of its credibility. Nature and grace intermingle, and unite in chanting to the Author of both a hymn of adoration and thanksgiving. Political economy and sociology are so akin to moral theology that I should bring them into the closest quarters with it. Literature should be called upon to unfold in seminary halls the treasure of its graces and elegance of form [Moynihan p. 245; cf. White, 1989, p. 243].

Professional courses were added to address the duties of the modern priest, including a two-year homiletics course "in which theory was combined with practice" (White, 1989, p. 252). The school became the first in the nation to affiliate with Catholic University, which bestowed a bachelor's degree upon its graduates, and allowed for an advanced licentiate with one more year of study in Washington, D.C. (p. 202). Ireland followed closely the guidelines of the Third Council of Baltimore, even though he failed "to see the good" in a strictly Thomistic theology (p. 244). St. Paul's was truly a graduate institution, and it was the first seminary in the region, Catholic or Protestant, to earn a "secular" accreditation by the North Central Association.

Although the academic program at St. Paul's was rigorous, the daily regimen still reflected Sulpician discipline, American style. Students rose around 5:00 A.M. and had morning meditation, mass, then breakfast. Classes ran through the morning and early afternoon, interrupted by lunch and some physical recreation. The afternoon ended with more recreation, a popular devotion, and dinner. Evening consisted of personal examination, rosary devotions, and evening prayer followed by a period of study (White, 1989, pp. 220–221). The seminary was equipped with a modern gymnasium, providing seminarians an hour or two of freedom from their cassocks (p. 230). A vigilant chapter of the Catholic Abstinence League reinforced a strict policy of no smoking and no drinking. Although near the College of St. Thomas, the seminary was entirely self-contained, and off-campus privileges were restricted. The priest-only ethos reflected the *esprit ecclesiastique* Ireland had known in France: "I offer the best tribute of love I can to my seminary of Meximieux, by striving to reproduce it in the seminary of St. Paul" (O'Connell, p. 54).

Catholic Pedagogies of Formation

Classroom pedagogies of late-nineteenth-century Catholic seminaries still relied on the daily recitation and discussion of approved manuals and textbooks. Whereas most manuals in the fields of philosophy and theology came from Europe, new manuals in pastoral theology written in the United States emphasized the public role of the American priest as "preacher and teacher" in the pulpit and parochial school (White, 1989, pp. 214–216). Likewise, new manuals in moral theology applied Catholic teaching to American pluralism, democracy, and church-state relations. In 1896, John Talbott Smith wrote that the new modern seminary stressed the professional skills and the "spirit, ability, education and refinement" fitting an American priest (White, p. 218). When Smith's monograph was read to Ireland's students, they proclaimed, "The author must have had St. Paul Seminary in mind when he wrote this book" (p. 219).

The unique pedagogies of the Catholic seminary lay in its *telos* of formation. At St. Paul's, Ireland spoke regularly of the "model priest" as *gentleman, scholar,* and *saint* (White, 1989, pp. 213–14, 219). By "gentlemen," Ireland meant men of their age, "who know the period, the condition of people's minds" such that "no man of education need to be ashamed to acknowledge [him] as pastor" (p. 212). By "scholar," Ireland had in mind the liberally educated priest, not the specialist. The strong liberal arts and science curricula of the seminary were designed to cultivate a "passion for books," and "good preaching and writing" to speak to the people's interest (pp. 213–214). By "saint," Ireland shared the views of Cardinal Gibbons, who described the priest in *The Ambassador for*

Christ (1896) as one who exhibits not only the supernatural virtues of prayer and contemplation but also the outward, human virtues of humility, truthfulness, politeness, and cheerfulness. Both Ireland and Gibbons endorsed Paulist founder Father Isaac Hecker's emphasis on the "natural and social virtues" of active public service in the life of the priest (White, p. 233; cf. O'Connell, pp. 288–89).

The nineteenth-century Catholic seminaries set the precedent for the *interpretive* and *formative* pedagogies of the twentieth-century seminaries. Ireland sought to combine the interpretive frameworks of ecclesiastical tradition and modern, liberal education in the formation of a new kind of priest. Above all, the priest would become an interpreter of the church in the modern age of science and advancement. In contrast to the specializations of the university, modern priests were to be well-rounded generalists, grounded in the classics and familiar with their times. Although the *telos* of seminary education remained the *formation* of ecclesial representatives, priests had to also be leaders of their age. The spiritual and ecclesiastical formation of the priest had to be combined with the civic-minded requirements of a public leader.

Two Patterns of Priestly Imagination

The cross-curricular framework that marked St. Paul Seminary was that of *liberal education*. Becoming a "gentleman priest" meant that one had to relate the Catholic tradition to Western classics as well as modern sciences. Thomas Aquinas was taught alongside Virgil and modern biology. This alliance of Catholicism, classic humanism, and modern science was seen as integral to the advance of "Western civilization" in the Americas. Ideally, young seminarians developed an interdisciplinary framework of interpretation and a passion for continued self-study that would continue. As they began to serve parishes and mission sites, they were expected to converse with the most educated members of these societies and the wider public. If Ireland was the example, the ultimate success of the educated priest lay in his ability to become a civic leader in his own community, beyond the confines of parish or charge.

The most influential cross-curricular pedagogies in all the Catholic seminaries, however, were the communal practices of spiritual formation, developed from Sulpician or religious order regimens. Regular practices of morning and evening prayer, daily mass, self-examination, devotions, and corporate readings continued throughout the twentieth century in most schools. Seminarians were expected to adopt the sacramental and devotional practices that would sustain them throughout their priesthood.

They were carefully socialized into a way of life and a brotherhood that would last a lifetime. As we saw in the chapter on formative pedagogies (Chapter Four), learning to embody the presence of God and the virtues of a priestly way of life is crucial to such formation. Regardless of changes in curricula, supervision, and field education, the daily regimen of the spiritual life served as the integrating framework for most Catholic seminaries.

What emerged in the nineteenth century were two distinct patterns of the priestly imagination (Schuth, 1989, pp. 141–51). Father Hecker, Ireland, and the Americanists argued for a priestly imagination that is *liberal minded* and *missional,* which allows one to be both apologist and activist for the Catholic Church. Knowing and praying the tradition was important, but so was acting on its implications for a new, democratic society. In this view, priestly formation emphasized a *personal integration* of the tradition with the natural virtues of public service and activism. The traditionalists proposed another view of the priestly imagination as *representational* and *sacramental,* in a way that embodied in sacramental office and devotion the presence of Christ. Priests, they maintained, must embody the supernatural virtues of contemplation and prayer to serve as models of the Christian life. The view of formation among the traditionalists emphasized the *identification* of seminarians with a spiritualized Christ and the model of the priesthood seen in those who taught them.

Renewing Tradition and the Modern University

Solomon Schecter and the Jewish Seminaries

By the dawn of the twentieth century, modern science and history were making their impact on American seminary training. As Darwinism drove a wedge between those religious traditions that would adapt and those that would resist the new science, more subtle changes in the canons of knowledge and education began to seep into all religious traditions. The dominant paradigm of Scottish Common Sense philosophy—with its Baconian emphasis on facts and moral intuition—was giving way to views of knowledge influenced by philosophies of idealism, romanticism, and pragmatism (Kuklick, pp. 128–39, 191–202). History was increasingly viewed as a dynamic process, whether as a function of the Absolute Spirit (Hegel), natural evolution (Darwin), or proletariat revolution (Marx). Canons of research shifted from making factual statements about the world to developing strategies of intervention and change through industrial technology, educational reform, and social and political reconstruction.

Religious traditions in America responded to this modern transformation along a spectrum: from more accommodating (*modernist*) responses to more reactionary (*fundamentalist*) responses. Methods of theological research followed in kind: from historical-critical reconstruction of religious texts to empiricist reiterations of basic textual "facts" and doctrinal "truths." The accommodating response often dismissed cherished claims of "miracles" or "revelation," and the reactionary option often barricaded itself against modern historiography and epistemology. Both sides embraced technology and industrialization as a sign of their openness to progress, but one movement (the modernists) aligned itself more with urbanization and the other (the fundamentalists) with the ideals of the preindustrial township. Most responses included some degree of adaptation to modernity, as long as it did not compromise their core religious identity. One of the chief mediators of modernity and religious tradition in the education of clergy was Solomon Schechter.

From Yeshiva to University

Schechter (1847–1915) was born into a Hasidic Jewish family that fled Russia for greater freedom in Romania. The Hasidim began as a pious rebellion against the yeshiva tradition of intellectual rigor, but the Schechter family belonged to the Habad sect known (at least in the nineteenth century) for its love of learning and less excessive devotion to its *zaddik* (leader). The scope of learning in this Hasidic community, however, lay within the strict confines of Ashkenazi Judaism of central Europe, which, unlike the Sephardic Judaism of Spain, eschewed modern science and philosophy for a singular focus on the Talmud. Schechter left home, against his father's wishes, to attend a Romanian yeshiva devoted to the study of the Talmud. Like any yeshiva of the day, this school was patterned after the great Talmudic schools of Lithuania, which had survived Napoleon's closure of other yeshivot in Europe. The traditional yeshiva was devoted to the study of the Talmud for its own sake (Torah *lishma*), as an act of devotion as well as intellectual growth (Helmreich, 1986). Since the post-biblical literature was so vast, the yeshiva could hope to instill only basic principles and study habits that the student could exercise over a lifetime of learning. Students spent twenty-five to thirty hours per week studying these classic Jewish texts. The only secular studies included in the yeshiva were those demanded by the state.

As a scholarly prodigy, or *ilüy*, Schechter pursued further study in Vienna, where he was exposed to the Jewish Haskalah, or Enlightenment.

This movement originated in eighteenth-century Germany under Moses Mendelssohn, who advocated the incorporation of modern learning into Jewish education. In Vienna, Schechter continued Talmudic studies with scholars who explored the Talmud in a scientific vein (Bentwich, 1938, p. 36). After four years, he received the rabbinical ordination, though he would never exercise the office in a synagogue. He then went to one of the most renowned schools of the new "Science of Judaism" in Berlin, the *Hochschule fur die Wissenschaft des Judentums* (Academy of Jewish Science), founded by the leader of Reform Judaism, Abraham Geiger. There he continued studies of Bible, Talmud, and rabbinical literature in a strict historical-critical approach and simultaneously took up studies at the famed University of Berlin in psychology, ethics, pedagogy, aesthetics, philosophy, Hebrew, Syriac, and textual criticism (Bentwich, 1938, pp. 44–45). The compatibility of Talmudic study with modern scholarship began to form in Schechter's mind.

Wissenschaft *Versus Tradition in the Modern University*

The University of Berlin was founded in the early 1800s as the quintessential university of the Enlightenment. In all fields of study—from the humanities to the natural sciences—modern canons of inquiry, or *wissenschaft,* would reign. For the "pure sciences," like philosophy, universal canons of reason were established to provide a comprehensive foundation for the other disciplines. For the natural sciences, empirical data was identified, catalogued, and organized by categories of universal reason. In the human sciences, like history or religion, the texts and traditions of a given culture or religion were examined by historical-critical methods and interpreted by rules of interpretation that laid out the content and various meanings of such texts. As a "positive" science, religion was examined historically and culturally apart from any traditional canons of "authority" or "revelation" (Kelsey, 1992, pp. 78–98).

Although Geiger hoped his new Academy of Jewish Science would be accepted as a graduate department at the University of Berlin on scientific grounds (Schwarzfuchs, 1993, p. 89), anti-Semitism was too strong, and his hope was not realized. His *hochschule,* however, operated as a Jewish college in the university. A number of scholars taught in both institutions, and gifted students like Schechter moved back and forth between them. In most respects, the methods of research and study at the *hochschule* were like those at the University of Berlin. Sacred texts of the Bible and Talmud were exposed to modern, historical critical methods of research.

Traditional understandings of authorship and divine revelation, like the Mosaic origin of the Pentateuch, were regularly challenged. Historical criticism contextualized ancient ritual practices and moral teachings, but in so doing it distanced most students from religious practice. Most important, perhaps, the study of the Torah was no longer viewed as an act of devotion but rather as an act of objective, scientific inquiry. Geiger himself carried out historical critical studies of the Talmud, the prophets, and even the Pentateuch, in a way that raised radical questions of origin, authorship, and the viability of religious practice. Unlike the Christian school of theology at the university, however, the *hochschule* did not have the integrating field of "professional practice" because it did not focus on the training of rabbis.

For two reasons, Schechter never embraced the secular form of *Wissenschaft des Judentums* in the *hochschule*. First, he saw Geiger's historical-critical work as serving the German university more than Jewish tradition. He perceived that it cut living Judaism from its moorings, and its message of universal salvation facilitated the assimilation of many in the Jewish community into German Christian life and culture. Second, and more important, Schechter watched the methods of scholarship in German universities being used against Jews. He saw in the "higher criticism" of scholars like Julius Wellhausen a "higher anti-Semitism" (Schechter, 1915, p. 37), because it historicized Israel's development into a sterile religion of law and "took the soul out of religion" (Bentwich, p. 45). The views of the famous church historian Adolph Harnack displayed "not so much his hatred as his ignorance of Judaism" (Bentwich, p. 37). In short, Schechter despised those modern scholars—Christian or Jewish—who, with only a smattering of Hebrew and complete ignorance of the Talmud, claimed to sum up "the Jewish spirit" in a paragraph or two. Schechter knew that modern, historical methods of scholarship would not serve Judaism, or any religion, unless they respected an historical understanding of "tradition" as a living reservoir of knowledge, again made accessible to modern life.

Wissenschaft *in the Service of Tradition*

Schechter found that living sense of tradition at Cambridge. First invited to England by a friend in 1882, he was recruited to join the university faculty as a lecturer in 1890, and in 1895 he became a reader in Semitics and Hebrew literature. Although Cambridge was a bastion of classical learning and clergy formation for the English church, it also housed fine rabbinic scholars such as Charles Taylor. British museums and libraries held over half of the known Hebrew manuscripts in the world, simply waiting to be mined by a scholar of Schechter's ability. Schechter's fame as a scholar was enhanced by his discovery of one of the greatest storehouses of ancient Hebrew manuscripts, the Cairo *geniza*, or repository for buried Torah scrolls (Bentwich, pp. 126ff). With a tip from two English women travelers who brought back a page of *Ben Sira* in Hebrew—the first known to the modern world—he traveled to Cairo, and he negotiated for months to have over one hundred thousand manuscripts returned to England. For years he combed the manuscripts, publishing the first modern edition of *Ben Sira* in Hebrew, with commentary, and numerous articles on the *Geniza* manuscripts (Schechter, 1915). With such success, and an environment hospitable to the wedding of scholarship and religious devotion, Schechter could have remained at Cambridge for years.

However, he longed for a stronger Jewish environment for his family and sensed that the destiny of Judaism lay elsewhere. He came to believe that America would be the site of a new Jewish Renaissance. When the invitation came to lead a newly reorganized Jewish Theological Seminary in America, he accepted the challenge. There he found a place where he could combine modern research methods (*wissenschaft*) with the piety of studying for God's sake (yeshiva).

The Jewish Theological Seminary in America

With the hope of bringing Schechter from England, some Jewish leaders in New York had planned a reorganization of the Jewish Theological Seminary to become the kind of center for Jewish scholarship that Schechter had envisioned (Raphael, 2003, pp. 142–44; Sarna, 1997). In 1902, a coup d'etat wrested the seminary leadership from clergy control. The new charter called for "the perpetuation of the tenets of the Jewish religion, the cultivation of Hebrew literature, the pursuit of Biblical and archaeological research, the advancement of Jewish scholarship, the establishment of a library, and the education and training of Jewish rabbis and teachers" in the spirit of the first modern Jewish seminary at the University of Breslau (Schwarzfuchs, p. 113). The clear priority was scholarship in service of Jewish practice and culture to include training religious leaders. This model was closer to the modern university than to the yeshiva, and it was expected that rabbinical students would already have a bachelor's degree from a secular university before admittance. Jewish Theological Seminary established a moderate Orthodoxy, somewhere between the Reform seminary at Hebrew Union College and the Orthodox seminary, which later joined Yeshiva University.

When Schechter arrived in the United States, three rabbinical seminaries had already been established in the country. In 1875, Isaac Wise had founded Hebrew Union College in Cincinnati as a center of Jewish learning and rabbinical training for all American Jews. Within a decade, however, Hebrew Union's main constituency of German immigrant and Reform Jews had made major changes in liturgy, jettisoned the dietary law, and emphasized the universal messages of the Bible. Although Wise maintained strong rabbinical studies in his curriculum, by 1900 the school had evolved from a broad-based center of Jewish scholarship to a more traditional American seminary serving the needs for denominational leadership. Jewish Theological Seminary had been founded in New York in 1887 as a direct response to Reform Judaism by Sabato Morais and others who sought new leadership for the masses of new Jewish immigrants to the city. It was patterned after European seminaries, like the Jewish Theological Seminary of Breslau, which combined a moderate *Wissenschaft des Judentums* with Orthodox religious practice and rabbinical studies. Some Orthodox communities wanted a more traditional yeshiva, so with the arrival of the great Lithuanian Talmudist Bernard Revel, the Rabbi Isaac Elchanan Theological Seminary was established in New York in 1896. Eventually, this school allowed some *hokmah,* or secular studies to prepare Orthodox rabbis to function in an English-speaking society, and it joined Yeshiva University in the 1920s.

Under Schechter's leadership, Jewish Theological Seminary became the center of *Wissenschaft des Judentums* in America and the Conservative movement in Judaism (Schwartz, 1997). He gathered scholars of international renown who firmly established the reputation of the school (Ellenson and Bycel, 1997), including Levi Ginzburg in Talmud, Israel Friedlaender in Bible, Alexander Marx in history, and Joseph Mayor Asher in homiletics. They were not only great scholars but also devout practitioners. Schechter established the primacy of textual research, as "many a Seminary graduate was expected to demonstrate his prowess at editing a manuscript text" without commentaries (Sarna, 1997, p. 59). Jewish Theological Seminary promoted a view of the rabbi as scholar to help revive contemporary Judaism. The faculty embodied this tradition by publishing scholarly editions of classic Jewish texts, especially in the Schiff Library collection.

Rabbinical Pedagogies of Cultural Renewal

Schechter raised rabbinical studies in America to a post-baccalaureate level marked by two traditions of teaching and learning. After preparatory study and exams, the rabbinical student at Jewish Theological Seminary began a four-year immersion in the linguistic and textual study of classical Jewish texts, which marked the first tradition. Unlike the traditional yeshiva, the texts at Jewish Theological Seminary included "almost every branch of Jewish literature" (Ellenson and Bycel, p. 543), from Bible and Talmud to Jewish philosophy and mysticism. Seminary pedagogies became a means of retrieving and reclaiming classic Jewish literature. The formal, text-based curriculum at Jewish Theological Seminary included twenty-five hours per week and was based on classical texts in their original languages.[14] Well into the twentieth century, students were expected to write a scholarly commentary on one of the classic texts; many of these were published.

The second tradition of teaching and learning at Jewish Theological Seminary involved the preparation of the rabbi as a cultural and religious teacher who "should know everything Jewish" (Ellenson and Bycel, p. 540), including traditional folklore and contemporary issues. Schechter envisioned the rabbi as a consummate "doer" who extended *gemiluth chasadim,* or social work, to the community as "an organizer, a social agitator, and expert on all topics of the day" (Ellenson and Bycel, p. 540). The Teachers Institute, run by Mordecai Kaplan, especially prepared rabbis and Jewish educators to renew Hebrew learning and Jewish culture and causes in these ways. Both scholarly traditions at Jewish Theological Seminary worked in tandem to prepare rabbis who were "traditional at their core and modern in their forms" (Sarna, 1997, p. 65). Thus the school held together modern textual scholarship with the development of leaders for "Catholic Israel," by which Schechter meant all Jewish civilization.

Consequently, the nineteenth-century rabbinic schools set the precedent for *interpretive* and *contextual pedagogies* that continued into the twentieth century. On the one hand, the interpretation of classical texts, informed by modern scholarship, remained the hallmark of rabbinical seminaries until late in the century.[15] Rabbis educated in America became community scholars of classic Jewish literature, through their command of original languages, textual structure, and histories. On the other hand, the seminaries increased their emphasis on *contextual* studies of Jewish civilization, including Hebrew studies, Jewish literature and folklore, and contemporary Jewish issues. American rabbis, in particular, mobilized Jews in the United States to become informed and active around the causes of Russian persecution, immigrants, anti-Semitism, the Holocaust, and the founding of Israel. Instead of being sidelined to a cultural enclave, however, these studies and causes were brilliantly linked by seminaries and their graduates to larger issues of human rights, social justice, and

Western democracy. Modern rabbis became leaders in the cultural renewal of Judaism as a force in the modern world.

Legal Disputation and the Rabbinical Imagination

The centrality of *halakhah* (law) in early rabbinical education in America cannot be overemphasized. The yeshiva tradition inherited by the seminary focused on "halakhic application" of the Talmud (Liebman, 1974, p. 42), as it culled legal directives and principles of judgment from the text, through ongoing argumentation. Traditional methods focused intensely on every minutia of the text, while others involved an "extremely clear and sharp analysis of basic principles which, as if in a flash, illuminate entire subjects and many difficulties" (Berkovits, 1975, p. 291). A professor's arguments with the rabbinic literature drew students into the debate and served as a model for their own debates with each other. Above all, the study of the Bible and Talmud was "at one and the same time a religious obligation, a spiritual exercise, a mode of worship, and a moral as well as an intellectual discipline" (Sarna, 1997, p. 69). In the twentieth century, the rules of this disputational style became more clearly defined to include patterns of "inner Biblical exegesis" (Sarna, 1997, p. 69), intratextuality between different rabbinical works, rhetorical analysis of each section of the Mishnah and Talmud, and complex patterns of halakhic judgment (Neusner, 2003).

What emerged is a form of the rabbinical imagination marked by *dialogue* and *disputation*. The interpretive practices of argument and debate—both within and outside the classroom—constituted a dialogical practice of reading the Talmud and engaging contemporaries. Talmudic patterns of exposition are extended to community life by juxtaposing sacred texts with contemporary issues. The goal is not to yield a definitive interpretation, but to continue the process of debate and dialogue within the living context of "Catholic Israel." Although the study and debate of sacred texts is, in itself, a devotional act, it also has direct implications for religious practice in the community. Reform and Conservative seminaries, each in their own way, for example, debated the halakhic and societal issues, including the entrance of women into the rabbinate.

Legacies in Seminary Education

The pioneers of these five traditions of seminary education exerted a lasting influence on the way clergy have been educated in the United States. The mission, ethos, and pedagogies of each type of institution reflect the unique experience and concerns of the founders and their religious communities. Often seminary traditions combined, with unusual strength, two of the four pedagogies we have described in earlier chapters. For example, mainline Protestant seminaries sought to balance *intellect* and *piety* by stressing the pedagogies of *interpretation* and *performance,* which linked text-based studies to rhetorical skills and professional roles, while relegating personal piety to corporate worship and student associations. Fundamentalist-evangelical seminaries, by contrast, stressed *Biblical piety* and *mission work* through pedagogies of *formation* and *performance,* which joined communal pedagogies of millennial devotion with skills-oriented training in social service and marketing. African American seminaries emphasized *social uplift* and *exemplary leadership* through pedagogies of *contextualization* and *formation,* thereby linking the social struggle of an emancipated people with the development of clergy who identified themselves as "race men and women" (Mamiya, p. 45). Catholic seminaries, especially of the Americanists, combined *monastic rigor* and *the liberal arts,* through pedagogies of *formation* and *interpretation,* which shaped priests as "gentleman scholars" steeped in Catholic tradition and modern learning. Jewish seminaries sought a new mediation of *tradition* and *wissenschaft* through pedagogies of *interpretation* and *contextualization,* combining legal disputation and strategies of cultural renewal in the work of the rabbi. Within each tradition of seminary education, distinct pedagogies emerged to address the founders' concerns for professionalism, skills and piety, emancipation, formation, and cultural renewal.

ENDNOTES

1. The curriculum of the Greenfield Academy included reading, penmanship, composition, spelling, English grammar, arithmetic, algebra, spherics, calculus, Newton's *Principia,* Greek New Testament, natural philosophy, declamation and belles lettres, geography, and history (Cunningham, p. 144).

2. These were followers of the strict disciple of Edwards, Samuel Hopkins, and were called "Hopkinsians" in their day.

3. By the year of Dryer's departure, in 1872, Illinois State Normal University exceeded the enrollment, vision, and annual expenditures of any other normal school in the nation (Harper, p. 80).

4. By 1877, Dryer could report 673 cottage prayer-meetings, 78 mother's meetings, 165 school prayer-meetings, 502 sessions of the Sewing School,

2,820 calls for Bible reading, 479 visits to the sick, and 10,625 tracts distributed (Getz, p. 34).

5. Mildmay was established by Rev. William Pennefether in 1864. He also founded the Mildmay Deaconess home in 1869. The work of the Mildmay Deaconesses was so successful that it became the model for the Deaconess movement throughout the Methodist church in England and the United States (Dobschuetz, p. 46).

6. Darby founded the unique theology of the Plymouth Brethren church in 1830. It was based upon a combination of literal biblical interpretation, Puritanical morals, and futuristic predictions about the end times.

7. A cross-denominational conference for evangelicals, founded at Keswick in 1875, stressed "practical holiness" in all aspects of the Christian life.

8. The Sulpicians emphasized shaping the seminarian in a pattern of self-identification with Christ through "spiritual states" that corresponded with stages of Christ's own life: his infancy, teachings, and crucifixion.

9. Only with the opening of new archdioceses in the expanding United States were lasting, freestanding diocesan schools founded in numbers: Mt. St. Mary's, Maryland (1809); St. Mary's in Missouri (1819); St. Charles Borromeo, Philadelphia (1838); St. Joseph's, New York City (1840); St. Francis de Salle in Milwaukee (1856); Mount St. Mary's of the West in Cincinnati (1857); and others.

10. Formation houses were established by Vincentians in Missouri (1818), Jesuits in Missouri (1823), Dominicans in Ohio (1834), Benedictines in Pennsylvania (1846), Redemptorists in New York (1849), and Franciscans in Santa Barbara (later Berkeley), California (1854).

11. Although a diocesan order, the Vincentians also established their own houses in Missouri (1818) and later at their colleges in Niagara Falls, New York (1857), and Cape Girardeau, Missouri (1858). The Jesuits began a novitiate in Missouri (1823), trained at their fledgling universities— St. Louis and Georgetown—and finally centralized advanced training at Woodstock in Maryland (1869). The Dominicans established a *Studium Generale* at Somerset, Ohio (1834), and another in Monterey, California (1860). German Benedictines set up holistic communities including monastery, farm, lay school, and seminary training at St. Vincent's in Pennsylvania (1846), at St. Meinrad's in Indiana (1854), and at St. John's in Minnesota (1857). The Redemptorists opened a house of studies in New York (1849). Franciscans began a house of study in Berkeley, California (1854), and in New Jersey (1876).

12. The Americanists included John Keane, archbishop of Dubuque and first rector of Catholic University; James Gibbons, archbishop of Baltimore; and Dennis O'Connell, bishop and rector of North American College in Rome. Prominent traditionalists included Michael Corrigan, archbishop of New York; Bernard McQuaid, bishop of Rochester; and Frederick Katzer, archbishop of Milwaukee.

13. The Third Plenary Council of Baltimore was the third meeting of American archbishops and bishops in the nineteenth century, approved by the Vatican, to chart the course of the Catholic Church in the United States. The council shored up American Catholic faith with the Baltimore Catechism, reasserted the authority of the episcopate, streamlined clergy education, established a system of parochial education, and approved plans for a future Catholic University in America.

14. The twenty-five hours of curriculum at Jewish Theological Seminary consisted of

    7 hours Talmud

    4 hours codes (Shulhan Aruch)

    3 hours Bible and rabbinical commentaries

    2 hours lecture in Jewish philosophy

    1 hour *Midrash*

    1 hour each (total 5) Judeo-Aramaic grammar, Hebrew grammar, Jewish literature, Jewish history, Jewish philosophy

    1 hour lecture in Jewish theology

    1 hour liturgy and Jewish calendar

    1 hour practical rabbinate (called homiletics)

    By 1912, practical rabbinics had risen to 3 hours per week.

15. Liebman's classic study (1974) of U.S. rabbinical seminaries in the 1960s confirmed the increase in student unrest over the heavy emphasis on text studies, especially at Jewish Theological Seminary. The required curricular changes did take place in the 1970s to include more practical rabbinics (Ellenson and Bycel, pp. 569ff).

8

CONTINUITY AND CHANGE
IN THE TRADITIONS OF
SEMINARY EDUCATION

THE DIVERSITY OF SEMINARY EDUCATION TRADITIONS is unmatched in other forms of professional education. Two sources of this diversity are especially pertinent to this discussion. First, mainline Protestant, evangelical Protestant, African American, diocesan or religious-order Roman Catholic, and Reform and Conservative rabbinical seminaries continue to identify with the legacies of their eighteenth- and nineteenth-century pioneers. Second, seminaries have responded differently when negotiating the influence of the university on their missions and in their cultures and teaching practices around social issues of class, gender, and race, and cultural issues associated with modernity, pluralism, and democracy.

Historically, the divisions among the seminary traditions have often been quite deep. During the latter decades of the twentieth century, however, new collaborations and movements in the U.S. religious community (for example, the ecumenism of mainline Protestantism, the interdenominationalism of Protestant evangelicals, the black civil rights and Catholic conciliar movements, and post-war Zionism) created the conditions for more cooperative approaches or shared agendas in educating clergy.[1] Broader educational influences from the university, faculty guilds, and accrediting agencies, and the growing competition among schools for faculty and students beyond a school's traditional constituency have also contributed to the blurring of the lines among them.

As part of the study we considered how the interaction of these two forces—continuing commitment to religious tradition and response to new and emerging challenges, especially from the university—shape the pedagogical cultures and practices of seminaries. In this chapter we explore some of the continuities and changes we observed in these seminary education traditions. We begin this chapter by describing persisting emphases in the mission, culture, and teaching practices of each of the five traditions described in the previous chapter. We then explore how the mission, culture, and teaching practices of these seminary traditions have responded to new challenges and influences.

Legacies of the Traditions

The legacies of seminary traditions continue to influence contemporary seminary education, even as increased collaboration and the forces of modernization blur the boundaries among them. The classic Protestant seminary set standards of academic and professional excellence that have been adopted by most seminaries; the religious training schools developed strategies of field work and popular piety that many seminaries have adapted; the African American seminaries upheld a vision of social advocacy and justice that continues to challenge most seminaries; Catholic seminaries maintained a rapprochement of tradition and the liberal arts to which many seminaries are returning; and Jewish seminaries established levels of text study and patterns of mediating tradition and modernity that many Christian seminaries seek to emulate.

Dwight's Legacy in Mainline Protestant Seminary Education

Despite Dwight's contributions to politics and theology, his educational legacy overshadows them.[2] His continuing influence may be traced, in part, to Andover's success as a graduate-level school for the professional education of clergy. The Presbyterian General Assembly, for example, invited Dwight to help organize a seminary at Princeton in 1812 (Miller, 1990, p. 104). The Dutch Reformed Church simultaneously opened a divinity school associated with Queen's College, later to become Rutgers University (p. 99). Other denominations soon followed their example. [3] At the time of the Civil War, in the early 1860s, more than fifty-five Protestant seminaries had been established (pp. 201–2). When Robert Kelly conducted the first national study of clergy education in 1924, the number of Protestant seminaries had increased to one hundred and forty.[4]

Dwight's view that education should develop both "piety and intellect" dominated the imaginations of nineteenth-century Protestant college and seminary educators. For Dwight, education was a primary means of "forming" or "reforming" the understanding and will toward a higher aim. Through a combination of rhetoric and exhortation, educators could reach both the minds and hearts of students, thereby influencing both intellect and moral action. With the alignment of intellectual content and moral action, a person would grow in piety, in the knowledge and love of truth itself—namely, God. In Dwight's "education of the heart," both knowledge and right action were viewed as products of virtue or character (Wenzke, 1989, p. 79). Although some seminary educators found tensions in this "hybrid" commitment (Lynn, 1981; Miller), it held the allegiance of Protestant seminary faculties as long as they saw themselves as pastors *and* scholars engaged in both classroom teaching *and* the communal pedagogies of seminary worship, mission societies, and student devotional groups.

By the early twentieth century, commitments to the interdependence of piety and intellect were being challenged. University trends that emphasized academic specialization and professionalism increasingly dominated both the structure and the pedagogy of the seminaries. Traditional literary categories of Bible, history, and theology were differentiated into scholarly disciplines, hastening the specialization of faculty teaching and research. To these three traditional fields—now independent of the arts of ministry—was added practical theology to form the "fourfold curriculum" of theological education. This movement toward scholarly specialization eventually became an end in itself, dissociating piety from intellect in the practice of the profession (Farley, 1983, 1988; Gilpin, 1996).

Over the course of the twentieth century, most Protestant seminaries conceded the dominance of either the academic or professional poles of this new curricular configuration. Union Theological Seminary of New York, Hartford Theological Seminary, Oberlin Theological Seminary, and many denominational seminaries tried to *close* the gap between the academic and professional dimensions of the curriculum by championing a "clerical paradigm" for clergy professionalism.[5] In this effort, the seminary administration and faculty identified distinct tracks of study according to specific skill-sets and ministerial roles: homiletics, religious education, pastoral care, or social work (Kelsey, 1993, pp. 49–63). "Academic" fields were taught as "resources" or "theory" for specific practices of ministry (Kelly, 1924). The professionally oriented school might turn to one of the social sciences, such as social ethics, as a unifying focus, but more often each ministerial "track" or field adopted one of the social sciences as its cognate or legitimating discipline: for example, progressive education theory for religious educators, psychology for pastoral counselors, communication theory for preachers, sociology or ethics for urban pastors, or language and culture studies for missionaries.

Protestant divinity schools within universities and some of the larger Protestant seminaries (eventually including Union Theological Seminary) sought to address the relationship of academic and professional learning by focusing on the academic pole through specialized knowledge in ancient languages, historical criticism, psychology of religion, and philosophical theology. The goal was to prepare students in the *academic foundations* for ministry, leaving the development of professional skills primarily to field work or summer institutes. In their important 1957 study of theological education, Niebuhr, Williams, and Gustafson took this stance, advocating a model of academic foundations for ministry as an antidote to the plethora of disciplines and specializations to be found in the mid-century seminary.

In both the professional and the foundational models of Protestant seminary education, various "cross-curricular" discourses—the social gospel, biblical theology, or neoorthodoxy[6]—were championed by given schools or departments in a school. But the university and guild pressures for the freedom and integrity of each discipline usually limited their influence to a decade or two, at most. Whether a school adopted the professional or foundational model of curricular unity, it perpetuated a gap between academics and ministry practice and, more generally, between intellect and piety.[7]

The most significant legacy of Dwight and the mainline Protestant seminaries may be seen in the use of newer university disciplines to link foundational, text-based studies to focused practices of ministry. In Dwight's day, new studies in literary criticism and the rhetorical arts served as a bridge between textual studies of the Bible and tradition to the oratory of ministry practice in pulpit and parlor. When bolstered by a cross-curricular, theological discourse on the nature of the will, this movement from text to practice was rationalized as the art of clergy persuasion and conversion. During the twentieth century, this educational movement from text to practice to rationale was reiterated in various forms in Protestant seminaries. In the 1920s and 1930s, the "social gospel" adopted sociology and ethics to shape the educational movement from text to practice in the clerical art of social reformation and public service. During the 1940s and 1950s, American neoorthodoxy used relational existentialism and dialectical philosophy to construct a text-to-practice movement that emphasized clergy practice as social critique and transcendent witness. In the late 1960s to 1980s, liberation theology used a Marxist social analysis and philosophy of history to create a new movement from text to practice to rationale, advocating the clergy art as solidarity with the poor and social transformation (Ziegler et. al., 1979). Finally, post-liberal theology has more recently used realistic hermeneutics and anthropology to generate an educational movement (from text to practice), fostering the clergy practice of reclaiming and renewing tradition.

Other educational trends have brilliantly illuminated texts—including philosophical hermeneutics, process philosophy, and deconstruction—but they have not, to this point, generated the full educational movement from text to practice in a way that similarly reconstructs clergy practice itself. Missing generally from these educational trends has been any significant attention to piety as an integrating feature in the education of clergy. This legacy of Dwight's vision for the education of clergy instead became a primary feature in the education of the Bible and religious training schools.

Dryer's Legacy in Bible Schools and Evangelical Seminaries

The Moody Bible Institute became the flagship institution of the Bible and religious training school movement in the nation. In its first fifty years, Moody educated over one hundred and twenty thousand students through its residential and correspondence courses.[8] Funded by a steady stream of donations from major Chicago businessmen, it helped shape a new style of "mass media" evangelism through radio, book and tract publishing, Bible curricula, and public lectures that appealed to a working-class, immigrant population. A host of newly established Bible and mission training schools[9] emulated Moody's mission and strategy.

Kelly's national study in 1924 warned mainline Protestant seminary leaders that the Bible and training schools "now enroll as many students as all the seminaries" combined (p. 229). And yet these schools struggled for years to establish their academic identity and credibility. A commentator from the 1930s pondered Moody's ambiguous status: "Certainly it is not a theological seminary; and certainly the work is of too high a grade to be dismissed as a mere Bible institute" (Day, 1936, p. 261). Later in the twentieth century, many of these schools would follow the lead of Fuller and Gordon-Conwell seminaries in accepting the academic standards and procedures established by regional accrediting agencies and the Association of Theological Schools for their educational programs.

The struggle for academic credibility was complicated by the role of the religious training schools in the larger conservative Protestant movement. During the fundamentalist-modernist controversy in the early decades of the twentieth century,[10] some conservative Bible schools began to operate like quasi-denominations by creating the ideology and mobilizing the institutions for a national populist movement (Brereton, 1990; Carpenter, 1997). With the publication of the Scofield Bible, leaders in the movement had a popular framework for propagating a dispensational theology[11] and an approach to Bible study insulated from modern, historical-critical methods. The Bible schools also laid the groundwork for a militant, anti-modernist network of "total institutions," including Christian day schools and academies, Bible colleges, publishing houses, training networks, and newly organized seminaries for the education of clergy (Peshkin, 1986; Carpenter, 1997) for developing an evangelical alternative to mainstream American culture.

During the twentieth century, many of the Bible schools and the evangelical seminaries that arose from them became adamantly antievolutionist, antihistorical, anticommunist, and antifeminist. Between 1910 and 1915, Reuben A. Torrey, formerly of Moody and later president of the Bible Institute of Los Angeles, helped edit the manifesto of the movement, *The Fundamentals,* financed by oil magnates Lyman and Milton Stewart and shipped to thousands of U.S. congregations.[12] In it, conservative Protestant leaders laid out a litmus test for Christian orthodoxy that denied any accommodation of evolution, historical criticism, or symbolic interpretations of Scripture. Moody continued to provide leadership to this expanding movement by helping found the World's Christian Fundamentals Association in 1919 and, after World War II, a broader coalition called the National Association of Evangelicals as a counter to the mainline Protestant Federal Council of Churches (later, the National Council of Churches).

Emma Dryer's vision of a populist, coeducational evangelical training institute in the normal school tradition was not altogether lost, however. Many evangelical seminaries held on to a vision of lay theological education for ministries of Christian education, youth work, and missionary service. Training schools for deaconesses and other religious training schools were established by women and men of similar vision: the Christian Workers School (1885) in Springfield, Massachusetts; the Chicago Training School (1885); and Boston's New England Deaconess School (1889). These schools emphasized pedagogies of practice and kept biblical witness closely tied to social service, as Dryer had envisioned.[13] Over the next fifty years, most of the religious training schools that survived either evolved into liberal arts colleges (for example, Springfield College), merged or collaborated with seminaries (for example, the Chicago Training School with Garrett Biblical Institute), or became university divisions (for example, Boston University's School of Social Work).

Eventually, a new "neo-evangelical" seminary pattern developed, led by institutions like Gordon-Conwell Theological Seminary and Fuller Theological Seminary (Marsden, 1987). It combined the biblical mission of the Bible Schools with the rational orthodoxy identified with the old

Princeton theology. The popular revivalism of Billy Graham created a broad-based coalition for these new schools. Their intellectual strength was established by scholars such as Carl Henry and Edward Carnell. Unlike traditional fundamentalists, these new evangelical schools adapted in their courses of study certain aspects of modern thought ranging from the social sciences to moderate forms of historical criticism to affirmations of cultural pluralism (Hunter, 1987).

Jews appropriated the training school format for Teachers Institutes at Hebrew Union College and Jewish Theological Seminary to train leaders for *Talmud Torah* programs and Jewish day schools (Philipson, 1925, pp. 58ff). Catholics also adopted and adapted the training school format (without the dispensational theology) as religious orders founded numerous "normal schools" and "apostolate training schools" for such specialized ministries as the social work of Catholic Charities or St. Vincent de Paul (Carey et al., 1989).

Bible and training schools pioneered early forms of field work, mass communication, and skills training for the ministry, but among their most significant contributions to seminary education may be in the emphasis Dryer and others in the movement gave to the nurture of popular piety. The development of religious leaders with strong Christian character— who would, in turn, develop Christians of exemplary character and piety among those they served—established a unifying focus for the education of students. Small group devotions and peer reflection on the community work of students contributed to an egalitarian framework in the schools for developing Christian piety and character, whether as educator, missionary, or preacher. The biblical and missional emphases in their pedagogies influenced emerging models for seminary education (cf. Banks, 1999).

Men and women continued to enroll in most of these schools, and increasingly they worked and studied side by side in their Christian duties. Although gender roles remained clearly defined in public and in family life, the religious training schools provided greater access for women to enter certain arenas of ministry (for example, education, mission work, and evangelism) than did many of the traditional seminaries. And unlike "highbrow" seminaries, where dating and marriage were often frowned upon (Handy, 1987, p. 177), the Bible schools celebrated exemplary Christian couples as coworkers and model families.

Payne's Legacy in African American Seminaries

Daniel Payne had a profound impact on the development of African American seminaries, first through his own denomination and then, by

example, through others. Following Wilberforce, the African Methodist
Episcopal Church established eleven more schools with theological departments and became the leader of theological and collegiate education for
the black church.[14] Two sister denominations in the Wesleyan tradition
also opened schools: Livingston College in North Carolina (1882), by the
African Methodist Episcopal Zion Church; and Lane College in Tennessee
(1882), by the Colored (now Christian) Methodist Episcopal Church.
Over the next hundred years, these three black Methodist denominations
maintained numerous institutions for the education of clergy and provided
much of the leadership for the black suffrage and civil rights movements.

The other primary source of black clergy leadership came from the
more than one hundred schools founded by black Baptist denominations
across the South, from Houston College in Texas (1885) to Morris College in South Carolina (1905).[15]

The story of these African American seminaries involves both struggle
and success. Most did not survive into the twentieth century due to economic hardship, the massive urban migration of blacks, and the resurgence of white supremacy after Reconstruction. The primary institutional
legacy of Wilberforce is evident in those that survived. Most were "yoked
institutions," linking the formation of pastors to the social uplift of
African Americans through a larger program of liberal and professional
education or industrial and vocational education.[16] A national study of
African American seminaries in 1925 found only two of the fifty-two
schools were freestanding (Daniel, 1925, p. 15) compared with the large
number of freestanding seminaries in white denominations (Kelly, 1924).
Howard's Divinity School was part of a liberal arts college, Simmons tied
its seminary to a normal institute, and Wilberforce yoked its seminary to
both. Even black technical and industrial schools such as Hampton, Livingston, and Lane included a seminary or theology department for the
training of clergy (Hampton, 1893; Washington, 1905, pp. 41–42). The
most famous of these schools, Booker T. Washington's Tuskegee Institute,
also had one of the largest "Bible training schools," graduating seventy-
seven ministers by the turn of the century (Washington, pp. 41–42).

The impact of these yoked institutions has been significant. They educated an increasing number of black church leaders with each new generation. By emphasizing the full emancipation of black Americans as a
larger, shared concern, they avoided the schisms between holiness and
Calvinist traditions of the white Protestant community in the nineteenth
century and between the fundamentalist and modernist movements in the
twentieth. They forged and helped sustain the identity and mission of
black churches, provided key leaders for African American communities,

and trained many pastors and laity who gave local leadership to the civil rights and black theology movements. Although African-American churches continued to maintain a strong system of clergy apprenticeship, by the 1980s more than one-third of Black clergy had some seminary training (Lincoln and Mamiya, 1990, pp. 128-131).

The ethos of black seminary education, shaped by a mission of full emancipation and social uplift, culminated in a distinctive theological framework for the training of clergy in the American context. It emphasized a pattern of biblical interpretation infused with transformational hope and social vision in the face of horrendous odds. Eventually, through such diverse voices as Howard Thurman of Boston University (Thurman, 1954), his student Martin Luther King Jr., and James Cone of Union Theological Seminary (Cone, 1970), it gave form to black liberation theology and inspired liberatory theologies in North America grounded in different communities of struggle (for example, feminist, womanist, Latino-Latina, and Asian American liberation theologies). These transformational theologies, allied with related theological movements of liberation in Europe, Latin America, Asia, and Africa, have in turn drawn attention to the global dimensions of all forms of theological education and discourse.

Ireland's Legacy in Catholic Seminaries

During the Romanist era of the U.S. Catholic Church, from 1910 to 1960, the vision of seminary education held by Ireland and the Americanists diminished but did not disappear. After Father Hecker's views were translated into French, the Vatican could no longer ignore them. Leo XIII, having failed to unite the church with French republicanism, saw two problems with the Americanists: they accommodated too much to the thought of the age, and they overemphasized priestly activism. "Natural virtues" are not be extolled above "supernatural," he proclaimed in *Testem Benevolentiae* (1899) when condemning the "Americanism" of Hecker and his followers. His successor, Pius IX, reiterated the virtues of "personal sanctification of the priest" over "dedication to the service of others" (White, 1989, p. 235). For the American Church, Rome's response gave precedence to the traditionalists, who had claimed all along that the Church was "in" but not "of" the world, including the world that is American society.

After Leo XIII's condemnation of "Americanism" in 1899, Pope Pius IX proclaimed modernism a heresy in *Lamentabili* (1907). This "one-two punch on the American Church" (Reher, 1988, p. 457) quieted many cultural and intellectual innovators in the seminaries, but it did not terminate the Americanist spirit altogether. Religious orders and lay leaders, exemplified by the St. Vincent de Paul Society and Dorothy Day, initiated active social missions in the early twentieth century. A pool of "labor-priests" educated in sociology at Catholic University organized labor unions, settlement houses, and American chapters of Catholic Action (Dolan, 1995). Some seminaries (for example, St. Mary of the Lake, in Chicago) developed courses in Catholic social teaching, and by 1950 more than thirty-two seminaries included Catholic Action teaching in their curricula (White, 1989, pp. 350–54).

A new liturgical movement, spearheaded by St. John's Abbey in Minnesota, inspired new forms of Catholic social witness. Catholic scholars developed journals and professional associations parallel to those of the American university; for example, American Catholic Historical Association (1919), American Catholic Philosophical Association (1926), Catholic Biblical Association (1936), and Catholic Theological Society of America (1946) (White, 1989, pp. 371–73; Carey et al., 1989, pp. 151–53). By the 1940s, Pope Pius XII was encouraging more biblical studies and increasing numbers of Catholic seminaries were introducing students to methods of historical criticism (White, 1989, p. 284).

When Pope John XXIII convened the second Vatican Council (1962–1965), the American Catholic Church was poised for a number of transformations. The council's call for the Church to engage contemporary modern society (*Gaudium et Spes*) vindicated many of Ireland's ideals. John XXIII's emphasis on "inculturation" made official the more contextual approach of translating the faith according to the given culture— much as the Americanists had argued. Vatican II's *Optatum Totius* upheld the diocesan priesthood as the primary form of ministry in the Church, and it standardized seminary education in ways the Americanists might have applauded.

Since Vatican II, many seminaries have emphasized one view of the priesthood over the other. Some religious order and diocesan seminaries adopted the missional emphases and personal integration pedagogies cultivated in Ireland's seminary (Schuth, 1989), whereas some other diocesan seminaries adopted the sacramental emphases and identification pedagogies historically identified with the traditionalists (O'Malley, 1990, p. 65). Both traditions of Catholic seminary education kept some version of the liberal or humanities education that Ireland valued as part of their curriculum.

The pedagogies of liberal education that Ireland espoused, however, were transformed during the twentieth century by newer approaches to Thomastic studies. At the beginning of the century, traditional Thomism reinforced Vatican control and guaranteed distance from modern thought in the seminary curriculum. In a renaissance of interest in neo-Thomism, Jacques Maritain, Karl Rahner, and other Catholic scholars integrated the deeper humanism of modern philosophy in topics ranging from phenomenology to hermeneutics with the works of Thomas Aquinas. By the 1980s Catholic seminaries, in the spirit of this resurgence of attention to Thomism, established a two-year prerequisite in philosophy for advanced seminary education, thereby establishing a strong link between priestly formation and classical, medieval, and modern philosophy (Schuth, 1989). In contrast, in most mainline Protestant seminaries this broader engagement with the humanities had all but disappeared from the curricula. At the same time, Catholic seminaries were encouraged by John Paul II (*Pastores Dabo Vobis,* 1992) to embrace the resources and methods of the social sciences (especially sociology, psychology, social ethics, and cultural anthropology, altering academic approaches to theological and biblical studies, revising views of the lives of seminarians, and reshaping the ethical and psychological dynamics in pedagogies of human and spiritual formation (Hemrick and Hoge, 1985, 1987; Hemrick and Wister, 1993).

The abiding influence of the nineteenth-century Catholic seminary is evident today in the increasing attention to priestly formation as the overarching framework for Catholic seminary education. A daily rhythm of sung prayer, mass, and private devotions along with spiritual direction continues at most seminaries, in the tradition of the Sulpicians or the religious orders (Hennessey, 1997). The entire educational process, however, is conceived as one of comprehensive and balanced formation in five areas: intellectual, academic, spiritual, human, and pastoral. With the establishment of the national Program of Priestly Formation (commonly referred to as PPF) by the U.S. Conference of Catholic Bishops in the 1970s, this comprehensive vision of seminary education has become the standard framework for diocesan and religious-order seminaries throughout the country. PPF requires two things that seminaries in other traditions often struggle with: (1) the coordination of the formal academic curriculum with the larger communal curriculum of worship, community life, and field education; and (2) the concentration of pedagogies in forming the personal and vocational "character" of the seminarian in an ideally balanced and integrated way. Although some Catholic seminary educators describe the requirements of the PPF as burdensome and even constrictive—especially in its elevation of the diocesan priest as the standard for other forms of ministry (O'Malley, p. 67)—it also provides a working framework for curricular coordination and personal integration.

Schechter's Legacy in Rabbinical Seminaries

Although Schechter hoped Jewish Theological Seminary would continue to serve the Orthodox Jewish community, he soon realized it was a new mediation between Orthodox yeshiva and Reform *wissenschaft*. It also required a new kind of synagogue. Following the pattern of the Reform movement that had established the Union of American Hebrew Congregations (1873) and the Central Conference of American Rabbis (1889) alongside Hebrew Union College (1875), replicated by the Orthodox at Rabbi Isaac Elchanan Theological Seminary in 1906 (Schwarzfuchs, p. 116), Schechter formed the United Synagogue of America (1913), and Jewish Theological Seminary alumni formed the Rabbinical Assembly of America (1917).

This threefold pattern of school, synagogue union, and rabbinical organization established Conservative Judaism as a distinctly American denomination. Although the Conservative movement has no explicit creed or platform, it does share with the Reform movement a commitment to a "new synthesis of tradition and the modern spirit," in an American mode (Raphael, 1985, p. 92). Within a generation, Schechter's Conservative movement became the mediating tradition between modernism and ultra-orthodoxy in worldwide Judaism.

Schechter established the seminary as a leader in the development of Jewish scholarship. With Hebrew Union College, Jewish Theological Seminary advanced developments in *Wissenschaft des Judentums* to the point that one rabbinic educator proclaimed, "Judaism has made science the sister of our faith" (Philipson, p. 75). Overall, the Jewish *Wissenschaft* movement emphasized the modernization of received traditions to give "new shape to the inherited content of Judaism" (Meyer, 1988, p. 75). Both schools elevated the rabbi as teacher of an entire cultural and religious tradition. By the 1920s Hebrew Union broadened its curriculum to include more Bible than Talmud, social studies, modern philosophy, more history, and elocution (Philipson, pp. 30, 74). Jewish Theological Seminary expanded the traditional curriculum to include all forms of Jewish literature and Jewish communal studies (1919) as a reflection of a new rabbinical charge to serve wider social and communal functions (Ellenson and Bycel, p. 545). It also advanced the study of Hebrew by conducting all teaching—and publishing most scholarly works—in modern Hebrew. Although Jewish Theological Seminary maintained a text-based curriculum, it continued to add such programs in "practical rabbinics" as pastoral psychology and education (Liebman, 1974).

The pedagogies dominating the curriculum of the seminary at the beginning of the twentieth century influenced rabbinic education for decades. Liebman reports in 1968 that both Jewish Theological Seminary and Rabbi Isaac Elchanan Theological Seminary continued to have text-based curricula built around pedagogies of dialogue and disputation, but the cultural context for these studies had completely changed. On the one hand, as Judaism increasingly participated in the mainstream of American society, students were clamoring for courses in practical rabbinics. On the other hand, the fusion of cultural and spiritual Zionism with political Zionism after the Holocaust placed the existence and viability of the state of Israel at the center of rabbinic education for the Conservative movement, quieting earlier dissent from both Reform and some Orthodox corners. More recently, Jewish theories of text interpretation and halakhic development have incorporated broader hermeneutical theories of narrativity, intertextuality, rhetoric, and legal interpretation (Neusner, 2003; Roth, 1986) into the canon of the seminary curriculum, even as traditional pedagogies of dialogue and disputation continue to predominate in the classroom.

Jewish Theological Seminary and Conservative Judaism hold a unique place in the story of American seminaries caught between religious tradition and the modern sciences. The drive to establish a new institution for the renewal of an ancient religious tradition, along with the need to professionalize clergy education, created an unparalleled opportunity for mediating tradition and *wissenschaft,* without compromising either. Most Protestant seminaries identified with one side or the other of the fundamentalist-modernist divide until the 1930s, when theological neoorthodoxy began to mediate between them. Most Catholic seminaries, under the watchful supervision of Rome, allowed the social sciences to seep gradually into their bulwark of tradition until Vatican II, when the call for thoroughgoing reform encouraged the rigorous engagement of social science and theology.[17] More recently that engagement has been tempered (Baum, 1986).

Judaism, however, had a strong mediating tradition in Conservative Judaism and its seminary that allowed differences between Orthodox traditionalists and Reform modernists and between tradition and *wissenschaft* to be addressed in more systematic fashion. Both Conservative and Reform Jewish rabbinical education appropriated the scientific and research standards of the modern university without conceding the constitutive power of religious tradition, although to quite different effect.

In this regard, their experience contrasts with Catholic and Protestant seminary education. With the founding of research-centered universities patterned after the University of Berlin at Johns Hopkins and the University of Michigan, and in the transformation of Harvard, clergy education, along with other forms of professional training, was altogether altered. As we observed earlier, Protestant seminaries, in particular, attempted to respond to these changes in the university by adopting the Berlin model of the *theological encyclopedia,* which organized the curriculum into historical foundations (Bible, history, dogma) and professional application (practical theology). They also added disciplines from the human sciences (sociology, psychology, and education), reorganized their curricula to offer numerous electives, and weakened the liberal arts emphasis on classical languages to make room for curricular innovation (Kelsey, 1993; Kelly, 1924). Bible schools and evangelical Protestant seminaries, on the other hand, resisted the disciplines and curricula of the universities, opting instead for models drawn from business and vocational schools. Catholic seminaries, meanwhile, slowly incorporated such modern disciplines as sociology within a definition of "tradition" that resisted accommodations to modernity.

Jewish seminaries, in contrast, incorporated modern historical, linguistic, and eventually social studies into the service of rejuvenating their textual, religious, and cultural traditions. They envisioned their seminaries as "Jewish universities" with multiple departments, faculties, and schools, even when they did not have that official designation. In short, rabbinical seminaries incorporated many disciplines and organizational forms of the modern university, without conceding the place of Judaism in academic study or a religiously pluralistic society.

Negotiating Tradition and Modernity

The seminary education traditions just described continue to profoundly shape and direct seminary life. They influence and shape in distinctive ways the pastoral, priestly, and rabbinic imaginations of students and establish perspectives and priorities for student engagement with the bodies of knowledge and the range of skills, dispositions, and habits associated with the education of clergy. These traditions are not only dynamic and changing, they are persistent. Their persistence helps explain differences of perspective and practice in the education of Jewish and Christian clergy.

A common emphasis in each tradition is the commitment to prepare leaders to build and maintain local symbolic cultures that ground the religious communities they lead in their religious traditions, while at the same time equipping them with patterns of action for engaging modern demands and global changes. This is both a representative and a constructive enterprise. However, at stake in this commitment are three issues that seminary faculties in each of these traditions have often negotiated—and renegotiated—quite differently: (1) the relationship of seminary education to the modern university, (2) the influence of social context on educational ideals, and (3) the pedagogical reconstruction of theology and tradition. These negotiations have influenced the mission of American seminaries and given form to a variety of institutional cultures that, in turn, have diversely shaped seminary educator intentions for student learning.

Seminary Education Engages the Modern University

During the twentieth century, seminaries responded selectively to the changing mission and standards of the American university, in some cases taking ideas and practices *from* the university, in others giving ideas and practices *to* the university. This interchange may be illustrated, in Christian seminaries especially, by the adaptation of the European model of theological education developed at the University of Berlin at the beginning of the nineteenth century, the acceptance of accrediting agency standards, and the invention of new patterns of collaboration between university and seminary.

Curricular Adaptations

With Protestant and Catholic adaptations of the European organization of the fourfold curriculum, much of American Christian seminary education aligned itself, as we have noted earlier, with the curricular structures of the research university (Farley, 1983, 1988; Schner, 1993). The older, liberal arts arrangement of the theological literature in Bible, doctrine, church history, and pastoral studies was gradually reorganized into the "positive sciences" of biblical, systematic, historical, and practical theology, each with its own methodology and subject matter.[18] Farley has marshaled a powerful critique of the splintering effects of specialization and the accompanying "guild mindset" encouraged by the fourfold curriculum on a unified theological vision or habitus (1983, 1988). During this study, we also saw how the fourfold pattern provided a pragmatic and flexible curricular structure for seminaries to adapt and organize their proliferating disciplines and expanding faculties.[19]

However, the various Christian seminary traditions appropriated the fourfold curriculum in different ways. Mainline Protestant seminaries linked disparate areas of the curriculum through cross-curricular disciplines of historical criticism, psychology, hermeneutics, or social theory. [20] Evangelical Protestant seminaries perpetuated the structures of the fourfold curriculum to provide a pragmatic rationale for biblical authority.[21] African American seminaries oriented the various areas of study in the curriculum toward the mission of racial emancipation (Daniel, 1925). Although U.S. Catholics were slower to adopt the fourfold curriculum in its strictest sense,[22] they finally adapted it to a strong tradition of philosophical and priestly formation (Schner, 1993). This allowed them to claim a unity of theology and ministry in each of its programs of formation (human, spiritual, intellectual, and pastoral). The only tradition to tilt the fourfold curriculum toward a "functionalist version of the clerical paradigm" (Farley, 1983, p. 127), focused on skills development, was the religious training and Bible School tradition.

New Standards, Structures, and Disciplines

Through the efforts of the Association of Theological Schools and regional accrediting associations, seminaries raised academic standards, increased library quality, and framed the terms of faculty advancement to be more in line with the general standards of higher education (Carroll, 1981). In the process, they also adapted other features of the university. Although the seminaries managed to avoid some of the pitfalls of the university structure and experience, the features they adapted had significant implications for the seminary pedagogical culture.

Seminaries incorporated the new social sciences into the curriculum, generally without conceding to the positivism that accompanied them in the academy. For example, Catholic, Jewish, and mainline Protestant faculties added chairs in education, psychology, and sociology but kept the disciplines grounded in a strong tradition of theological education. Seminaries with roots in the religious training tradition, like Fuller, added departments or schools of psychology, adapting them to Biblical literacy and piety and spawning a new movement of "Christian counseling" (Marsden, 1987, pp. 233–37).

Even though seminaries followed the expansion of disciplinary and curricular structures of the American university, they also retained a core canon of literature, primarily the Bible and Talmud. This core canon not only provided a cross-curricular discourse within the seminary community, but it also contributed to and facilitated seminary resistance to some of the fragmenting specialization occurring in other branches of the academy. Seminary educators adopted models of interpretation from the humanities, for example—from Gadamerian and narrative hermeneutics to existential and analytic philosophy—as frameworks for cross-disciplinary study, but they also relied on theologies, ranging from the social gospel to neoorthodoxy to liberation, to keep various parts of the curriculum grounded in Biblical reflection.

Collaboration

Throughout the twentieth century, university-based seminaries continued to reinvent their relationship to the wider university by adopting public religious education programs, developing new academic disciplines and collaborative programs with other professional schools, raising expectations for faculty research and publication, and expanding their mission to include the education of both "clergy" and "scholars" (Lindbeck, Deutsch, and Glazer, 1976; Cherry, 1995).

In the latter part of the century many freestanding schools, for example, affiliated with nearby universities to increase academic standards, expand academic resources, and engage new disciplines of inquiry. At about the same time, seminaries began to forge collaborations with each other for the same purposes. From Boston to Washington, Chicago, and Berkeley, and many places in between, schools expanded their resources by establishing "clusters" or federations of schools to share faculty, libraries, and curricula. Typically, these clusters created programs bringing faculty and students from various traditions together in class, often in jointly sponsored academic programs.

In collaboration with the National Council on Religion in Higher Education,[23] many seminaries sought to influence the university through the middle of the last century by promoting the study of religion, facilitating religious practice, and fostering a new vision for unifying the university (Cherry, 1995, p. 47). The council developed an extensive fellows program, for example, funded by the Hazen, Lilly, and Danforth foundations, for the graduate education of quality teachers of religion for American colleges and universities. This initiative contributed to the expansion of seminary programs for training scholars to teach "beyond" the seminaries as a distinct vocation. The council also established the first schools of religion dedicated to the "scientific study of religion" at public universities in Indiana, Michigan, Oklahoma, and, most notably, at the University of Iowa (Cherry, 1995, pp. 100–101).[24] These schools developed their own doctoral programs and were soon educating many of the new candidates for the doctor of philosophy in religious studies.

During the 1930s, the council[25] began promoting religious life on campus through denominationally sponsored noncredit courses to the university curriculum, campus pastors, and university chapels (Cherry, 1995). Protestant denominations, often cooperating ecumenically, expanded this effort with campus ministries at state universities (Marsden, 1994, pp. 335ff), leading some seminaries to add courses on religion in higher education for students interested in becoming campus ministers. After World War II, the council advocated the study of religion as a "unifying vision" for the modern university: first, by its inclusion in the general education curriculum, and second, by pursuing a Protestant, Catholic, and Jewish alliance for developing a "Judeo-Christian tradition" of religious scholarship and practice.

In retrospect, the council's efforts primarily facilitated the study of religion as a distinct academic discipline, laying the groundwork for the expansion of the field of "religious studies" in the 1970s and 1980s (Cherry, 1995, pp. 112–23; Kitigawa, 1992). It failed to provide an emerging framework or paradigm, however, for grounding the lively debates about the relationship of faith, science, and modern knowledge taking place among the faculty and students on mainline Protestant college, university, and seminary campuses (Sloan, 1994). Even though denominationally sponsored programs for the student practice of religion and the seminary programs that provided their leadership have ebbed and flowed since the 1950s, the council's vision of the study of religion as a unifying vision for the modern nonsectarian university has all but disappeared.

The increasing emphasis on clinical education, especially in medical and other professional schools, reshaped seminary education as well. Seminaries developed numerous "apprentice" sites in collaboration with community agencies to engage students in practical and professional training. The settlement house movement in the late nineteenth and early twentieth centuries was strongly supported by Protestant seminaries (Williams, 1941; Handy, 1987). By the 1950s, many had evolved into "urban work" sites of skills training and supervision. By the 1970s, sites for "field work" in parish, social, and clinical settings had been combined with patterns of careful supervision and curricular credit in the "field education" movement to develop pastoral, priestly, and rabbinic skills and identity (Hunter, 1982). During the 1940s and 1950s the clinical pastoral education movement brought seminary students and specialized faculty members into community and hospital settings with specially trained and credentialed supervisors (Hall, 1992). The emphasis on "globalization" in the 1980s and 1990s led to the creation of international sites for mission education and cultural immersion (Stackhouse, 1986, 1988; Browning, 1986). Finally, the emergence of congregational studies as a distinct field within the sociology of religion refocused the attention of seminaries on the congregation as a site for both ministry formation and scholarly research (Hopewell, 1984; Hough and Wheeler, 1988). The development of a wide array of clinical settings for clergy education significantly extended the collaborative network of agencies involved in seminary education.

The Influence of Social Context

Tumultuous social change throughout much of the twentieth century—urbanization, war, economic crises, quests for civil rights—intensified the contextualization of each seminary tradition. Seminaries were increasingly expected to prepare clergy who could effectively address public issues and bring their influence to bear on the alliance of congregation or synagogue and society. A national study in 1934, for example, charted a trend among Protestant schools to link Christianity to social issues of capital, labor, race, and war (Brown and May, 1934). In a review of clergy education literature in the 1980s, Gustafson observed that expectations of clergy were increasingly being influenced by changes in the academy, rising ethnic and gender consciousness, and globalization (Gustafson, 1987, 1988).

The expansion of attention to society in the academic disciplines, curriculum, and pedagogies of seminary education was fueled, in part, by the philosophical turn toward pragmatism through Protestant "social gospel" theologies, Catholic social ethics, and the increased emphasis on *gemiluth chasadim* or Jewish social work (Wertheimer, 1997, p. 540). Seminary scholars began to use new forms of social analysis adopted from sociology, Marxist theory, and ethics. Christian urban work, Sunday school missions, and Jewish settlement houses helped socialize new immigrants. Teaching institutes trained teachers to spread Jewish culture and Hebrew learning (Mintz, 1997, pp. 85ff). Catholic religious orders and lay movements, exemplified by the St. Vincent de Paul Society and Dorothy Day, began new social missions (Carey et al.), and "labor priests" organized labor unions, settlement houses, and American chapters of Catholic Action. The quest for "social efficiency" in these movements did not involve a narrow or functionalist view of the clergy (Gilpin, p. 97), but rather a public reorientation of priests, pastors, and rabbis toward the broader society.

Among the social movements and influences impacting the education of clergy during the latter part of the twentieth century, three have significantly affected seminary curricular structures and the teaching practices of faculty: an emphasis on professionalism and professional competency, the presence of women and feminist perspectives, and a growing consciousness of the dynamics of globalization.

A Quest for Professional Competency

The contextualization of seminary education took a distinctive form in the "professional competence" movement of the late 1960s and 1970s (Martin, 1977). This movement originated as a response to several internal and external pressures: the widening gap between "foundational" disciplines (Bible, theology, history) and the practical fields; higher education's growing movement toward *professionalism*; and the public cry for "social relevance" in the midst of the cultural, civil rights, and antiwar struggles of the 1960s. Calling on the clergy to become a modern profession, such Protestant advocates as Seward Hiltner and Charles Fielding linked clergy knowledge and skills with wider public service by building key competencies and assessment into the seminary curricula for the various roles of ministry: teaching, preaching, counseling, community organizing, and administration (Fielding et al., 1966; Brekke, Schuller, and Strommen, 1976; Carroll, 1985).[26]

Implications for the movement were clear: "relate the whole curriculum to ministry" (Fielding, p. 71). The Association of Theological Schools took up that challenge in a comprehensive plan of "Curriculum for the '70s" (Ziegler and Deem, 1969) and later in an ambitious survey, "Readiness for Ministry," given to seminary faculties, denominations, and church and synagogue members in an attempt to identify skills and traits for ministry (Schuller, Galloway, and O'Brien, 1975; Schuller et al., 1976). Both projects stirred considerable debate, but were spottily adopted, due in part to resistance from larger seminaries and university divinity schools (Hough, 1981; Ziegler, 1984).

Catholic and Jewish seminaries' responses to the pressures toward professionalism were somewhat different from that of Protestants. Catholics pioneered the sociological study of the priesthood as a profession (Fichter, 1961; Potvin and Suziedelis, 1969) and folded issues of professional competency into a national program of academic, spiritual, and pastoral formation for priests (Schuth, 1989, 1999; Schner, 1993). Although Liebman lamented, in his study of Jewish seminaries, that none were "actually oriented toward professional training" (1974, p. 104), "demands for professionalization were heard" even at the Orthodox Rabbi Isaac Elchanan Theological Seminary (Ellenson and Bycel, pp. 569ff). Generally, the Jewish seminaries added psychology and clinical programs to their curricula and offered such new courses in the "practical" arts of the rabbinate as speech, education, and homiletics (Liebman, pp. 51–60).

Although the "professional competency" movement as such was relatively short-lived, it secured a place for clinical and action-reflection pedagogies in the seminaries that continues to the present.

The Presence of Women and Feminist Perspectives

During the latter decades of the twentieth century, seminary education felt the profound impact of the increasing presence of women in seminary programs and the accompanying expansion and influence of feminist, womanist, and Latina theologies. After 1960, women, in increasing numbers, were gradually admitted to ordination in all mainline Protestant and some evangelical Protestant, as well as Jewish Reform and Conservative denominations. New lay ministry options, especially for Catholics, further contributed to the increased presence of women in seminaries (cf. Dolan, 1989) . Despite a number of seminaries that still only admit men, by 2002 the proportion of women students had increased to 36 percent of the total enrollment in all degree programs.

The impact of women students and faculty has been not only demographic. They introduced new perspectives to disciplinary thinking. Feminist, womanist, and Latina theologies provided a fresh critique of seminary curricula, methodologies, and pastoral roles (Cornwall Collective, 1980; Cannon et al., 1985). Although this new scholarship has generally been incorporated into the educational programs of most mainline Protestant, Reform Jewish, and religious order Catholic seminaries, it has also been strongly resisted in many evangelical and diocesan Catholic schools (Marsden, 1987; White, 1989; Schuth, 1989).

At the same time, the growing presence of women students and the gradual increase in women faculty expanded the pedagogies and practices of most seminary communities by the 1990s to include more experiential learning; social and communal epistemologies; feminist, womanist, and Latina interpretations of sacred texts; and gender analysis and reconstruction of tradition (Ackermann and Bons-Storm, 1998). For example, in her 1995 study of feminist practices of theological education in the mid-1990s, Rebecca Chopp explored the transformation she observed women effecting in Protestant theological education through such distinctively feminist pedagogical practices as "narrativity" and community (or *ekklesia*). We observed something of the influence of the presence of women in the schools we visited in the attention given by faculty (to varying degrees, and despite resistance to feminist, womanist, and Latina scholarship among some faculty) to such themes in feminist pedagogy as building learning communities, honoring different styles of learning in assignments, and engaging students in narrative modes of learning.

Globalization

Seminaries have also responded to the rise of social, political, economic, and religious global movements in the late twentieth century. The responses have included action-reflection pedagogies to introduce students to the dynamics of poverty, racism, and oppression (Rhodes and Richardson, 1991); programs of immersion in the cultures of emerging nations (Evans et al., 1993); engagement with political Zionism (cf. Lederhendler, 1997); and the resurgence of Vatican oversight of U.S. Catholic education (Baum, 1986). In the 1970s and 1980s, the rise of black, liberation, and contextual theologies in Catholic and Protestant communities raised new questions about the composition of the seminary community and traditional methods, social organization, and epistemologies of seminary studies. Programs were established to increase the number of black, Hispanic, Asian, and Native American faculty. Minority students were explicitly recruited to historically white seminaries. Faculties sought to broaden the social location of the education they provided all students by expanding curricular offerings, adding seminars in cross-cultural and global "immersion" to reorient student and faculty reflection upon their traditions. By sending students and faculty to Appalachia, urban America, South and Central America, Africa, and Asia, faculties hoped to create a multicultural and global perspective on theological learning and the ministry (Shriver, 1986; Lesher, 1994). These curricular and pedagogical innovations culminated in proposals to reorganize seminary education around global themes and utilize pedagogies of immersion (Hough and Cobb, 1985).

Under the impetus of Zionism, during the 1960s Jewish seminaries began developing "studies abroad" and exchange programs with Israel. Hebrew Union College, Jewish Theological Seminary, and Rabbi Isaac Elchanan Theological Seminary established "study houses" in Israel for the year-round involvement of faculty and students in the Holy Land to link spiritual and cultural Zionism with political Zionism as an expression of loyalty to the state of Israel (Lederhendler, 1997, pp. 192–99).

The global pressures on Catholic seminaries came from opposite directions: from the global nature of the church through increased enrollment of international students and a focus on multicultural education, and through closer oversight of American seminaries by the Vatican under Pope John Paul II, especially to keep some post–Vatican II movements—including calls to allow priests to marry and women to be ordained—under control. Papal visits were catalysts to streamlining curricular developments, improving fidelity to established Catholic teachings (especially in moral theology), elevating the status of priest-centered pedagogies in pastoral formation, spiritual direction, and clinical education (Baum, 1986; Schuth, 1989), and promoting priestly identification with a worldwide brotherhood.

Even as each of these movements tried to "situate" pedagogies integral to the various American seminary traditions within a larger, global context, student and faculty encounters with different cultural expectations for teaching and learning in the classroom and the seminary community also challenged the efficacy and authority of their inherited pedagogical practices. Those new expectations provided a primary impetus to the pedagogies of contextualization we described in Chapter Five, to increase student consciousness and capacities for working sensitively and constructively in the encounter of meanings and practices originating in diverse cultural, religious, or socioeconomic contexts in traditional clergy roles and responsibilities.

Pedagogical Reconstruction of Theology and Tradition

Each of the five historic seminary traditions originated, in part, as their pioneers reshaped inherited theologies and religious traditions by changing or developing pedagogies for clergy education. This "pedagogical reconstruction" of theology and tradition continued into the first half of the twentieth century; for example:

- Faculty in mainline Protestant schools adopted social epistemologies and pragmatic pedagogies (for example, those of Dewey) to create new *intertextual methods* of study that linked fields such as sociology and psychology with the theological disciplines to equip clergy as cultural leaders with a socially critical and intellectual gospel.

- Early evangelical seminary faculties refined the application of empiricist methods[27] in the study of Bible and doctrine with insights from communication and marketing strategies, to emphasize the *intratextual* integrity, rational coherence, and certainty of biblical texts.

- African American theologians emphasized biblical devotion and oral pedagogies to prepare moral exemplars and "race leaders," to demonstrate the *social efficacy* of biblical and black cultural narratives.

○ The faculties in Catholic seminaries gradually integrated church teaching with new forms of social thought, historical criticism, and philosophy to *recontextualize* modern knowledge in Catholic tradition.

○ Rabbinic scholars incorporated higher biblical criticism (including source criticism[28]), modern and Jewish philosophy, and a spiritual and cultural Zionism to prepare Jewish cultural leaders to *mediate* modernity and tradition.

Seminary educators, in other words, have not passively transmitted their religious traditions. New pedagogical emphases have significantly contributed to the reconstruction of those traditions. This influence of pedagogy in shaping theological perspectives may be seen most recently in two movements in seminary education: (1) in Jewish and Christian seminaries, a renewed interest in spirituality, or spiritual formation; and (2) in particular among Christian seminaries, a renewed interest in practical theology.

Spirituality

The appropriation and expansion of the traditions and practices of *spiritual formation* has had several catalysts. A growing interest in the popular and academic study of world religions (for example, Hinduism, Islam, Buddhism) has highlighted alternative ways of conceiving the religious life. This new interest and knowledge has, in turn, yielded resources to address a pervasive cultural and spiritual quest: as new technologies, globalization of economic structures, and significant shifts in social values and structures seem to subvert familiar modes for making meaning and establishing social order, they also seem to intensify a deep spiritual hunger. At the same time, in the midst of this widespread quest for spirituality among the laity, and partly in reaction to the variety of social and public roles clergy had assumed during the 1960s and 1970s, religious communities have increasingly looked for signs of the spiritual dimensions of faith or observance, devotion, and integrity in their clergy.

Jewish and Christian seminaries and denominations have responded to this popular revival of interest in spirituality with new requirements for self-examination and self-disclosure in the processes leading to ordination. Although not entirely new in some Roman Catholic seminaries, spiritual autobiographies, faith journals, and other instruments of self-discovery have become commonplace across the spectrum of Protestant, Catholic, and some Jewish seminaries. New prayer and meditation practices, devotional Bible studies and *lectio divina*,[29] the revival of popular devotions in Catholicism, and the resurgence of traditional Jewish practices of observance at home and in the synagogue have reshaped seminary campus life and classroom practice. Various proposals for making spiritual formation the unifying center of Protestant and Catholic seminary education were put forth and debated, but rarely fully adopted (Schner, 1985; Hall, 1988; Kelsey, 1988; Lindbeck, 1988; Meye, 1988; Mouw, 1987; Tracy, 1988).

This resurgence of interest in spiritual formation has expanded the range of curricular offerings and altered the focus of existing courses in many seminaries to include attention to new disciplinary studies in spirituality (Holder and Dahill, 1999). Among the one hundred and twenty-nine seminary educators responding to the study survey, for example, eight described a course explicitly exploring some aspect of spirituality, ranging from "Jewish Mysticism" and "Biblical Foundations of Spirituality" to "Introduction to Spiritual Theology" and "Islamic Mysticism and Spirituality." New scholarship in Christian and Jewish mysticism has produced a new literature probing spirituality both within various religious traditions and at their intersection (for example, Schneiders, 2000; Downey, 1997; Dreyer and Burrows, 2005; Ochs, 2001; Green, 1997; Hoffman, 2002). This new scholarship—again often developed, in part, in seminary classrooms—has been accompanied by the revival of ancient prayer and worship forms in the worship life of the seminary community and the development of companion studies in liturgical theology—all designed to prepare clergy to give leadership to the spiritual formation of the communities they serve.

Much of the attention to spirituality and to spiritual formation in contemporary seminary education occurs outside the classroom. In the next chapter we will explore community worship, the use of small groups, and programs of spiritual direction as primary venues in the contemporary seminary for cultivating seminary student spirituality. The emphasis on spirituality, however, moves beyond the programmatic or curricular to permeate classroom teaching practices as well—despite the observation of one seminary educator that "God smiles on the superficiality of it all" and comments from several faculty members that attention to spirituality is difficult in classes that include some students preparing to be clergy and other students more interested in the academic study of religion than spiritual practices.

When we asked faculty survey respondents to identify three intentions for the "usefulness" of a course they enjoyed teaching "for students' present and/or future ministries," we provided a list of ten possible answers and asked for three responses. More than 30 percent among this faculty sample indicated they hoped "students would acquire resources" from the course "for their own spiritual growth and for fostering that of others." Nearly 30 percent had created assignments to engage students devotionally with materials in the course. Some described their teaching as "deeply spiritual." They also indicated quite different things by that claim. A teacher of Talmud, for example, pointed out that for Jews "study of the sacred text is itself a religious obligation" and "there is hardly a class in which the theological, spiritual, and/or ethical implications of the talmudic text do not surface." A Christian Bible teacher, although expressing caution about linking insights in class with the activity of God, also seeks to bring "my adoration of God into the classroom" and "model it in my passionate engagement with the Bible."

Many teachers—especially among Protestant seminary educators in freestanding schools—invite students into explicit spiritual practices of prayer or meditation in class. One seminary educator among this group, for example, said "we pray before every class session. The students share very brief concerns, and a different student prays each day." Even in a large class "this builds community." In a university divinity school, another seminary educator begins each class session with "centering silence"—a practice "integral to my discipline."

All this attention among participants in this study suggests that this trend is more generally reshaping the assumptions and practices of contemporary seminary education not only as a new focus of scholarship for research and teaching but also as a mode of discourse and practice in some classes and in programs explicitly designed to cultivate student spirituality. This has all the appearances of a major reform movement in seminary education.

Practical Theology

The contemporary movement in practical theology in Christian seminaries originated, in part, as a response to the challenges of educating Christian clergy for their complex roles and responsibilities in contemporary religious communities. Discussions about practical theology began in the 1970s when Protestants and Catholics began to critique the adequacy of the "professional competence" model of clergy education.[30] Farley, for example, observed that although the competence model had increased attention to the range of technical skills clergy needed, it did little to integrate the concerns of clergy practice with the classic disciplines (1983, pp. 114–16). Instead, it had widened the theory-practice gap. The discourse on practical theology tried to address that gap and restore curricular unity by reorienting the entirety of seminary education toward reflection upon the religious and social praxis of faith communities.

The range of practical theology proposals from scholars in a variety of fields included two predominant strategies: to shift the primary context of theological reflection from theory to issues of practice and to redefine theological reasoning itself as inherently practical. Four basic types of practical theology predominated in the discussion, each with its own model of practical reasoning (Poling and Miller, 1985).[31] The first type employed *social scientific* models of reason to highlight *either* the person-forming power of religion (Hiltner, 1958) or its place in shaping civil society (Bellah, 1975). The second employed a *critical correlation* between tradition and social location *either* to revitalize Christian communities and practice in the public sphere (Fowler, 1985; Palmer, Wheeler, and Fowler, 1990) or to form a *public theology* (Browning, 1983, 1991; Osmer and Schweitzer, 2003). The third uses *critical-confessional* models of practical reason *either* to reconstruct Christian identity and mission (Mudge, 1984; Hough, 1984; Hough and Cobb, 1985) or to provide a vision for the wider society (Groome, 1980; Farley, 1983). The fourth type emphasizes a *transformative praxis* to mobilize faith traditions in the service of *both* ecclesial and social change (Chopp, 1987; Taylor, 1990). These proposals have been catalysts to lively cross-curricular conversation in some seminaries, as we discovered at Catholic Theological Union when Bergant described herself as a "practical theologian," someone who is "practice oriented," or, more precisely, as a "thinking Christian practitioner." For her students in Old Testament, that means she seeks to cultivate "a *habitus* way of thinking" for crossing the disciplines of the seminary curriculum so that when her students are in Fragomeni's class they will be able to "think biblically in a liturgical context," and when in Nairn's class they will be able to "think biblically as ethicists."

The emphasis on *practical reasoning* as a way of thinking in each of these practical theology proposals has shifted the attention of some seminary educators away from nurturing in students the ability to apply theory to the activities of professional practice and toward developing in students the capacity to move back and forth, as William Sullivan has written, through a "three-fold pattern" of thinking and action from "engagement with the concrete situation" of a ministry event "through detached observation and analysis" of that event "and back again to more informed engagement" with the persons or situations involved in it (Sullivan, 2005, p. 244). At Catholic Theological Union, Nairn explicitly seeks to cultivate this pattern of thinking in the study of medical ethics cases as he guides students through the pedagogical activities of *reacting* to the facts in the case, *retrieving* insights from religious tradition with the potential of illuminating the case, and *reconstructing* a response to address issues in the case. Lyman fosters a similar pattern of thinking in her church history class at Church Divinity School of the Pacific; she moves students through an encounter with a text to an exploration of that text in the dialectic of its original and contemporary context, to an examination of its meanings and significance in the present situation. The modes of practical reasoning in seminary education vary—due, in great part, to the variety of settings for learning professional practice. These range, for example, from clinical and pastoral care settings to community rites and liturgy, from education in congregations to global mission, from symbols of civil religion to ethics of public discourse, and from the liberatory concerns of mainstream women to those of the poor and oppressed.

A few contributors to the discussion of practical theology have pushed the conversation beyond the situational practice of practical reasoning in courses like those taught by Nairn and Lyman or the discussions among students and field education supervisors about some ministry experience, to specific proposals for the reform of seminary education (Hough and Cobb, 1985; Fiorenza, 1987; Mudge and Poling, 1987; Browning, Polk, and Evison, 1989; Chopp, 1995). Among these, perhaps the most prominent emphasized the congregation as the primary social location for action and reflection in seminary education (Hough and Wheeler; Hopewell, 1984). We saw this alternative way of thinking about how to engage students at the intersection of the academic and professional most explicitly in the interplay of congregation and school in Trinity Lutheran Seminary's program. Other seminaries have incorporated the study of congregations into some courses. A few schools have appointed a faculty member in a field of "congregational studies."[32] However, discussions on the pedagogical possibilities in practical theology—and of congregational studies more specifically—in shaping the future of seminary education are still relatively new. Whether or not they will be the subject of another chapter in the story of seminary education or lead to the establishment of a new framework of practical reasoning in seminary education is not yet clear.

The Pastoral Imagination: Its Contribution to Public Life and American Modernity

Throughout the twentieth century, changing expectations about clergy roles and responsibilities have increasingly challenged the adequacy of the pastoral, priestly, or rabbinic imaginations that the various seminary traditions were attempting to nurture. During the early decades of the century an increasing consciousness of social pressures—from industrialization, urbanization, immigration, and other modern social processes—intensified expectations for social advocacy and relevancy among clergy educated in all seminary traditions.[33] These expectations ranged from the growing attention in some religious circles to problems of labor, poverty, and civil rights to deepening concern in others about the influence of secular, antireligious forces like communism.[34] By the 1950s, clergy were increasingly expected to see themselves as institution builders and managers of full-service congregations supporting a range of ministries of worship, education, pastoral counseling, social welfare, and community organizing.[35] After the 1960s, new social movements of civil rights, women's liberation, pacifism, and sexual liberation often led to views of clergy as social mediators among the traditional institutions of school, church, family, and sometimes the state. More progressive priests, religious sisters, rabbis, and pastors, like Martin Luther King Jr., sought to expand and transform existing institutions to embrace these new movements, while neoevangelicals, like Billy Graham, cautioned against godless change and the jettisoning of traditional values (Carpenter). By the end of the century clergy were also being asked to become spiritual therapists and guides to heal wounds of social division, urban decay, economic disruption, and suburban isolation.

The polarization of religious and seminary education traditions into modernist and liberal or fundamentalist and traditionalist responses to modernity in the early twentieth century concealed how they all adopted aspects of modern social organization and cultural reproduction that had direct impact on the way they viewed and approached the education of clergy. For example, while Jewish "modernizers," both Reform and Conservative, were appropriating methods of higher learning and developing rabbinical associations and denominations, traditional Orthodox were invigorating *yeshivot* and Yiddish newspapers with modern institutional forms (Raphael). While denominations like the African Methodist Episcopal Church embraced modern colleges and seminaries for educating the clergy, many independent Baptists and Pentecostals continued to rely on "spiritual leaders" called and apprenticed in the local congregation. While liberal Protestants were using, in seminary education, forms of "high-culture" literacy and the arts, fundamentalists were mastering the tools of popular culture and advertising in radio, mass rallies, and tracts (Carpenter). And while Catholics advocating "Americanism/ modernism" were embracing the social sciences, voluntary associations, and labor unions, traditionalists were enhancing the congregation, parochial school, and college with modern forms of organization. In other words, despite differences in the ways each seminary education tradition responded to these various challenges of modern cultural production, each also emphasized pedagogical practices designed to prepare clergy to represent their religious traditions with distinctive symbolic practices and world views, while responding constructively to new and challenging circumstances with distinctive symbolic practices in the encounter of their religious traditions and modernity.

More recently, the transformation of "modernity" by contemporary forces of globalization has created new challenges for seminaries educating clergy to be both representatives of the cultures of their religious traditions and agents or builders of those cultures in the changing dynamics of globalization in the modern world. With the onset of what Appadurai has called the "global flows" of mass media, ideology, technology, finance, and immigration, the "acids of modernity" corroding inherited religious and cultural traditions have taken a new form (1996, p. 33). Seminary educators, like their peers in all other modern institutions, find themselves caught in the tension between these "global forces" and the needs of "local" human communities. A pervasive response for negotiating the tension between the overdetermining dynamics of these "global flows" and heightened awareness of human needs for identity and action in local communities has been the construction of symbolic worldviews in what Appadurai has called "sites of locality" or "neighborhood" for human engagement (Appadurai, pp. 178ff).[36] These world views become resources for interactions with and, sometimes, resistance to the global forces impinging on local communities.[37]

The challenge for contemporary seminary educators is finding ways to cultivate the pastoral, priestly, or rabbinic imaginations of their students as cultural representatives and builders of their religious traditions in the midst of the interaction of these global and local movements (Schreiter, 1997). One way to understand these challenges is to think of two axes of interaction. The first axis describes the cultural tension between forces of "the global" and "the local" in which the pastoral imagination reconstructs a symbolic world view as a relatively stable, but responsive mediation or "glocalization" (Robertson, 1995) between these two forces. Pedagogies of interpretation, for example, can facilitate a reading of global trends in relation to the "universalizing" symbols and practices of religious traditions. Pedagogies of contextualization, on the other hand, can encourage the development of local strategies of inherited community practices and symbolizations for appropriating or resisting encounters with global flows. What emerges in the interplay of both pedagogies is the cultivation of a symbolic imagination for rendering "local community" in terms of a "global" mission and world view.

During the course of this study, we observed, for example, evangelical seminary educators nurturing a strong sense of local community poised for evangelization of the world; Jewish seminary educators cultivating Jewish identity supporting worldwide Jewish civilization and nationalism; and Catholic seminary educators emphasizing an appreciation for local cultures, institutions, and communities, with respect, at the same time, for a global institution and the authority of a historic symbolic tradition.

The second axis describes the tension of forming clergy persons as both cultural representatives and culture builders. In order to make concrete "the local" in the midst of changing "global flows" (Tomlinson, 1999), clergy must also be formed as representatives, even icons, of the symbolic cultural world they stand for. At the same time, they must equip local communities with the practices and discourses of that symbolic world for living in and engaging their own settings with meaning and purpose. Consequently, pedagogies of formation focus on shaping the person of the pastor, priest, or rabbi as a cultural representative who inspires local community practice as an extension and expression of a religious tradition and serves as an implicit or explicit norm of faithfulness. Pedagogies of performance, on the other hand, cultivate in clergy the skills and role identities as culture builders to equip community practice and symbolic discourse for encounters with impinging global forces.

What emerges is the profound interaction between a form of *paideia*—embodied in the person of pastor, priest, or rabbi—that inspires and equips an imaginative habitus, or way of being in the world, for a religious community. We have seen how Protestant clerics, historically, embodied the rhetorical arts in a way that empowered the community's culture-building mission of education and social reform; how traditionalist Catholics forged a sacramental understanding of the priest to model a sacred space and way of life for being both Catholic and American; and how rabbis embodying a level of Jewish practice and devotion have helped many Jewish communities solidify their identity and practice as a distinct religious and cultural tradition in the global landscape. This deeply symbiotic, even spiritual, relationship between the *paideia* of the cleric and the habitus of the local community is one of the distinctive marks of the clergy profession.

ENDNOTES

1. Of all these, Zionism is the most complex, as it caused dissension as well as cooperation among Jewish communities and their seminaries. Increased collaboration and shared agendas among Reform, Conservative, and modern Orthodox seminaries, however, were enhanced by their support of Hebrew teaching and learning, Jewish colonization of Palestine, the establishment of study institutes in Israel, an extension of Judaism as a pan-national "civilization," and the political support for the new state of Israel that followed the Holocaust (Lederhendler, 1997; Meyer, 1988, pp. 293–97, 326–34).

2. Dwight's "federalism" was eclipsed by Jacksonian populism, and his version of "New Divinity" was displaced by the "Yale Theology" of Nathaniel Taylor (Fitzmier, 1998).

3. Lutherans opened schools in Hartwick (1815), Gettysburg (1826), Columbus (1830), and Lexington (1835). Episcopalians opened General in New York (1817), Virginia Theological (1823), and Kenyon in Ohio (1828). Congregationalists continued with schools in Bangor, Maine (1816), Yale Divinity School (1823), Hartford (1833), Oberlin in Ohio (1838), and Western Reserve in Ohio (with New School Presbyterians) (1838). After Princeton (1812), Presbyterians established seminaries at Auburn, New York (1820), Maryville in Tennessee (1821), Union in Richmond (1823), Columbia in South Carolina, and Southern (later, Louisville Seminary) in Louisville (1832). In light of a schism, New School Presbyterians opened Union in New York (1836), Western Reserve (1838), and Lane in Cincinnati (1839). Baptists opened Newton in Massachusetts (1819), Hamilton in New York (1820), Virginia Baptist (1832), Baptist Literary and Theological Institute (later Mercer) in Georgia (1834), and Southern Baptist in Kentucky (1850). Smaller groups began Harvard Divinity School (1824, Unitarian); a seminary at Mercersburg, Pennsylvania (1825, German Reformed); Pittsburgh Theological Seminary (1818, Associated Presbyterians); and Western in Pittsburgh (1828, American Presbyterians). Methodists built seminaries at Newbury (1839), Concord (1847), Vermont (1834), Garrett in Chicago (1855), and Drew in New Jersey, right after the Civil War (1867).

4. The 1860 census report, by way of comparison, reports more than two hundred colleges in the country. By the 1920s the number of colleges and

universities in comparison to the number of seminaries had increased dramatically.

5. Farley documents the rise of the academic specialties and the failure of a professional "clerical paradigm" to unite them in *Theologia* (1983, pp. 87, 127–35). As we discuss later, however, each of the seminary traditions tried to unite the various disciplines in their own ways, so that the functional view of the "clerical paradigm" was only one option.

6. In Europe, neoorthodoxy was dominated by Karl Barth, but in America the dominant influences were Reinhold Niebuhr (Union New York), H. Richard Niebuhr (Yale), and the Swiss theologian Emil Brunner, especially at Princeton. Paul Tillich, although originally identified with the theological movement of neoorthodoxy in Europe, developed what he called the "correlational method" while at Union New York. It would later become a hallmark of liberal and contextual theologies (Ahlstrom, 1976, pp. 932–48).

7. Farley (1983) and especially Kelsey (1993) acknowledge the pull of both "poles" of the tension, but they do not distinguish the "foundational" and "clerical" models enough as distinct strategies adopted by different seminaries. Furthermore, each in its own way is a response to the larger university pressures of specialization and professionalization.

8. During those first fifty years, Moody had 19,785 students enrolled in residence, 17,219 as evening students, 83,257 as correspondence students, and 9,469 in the WMBI Radio School of the Bible, for a total of 129,730 (Day, p. 265).

9. The earliest schools included the Alliance Training School in New York (later Nyack, 1882), Conwell Bible School in Philadelphia (1884), Gordon Bible Institute in Boston (1889), and the Bible Institute of Pennsylvania (1894).

10. Early-twentieth-century schools in the fundamentalist-evangelical movement of higher education included the Northwestern Bible and Missionary Training School in Minneapolis (1902), the Bible Institute of Los Angeles (1908), The Philadelphia School of the Bible (1913), Prairie Bible Institute in Alberta (1922), and Columbia Bible School in South Carolina (1923) (Carpenter, p. 17).

11. In 1909 Oxford University Press published what has been known since as the *Scofield Bible*. In preparing this version of the Bible for publication Cyrus Scofield added extensive notations to the King James Version of the Bible to mark the various "dispensations" of God in history, according to the teachings of John Darby, Scofield's teacher.

12. After working with the project for two years, Torrey assumed responsibility for editing the last two volumes. He then edited with A. C. Dixon a new four-volume edition called *The Fundamentals* published by Baker House in Grand Rapids in 1917.

13. A Yale study in 1916 documented sixty-one training schools in the United States, dominated not by the Bible institutes but by deaconess, social work, and YMCA schools (Behan, 1916).

14. The AME Church reestablished Wilberforce in Ohio (1863), and founded Western University in Kansas (1864), Morris Brown in Georgia (1881), Paul Quinn in Texas (1881), Allen University in South Carolina (1881), Shorter in Arkansas (1886), Kittrell in North Carolina (1886), Edward Waters in Florida (1888), Payne University in Alabama (1889), Campbell College in Missouri (1890), Turner College in Tennessee (1890), and Lampton College in Louisiana (1911). In 1924, all of these except Turner still had theological departments (Daniels, 1875, pp. 23–25). The AME Zion began Livingstone College in North Carolina (1882), and the CME opened Lane College in Tennessee (1882), its primary seminary, and Texas College (1894), Mississippi Industrial College (1905), and Miles Memorial College in Alabama (1905), all of which had theological departments at one time.

15. Black Baptist denominations founded over one hundred schools, of varying sizes and strengths. Some of the largest and most lasting were Houston College (1885), Virginia Theological Seminary (1888), Western College in Michigan (1890), Friendship Baptist College in South Carolina (1891), Meridian Baptist Seminary in Mississippi (1897), Central City College in Macon (1899), Central Texas College (1901), Conroe Normal and Industrial College in Texas (1905), Morris College in South Carolina (1905), Central Baptist in Kansas (1921), and Northern Baptist University in New Jersey (1913).

16. Many African American seminaries that followed Wilberforce began under the auspices of white denominations and missionary organizations. American Baptists founded six black institutes, such as Shaw in North Carolina (1865), and five more with black Baptist denominations, such as Simmons in Kentucky (1873). Northern Methodists founded six black schools, such as Rust in Mississippi (1866) and Gammon in Atlanta (1883). Presbyterian groups centralized their black seminary training in four schools, including Biddle University (later, Johnson C. Smith) in North Carolina (1867) and Knoxville College (1875). The American Missionary Association, spearheaded by Congregationalists, began twenty-one schools by 1870, including many lasting institutions, such as Hampton Institute in Virginia (1868), Fisk School (later Fisk University) in Nashville (1866), and Howard

Normal and Theological Institute (later Howard University) in Washington, D.C. (1867). The Federal Freedman's Bureau helped build the facilities of larger black schools, while missionary and church bodies provided faculty and program (Daniel, 1925, pp. 19–21). Some Southern white denominations founded black schools, such as South Paine College (Southern Methodist, 1883), the Tuskaloosa Institute (Presbyterian, later Stillman) (1876), and the Southern Baptists' Divinity Seminary, in cooperation with the National Baptists. In almost all instances the education of clergy in these institutions existed as a part of the institutional mission.

17. University theology programs and seminaries were usually far ahead of freestanding seminaries in the interface of theology and the social sciences (White, 1989, pp. 318–35).

18. Farley offers a powerful analysis of this shift in theological study from "habitus of wisdom" to "clerical paradigm," from literary avenues in the service of "theologia" (a sapiential knowledge of God) to distinct theological "sciences" with their own rationales and faculties for educating clergy (1983, pp. 29–124). This shift in the fourfold curriculum also provided a blueprint for organizing theological faculties into academic guilds like their counterparts across the university; for example, the American Society for Church History, the Society of Biblical Literature (Miller, p. 638), the American Catholic Philosophical Association, the Catholic Theological Society of America (1946) (White, 1989, pp. 371–73; Carey and Muller, 1997, pp. 151–53), and the Society of Jewish Academicians of America (Wertheimer, 1997, I, p. 347). Although many scholars find Farley's analysis of the fragmentation of theologia into discrete disciplines and guilds compelling (Handy, 1982; Kelsey, 1993; Chopp, 1995; Gilpin, 1996), we attribute this narrowing of the focus of the study of the theological literature as much to the increasing alignment of the seminary with the research university as to the increasing dominance of a "clerical paradigm."

19. Farley lamented the "pedagogical" and "curricular" nature of the fourfold curriculum (1983, p. 136), but in the pluralistic and pragmatic landscape of American Christianity, that was its strength.

20. In passing, Farley (1983, p. 108) does note that the nineteenth-century encyclopedists established the methodological precedence of unity by retaining "historical methods in each of the four theological sciences."

21. Farley acknowledges this original unifying feature in the American context (1981, p. 100) and Gilpin emphasizes the affinity of the encyclopedic tradition in American evangelicalism because both emphasize biblical authority (Gilpin, pp. 55–57). But neithers see this as a viable option for

late-twentieth-century theological education. Evangelicals, of course, disagree (Hart and Mohler, 1996, pp. 20–21).

22. Compare the Kelly study of Protestant curricula in the 1920s (Kelly, pp. 113–27) with the Heck study of Catholic theologates in the same period (White, 1989, pp. 364–70).

23. Originally the council was called the National Council of Schools of Religion, a name that it held for only two years.

24. By 1971, the "Welch Report" of the American Council of Learned Societies highlighted the influence of these schools, observing that of the fifty-two Ph.D. programs in religion in the United States, nineteen did not rely on a divinity school faculty.

25. The council was renamed the Society on Religion in Higher Education in 1962.

26. Fielding lists no fewer than twenty-three specialized ministries of the clergy (Fielding et al., pp. 79–80)!

27. These methods were especially influenced by nineteenth-century advocates of Common Sense Realism (Carpenter, pp. 5, 32; Kuklick, 1985, pp. 128–39).

28. Source criticism identifies different literary-historical threads in the Hebrew Scriptures—J (Yahwist), E (Elohist), P (Priestly), and D (Deuteronomic)— which in turn demonstrated such things as that Moses was not the author of the Pentateuch.

29. *Lectio divina* is a method of reading holy Scripture as a devotional, meditative exercise.

30. The more historic term for this "field" is *pastoral theology,* which is meant to cover the full range of clergy service, and it is still used in many Catholic and European contexts. In the United States, however, pastoral theology in Protestant seminaries has been dominated by members of the pastoral care and counseling field; in Catholic seminaries it includes canon law, homiletics, liturgical practica, and sometimes religious education and spiritual direction.

31. Poling and Miller (1985) identify three methods in practical theology: critical-scientific, critical-correlational, and critical-confessional, each with two versions. We add a fourth method, based in "transformative praxis" (Chopp, 1987; Taylor, 1990).

32. Some of the drawbacks of the ethnographic focus of "congregational studies" have been its reticence to engage "action-research" oriented toward the transformation of congregational systems and its reluctance

to support normative or prescriptive understandings of theology or sacred text.

33. These intensified expectations were especially true of the Federal Council of Churches and its member denominations before World War II.

34. Conspiracy theories against communism were common among early fundamentalists (Carpenter, 102–105), and neoevangelicals like Billy Graham spoke out against the threat of communism (Hudson, 1981, pp. 385–87).

35. The demands of the multipurpose congregation led to H. Richard Niebuhr's call in the 1950s for modern clergy to become "pastoral directors" of this all-service institution.

36. Appadurai calls the radical form of this social-symbolic response the creation of "cultural primordia," which strengthens localism in the face of modernity's global onslaught (Appadurai, 1996, pp. 139–42).

37. Clergy became major players in the "culture wars" of the late twentieth century (Hunter, 1990) because they are so effective in building and reinforcing local pockets of cultural identity, which are in reality as much a response to global forces as to the cultural "other" around them who hold a different symbolic world view.

9

CULTIVATING SPIRITUAL PRACTICES FOR CLERGY LEADERSHIP

AN ESSENTIAL CAPACITY OF CLERGY PRACTICE—and perhaps its most distinctive—is facility with the spiritual dimensions of human life and experience. Clergy are routinely expected to exercise this capacity in ordinary actions and rituals: teaching, preaching, leading liturgy, and even conversing. They are sought out in times of personal, community, national, or global crises. Clergy are expected to expertly field questions about sacred texts and ethics; to preside competently at public rituals; to evoke, welcome, and respond to often fumbling articulations of highly intimate spiritual experience and deeply personal need. In dealing with people's questions, fears, and hopes about the ultimate meaning of their lives and experiences, clergy require sensitivity and skill. They must sense which aspects of their particular religious tradition might best provide resources for healing or liberating; they must know how to be prophetic in given situations and how to frame appropriate responses for changing situations and circumstances in congregations and communities.

How are clergy prepared to exercise this capacity? In what ways do seminaries cultivate the knowledge and skills and nurture the dispositions and habits associated with the spiritual dimensions of clergy leadership?

Clergy who graduated from the seminaries participating in this study described the influence of their seminary education on their response to the national crisis precipitated by the attacks of September 11, 2001, on the World Trade Center and Pentagon:

o A rabbi in Manhattan who, among other things, had disseminated information "about bereavement services and planned an observance on the thirtieth day after the catastrophe in keeping with the Jewish tradition of *sheloshim,* an observance that occurs thirty days after the burial of a loved one," wrote that her seminary education had prepared her to respond in this way "by reinforcing my sense that Jewish tradition is rich in rituals to help the mourner."

○ A vocation director at a Florida Benedictine monastery recalls that "All I could think of as the events were unfolding was how I could be the compassionate presence of Christ to those who were frightened, worried, or doubtful of God's presence. My next thoughts were how to diffuse the almost certain anger that would erupt and how to teach non-violent responses to said anger. I turned to prayer, scripture, to my non-violent-conflict-resolution training, and to my community in order to implement all of the ideas and I continue to do so as new and perhaps related events arise. The primary way my graduate theology education prepared me was by the community atmosphere that is prevalent at St. John's. [Through] my Benedictine training . . . this kind of response has become almost second-nature to me. The secondary way is how my prayer life deepened during my years there. It has given me much more of an inner peace which I can bring to stressful situations."

○ "Perhaps my training in spiritual direction [during seminary] gave me confidence to plan" two events, wrote an Indiana Mennonite pastor: the first an "evening prayer service" as a "way to respond to the shock of the event and to reaffirm that we place our ultimate trust in God," the second a "lament service the following Sunday," which gave the congregation the opportunity "to truly mourn and read uncomfortable scriptures, be honest about asking God hard questions all within the context of the worshipping community," and to preach the peace sermon "central to the Mennonite theology of the gospel." This respondent continued: "There is no emotion or experience God cannot handle; no rage or fear that makes God turn away. The seminary emphasized over and over again that platitudes do not invite people to really experience God," but that extending an "invitation to explore their real experience in the presence of God does."

For these seminary graduates, several key elements had been instrumental in preparing them to engage the spiritual dimensions of this moment of national crisis: (1) an immersion, during their schooling, in the spiritual resources of their religious traditions, (2) sustained participation in the spiritual practices of those traditions, and (3) opportunities to exercise the knowledge of those religious traditions in the rituals and practices associated with their work as clergy.

Spiritual leadership, however, does not consist solely of responding to others or putting together ritual or teaching events, crucial as these are. As we described in the chapter on the pedagogies of formation, a primary goal of spiritual formation is the capacity for personal *transparency* in relation to God or the ultimate truths of one's religious tradition. The capacity of the priest, rabbi, or pastor for authentic spiritual presence in the face of others' needs emerges from the depths of his or her encounters with the ultimate mystery of God and from the depths of religious tradition, as well as from experiences of loss, suffering, joy, transition, or death. In crises and in everyday life, clergy are expected both to embody the life of faith or observance in ways that are somehow paradigmatic and to invite others into the most sacred practices of their tradition to provide sustenance, orientation, mutual presence, and hope in the face of chaos and death. In short, in a complex world, future clergy need both personal and professional grounding in what we are broadly referring to as "spiritual practices."

As part of the study, we explored how seminaries organize themselves to cultivate in students the numinous or transcendent dimensions of their religious traditions that would provide this personal and professional grounding in spiritual practice. We discovered great variety. Indeed, we found much more variation in ways of cultivating spiritual practice than we did in approaches to classroom teaching. In some schools communal worship is central: taking place several times a day, involving all or nearly all the community membership in various roles, and providing an encompassing liturgical or interpretive framework for what goes on in classrooms and the life of the community. In other seminaries, worship seems to be almost tangential: it takes place once or twice a week, attendance is spotty, and contributions to the larger culture or to pedagogical practices are not particularly visible.

In some seminaries, most of the student community practices selected spiritual disciplines in small groups—some highly structured, others quite informal. In other seminaries such groups are rare. Some seminaries engage students in formal programs of spiritual direction. In other seminaries, students are supervised in their spiritual growth primarily by their denominations through candidacy processes for ordination. Despite these variations, the faculties we observed seemed to emphasize one or more of these three strategies for cultivating among their students the spiritual dimensions of clergy leadership: community worship, programs using small groups and peers in spiritual formation, and programs of individual spiritual formation.

Cultivating Spirituality Through Community Worship

Every school in the study sponsors some sort of program—chapel or common worship—that becomes a primary site for cultivating shared or communal spiritual practices. Although we found great diversity in the forms such programs take, one feature common to all is that they provide, to some extent, a locus of community interaction, training (implicit or explicit) in performance, and a (or the) symbolic center of the school. In the setting of common worship, students experience faculty and administrators not only as lecturers or advisors but as preachers and liturgists. Conversely, the faculty, staff, and administrators watch students grow from novice acolytes into seasoned assistants, deacons, ritualists, and, in some seminaries, preachers. In common worship, the community members together weather its crises and those of the world, share needs, celebrate joys, mourn losses and other tragedies, and observe the ritual cycles of the tradition.

Worship patterns vary not only from seminary to seminary but within many of the seminaries we visited. From the highly structured, formal, and symbolically complex services of St. Vladimir's cycles of matins, vespers, vigils, and Eucharist to the devotional, emotive tone of Fuller's Advent service, the liturgies of seminary worship span a range of styles not unlike those to be found in the congregations their students will eventually serve. Worship has as its primary values nurturing spiritual bonds among members of the community; doing "primary theology"—that is, providing places for individuals and the community to experience, celebrate, taste, sing, proclaim, confess, or adore that to which (or the One to Whom) the rest of their intellectual, ministerial, and logistical activity is directed;[1] and nurturing dispositions, sensibilities, and habits associated with such spiritual practices as praise, confession, and thanksgiving. Seminary worship has the additional function of cultivating the spirituality and the spiritual leadership of future clergy leaders, most explicitly by fostering in students an awareness of the range and depth of their religious liturgical tradition, a variety of worship styles, and the musical idioms of different cultures while at the same time cultivating and increasing confidence and skill in worship leadership.

In the seminaries we visited, we found that the role of community worship in the students' spiritual formation was significantly influenced or determined by shared assumptions among the members of the faculty about the larger role of the seminary in the students' spiritual formation; the place of worship in the life of the seminary community; the assignment

of responsibility for community worship (who plans, leads, and participates); and the extent to which community worship is viewed as having a
pedagogical as well as a liturgical function in the life of the seminary. These
assumptions, we also discovered, are influenced by the liturgical traditions
of the sponsoring school, by the extent to which students reside in or commute to school, and the religious and cultural composition of the seminary
community.

A Shared Liturgical Tradition

Among the schools we visited associated with denominations with strong
liturgical traditions—Christian Orthodox, Lutheran, Roman Catholic,
Anglican, and Conservative Jewish—most students and faculty identified
strongly with those religious traditions. A large percentage of the seminary community participates in community worship. Worship typically
functions at the center of the life of the school and is viewed as a primary
site of academic, professional, and spiritual formation.

The chapel program at the Church Divinity School of the Pacific in
Berkeley provides an example of a carefully constructed liturgical apprenticeship that contributes to the students' spiritual formation. (Our description is drawn from a focus group conversation with students in their final
year of seminary and the Chapel Formulary.) In the first year, students
take a course, "Fundamentals of Worship." The students remember that
the course deconstructed many of their cherished notions of worship and
introduced them to the wider liturgical traditions of their denomination.
Students had a rotation of assigned participation in planning and leading
the fifteen worship services each week of the school year. During the worship services, they observed faculty preaching and celebrating the
Eucharist. In their senior year, students preach in chapel and, in their final
semester, take another course on worship, where they "put together liturgies" and "see how each person has developed" over the course of their
seminary experience.

As one Church Divinity School student observed, "a lot of time is spent
in chapel." The offices surrounding the atrium of one of the campus buildings may function as the administrative center of the campus. The dining
hall and adjoining courtyard may function as the social center of the campus. Classrooms are scattered across the campus. However, the chapel,
which sits off to the edge of the campus, is not only its liturgical center;
it may also be its pedagogical center. In this place, the secular rhythms of
the academic calendar are transformed as the seminary community moves
through the liturgical events of the Christian year and the liturgies of each

week. The eleven ordained faculty members preach regularly and share leadership (along with invited guests) of the five daily eucharistic liturgies. Prior to each worship service, the dean of the chapel physically models and then guides the students and faculty members involved in its leadership through each movement in the liturgy in what is undoubtedly the most consistent pedagogical activity students experience. Community investment in the worship life of the community is high. Attendance is not required, but is expected, and participation is significant—especially for the mid-morning and Thursday afternoon eucharistic liturgies.

Among several influences on the community worship in the education of Church Divinity School students, two are especially important: the commitment of faculty to the role of worship, and the homogeneity of the seminary community. The faculty is committed to the centrality of worship in seminary life and to the importance of mentoring students as liturgical leaders over the course of their studies. They invest time in the worship program. Offering fifteen services a week (five of which require ordained leadership) requires oversight and planning. Faculty members prepare sermons, work with students assigned to the services, approve student prayers, lead rehearsals, and later provide feedback. All this is in addition to the actual time spent in chapel, in the classroom, and on committees. For the members of this faculty, academic responsibilities and roles of formation clearly overlap.

The school's religious homogeneity also significantly shapes community worship in the education of Church Divinity School of the Pacific students. The seminary is part of a consortium of seminaries, the Graduate Theological Union in Berkeley. This participation puts the Church Divinity School in a larger ecumenical environment. Students from any institution in the consortium are permitted to take courses at any other consortium seminary. However, the vast majority of the students admitted to the Church Divinity School of the Pacific are related to one of the member churches of the Anglican communion around the world. This shared identity provides a common theological and ecclesiastical heritage within which the intensive deepening of liturgical practice unfolds. There is no debate about which denomination's order of worship should be used in a given week, whether nonliturgical worship styles should be given a higher profile, or whether the services are becoming "too Christian" in the interreligious world that makes up the larger Berkeley community. We discovered that among the few students, staff, and faculty in the seminary who are not Anglican, worshipping only in the Anglican way can be experienced as marginalizing for some. At the same time, for the majority of the seminary community, and for Anglicans in the Graduate Theological

Union who participate in the worship program at the Church Divinity School, this shared liturgical life enhances and deepens their formation in the communal spiritual practices of that religious tradition.

Diverse Liturgical Traditions

In more religiously diverse contexts, such as those at Candler, Fuller, Yale, and—to a significant extent—in free-standing Protestant seminaries with students from several denominations (Louisville Presbyterian Theological Seminary, Garrett-Evangelical Theological Seminary, and North Park Theological Seminary, for example), the chapel program has a somewhat different role. In these seminaries, the community is confronted with the challenge of being responsive to the *diversity* of the students' religious traditions and cultures at the same time it is engaged in their academic, spiritual, and pastoral *formation*. Faculty and administration in these seminaries must consider complex and difficult questions about the role of worship in their education:

o How much diversity of liturgical form, language, musical style, or personal and cultural expression is conducive to students' formation in their religious traditions?

o How much diversity is needed to stretch students' imaginations beyond the limits of their own backgrounds and into new expressions or different conceptions of their traditions?

o At what point does diversity of worship forms (or of students' own religious affiliations) limit the ways in which shared worship can be formative to any?

o *Which* religious, cultural, and national diversities in the student and faculty community are to be viewed as most beneficial in the seminary's intentions for student formation?

Church Divinity School of the Pacific addresses these questions, in part, through its participation in an ecumenical consortium of schools that provide alternative liturgical approaches to the religious formation of students. Some seminaries with significant religious and cultural diversity negotiate the relation of religious and cultural diversity and the spiritual formation of their students in more direct fashion. The assistant dean of worship and music at the Candler School of Theology, for instance, notes that in its chapel program, oriented broadly within shared Christian lectionary and sacramental practice,

[W]e weave a variety of services. Some are particularly denominational—United Methodist, Episcopal, AME, Lutheran—and are taken
intentionally from those worship books. Other services are more culturally based: Korean, pan-African, African-American ("black
church"). And some are "event" driven: Women's Week, Heritage
Week, etc. These particular services/weeks are all held together by,
nested in, what the students tend to call "Candler worship," that
unique blend of music, prayer, preaching, artistic expression that looks
and sounds like "us." This variety invites the community to both experience what they know (their "heart language" as Hoyt Hickman says)
and to expand their liturgical language and their relationship to the
whole church.

In a similar fashion at Yale, worship on any given day may represent a
typical "service of the Word" in the style of one of the Christian traditions
represented on campus, or something else entirely. For instance, on one
day of our visit, during the season of Lent, the pews in the worship space
were configured to form a labyrinth. To the sound of quiet organ music,
worshipers moved slowly and in silence along a path laid out as the Sta-
tions of the Cross. Each station included a painting by a local artist and
text about the significance of the station in light of some contemporary
reality. The chapel program at Yale emphasizes musical quality (a contribution of the Institute for Sacred Music), ecumenical and cultural diversity, creativity, and intellectual rigor.

Indeed, both Yale and Candler must address the challenge of including
people meaningfully from diverse religious backgrounds without devolv-
ing into either a "lowest common denominator" or a mere series of daily
events, each from some new perspective yet disconnected from one
another. Yale Divinity School does not intentionally apprentice all students into liturgical leadership nor view their participation in chapel as
essential to their preparation for clergy practice. Yet in a theological world
strong on critical methodology and academic excellence, its chapel program provides a locus for experimentation with old and new prayer forms
in an intellectually rigorous and very "real world" of religious diversity.
Although attendance on any given day in any of the scheduled worship
services may only be twenty percent of the total student community,
nevertheless, over the course of a week, about half the students and many
faculty members participate in community worship—including a significant number each day. Worship is undoubtedly as *formative* for some in
the Yale community as it is for those with whom we talked at the Church

Divinity School of the Pacific, but the intent and content of that formation looks quite different.[2]

At Fuller Theological Seminary, chapel programs for the full seminary
community did not, at the time of our visit, represent the kind of institutional investment we observed at either Church Divinity School of the
Pacific or Yale Divinity School.[3] Chapel services designed for the whole
community were held twice a week. One service in the sanctuary of the
First Congregational Church and just beyond the campus emphasized historical Protestant worship traditions. The other, held in a campus audito-
rium, reflected the influence of contemporary praise services. Especially in
this latter (and more popular) service, students were granted considerable
authority to create, change, critique, discard, or improvise the elements of
worship. Only a fraction of this large seminary community attended either
service—indeed, many students were not on campus when they occurred.

Other opportunities for worship for different constituencies of the seminary community continue to be offered throughout the week. Some follow denominational liturgical forms. One follows the worship patterns of
the black church. Others are in Spanish, Japanese, and Korean. A Taize
prayer service[4] is offered on occasion. During our visit some students described the role of seminary community in worship as important in their
formation for ministry, but both faculty and students placed more emphasis on small groups and course work as primary sites for cultivating spiritual practices.

Cultivating Student Spirituality Through Small Groups

Seminaries also engage students in a variety of small groups established
to facilitate the development of a range of spiritual disciplines and practices. These small groups, present in some form at every school we visited, often exist in service to other features of community life, but they
are used to cultivate spiritual practice. In the seminaries we visited, these
groups vary in form and purpose; for example, the *havrutah* study pairs
at Jewish Theological Seminary, the Bible study and prayer groups at
Southwestern Baptist, the community service at St. Vladimir's, Trinity's
integrative groups, St. John's small-group faith-sharing processes on quiet
days and retreats, Candler's contextual education groups, and Howard's
faith formation classes.[5]

The purpose, structure, and focus of these small groups are, if anything,
even more complex than are the liturgical styles and traditions of the seminaries in which we observed them; for example:

o All first-year students at Southwestern Baptist Theological Seminary participate for a full academic year in weekly "spiritual life groups" led by faculty members and other staff. They use a comprehensive and well-organized notebook, entitled "The Journey," to provide a common, but also intimate experience of spiritual practice. The notebook includes daily scriptural devotions organized around weekly themes, accompanied by reflection questions and space for journal entries.

o Students at every stage of Trinity Lutheran Seminary's three-year program are gathered into "integration groups." Led by faculty and students, these groups meet weekly. Throughout their seminary careers, students can turn to the group for mutual support and academic consultation, spiritual growth, and vocational reflection. Each group also takes responsibility for planning and leading the daily worship services for one of the weeks in the school year.

o All students in the Master of Divinity program at Howard University School of Divinity participate in a series of faculty-led small-group courses designed to engage students in the practice of spiritual disciplines. Despite their location in the formal academic program, these groups illustrate many of the features of small groups more generally in the cultivation of spiritual practices among the seminaries in this study.

Although we found no uniform practices in the use of small groups to foster students' spiritual formation, we discerned two basic uses of small groups for this purpose: small groups can be used to create a space in a busy seminary calendar to tend to students' spiritual growth and they can center the spiritual life of the seminary community, thus contributing to students' spiritual development. We also wondered to what extent small groups might facilitate a public as well as a personal spirituality.

Creating Space for Spiritual Growth

Dr. Dolores Carpenter, professor of religious education, designed Howard's six-semester course sequence on faith development and spiritual formation in the 1990s. Students receive one-half of a course credit for each semester, and all members of the faculty teach in the sequence. The overarching purpose of the program is to provide a place where students can, as one professor told us, "bridge the abstract and the concrete"; that is, make connections among academic work, ministry context, and personal and spiritual growth. In groups of eight to ten, students are introduced to spiritual disciplines and the literature of Christian spirituality with the intention of helping them move toward encompassing models of wholeness that include attention, first, to their health and self-care, and second, to their capacities for "prophetic ministry," a major theme in Howard's educational mission. The small group provides a safe place for faculty and students to experience each other as "fellow pilgrims." Faculty members often assign personal writing, such as journals or reflections; at least one professor asks students to write poetry. Although it's a matter of dispute in the faculty, student work is graded.

The program has a basic curricular structure for the three-year sequence of courses, but professors typically develop their own variations on its original design. Sanders, for instance, usually introduces students to classics in spirituality. During the semester we visited the campus, her students were reading *Centering Moment,* a book of daily meditations by Howard Thurman. Before class, students read one of the meditations; in class, they discuss their reactions and share their experiences with the meditation. Written assignments included two short reflection papers: one an overall reflection on the experience with the Thurman meditations, the other a reflection on how a particular biblical book (in its entirety, not just a few passages) "speaks to me."

Kortright Davis, professor of theology at Howard, who considers his experience with the faith development groups as particularly "precious" in his experience as a seminary educator, takes another approach. He does not have students read outside their class sessions, and during their meetings they use only one book: the Bible. He and the group read closely a section of Scripture over the six weeks of the course. In the semester we visited, members of the group were reading Romans 12, often spending the entire hour on just a few verses, digging deeply into the personal and spiritual implications they found there. Typically, Davis noted, the hour ends with students wishing for more time.

We observed during our visit to the Howard campus that these groups filled more than an academic function in forming the spiritual practices of their students. Most Howard students work, many full-time, and most academic courses are offered in the evenings to accommodate them. For the most part, students arrive for their evening courses and depart again without any sustained nonclassroom interaction; those who come on Wednesday afternoon, when the weekly chapel service is held, represent the primary exception. As many as seventy students or more may be enrolled in many courses. The school offers no food service, the bookstore has limited (and solely daytime) hours, and we observed that the lounge is largely unused. So the intimacy of these small groups not only provides space for cultivating specific spiritual practices and nurturing professional identity, but it also deepens and intensifies the relational dynamics of students and faculty across the Howard seminary community. In a manner similar to the role of the liturgical life of Church Divinity School of the Pacific, the small-group courses at Howard not only cultivate the spirituality and spiritual practices of students, but also provide primary spaces for the interaction of students and faculty that in turn shapes, in distinctive ways, the culture of the seminary community.

Centering the Spiritual Life of the Seminary Community

At St. Vladimir's Orthodox Theological Seminary, we observed how small-group interactions facilitate cultivation of the spirituality of both the seminary community and the students preparing for the priesthood. The small-group experience here occurs in the context of six hours of service to the seminary community each week. Responsibilities include work in the kitchen and dining room, in the residence halls, and in some of the seminary programs. Both students and faculty report this time of service often becomes one of the most powerfully formative elements of students' seminary experience: "It's on the breakfast crew that people's real character comes out!" Quite practically, performing the basic services necessary to the seminary community holds tuition costs down. But the collaborative effort involved helps nurture in students a sense of devotion and service that they take into their future ministry. It occurs in the wider context of the daily rhythms of academic study, worship, and the fellowship of common meals—each meal preceded and followed by sung communal prayer and made possible by the labor of one's peers. Reflecting on the influence of serving others in the seminary community on his spiritual growth, one St. Vladimir student said, "I think it happens the way you don't really expect it to happen." It is about "how you talk to your fellow students and how you help them . . . because you are a Christ to your fellow students. That is spiritual growth. I've seen it. People have been Christs to me, and I try to be too in the way I can. . . . I never before realized that the presence of God comes through other people." It is "community life" and "your struggle here" in the midst of that community that "provides these things. . . . That is a new thing to me."

At Jewish Theological Seminary, alongside the communal *mincha* services stand two other pedagogically significant small-group practices that contribute to the formation of rabbis. The first is an interesting analogue to the Church Divinity School practice of apprenticing students into liturgical leadership. The seminary rabbi, Edward Feld, leads a Wednesday morning "learner's minyan" for ten to twelve students new to the ritual practices of Judaism or desiring a learner-friendly environment for developing confidence in prayer leadership. After the students have gathered and put on their prayer shawls, Feld sets the stage for the day's morning prayers and readings, providing historical background and some interpretive framework for the function of the texts for the day. Students take turns leading parts of the service, practicing in this nonthreatening environment the rather complicated sets of liturgical practices integral to the leadership of a congregation. The student who led the day we observed was remembering the anniversary of her mother's death, so a set of mourning prayers was included. This immersion in the practices of Jewish prayer gives students not only opportunities to become familiar with liturgical texts, but also, and perhaps as important, the texture and intonations of chanting that, with increasing familiarity, deepen over time their relationship to these ancient texts and prayers in the midst of their own grief, joy, questions, and struggle.

The learner's minyan involves a small number of students and is an optional part of the Jewish Theological Seminary experience (although regular observance of these morning prayers is expected). But another form of small-group practice may be the most deeply rooted Jewish pedagogical structure of all: involving all rabbinical students over the entire course of their curriculum and connecting them with students of Torah and Talmud through centuries preceding them. In our description of Lehman's course on Talmud in Chapter Three, we note the practice of study in pairs, or *havrutah* (from the Hebrew word *haver,* or friend). This practice of the highly dialogical encounter of two contemporary scholars with the voices preserved in the highly dialogical ancient texts under study provides a distinctively Jewish experience of the encounter with sacred text and the interactive, open-ended nature of rabbinic practice itself. Students study Talmud in all five years of their academic program, and they often continue in relationship with their *beit midrash* partner through several, if not all, of these years.

Thus the spiritual practice of the study of sacred texts at the heart of Jewish spirituality is, in and of itself, also a practice of profound encounter with other human beings. These two "forms" of encounter comprise one spiritual practice in the debating of truth and reality, in the present and across time—a practice in and through which (that is, not separate from the debating itself) one may speak of encounter with God as well. During our interview with Lehman, she said, "I do feel moved spiritually by it. And I do feel that when I uncover something that I hadn't actually seen the day before, it feels . . . revelatory." Not only is this practice of textual engagement one of the most ancient we observed, but also it emphasizes the inseparability of academic and spiritual practices within the preparation for clergy practice. That this practice is a rigorous intellectual process demanding students' very best critical acumen is obvious; and that it is intended to function in ways that form the heart and spirit in patterns of ancient rabbinic devotion to sacred texts and elders is equally clear. One can see how its present contours spring from the textual and juridical emphasis of the traditional rabbinate while still serving to form students toward such practice. And perhaps this historical grounding can help others to perceive parallel foundations of their own practices and to discern appropriately how to build on those foundations.

Cultivating Public Spirituality

We have referred previously to Eisner's distinctions among the three curriculums: (1) the explicit curriculum outlined in seminary catalogues and given specific form in course syllabi; (2) the implicit curriculum reflected in the values, the patterns of authority and relationship, and the resources and strategies that influence the interactions of teachers and students; and (3) the null curriculum, which includes what is not taught and is thereby missing in the interactions of teachers and students. During the course of this study we became increasingly aware that in cultivating the spiritual practices of students, seminaries explicitly focus on the personal relationship of students to the meanings and practices of their religious traditions, the ritual and relational practices of religious community, and the integrity of religious leadership. However, in deliberately structured small-group programs to cultivate spiritual practices, the null curriculum—what seemed most absent—was some attention to the dimensions of public spiritual leadership, especially those spiritual practices associated with the historic concerns for justice in both Jewish and Christian traditions.

We discovered, though, in almost every seminary we visited, one or more advocacy groups working on some justice issue, usually around matters of gender, racial, cultural, or sexual nondiscrimination. These advocacy groups ranged from small, student-initiated and student-sustained programs of social justice to something as large as the Louisville Presbyterian Women's Center, with its focus on gender inclusivity in leadership; from the emphasis on prophetic ministry at Howard to the deeply ingrained involvement of the Associated Mennonite Biblical Seminary community in its denominational heritage of peacemaking and nonviolence. Yet in our surveys of students, alumni and alumnae, and faculty, only small numbers of present and former students chose "engagement in social justice and advocacy" as one of their five most formative experiences during seminary from a list of twenty possible choices. In contrast, more than a quarter of *faculty* respondents considered student engagement in some form of social justice or advocacy program as central to their spiritual and professional formation.

Many of the faculty members in this cohort, of course, may be reflecting the importance of some social justice or advocacy program in their own seminary experience twenty and thirty years ago. However, whether it is a disparity of perception or difference of experience, the reports of both faculty and students suggest that the notion of spirituality that dominates the imaginations of seminarians, and many of their faculty mentors as well, is focused more on practices of personal piety and observance than on concerns for the care of the earth and human community—concerns equally embedded in the traditions of Jewish and Christian spirituality.

The Contribution of Small Groups to Students' Spiritual Formation

Seminaries employ small groups in a wide variety of practices that foster their students' spiritual growth. Whether meeting together to wash dishes, debate Talmud interpretation, study the Bible, or ponder classic African American devotional texts, students engage with their peers and their professors in processes whose intention and effect is spiritual formation. In considering these various approaches to small groups, we realized that it is not so much the form of the group that is important in the cultivation of student spiritual practices as it is the contribution they make to the total curricular experience of students.

In contrast to community worship, small-group practices provide many more spaces for spiritual growth and offer a wider range of practices through which individuals in a diverse faculty and student community may find an acceptable blend of structure and spontaneity, familiarity and novelty, trust and challenge for fostering their spirituality. Yet we also observed that the *function* of small groups for spiritual formation seems to reflect the approaches seminaries take to the presence of diversity more generally in the classroom and curriculum. In schools with a more religiously homogenous student and faculty community, small-group practices tend to derive from and flow back into the primary practice of shared worship (for example, at St. John's Seminary, the faith-sharing groups that meet on quiet days and during retreats move into and out of traditional

Catholic liturgical forms; Trinity Lutheran Seminary's integration groups include among their responsibilities the planning and leading of a week of chapel for the community).

Something different happens in more religiously diverse seminaries, where community worship often involves careful negotiation among the school's constituencies. In these seminaries small groups, despite common guidelines for their conduct, often take on a distinctive life of their own, reflecting the influence of the particular backgrounds, experiences, and expectations of their members in the ways they interact with each other, their shared perceptions of the purposes of their life together, and the practices they agree to develop together. Candler School of Theology's contextual education reflection groups are an example, as are small-group programs in seminaries such as Howard and Fuller, where ongoing community worship does not provide a unifying experience for the larger community. Consequently, even within the same program, not only may the purposes and structures of small groups in seminaries like these vary extensively, but their quality and depth may range widely as well.

Spiritual Formation Through Individual Guidance

Seminaries also provide individual guidance for spiritual formation. Again, their approaches vary widely, often due to significant differences in the relationship between the educational processes of the seminary and the denomination's process of moving students from candidacy to ordination.

For example, most Protestant Christian seminary students work through some of the candidacy processes of their denominations outside the programmatic structures of the seminary. Some denominations screen students for admission into the candidacy processes as a prerequisite for admission to seminary. In others, screening for ordination is concurrent with the seminary experience. In still other denominations, candidacy is not connected to education at all.

Similarly, many denominations conduct evaluations of student progress through seminary alongside those conducted by the seminary. Others rely on seminary faculty to weave denominational evaluative procedures into their curriculum. Most denominations require additional work from students, beyond their academic program: giving exams, assigning position papers, and conducting interviews. In addition to assessing students' academic and ministerial competence, Christian denominations also often establish processes to further assess the depth of student personal practices of faith (what Catholics refer to more narrowly as "spiritual" formation) and provide mechanisms for monitoring students' personal psychological, physical, and integrative fitness for spiritual leadership (also described by Catholics as "human" formation).

In the Jewish context, there is no external denominational authority— such as a bishop, committee, or approval exam process—that screens students as to their suitability for ordination; rather, the faculty admits students to rabbinical school. Faculty make decisions about the requirements students must meet. At the conclusion of their education, the faculty approves them for ordination. At Jewish Theological Seminary, the chancellor conducts the ordination service. In a statement broadly comparable to those of many Christian denominations, the Jewish Theological Seminary's 2002–2004 *Academic Bulletin* spells out criteria for students' "good standing" toward ordination: "All students in the Rabbinical School are expected to be committed to and live an observant Jewish life. Standards of personal and professional conduct and interpersonal relations are a significant part of the tradition to which the school is committed. Accordingly, the dean of the Rabbinical School reserves the right to deny admission, registration, readmission or ordination to any student who in the judgment of the Rabbinical School faculty committee is determined to be unsuitable to the profession of the rabbinate" (p. 90).

Pedagogical practices and programs designed to nurture the individual dimension of what Catholics call "spiritual and human formation" tend to be implicit and idiosyncratic in most Protestant and Jewish seminaries. Trinity Lutheran and Church Divinity School of the Pacific both provide voluntary programs of spiritual direction. In most Protestant and Jewish seminaries, some faculty and some staff members provide spiritual direction or counseling, often in relation to a course they are teaching. Many students look to a clergy person they admire or a supervisor of field education as a spiritual mentor or director.

In Catholic seminaries, processes of individual spiritual and human formation are explicitly folded into the curricular structure. We observed well-developed and extensive—but quite different—programs of spiritual and human formation in both St. John's Seminary and Catholic Theological Union. Like all Roman Catholic seminaries, they follow the U.S. Catholic bishops' official broad guidelines and standards for the four major elements of "formation" (human, spiritual, pastoral or priestly, and academic). Within these encompassing and detailed guidelines, each has developed programs of formation to meet the Vatican-approved formational goals in relation to the students and the church constituencies they serve. At diocesan schools like St. John's, where all or most students are candidates for the priesthood and have been admitted through the associated diocesan offices, these formation programs are integrated into the full life of the school.

In contrast, each of the religious orders that make up the Catholic Theological Union assumes significant responsibility for much of the formation of their candidates.[6] This means that much of their "religious" formation[7] occurs prior to matriculating in the seminary and much of it continues alongside their theological studies, following guidelines that reflect both the general requirements of the church's "Program of Priestly Formation" process and the order's unique charism. At Catholic Theological Union, students typically are living in a house or other community setting with peers and religious superiors, so the formation process includes a residential dimension as well.

A Program of "Holistic" Formation

A particular program of individual formation at Catholic Theological Union illustrates features of other programs cultivating individual spirituality that we observed. It also illustrates a common emphasis on "holistic" formation. Further, because the order that runs this program, the Society of the Divine Word, addresses a need and reality that many Christian and Jewish communities in the United States and, increasingly, abroad must take into account—namely, how to live faithfully and fruitfully in contexts of cultural and religious pluralism—we found the experience of individual formation among Society of Divine Word students especially useful as an example.

In general, directors of the programs of religious formation across Catholic Theological Union told us that contemporary formation processes are "a total reversal" from those they had experienced as students prior to Vatican II. At that time, processes of formation emphasized the candidates' increasing conformation to the charism, structures, and institutions of their religious orders. Questions of personal discernment or a focus on individual experience were foreign. Now those questions are emphasized and the processes are highly individualized, focusing on the gifts, needs, and growth of each seminarian. Giving individual oversight and spiritual direction to students now requires a much greater investment of staff time and energy, a level of personal investment possible today, in part, due to significantly smaller numbers of candidates preparing for the priesthood. Smaller numbers, one spiritual director observed, has meant "there's more emphasis on holistic formation right now."

The Society of the Divine Word focuses on this more holistic formation. The order is represented at Catholic Theological Union by approximately thirty-five students, three faculty members, the academic dean, and several community staff members, including four who direct formation through small groups. The order, founded in 1875, is international in scope and is engaged in mission work around the globe. Its students in the seminary come from many countries; in fact, most come from outside the United States. They are preparing for cross-cultural mission work in any of sixty countries, typically working in multicultural teams. Thus, both the community life the students experience in the seminary and that for which they are preparing after graduation take place across cultural boundaries and often with persons who do not share their religious traditions.

Students live in four "small communities" of eight to twelve members each, within the larger Society of the Divine Word house in Hyde Park. Each small community has a common living area, kitchen, dining room, and chapel. Each group of students and their formation director, who lives with them, share chores and eat all meals together. They celebrate liturgy three days a week in their small communities, and they join the "large community" (all persons associated with the order in the seminary) on three others. In either setting, students often lead the scriptural reflection as part of their practice of preaching, a practice important to their order's focus on the Word of God. On Sundays, students are in their parish field education assignments. Each small community meets every Thursday evening for theological reflection: students examine together their ongoing field education experience, engage in Bible study and faith-sharing, and discuss formation issues.

In the small community we visited, only one of the eight students had been born in the United States, and his family had emigrated from Vietnam. Of the rest, most were from the Philippines, two from Latin America, and one from Russia. Their small community chapel has the look of a living room, with a fireplace, couches, chairs, and a few pieces of religious art. Their service was an informal liturgy in which everyone, including the presider (the small community's formation director), remained seated for the entire service. The presider's homily, or reflection, on the appointed biblical texts seemed directly connected to the candidates' ongoing instruction in religious and community mores and life.

As part of their degree program, students of the Society of the Divine Word take an academic concentration in world missions (an academic emphasis in the curriculum that the order helped to create) that includes two years in residence in the Chicago seminary, followed by a cross-cultural training program that consists of a year-long immersion in missionary pastoral activity. Back in the seminary for another one and a half to two years, students complete a mission integration seminar, in which each student reflects on his experience in the training program to become increasingly aware of the patterns of his personal and pastoral interactions with others and his own needs of self-knowledge, self-acceptance, and self-esteem, and to further understand God's call. The students resume participation in their small community, but this time under the supervision of the director of formation for the entire house as they enter the last stretch of preparing for ordination, perpetual vows, and their first missionary assignment.

A primary objective of the entire formation program is "human maturity." This is developed and occurs in "a progressive deepening of self-knowledge, in the unfolding of one's personal qualities, and in the achievement of that inner freedom which makes responsible decisions possible." Work toward these three goals depends on developing "an atmosphere of mutual trust" to provide a place for honest, nondefensive self-examination and feedback from others. During this process, each student meets individually five times a year with the director of formation for the Chicago house. These meetings, called *ratios,* are intended to "evaluate the consistency between vows/goals and the actual choices made, and to integrate the various aspects of the individual's activities."

The Society of the Divine Word's handbook describes the order's intention of helping students' personal growth flourish, within the various dimensions of spiritual life, physical health, clarity of boundaries, psychological maturity, and cultivation of professional or peer supervision in ministry. All this takes place within the context of small communities. Life in the mission setting, like that in Chicago, will be communal, so skills in friendship, communication, trust, and accountability are central to the formation process and are a central focus of the small community meetings. A basic principle is that strong and effective ministry in the real world—especially in the challenging context of cross-cultural and missionary work—depends on having one's human needs met as fully as possible all along the way. Thus, the formation process is intended not only to enable that to happen while the student is in Chicago, but also to give students the tools they need to continue in this process for themselves and one another while in ministry.

This is rarely easy. Particularly in a cross-cultural community like the Society of the Divine Word—and in most of the religious orders at Catholic Theological Union—a major challenge when "there is trouble," as one of the formation directors observed, is "distinguishing" whether it is "an issue of culture or personality." He and his colleagues have "come to the realization" that the major factor is typically personality. "Most people handle cultural stuff pretty well," but all too often when some problem is identified they "call it a cultural issue" so they do not have "to face it."

At times these personality problems are severe enough that the challenge of addressing them while taking on the steep demands of cross-cultural mission ministry would be overwhelming, so the student is asked to leave the program. A student is informed as soon as questions of compatibility are raised and then works with the director and community to sort out the consequences of that decision. "The thing about [being] the formator is, I've learned, you can't be afraid to make a tough decision about asking a person if this life is not for them. . . . It's difficult to let someone go. Some cases are black and white and that is easy, but others are tough." Here, he pointed out, the criteria spelled out in the handbook for acceptance into full membership in the order through perpetual vows, and the conversations among formation directors both within the order and among Catholic Theological Union's various communities, prove invaluable. One "can't do it in a vacuum." That would be a "terrible burden." And "that's why we don't do formation alone."

Obviously, the program of individual formation in the Society of the Divine Word at Catholic Theological Union is a distinctive one. Its primary features are possible because of the particular conditions of the Catholic Theological Union setting (full-time, trained formation directors; full-time residential students who spend up to five years in the program; and funding), and ideals (the charism of cross-cultural and cross-religious missionary service of the Society of the Divine Word; a celibate, male Catholic priesthood; devotion to the Word of God experienced as alive in Jesus Christ). Such a program would be difficult to duplicate in a school where, for example, the program of formation involves men and women, in which most students are married and many commute to class, and with limited funding for supervisory personnel and support staff.

Nonetheless, the elements of the program are not unique. It shares the features of many seminary programs to support individual spiritual formation: small and larger group worship, faith sharing, community service and chores, friendship, ministry practice in field assignments, spiritual direction, and religious supervision.

Aligning Practices for Spiritual Formation

Community worship primarily emphasizes the spiritual formation of the whole community—with the result that the goals of religious diversity and of formative depth into a particular tradition can be difficult to reconcile. Small-group strategies focus explicitly on the formation of persons in relation to others, with correspondingly greater space for diversity of spiritual practices formative across many particular traditions. Programs of individual spiritual formation provide the greatest attention to the particularity of each student within the seminary community. Through these programs and processes, the seminary faculty and staff can prepare candidates for clergy roles and responsibilities in ways that correspond to the needs and expectations of a religious tradition or denomination for its clergy. They can give special attention to supporting student quests for authentic and life-giving vocations in relation to the knowledge and skills, traditions and disciplines, norms and gifts, freedom and responsibilities of ministry. At the same time, they can address the blind spots, projections, wounds, and other individual problems that can subvert or undermine the realization of the vocation. Taken together, in other words, these programs of spiritual development can contribute both to the personal development of student spirituality and apprentice students more generally into the spiritual practices of their religious traditions.

We encountered some sense of the interrelatedness of the practices of community worship, small groups, and individual formation in each of the schools we visited. Every school had some sort of chapel program, every school had formally or informally structured small groups, every school or candidacy process had some means for individual growth and for assessment of readiness for ministry. When these different sites for cultivating the spirituality of clergy were aligned in some more or less intentional way, the effect seemed most powerful. That is, when the spiritual practices that are fostered in these ways—chapel, small groups, processes of individual formation, and, in some seminaries, the steps of candidacy toward ordination—reinforce or in some way function with one another, the contribution of the seminary to linking the development of spiritual practices with the emerging professional clergy identity of students seems to take place most easily.

Consider, for instance, Catholic Theological Union's lay formation program, which incorporates individual spiritual direction, weekly group processing and faith-sharing, and regular worship planning and leadership; Trinity's integration groups, whose members plan and lead a week of worship in the seminary chapel program and help each other through personal struggles, academic advisement, and pastoral growth; and St. John's or St. Vladimir's highly intensive residential experience, in which a near-monastic round of daily chapel services is the framework for complex individual and small-group spiritual development. All these, precisely in their capacity to simultaneously hold together (or simply provide space for) spiritual practice at the communal, the small-group, and the individual levels, illustrate alignment of approaches to the cultivation of spiritual formation. Such alignment, we found, significantly addresses students' hunger for spiritual growth as they prepare for clergy practice.

Throughout the study, we saw the importance of the alignment of various aspects of a student's theological education. This is also a finding of the larger study of professional education. In the case of seminary education, the alignment of approaches to spiritual practice that reinforce and support one another—with student engagement in the rest of the seminary curriculum and with the overarching values and ideals of a given religious tradition—can be especially effective. Indeed, the clergy quoted in the opening of the chapter, describing their spontaneous, creative, and spiritually grounded ministry responses to catastrophe, suggest the results of such alignment.

Whether an approach to develop students' spiritual formation works effectively with actual students in actual preparation for the complex practice of ministry depends, we were often told, on equally complex factors, such as (1) the experience, maturity, and training of those overseeing the programs or doing spiritual direction; (2) the degree to which the seminary as a whole and particular leaders within it foster a climate conducive to personal growth, authentic prayer or observance, and the intimacy of real faith-sharing; (3) the effectiveness of mechanisms designed to help students address their blind spots and find ways either to grow through them or to exit the candidacy process; and (4) the degree to which seminary educators and other leaders are perceived to be truly transparent to the Holy in their own faith or observance. This suggests that, given appropriate investment and careful oversight and boundaries, the cultivation of spiritual practices for clergy leadership ministry involves faculty attention to the mutuality of worship, small groups fostering spirituality, and individual spiritual guidance in educating seminary students.

ENDNOTES

1. The language of "primary" theology to describe worship (as distinct from the "secondary theology" that constitutes formal or systematic theological reflection) comes from Aidan Kavanagh's study, *On Liturgical Theology* (1992, pp. 74ff).

2. This formative dimension may take place for some as much through coffee afterward as through the worship itself. Daily chapel services at Yale function as one of the only ongoing communal gathering points; the tradition of coffee and doughnuts after chapel allows the worship services to

open into conversation, creating a space for unstructured faculty-student encounter otherwise rare in this busy and highly scheduled place.

3. Following the visit of the research team to the Fuller campus, significant changes have occurred in the worship life of the seminary community. An All-Seminary Chapel is now held once a week with faculty, staff, and student leadership. Faculty members preach in all services. Options have been expanded for the various constituencies in the seminary community. A chapel for the campus is in the planning stages.

4. The Taize liturgies originated in the international and ecumenical Taize Community in France. They are widely used in Christian circles around the world.

5. We discovered these small groups often created the conditions for the development of deep and lasting friendships among seminarians. Students and alumni consistently ranked friendship next to coursework in assessing the contributions of the seminary to their formation for ministry.

6. Most of the religious orders at Catholic Theological Union are male, and nearly all their students are preparing for the priesthood. The women's orders at the seminary prepare students for other forms of ministry in parishes or other settings; like the priestly candidates, they too experience their primary spiritual formation through their orders. Lay students in all degree programs are required to participate in spiritual formation as well. They take part in one of three programs geared to students of different racial and cultural backgrounds. Each program is overseen by its own director and includes components of individual spiritual direction, quarterly day-long retreats, and weekly or biweekly group sessions integrating prayer, worship (the opportunity for sustained worship leadership is a novelty for many lay students in the clerically oriented Catholic tradition), and reflection on questions arising from their studies and field education.

7. Within the Catholic Church, the language of "religious" formation typically refers not to growth in a person's religious faith or observance in general, but specifically to formation within a religious order. Thus to speak of persons as "religious" typically has the specific meaning that they are nuns or sisters, monks, brothers, or order priests (such as Jesuits). Within each order, formation is more or less tailored to the "charism" of the order—that is, its distinctive mission and spirituality.

CULTIVATING PROFESSIONAL PRACTICES: FIELD EDUCATION

SEMINARIES USE ANOTHER SET of communal teaching practices. Embedded in the structures and processes of seminaries, these are variously called *field education, supervised ministry,* or *contextual education.* The terms reflect variations in seminaries' efforts to move students from the classroom into the kind of professional practices they will be assuming as clergy. Although a broader and deeper discussion of the particular meaning of these terms in pedagogical practice is warranted, our attention in this study focused on practices of engaging students in learning on site. We therefore use the term *field education* to identify these practice-oriented programs, simply because it is the oldest and most common term in use.

Field education programs are generally designed as a bridge between seminary and the congregation or other sites of clergy practice. Their purposes originate in the mission of seminaries—a mission shared by other professional schools—to educate leaders for service to various publics. This mission requires that seminaries link, in some fashion, teaching in the classroom and communal ethos with teaching in the field or sites of clergy practice. Yet, because seminaries balance this mission alongside others, such as updating theological scholarship and preserving a living religious tradition, efforts to establish and maintain that link are fraught with challenges.

Some challenges are shared with professional education in general, as in negotiating curriculum values and practices identified with cognitive and skill apprenticeships. For example, academic guilds expect evidence that seminaries contribute to the advancement of knowledge, thus focusing on the students' academic knowledge; sites of professional practice, like a congregation, expect evidence that the seminaries' graduates have knowledge they can use. Seminaries must respond to the expectations of both constituencies. Other challenges have to do with seminary education in particular, like the integration of Talmudic or biblical traditions and practices into a seminarian's identity, roles, and skills. Such integration cuts across all three of the professional apprenticeships: cognitive, practical, and normative.

Other challenges are embedded in the structures of the seminary. For example, we found significant variations in the position of field education staff on the faculty. During this study, we met field education directors with academic doctorates and professional ministry experience, but no faculty status; others with a professional academic education, years of ministry practice, and full faculty standing; and still others with years of experience in the academy, albeit without academic doctorate or experience in congregational ministry—all giving oversight to the formation of clergy professional practice. We saw similar variation in the academic roles of those in the field who supervise students: in some schools they are called (and considered) adjunct faculty; in other schools they have no official standing.

The position of field education directors is complicated by the various roles they fill in the seminary community. Most of those we interviewed had some experience in local ministry, helping them serve as advocates for the world of ministry within seminary walls. As administrators of field education programs, they also serve as ambassadors of the seminary to congregations, hospitals, and community agencies. Their contacts in the community mean they typically know more local ministry practitioners than anyone else in the institution. They invite many of the ministry practitioners they meet to be field education supervisors; sometimes they include them in seminary colloquia to enrich their own continuing education. They structure programs to equip students to negotiate the huge shift between the culture of the seminary and the culture of the local congregation or ministry site. And some field education directors take on the "secret mission" of helping faculty members bridge these cultures as well by involving them in field education seminars, site visits, and assessment.

Still other challenges for field education programs have to do with the relationship of seminaries to the denominational bodies and other agencies receiving their graduates. For many, that relationship involves a twofold charge: to assess the *integrity of a student's calling* to ministry and to facilitate the *professional readiness* of the students. As noted in the previous chapter, some schools in the study—most notably St. John's Seminary and Catholic Theological Union—foster spiritual and human formation through specialized programs. In some Protestant schools like

Trinity Lutheran Seminary, an extensive candidacy process in the denomination shares this obligation with the seminary; the church body and seminary work hand in hand on matters of admissions, internship, and readiness for ordination. But in most seminaries we visited, Jewish and Christian alike, the field education program carries much of the responsibility for both assessing vocational integrity at the "front door" and preparing for professional readiness at the "back door."

Bridging the Classroom and the Congregation

In studying the role and function of field education in preparing students for professional practice, we found three persistent questions:

o Is field education primarily a phase of a *practical or skill apprenticeship* in an otherwise academic program? If so, why are some field education departments given the task of discerning the vocation of incoming students?

o Is field education the primary site for the *integration* of learning, in which the various disciplines of seminary education come alive and commingle for the student in professional practice? If so, why are so few faculty members in such "traditional" disciplines as Bible, history, and theology directly involved in the field education work with students?

o Is field education more aptly called *contextual education*—in the case of clergy education, a curriculum-wide orientation toward teaching and learning emphasizing the preparation of leadership within concrete communities of faith and public life? If so, why are there generally so few new faculty hires required to have either some experience as practitioners in ministry or academic preparation for "reading contexts" in and through their own disciplinary specializations?

We carried these questions through our investigation of field education in the schools that we studied. In addition, we found in Gardner, Csikszentmihalyi, and Damon's discussion in *Good Work: Where Excellence and Ethics Meet* a way to think about the common theme of the relationship of classroom and field pedagogies running through each of these questions, for they describe the optimal interaction of the institutional ethos, social practices, and roles of professional education as an "alignment" wherein each reinforces and draws upon the other (2001, pp. 26–27).[1] The implication is that if the ethos, teaching practices, and professional roles of the educators, staff, students, and field supervisors are in alignment, then teaching practices in field education are genuine extensions of the larger cultural ethos and teaching practices of the seminary.

We explore these questions and ideas by describing three approaches to linking or bridging the cultures and the pedagogies of the classroom and the ministry site. Examining the field education programs at Yale Divinity School, Trinity Lutheran Seminary, and St. John's Seminary, we compare structural differences among the programs and different expectations about student learning. We selected them as examples because each program emphasizes, albeit in different ways, strong linkages between the academic and ministry experiences of students. At Yale Divinity School, students pursuing the master of divinity degree can fulfill the "supervised ministry" requirement in two semesters, either while taking classes or during the summer. The program is distinguished by the range of ministry sites (from urban ministries to local parishes to hospitals) and denominational traditions and its disciplined use of reflective-practitioner pedagogies. Interpretive pedagogies emphasized throughout the curriculum dominate the learning process in field education as well.

Trinity Lutheran Seminary, in contrast, has an integrated "ministry in context" requirement involving two years of part-time field placement in addition to at least one unit of clinical pastoral education in accordance with Lutheran ordination standards, one year in a full-time internship, and structured reflection on the intern experience in academic courses during the student's final year of school. The program is extensive; field placements are parish-centered; faculty involvement is relatively high; and the assessment process is comprehensive, engaging students in performance pedagogies directed to pastoral action.

St. John's Seminary requires students to participate in a ministry experience off campus along with course work during pre-theology, first and second year, an intensive three-week hospital ministry experience during their first year, a full-time internship in the third, and to take many required courses in pastoral ministries. As seen in the previous chapter, the program is thoroughly integrated into curricular and school structures emphasizing pedagogies of formation, in which the processes of evaluation are precise and patterns of theological reflection are well defined.

The pedagogies in each of these seminary programs are all directed to preparing students for clergy practice. On the surface, Yale, Trinity, and St. John's embrace methods of field education generally shared across seminary education: *field experience, supervision,* and *student reflection*— often with peers (Hunter, 1982; Pyle and Seals, 1995). These defining methods were refined through the clinical pastoral education movement earlier in the twentieth century and adapted to other clergy education placements, like congregations and social agencies, by field education specialists (Fielding, 1966; Hunter, 1982). In the discussion that follows, however, we are careful not to identify these instrumental methods with the patterns of pedagogical practice in the particular field education of each of these seminaries, as the latter are infused with theological traditions and ecclesial expectations that distinguish their purposes, content, and methods.

Yale Divinity School

As a *university* divinity school, the culture of Yale Divinity School emphasizes academic disciplines and habits. The explicit ideal of Yale's theological education—harkening back to the days of Jonathan Edwards and Timothy Dwight, whose portraits still adorn seminary hallways—remains that of the *learned clergy*. Pedagogies of interpretation, typically involving lectures peppered with lively, engaging discussion, predominate as members of the faculty model and practice disciplinary ways of thinking that are familiar to most students from their undergraduate academic programs and highly valued by the master of arts in religion students, who currently outnumber students enrolled in the master of divinity program.

The neocolonial design of the chapel, the numerous historic clergy portraits, the daily rituals of chapel and common-room gatherings, and especially the centrality of the interaction of teacher and students in the classroom all reflect the continuing legacy of cultured, New England clergy, with an important exception. In the past, Yale educated clergy primarily for mainline Protestant denominations. The current Yale student community was, with the exception of Fuller, the most denominationally diverse among the seminaries we visited. This range of denominational traditions defines "diversity" in the minds of many faculty members far more than do differences in race, ethnicity, class, and perhaps even gender.

The culture that fosters the ideals of a "learned clergy" in the school differs from the cultures students encounter in their ministry sites in surrounding communities and churches. New Haven, where Yale is located, is described in the *Supervised Ministry Handbook* as "one of the country's most interesting, but also most impoverished cities," with several distinct immigrant populations and signs of industrial decline and urban decay. A tense "town-gown" relationship with Yale University has been fueled over the years by labor struggles and disputes over university expansion.

To bridge this town-gown divide, and to expose clergy students to contexts of urban ministry, the Divinity School instituted a program of "community service and contextual education" for first-year students, called CityWorks. In this program, students "amidst and alongside the disenfranchised" practice social analysis in a theological context for three to five hours a week. They participate in after-school tutorial programs, programs serving the homeless and refugees, and activities of community organizing. Every few weeks they gather for dinner to share fellowship, engage in theological and social analysis, and practice spiritual reflection about their experiences. Although the program offers no academic credit, about twenty students participate.

Yale's supervised ministry requirement involves most master of divinity students in a part-time internship and practicum during their second or third year of seminary. When completed, they receive three academic credits. Internship sites are located "all around Connecticut, New York, Massachusetts, and Rhode Island." Two-thirds are in parishes ranging from struggling center-city churches, to small rural congregations, to thriving, "big steeple" congregations predominantly associated with mainline Protestant denominations (Episcopal, United Church of Christ, Presbyterian, Lutheran, and the like). The rest take place in social service agencies, like those of CityWorks, or in hospitals, nursing homes, prisons, or campus ministries. The director of supervised ministries, Barbara Blodgett, describes the student commitment as "fifteen hours a week total, including an hour and a half in class we call the practicum." Because the interdenominational character of Yale makes it hard to depend on church judicatories to locate and assess potential sites, the program relies on a combination of historic teaching parishes along with sites generated by alumni and alumnae networks, student initiative, and Blodgett's interactions with local pastors.

The key to bridging the cultures of seminary and ministry sites for Yale students lies in the kind of supervisor Blodgett seeks. Because their primary responsibilities include helping students identify ministry roles "appropriate to their status as students" and meeting with them weekly for theological reflection on their ministry experience, Blodgett is most interested in persons who (1) define what they do as ministry, (2) have been in their positions "long enough to have their feet on the ground," (3) "are excellent at what they do," and (4) can "*reflect on their excellence*" [our emphasis]. As an example, she cites a local priest "who takes contexts seriously" and "reflects on ministry vis-à-vis class difference, socioeconomic difference." She assumes that this priest "would share that with an intern." That assumption is crucial. For Blodgett, supervisors must have the capacity to reflect on the relationship of social context, theology, and ethics in ministry and the ability to help academically inclined Yale students do the same. This interaction is, for Blodgett, the most effective way for students to bridge the cultures of seminary and ministry site.

The other site for bridging these two cultures is the intern practicum groups. "Designed to enable students to think critically about ministerial practice in a group of colleagues," they exist to facilitate student reflection on ministry. Groups meet weekly and are formed around specific ministries, such as urban parish, campus ministry, and public-square ministries. Once a month, all practicum groups meet in plenary to hear ministry-practitioners discuss such topics of professional practice as class issues and ministry, spirituality and burnout, or the ethics of confidentiality.

Each practicum is cotaught by a Yale faculty member and a ministry-practitioner. Blodgett looks for faculty members who care about ministry and are comfortable with pedagogies of reflection *on practice*. Moving faculty members beyond a traditional theory to a practice model of teaching is a challenge because, she believes, it is "the one . . . most lodged" in their teachers' "toolbox or their psyche." This means that as program director, she works with students and faculty members from different ends of the spectrum: helping students reflect on their experiences and helping faculty "bring their disciplines" into the conversation as they teach toward clergy practice. Leadership of an intern practicum is not included in the teaching load of Yale faculty, however—accounting, in part, for the small number of faculty who participate in the program.

Blodgett's appointment—like that of many of her colleagues in other seminaries—is an administrative rather than an academic one. It is in some ways an awkward arrangement: her responsibility is predominantly academic but her role is primarily administrative. Blodgett is unusual among the field education directors we interviewed in that she brings to the position professional experience in ministry, an academic doctorate (in ethics), and a record of publishing. In other words, she herself bridges the cultures of the academy and ministry sites. She also bridges the cultures of the school and ministry sites by bringing to her own teaching and leadership in the program a sophisticated learning theory and a theologically grounded framework of ethical formation. Yet the academic marginalization of the position means she can have little direct impact on faculty searches, curriculum review processes, and other decisions affecting the relationship of the cultures of the school and ministry sites in the education of Yale students.

Trinity Lutheran Seminary

Trinity Lutheran Seminary presents itself as a church-oriented seminary educating "men and women for *leadership in God's mission to the world through the church*" [our emphasis]. The interior spaces of the campus are adorned with religious art work. The rhythms of seminary life are punctuated by numerous liturgies each day for small groups and the whole community. Two chapels—one old and one new—engage the community architecturally in the interplay of historic and contemporary expressions of being the church at worship. Chapel attendance was higher than in most schools we visited. When one of the research team members first arrived on campus, he asked two students, "Where is the dean's office?" They replied, "Which dean? The academic dean, or the dean of the chapel?" This response came to represent for us the way this seminary views the interdependence of the academy and church in its educational program.

Anticipating the merger of two Lutheran denominations, their Ohio seminaries merged to form Trinity Lutheran Seminary. The contemporary pedagogical culture of the seminary lies somewhere between a classical education, with a deep commitment to the academic disciplines inherited from one of those schools, and a contextual education, with strong implications for performance-practice from the other.[2] Both traditions persist in what appear on the surface to be parallel programs of academic coursework and contextual learning in ministry sites, but the faculty gives unusual attention to issues of integration along the way, challenging this perception. These integrative processes are implicitly embedded in a sequence of courses and field education experiences emphasizing first theory, then practice, then theory in practice. Interpretive and performance pedagogies are interrelated throughout.

In this teaching and learning environment, the field education program at Trinity is a highly defined and coordinated process of socialization into a pastoral identity and performance-practice primarily in congregational contexts. *Context* at Trinity refers especially to "the congregation," but it encompasses the local church in all its missional, relational, and organizational dimensions. This program is carefully sequenced alongside the academic curriculum, and moves from observation and shadowing in year one, to a participatory ministry in year two (coordinated with courses in practical theology), to a full-time internship in year three. Master of divinity students are expected to fulfill a unit of clinical pastoral education, usually in the summer after their first year. The seminary has invested heavily in its contextual education program, with two staff members (one of whom has faculty status) in directing roles, regular meetings of academic faculty with local supervisors, course assignments coordinated with field assignments, and the involvement of faculty in "integrative groups"—or "I-groups," as they are called by everyone in the seminary community—in evaluating student field work experience.

Trinity Lutheran Seminary struggled in the 1980s to clarify whether its program was a field education extension of the classroom, or a contextual education extension of the congregation into the seminary. Finally the faculty embraced both. The two-year ministry in context program, for example, is described as "an extension of the classroom into the congregation and an extension of the congregation into the classroom. The seminary expects and encourages students to use the one forum to explore and reflect on ideas and experiences they are encountering in the other. In this sense the MIC [Ministry in Context] program reflects Trinity's fundamental commitment to *integrated learning.* . . . This connection is valued because of the ways it *infuses pastoral practice with intellectual rigor,* and because of the ways *it focuses our intellectual pursuits on the real needs* of real people [our emphasis]" (*2001 Trinity Lutheran Seminary Catalogue*).

Students are in the ministry in context program as part of their first two years of seminary. It is designed to create a free flow between the worlds of seminary and sites, facilitated by lay committees in ministry sites, in which the student is the primary traveler between them. The program sets up learning processes and contexts to maximize the students' integration of their work into a pastoral identity. Ruth Fortis, coordinator of the program, requires students to "keep a reflective log on what they're discovering about their pastoral identity and the pastoral practices of the person who is their mentor." In the first quarter of the academic year, students observe different ministry sites and shadow practitioners in order to locate a site where they might serve for one or two years. Students also spend four Sundays in a non-Lutheran site to experience different styles of pastoral work and "being the church" and to "find out what it feels like to be "out of your element and in a strange place."

During the second year, students spend six to eight hours per week in the ministry site, using the site to fulfill classroom assignments, particularly in pastoral care, Christian education, and preaching. They meet weekly with supervisors who, as exemplary practitioners, model ministry as they listen to and pose questions for student reflection.

The year-long internship is a denominational requirement for all Evangelical Lutheran Church of America students. At Trinity Lutheran Seminary, emphasis is on the integration of academic learning and pastoral practice and identity. Following requirements of the denomination, the program consists of a "service-learning contract" identifying the student's goals, a wide range of student parish involvement, the participation of a lay committee in the student's learning process, and ongoing supervision. Although denominational guidelines stress the role of supervisors as models and mentors, the director of contextual education, Jane Jenkins, insists they should also be able "to facilitate theological reflection." The school's internship handbook reinforces the point. It describes supervisors as "adjunct members[s] of Trinity Lutheran Seminary's faculty" who have been identified as strong pastors with "the ability to reflect upon the practice of ministry and to lead in such reflection." Back in the seminary for their final year, students participate in courses designed to reflect academically back on their internship experience. The roles of intern supervisor and faculty member, in other words, reflect the commitment of the school to the reciprocation and integration of academy and church in the education of Trinity Lutheran Seminary students.

St. John's Seminary

The primary mission of St. John's Seminary is to prepare candidates for the priesthood in the archdiocese of Los Angeles (to which it reports) and a number of other Roman Catholic dioceses, including Fresno, Seattle, Tucson, and Oklahoma City. The relationships and procedures of diocese and school are interwoven in almost every phase of the educational experience, heightening the accountability of the seminary around issues of priestly formation. Faculty members, for example, define their educational mandate in relation to the "four pillars" of *intellectual, spiritual, pastoral, and human formation* set forth in the U.S. Catholic bishops' Program of Priestly Formation (PPF). Directors for each area of formation meet regularly to coordinate the overall experience of each priestly candidate.

Like many Catholic seminaries, St. John's places a distinctive emphasis on the human as well as the intellectual, pastoral, and spiritual formation of students. This emphasis is a response to Pope John Paul II's call for all Catholic seminaries to attend to the dynamics of human formation (*Pastores Dabo Vobis*, 1992) and to the need in the church for priests with the sensibilities and skills to collaborate with parish leaders and members, including women. This focus on human formation includes psychological testing, a vocation motivation questionnaire, workshops on sexuality and the celibate lifestyle, an individual development plan for each seminarian, and a personalized annual review process. "Formation advisors," assigned to students from the regular faculty, coordinate and advise on personal formation issues, and participate in the "external forum" for evaluating students, as distinguished from the "internal [more confidential] forum" of assessment by each student's spiritual director. Through this program of human formation, the seminary seeks to move the education of St. John's from an older "conformity model," emphasizing a shared priestly identity, to a "self-development model," stressing the exploration of unique strengths, weaknesses, and areas of growth for each seminarian.

This holistic approach to clergy education is rooted in and reinforced by ancient patterns of monastic formation. Admission depends on an affirmative decision by the student's diocese or order; for the most part, priest and religious faculty and students live on campus; liturgy, classes, meetings, and meals provide a shared rhythmic structure to each day; every student has a spiritual director; and student community responsibilities (from assisting in worship to cleaning up the dining hall) are designed to nurture the sensibilities and practices associated with the servanthood of priestly leadership. The campus reflects a Spanish, monastic design—marked by cut-stone archways and an inner quadrangle facing the seminary chapel—and a monastic distance from the world, as it sits pastorally secluded behind locked gates on a hilltop in the center of a large citrus grove overlooking the valleys below. In this setting—as its president, Monsignor-Rector Hefner, has stated in the 2001 seminary catalogue—the student is "invited to integrate his theological learning into his spirituality, not only to study the Scriptures, but also to pray them."

The faculty strives to bridge the cultures of school and local ministry sites in all phases of the seminary program, but two programs—language and cultural studies and field education—carry the primary responsibility for this task. Strategically, both emphasize the cultivation of a collegial style of leadership focused on learning to collaborate with laity and developing cross-cultural competencies. These two emphases are interwoven throughout both programs.

The language and cultural studies program, for example, places laity in primary instructional and evaluative roles. Directed by Aurora Mordey and taught by laypeople, including women, the program includes instruction in English and Spanish, and offers six pastoral theology classes and two theology courses in Spanish. Men and women from local parishes make up "local review boards" to evaluate the linguistic performance of students on their English language proficiency exams (mostly for international students) and Spanish language proficiency exams (for most students) and to suggest ways to improve their use of the language in public speaking.

The language and cultural studies program also figures centrally in facilitating student cross-cultural learning. The program has the threefold task of orienting international students to American society, requiring linguistic and cultural proficiency in English and Spanish, and challenging all students to affirm their own cultural gifts for ministry. A major emphasis of the program involves all students in a summer immersion in Latin America or Mexico, usually during their first or second year, and "integrative skills classes" in the latter years that emphasize language comprehension, vocabulary, pronunciation, reading, and conversational skills.

The bridging of academic and ministry site cultures at St. John's is also a primary emphasis of the field education program. Like the program of language and cultural studies, it emphasizes collaborative learning and feedback from laity in the various field placements students will have during their seminary career. In their first year, students spend several hours a week in a nursing home, learning not only how to listen to and assess the needs of patients but also how to work with medical and other personnel. In the second-year ministry site, seminarians spend a day a week in a social service agency. The options are many: women's shelters; teaching and campus ministries; programs on "skid row," in jails, or for the handicapped. Again, evaluations of their experience emphasize how well they work alongside lay professionals and workers whose roles and responsibilities tend to be more clearly defined.

At St. John's Seminary, the cultivation of this collaborative style of ministry culminates in a full-time internship during the student's third year of seminary, usually in a parish setting. An intern advisory board consisting of six persons from the parish has the responsibility of offering direct feedback, especially on the intern's "sensitivity and relational skills." Lay people use "reflection sheets" to give feedback on specific acts of ministry such as a liturgy, homily, or class. At the end of the year each member of the advisory board fills out an evaluation form on the intern, which becomes a part of the larger evaluation process in the student's pastoral formation.

The school's commitment to cross-cultural learning also permeates the field education program. Sister Regina Robbins, the program director, explained that, beginning with the first year of nursing-home work, "We . . . stress multicultural reality because multiculturalism doesn't just mean ethnic background; it also has to do with gender and age differences." She observed that attention to differences can often challenge student and staff assumptions. She recalled sending two seminarians—one African American and one African—to their first assignment. She encouraged the student from the United States to look after his African brother, with the expectation that this might be a strange cultural immersion for him. The African student, however, moved quickly to meet the staff and converse with the patients, while the U.S. student felt "lost" and had to rely on the international student for guidance. Contrary to Sister Regina's expectations, the African student was able to adjust more easily to the culture of the nursing home.

In weekly reflection sessions, students are invited to share strengths of their own cultural background, such as practices of hospitality or conversation, which may be assets to their own pastoral work. They can also examine experiences of being "lost" or disoriented in a new institutional or cultural context. The pastoral formation courses, which Sister Regina also oversees, include a required course, "Introduction to Multicultural Ministries," which identifies distinctive cultural practices of various communities in the Los Angeles area, and develops skills in cross-cultural sensitivity and interpretation. During the interview prior to placement assignments, Sister Regina asks students questions like, "[A]re you strong in Spanish? Do you want a parish that is multicultural? Do you want a Spanish parish in the inner city? What are your qualities? What are the things that you are afraid of? Where do you want to risk?" Consequently, traditional field education questions around personal "growing edges" are placed within the wider context of cross-cultural challenges and opportunities.

The strategies of bridging the cultures of seminary and ministry sites through collaborative and cross-cultural learning reinforce each other throughout the student's seminary experience. Collaborative modes of feedback and reflection prepare students for ministries in ethnically and linguistically diverse communities. Learning a second language, as a cultural and pastoral resource, prepares seminarians to remain in a learning mode. These pedagogical activities also underscore the commitment of the faculty and staff to cultivating the collegiality of the priesthood in a pluralistic school, church, and world throughout the student's seminary experience.

Pedagogies for Developing Clergy Practice

Although field education programs in seminaries share a common commitment to bridging the cultures of the academy and ministry sites, field educators bring to their leadership of these programs a variety of academic and experiential expectations. Consequently, the pedagogies of field education tend to be locally constructed, rely on a variety of theoretical sources, and emphasize a range of pedagogical practices. Most are considered to be *experiential* or to emphasize *action-reflection,* but the meaning of these terms tends to be influenced, positively and negatively, by the larger pedagogical ethos of the school.

Field education pedagogies in the three schools highlighted in this chapter, for example, reflect different ways of negotiating the relationship of school and ministry site cultures in the education of their students. Yale, for example, emphasizes a *professional* view of the clergy fostered through pedagogies of the "reflective practitioner." Trinity focuses attention on the *vocation* of clergy in pedagogies that correlate religious tradition and student vocation with pastoral responses to the needs of local congregations. St. John's emphasizes pedagogies that develop the *pastoral* habits and mind of the priesthood.

Although we did not have the opportunity to observe these pedagogies at work in field education settings, they were described for us in field education documents and through interviews and conversations with field education directors, faculty, administrators, and students. Our discussions with the students, faculty, and field education directors and their description of the pedagogies used in field education led us to frame three specific questions about the pedagogies:

○ To what degree are these pedagogies intensive, in the sense of being developed and monitored in the supervisor-intern relationship?

○ To what degree are they extensive, in terms of being used or reinforced within the larger school curriculum?

○ In what way are these pedagogies identified as a form of theological reflection owned by the rest of the seminary?

Pedagogies to Develop "Reflective Practitioners"

Blodgett describes Yale as "offering a professional education," entailing an apprenticeship phase of learning from "someone who calls [their work] ministry." Blodgett draws explicitly on the work of Donald Schön (1983, 1987) as she identifies and trains supervisors and prepares students for their internship year. Schön's work is appealing to her because he widened conventional action-reflection pedagogies to focus attention on the reconstructive function of practice in theory. By emphasizing "reflection-in-action," he privileges the improvisational use and adaptation of theoretical frames for understanding and responding to a given situation or event, often culminating in unanticipated results for theory as well as practice—indeed, with the possibility that practice may yield new theory.

Schön developed the model on the basis of his work with advanced professionals. The challenge for Blodgett is adapting it to the education of
seminarians who are still acquiring basic skills.

Blodgett does not train students and supervisors in a particular theological "method" to engage in this reflective practice as many field education programs do. Instead, she provides a book by Howard W. Stone
and James O. Duke, *How to Think Theologically* (1996), and tells supervisors and students that if they do not choose to use this book, she hopes
it "will at least prompt them to find their own way towards theological
reflection." The book, however, illustrates something of the reflection-in-
action process she would like to see. It guides readers into a threefold
process including (1) theological interpretation, (2) correlation of that
interpretation with others, and (3) assessing the adequacy of that interpretation. Creative and imaginative steps may be included at any point
throughout the process, but the pedagogy in the process emphasizes theology as an art of interpretation. It pays especial attention to the reflective side of Schön's "reflective practitioner."

As an ethicist, Blodgett expands the theological focus of this pedagogical framework to focus attention on the moral formation and the moral
imagination of students. She teaches in a program, required of all master
of divinity students, in sexual misconduct prevention. She asks practicum
instructors to raise moral and ethical issues in the case studies students
are presenting. In her own practicum and plenary teaching, she always
looks "for the moral dimension to any case or situation" under discussion. She adds that "in my own thinking and in my own practice, I would
say that I go back and forth between a principle-based approach and a
virtue-based, character-based approach. . . . I try to talk about the virtues
that the ministry needs . . . and the virtues they need to cultivate. But then
we also talk about what to do [in given ministry situations] and why."
This emphasis on the moral and ethical conduct required of the professional is part and parcel of the reflective-practitioner approach at Yale.

Pedagogies to Develop Pastoral Identity in Context

At Trinity Lutheran Seminary, we observed a cluster of pedagogical practices correlating the student's sense of vocation, church context, and religious tradition into a constructive relationship for pastoral identity. Three
distinct but interrelated pedagogical practices are directed to pastoral
identity: one emphasizing vocational exploration, a second doing contextual analysis, and a third engaging in theological reflection. These pedagogies reveal how the Trinity Lutheran Seminary faculty envisions the

contribution of pedagogies of formation, contextualization, and interpretation to the pedagogies of performance in student contextual education learning. Although the interplay of these pedagogies permeates the ministry-in-context program of the student's first two years of seminary, the pedagogies take center stage during the third-year full-time internship, which is typically in a congregational setting. In this setting students assume a wide range of ministry roles and responsibilities guided by expectations from the seminary and the denomination and negotiated in relation to the resources and needs of the congregation.

Early in the intern year, the student undertakes an intensified *exploration of vocation*, through a series of structured conversations with his or her supervisor. Together, they explore the "faith history" of the intern, guided by a set of questions about influential persons, experiences of conversion or faith commitment, and experiences of God's presence in the student's life. During these conversations the student is invited to draw on both academic and personal experience to share understandings of such things as church theology and sacraments, severe illness and evil, and the intersection of religion and politics. This exercise establishes a dialogical practice for the supervisor and intern, meant to form trust, model collegiality, and shape a primary learning environment for the year. Although the steps in the process are carefully outlined in the internship manual, the character and texture of the encounter between supervisor and intern are shaped by the practices and tone of each supervisor and the patterns of engagement by each intern.

Later in the intern year, the supervisor and student continue the process of vocational clarification with the aid of a three-part interview process called "discerning motivations for ministry." In the first part, they explore the past history of influences upon the intern's pastoral call from home church, high school, college, and work experiences. The supervisor poses questions, exploring such things as when the student first had the idea of becoming a minister, and what appeals to the intern about ministry and the lifestyle of a minister. In the second part, the supervisor and student explore the intern's self-perception about her or his personality, gifts, relational abilities, and coping mechanisms in the face of tension. In these conversations students are invited to reflect on their understanding of church authority and aspects of ministry they anticipate might frustrate or create tension for them. The third interview explores the intern's readiness for ministry. In this session, supervisors explore with interns their visions of the leadership needed in today's church and society and how they envision themselves in a number of ministry situations, such as dealing with needy persons, responding as a caregiver in times of crisis, interpreting the purposes of worship, and balancing personal and professional needs. Each of these supervisory conversations explores the student's movement from a sense of vocation to an emerging pastoral identity in pastoral practices.

During the intern year, students are also engaged in pedagogies that encourage *contextual analysis* of the local congregation as a primary site of ministry. This process actually begins in the first year of seminary as students visit different congregations, equipped with questions to help them reflect on such things as their experience of congregational hospitality. It continues during the middler year when the students focus attention on the contextual dynamics that influence specific ministry practices in courses on teaching, pastoral care, and preaching. During their third, intern year, supervisors and interns are trained in aspects of "listening to the context," with methods drawn primarily from ethnographic and cross-cultural models of missionary work. Interns are encouraged to explore the language and slang of a community; identify hopes, priorities, symbols, and values that make up its world view; find local interpreters of the community; spend time with people, listening and asking questions; and explore the formal and informal power dynamics of the community.

Contextual pedagogies appear most explicitly in the intern's "learning contract" and "covenant with the congregation." In these required assignments, student interns study the role-related aspects of congregational life that pertain to pastoral leadership and establish learning goals for each: worship, pastoral care, lay ministries and education, social ministries, stewardship, and judicatory and ecumenical relations. In turn, congregational leaders engage in a mini strategic plan to review the congregation's current sense of mission and corresponding needs for student leadership. When this preliminary work is completed, the supervisor, intern, and congregational representatives negotiate a learning contract for the internship period. The process helps the congregation know "that the student is there not only to learn but also to serve," Jane Jenkins told us. "And the congregation is not only to teach but also to be in ministry together so the partnership is . . . really healthy." This negotiation process is intended to model a style of pastor-congregation interaction for the student's future ministry.

Each side of this correlational pedagogy, emphasizing the mutuality of school and ministry site in a Trinity Lutheran Seminary education, has distinct processes of assessment. The clarification of vocation involves the student's use of congregational feedback for confirming and honing his or her sense of call. As Jenkins explains, "In our theology, we have an understanding of inner and outer call" whereby "a student's inner calling to ministry is tested and confirmed by the outer call in a given community." Contextual analysis involves an ongoing assessment of students' ability to respond to the needs they identify in congregations through the development of skills for pastoral action. Because an internship is "about skill exploration and enhancement," students wrestle with such questions as "What am I good at? What do I need to work on? What am I surprised that I can do that I didn't know?" Assessment forms emphasize the evaluation of skills development for performing pastoral actions in preaching and worship, pastoral care, education, and the like. Jenkins explains that these forms approach the question of assessment somewhat playfully to evoke conversation—for example, one rating scale asks whether or not, in relation to some pastoral action, the student "Can walk on water" or "Doesn't know where the water is."

Jenkins articulates the overall goal of contextual education of the seminary as shaping the pastoral identity of each student. It requires a third pedagogical focus: the art of *theological reflection*. Trinity Lutheran's intern manual lays out a clear three-step process: beginning with a *ministry experience,* then *correlating with the tradition,* and finally *constructing new meaning toward pastoral action.* Again, the process is a correlational one, but now between a student's ministry experience and the church's larger tradition, as a means of informing pastoral activity. The double sense of "pastoral identity" as performance-practice skills and theological reflection is highlighted in the regular supervisory practice of reviewing a "critical incident report." The intern brings a prepared report on a ministerial event and reflects upon it both practically and theologically with the supervisor. Jenkins explains that the critical incident report provides an opportunity for a student to say "This happened to me in my ministry this week" and for the student and supervisor to "look at it from a practical point of view as well as the theological point of view." Jenkins is clear that she considers a good pastor-supervisor to be someone who can "facilitate theological reflection" as well as "model ministry."

The goal of shaping a strong pastoral identity is one that contextual education shares with the rest of the seminary curriculum. "Integration groups" allow first- and second-year students to discuss issues of personal vocation, contextual learning, and theological reflection with fourth-year students. During the second year, courses in the "practical" fields offer assignments in preaching, teaching, and pastoral care that are often carried out in ministry in context field settings. After students return from their intern year, they take courses from across the curriculum, designed specifically to draw insights from their ministry practice into discussions of biblical, theological, and historical texts and traditions.

Pedagogies for Pastoral Skills, Character, and Lifestyle

Within the comprehensive framework of the Roman Catholic PPF, field education at St. John's Seminary is primarily about *pastoral formation* for ministries in a culturally diverse church and society. The notion of pastoral formation in the program, influenced by John Paul II's *Pastores Dabo Vobis* (1992), emphasizes the increasing communion of seminarians with the pastoral office of Christ as the Good Shepherd. "Hence," as the school's pastoral internship handbook states, the formation of priests "must have a fundamentally pastoral character." This is especially true of field education pedagogies that emphasize developing pastoral skills, character, and lifestyle.

The emphasis on *pastoral skills* at St. John's is most evident in the learning agreement and evaluation processes for the student's third-year internship at the seminary. In a fashion similar to that in Trinity, the learning agreement is negotiated by the intern, the supervisor, and a board of lay representatives of the parish. The agreement outlines the expectations, hours, and roles of pastoral performance, in sacramental (including pastoral visitation), service (including parish administration), and education ministries of the parish. Duties vary from greeting parishioners before mass to participation in first communion classes. Sister Regina uses the learning agreement in training supervisors because it identifies "what we want"—"the tasks," "the areas," and "the amount of time we want [interns] to spend." The goals of the learning agreement set up the elements of the evaluation process in the annual review. Evaluation forms identify pastoral skills and relational abilities to be assessed by the supervisor. An intern advisory board composed of six parish members observes the intern at work and meets with him monthly to give direct feedback on his relational and pastoral skills.

A commitment to developing *pastoral character* permeates the pedagogies of St. John's field education. Placements in hospitals and nursing homes, Sister Regina explains, "instill personal and pastoral qualities of compassion, ministerial presence, listening skills, slowing down." During the intern year, pastoral character is formed primarily through interlocking levels of accountability to others. During regular meetings with a spiritual director, interns seek divine help to address personal weaknesses and to strengthen gifts for ministry. With members of the intern advisory board, students receive feedback on their relational skills and explore ways to collaborate with lay people in the parish. With the supervisor, students examine their responsiveness to authority, cross-cultural sensitivity, and willingness to take responsibility, and the extent to which they show initiative, collaborate with clergy and lay colleagues, receive criticism constructively, and respond to situations with a sense of humor, flexibility, and resilience even when disappointed. The cultivation of professional ethics among students is understood largely in terms of developing these pastoral qualities.

Because during their intern year students live, for the most part, in rectories outside the compound of the seminary, field education becomes an ideal site for developing a *pastoral lifestyle*—a distinctive feature in the St. John's field education experience. This means the student's pastor-supervisor takes on the job of supervision in both "a rectory setting and a parish setting." At the beginning of the internship, supervisor and intern negotiate aspects of shared life in the rectory: the uses of common and private space (including areas of the house off limits to laity and family members), location and rules of office space, household duties, use of rectory or parish funds, times for socializing, and rules and times for house meetings. In this learning agreement, seminarians also identify aspects of the spiritual, intellectual, and physical lifestyle they plan to maintain: from daily prayer, to the reading of theological books, to regular exercise. In the midyear and final evaluations, these lifestyle agreements are reviewed by the supervisor and by the intern advisory board. Attention is given to simplicity and balance in one's lifestyle, healthy patterns of consumption, healthy friendships and forms of social interaction, and the nurturing of collaborative relationships with colleagues and laity to offset the isolation experienced by many priests. This attention to lifestyle issues has been intensified for the church and the seminary as charges of sexual misconduct and abuse of the pastoral office by priests have drawn attention to the importance of nurturing and assessing the personal and spiritual maturity of priests during their seminary years.

At St. John's, the strength of the bridge between the cultures of school and the ministry site comes from the attention to teaching toward clergy practice and "theological reflection." The process is similar to Trinity's. It moves students from the ministerial experience, through reflection on its meaning, to insights for pastoral action. But the emphasis at St. John's is more experiential, which is consistent with the seminary's approach to spiritual formation. In a first step, students describe an *experience* as "one source of truth," largely through narrative form. In a second, more complex step, they *reflect on that experience* from two perspectives: that of "personal values and levels of meaning" intrinsic to the experience, and in terms of the "economic, political, social, cultural or religious forces" to be found in it. In a third step, students *integrate the experience with faith and theology,* doing so in an expansive way that moves beyond personal interpretation to account for larger and relevant insights from Scripture and church tradition. The quest for integration of experience and tradition—different from Trinity's correlating sources of truth in each, or Yale's reflection on action—emphasizes the appropriation of the wisdom of Catholic tradition in and for specific ministry activity. In this final step of theological reflection, students are encouraged to *discern insight* for *new responses* in ministry. The process emphasizes the cultivation of their participation in the agency of that tradition.

The process of theological reflection at St. John's—like Yale's and, in some dimensions, like Trinity's—is communal. Early in the field educa- tion sequence, Sister Regina teaches the process to seminarians and super- visors. She puts them "in small groups" to learn to "write case studies" as a way of "sharing wisdom" rather than "case solving." Interns and supervisors continue this pedagogical pattern in a less formal way as part of the internship mentoring process. In order to assess that integration is occurring, formal "capstone sessions" are held for third- and fourth-year students, whereby students demonstrate, through case studies, their pas- toral knowledge and skill. Cases cover every arena of ministry, from sacra- mental practice to catechetical situations and crises of pastoral care. The format for writing and preparing cases is carefully outlined, directions for the presenter and a group facilitator are clearly laid out, and each case is reviewed by the director of field education prior to its presentation. Ele- ments in the group's reflection include prayerful preparation and careful listening and self-reflection as others share, all with special attention to how Scripture, tradition, and God's presence figure in the ministry case and their reflections on it.

Although the process includes instructions to integrate the discussion of cases with classroom studies, it most effectively socializes students into the discourse and community of priest-practitioners. A deeply communal process, it helps students internalize "a habitual way of reflecting and act- ing" associated with the lifestyle and ministry of the priesthood. The process is reinforced by an intern portfolio that each student submits, con- taining outlines of their work, demonstrations of pastoral competence, and written theological reflections.

Teaching Culture, Field Education Pedagogies, and Images of Clergy Roles

Two issues in field education emerged from our general review of the data from all schools participating in the study, and they became more appar- ent as we examined more closely the field education programs of Yale,

Trinity, and St. John's: first, how the pedagogies of field education are related to the dominant pedagogies of a particular seminary, and second, how field education pedagogies link knowledge and technical skill in professional practice to professional judgment.

The Relationship of Field Education and Classroom Pedagogies

Yale faculty responding to a survey question about their images of the clergy emphasized the roles of the pastor as teacher or proclaimer, spiritual guide or counselor, and community leader or advocate. Student and alumni and alumnae survey respondents echoed these images almost exactly. Linking these various images together in the pastoral role for the faculty at Yale is a way of "theological thinking." Blodgett put it this way: "I like to think that our students" come to Yale to be with a "strong theological faculty," and that when they leave, they know "how to think about something theologically." A student underscored her point when declaring that clergy with a Yale degree "bring a theological response to situations arising in the community." Blodgett refines this expectation for the pastoral imagination that the Yale faculty seeks to cultivate, with her observation that thinking theologically in this situation means learning to think within one's tradition—as in "an Episcopal way of thinking" or a Lutheran or Presbyterian one.

Images of clergy as teachers or proclaimers and as theological thinkers at Yale are embedded in pedagogies of interpretation that dominate the teaching practices in both classroom and field education. Indeed, the stated mission of the school is to "foster the knowledge and love of God" by equipping students with the scholarly tools to engage critically "the traditions of the Christian churches in the context of the contemporary world." Faculty attention, we heard in a variety of ways, centers on helping students develop a cognitive practice for monitoring, expanding, and changing frames of reference as they negotiate the interaction of scholarly knowledge and methods and viable faith traditions—that is, *wissenschaft* and *paideia*.

In a similar vein, field education staff and supervisors build on that practice to help students negotiate between the knowledge and skills of the classroom and the knowledge and skills of clergy practices in field education placements and in supervisory and practicum conversations. Some faculty members described the "clergy way of interpretive thinking" emerging from these pedagogical processes for students as "living in the midst of the tension" of "maintaining a critical edge" in their pastoral setting and a pastoral perspective in their theological studies.

At Trinity, images of the clergy held by faculty and students reflect the institution's historic emphasis on the interaction of academic and contextual patterns of clergy education. Faculty responding to our survey question highlighted the importance of three clergy roles: preacher and teacher, caretaker of pastoral relationships (that is, a lover of souls, loving critic, midwife), and leader of liturgy or sacraments. Student and alumni and alumnae survey respondents echoed their faculty mentors, although with more emphasis on the clergy as teacher. In a Trinity Lutheran Seminary education, these images cohere in the cultivation of a *pastoral identity*—something students describe as "a pastoral presence" or characterize as "an integrated person of faith."

In contrast to the experience of students at Yale, Trinity Lutheran students negotiate the relationship of school and ministry site predominantly through the interplay of pedagogies of *interpretation* and *performance*, stair-stepped through the curriculum. During their first year they develop a vocabulary through pedagogies of interpretation in Bible, theology, and church history classes to use in observing congregational life in the ministry-in-context program. During their second year, they engage pedagogies of interpretation and performance in classes on preaching, teaching, and pastoral care as they move back and forth between assignments and reflections in the classroom and practice in the ministry context. During their third year, they are engaged full time in ministry practice, primarily in congregations, along with formal reflections on that practice with a pastor supervisor. During their last year, students reflect on their intern-year ministry experience through the interpretive categories and methods in a range of courses, from Bible, theology, and history to ethics and a required course on preaching intended to function as a capstone in this interplay of interpretation and performance.

As students move through this structured engagement of both classroom and ministry site, the faculty expects them to internalize, with increasing sophistication and understanding, the cognitive and practical knowledge and skills associated with clergy roles of preaching, teaching, pastoral guidance, and liturgical leadership. This correlation of interpretation and performance pedagogies in the curriculum implies either the coordination or the mutuality of two fairly equal domains or sets of practices,[3] like those between a student's vocation and ministry context or between a ministry event and a theological tradition.

At St. John's, the faculty's image of clergy roles fits the post–Vatican II emphasis on priests as shepherds and servants to the whole people of God. Although they also used words like "healer," "teacher," and "worship or sacramental leader" to describe their images of priests, most emphasized the priest as servant, shepherd, and guide. Students and alumni shared these images, expanding the list to include such pastoral "characteristics" as compassion, caring, love, and discipline. Each of the St. John's programs of "formation" (intellectual, spiritual, human, and pastoral) embraces the *telos* in these images of the priest sharing in the pastoral office of Christ in ways that blend sacramentality with service. Pastoral or priestly formation, therefore, is the *telos* driving the interlocking elements in the St. John's education. It sustains the mutuality to be found in the levels of accountability of students to instructors in the classroom, supervisors and lay advisors in field education, and peers in the life of the seminary community. Seen in this light, *pastoral formation,* culminating in field education, is meant to be the capstone of the entire curriculum, as it seeks to socialize seminarians into roles of servanthood and leadership of communities of faith.

Linking Knowledge and Skill in Professional Judgment

Recent studies in nursing education suggest that teaching practices can move students from basic skills acquisition, to a fluidity and interchange of skills use, to the beginnings of internalized judgment and the improvisation necessitated by the constantly changing circumstances of professional practice (Benner, 1984). In the nursing field, this movement from beginner to intermediate to expert professional practice occurs largely through staged practice: exposure, under careful supervision, accompanied by ongoing reflective work upon practice. It models a mode of *practical reasoning* that emphasizes *judgment* in professional practice, as in the adaptation of knowledge and skills *while* engaging or addressing a given problem or situation (Benner, 1984; Schön, 1983, 1987; Sullivan, 2005). In other words, as William Sullivan has noted (2005, pp. 246–50), from this perspective a holistic view of practical reasoning involves the movement from theoretical *analysis* of a situation toward *concrete experience* in a fluid, intuitive way that allows practice to take the lead, even to the point of generating new theoretical insight. Although some models of theological reflection on ministry experience formalize this movement (Whitehead and Whitehead, 1995), few take into account the intuitive and improvisational nature of this practice among experienced ministers.

The formation of professional *judgment* and *action,* or *phronesis,* in this sense is akin to ancient patterns of education that aim at the development of professional *virtues* or habits of mind and moral action in the practitioner. This moves field education beyond the emphasis on skills or craft (*techne*), *to emphasize the cultivation of professional identity, judgment, and sense of authority.* The pedagogical issue at stake for clergy education centers on the progression of students from the inexperience of novices to the exercise of expertise in bringing both professional knowledge and skill to bear on specific pastoral, priestly, or rabbinic issues and situations. It involves, as Sullivan has also suggested, "a much tighter link among the three apprenticeships, not fusing them but giving a certain leading to the third apprenticeship as a way to embrace theoretic intelligence and technical skill in the service of fostering an enlightened practice" (2005, p. 242). The goal, in other words, is well-informed, proficient, and embodied practice.

Although most field educators and many seminary faculty members would generally affirm the importance of this notion of practical reasoning in the education of clergy, the mutuality of *techne* and *phronesis* at the center of the interdependence of the cognitive, skill, and professional identity apprenticeships has often been pedagogically elusive in seminary field education programs. Unlike Schön's advanced practitioners in psychotherapy, engineering, and architecture, who had had years of practice to integrate basic skills into professional competence (1983, p. viii), most seminary students—even those with prior experience in other professions—are, for the most part, novices at negotiating the interplay of the knowledge and skills associated with both the cognitive and skill apprenticeships of clergy practitioners, while at the same time developing a sense of their identities as priests, rabbis, or pastors.

Blodgett illustrated the challenge for seminary field educators while describing for us the learning agreements students create for their internships. She asks them to identify both goals (those long-term foundational aspirations for professional practice) and tasks (the concrete activities they will do to meet their goals). She has discovered students consistently fail to distinguish between the two. They will, for example, list "Learn how to celebrate the Eucharist" or "Learn how to lead a small group" as their goals, with "Assist with the Eucharist" and "lead a small group" as their tasks. She had always found their confusion frustrating, until she realized they were seeking "novice-level" knowledge and skills, and that their goals were really to practice these skills.

Yale students and alumni and alumnae responding to our survey questions indicated a high appreciation for the emphasis in the Yale curriculum on learning about the contextual aspects of ministry. This contextual focus is primarily introduced to students during course work, as faculty members in courses across the curriculum use historical-critical modes of scholarship to place a text or event in its larger sociohistorical context. It is reinforced in supervised ministry, as supervisors who take contexts seriously reflect with students on the meaning of their ministry experience. Yale students, in other words, practice making judgments about the contextuality of meaning in many courses and in formal reflections on their field education activities.

However, the task of establishing a link between, on the one hand, emphases on the contextuality of meaning in the professional judgments that clergy must make (as they prepare to preach, teach, visit persons in the hospital, speak out on some issue, or develop a committee meeting agenda), and, on the other, the technical skills required for proficiency or expertise in meeting these clergy responsibilities, is accomplished in a different way. Most Yale faculty with whom we talked assume that field education and several practical theology courses provide settings and occasions for developing the skills for making professional judgments in clergy practice. Many also assume the student has primary responsibility for initiating and negotiating, in his or her field education ministry sites, learning goals that facilitate the development of those skills—indeed, even for pastoral activities such as learning to lead small groups. Proficiency in making professional judgments emerges over time: in the reciprocity of student reflection on their actions in ministry, in conversations with their supervisors and peers in weekly practicum sessions, and as they assess the consistency of meanings in their judgments with their religious traditions and the appropriateness of their actions for their ministry contexts. In this way, professional judgment is rooted in the growing ability of the student to think theologically.

With a commitment to cultivating pastoral identity in the midst of clergy practice, the field education programs at Trinity and St. John's establish clear, although somewhat different, trajectories for student skill development toward the expertise of professional judgment. Like the program at Yale, they both resist modes of practical reasoning that engage students primarily in the application of theories to clergy practices.

The primary features of the Trinity Lutheran Seminary field education program parallel the five steps in the model of practical reasoning proposed by Hubert and Stuart Dreyfus, described by Sullivan (pp. 247–49). The Trinity faculty assumes, for example, that most students, as *novices,* lack the "perceptual grasp or ability to interpret a situation as whole." They are therefore introduced to the vocabulary of Christian ministry practice in courses in Bible, church history, and theology and sent out on structured observations of congregations to practice seeing congregational life through the lens of that vocabulary. Second-year classes in Christian education, pastoral care, and preaching move them into a second or *advanced beginner* stage of practical reasoning in which they begin to draw on knowledge in class and their knowledge of the ministry site to prepare for and practice clergy roles of teaching, preaching, and pastoral care under the supervision of both settings.

During the intern year, Trinity Lutheran students have opportunities to rehearse the interplay of their accumulating knowledge and developing skill in professional roles to the point that they begin to develop *competencies* in clergy practice. Depending on prior education and experience, some students in the intern year may even move through this third stage into the fourth stage of *proficiency,* demonstrating the capacity to make what appear to be intuitive judgments for some clergy tasks—based, however, on their interpretations and evaluations of prior judgments. During the intern year, few reach the level of *expertise* evident in the ability to make appropriate professional judgments "without either working through complex problem solving or devising an explicit plan." This level of professional judgment comes, Sullivan reminds us, only after "long training and practice," typically with much coaching and feedback along the way. Back on campus for their final year, students participate in classes through which they reflect back on their intern year, using it as a resource for anticipating future pastoral activity. Each step in this process is directed to the cultivation of a pastoral identity in pastoral action.

At St. John's, the field education program also establishes an agenda for learning specific skills for priestly ministries. As students move from a year of working in nursing homes to their internships in parishes, they develop skills in such pastoral practices as empathy and caring, teaching and liturgical leadership. But the focus of professional judgments in these activities is directed predominantly toward the spirituality and character evident in the practice of the student as future priest—that is, the extent to which the student internalizes, in his relationships and conduct with others at school and in the parish, the pastoral office of Christ.

"Doing" Practical Theology Through Field Education

In discussing the shape of practical reasoning, Sullivan observes that "in the teaching and learning of expertise, practice is often ahead of theory. It is expert practice that is the source of formal knowledge about practice, not the other way around" (p. 250). Sullivan is describing a cognitive process at the heart of practical theological thinking and pertinent to the role of field education in the seminary curriculum.

As we observe in Chapter Eight, a number of seminary educators from many academic disciplines have been engaged in a lively theoretical discussion about practical theology. This conversation has begun to influence how some seminary educators (in this study, notably at Catholic Theological Union) talk with each other about their teaching. In no seminary we visited has the discussion of practical theology led the faculty of a school to refocus its educational mission or revise the organizing framework of its curriculum. But we discovered that the notion of "practice"—and, indirectly, of practical theological thinking—has become the impetus to the intentions for knowledge and skill held by seminary educators responsible for field education. Implicitly, at least, in these settings students are engaged in "doing" practical theology.

This was certainly true of the field education programs at Yale, Trinity, and St. John's seminaries. In each of these schools, some observation, incident, moment, or case study of clergy practice provided the presenting question or issue for the formal interactions of teaching and learning in field education. The pedagogical activity, in other words, begins in practice.

The presenting question or issue in turn became the catalyst to formal reflection on that incident, moment, or experience, drawing on prior experience, resources from other classes in the seminary curriculum and other educational experiences, and the wisdom of supervisor and faculty member from their own reflections on practice. The interplay of these two pedagogical moments—which students repeat many times over throughout the course of the field education experience, both individually and collectively with peers—facilitates the movement from the naïveté of being novices in professional practice to some more advanced stage of professional proficiency.

Different expectations for the interplay of these two pedagogical moments in field education reflect alternative faculty assumptions about what knowledge, skills, habits, and dispositions should contribute to the operational practical theologies students are developing. At Yale, the pedagogical quest of faculty and supervised ministry supervisors—to help students become proficient in choosing and using appropriate methods for interpreting texts and contexts (preeminently appropriated and refashioned from literary and historical criticism) and methods for interpreting situations and practices (adapted from organizational theory and the social sciences)—emphasizes, among other things, clergy roles in facilitating the human quest for meaning.

At Trinity Lutheran Seminary, the movement is curricular as students move back and forth through academic and field settings and their associated bodies of knowledge and skills and move from introductory to increasingly more sophisticated engagements with their interdependence. At St. John's Seminary, the movement is centered on a plan of development that carries the student through programs of intellectual, pastoral, spiritual, and human formation toward priestly identification with the pastoral presence of Christ in whatever clergy roles he happens to be assuming in a given moment.

Although one will find, for the most part, the same academic disciplines in each of these schools and many shared curricular commitments among the members of their faculties, their graduates will generally bring a distinctive perspective to many clergy tasks. These differences may be illustrated by contrasting the responses of two seminary graduates to a question about how their seminaries had helped prepare them to make "professional judgments" in response to the September 11, 2001, attacks on the World Trade Center and Pentagon.

One expressed appreciation for the way the seminary had "invited me to think critically about how faith, the Bible and politics intersect" and "taught me to have a pastoral word and presence in a time of crisis." Another recalled how the seminary had nurtured "in me a pastoral sensitivity" by facilitating "a deep appreciation for God's missionary heart" and "God's persistence in reaching out to us in the midst of much pain" that culminated in the realization that "our call" is "to be God's people in the midst of life happening."

Both drew on the resources of their seminary educations for actions associated with the work of clergy. Both reflect a confidence in the professional practices they had developed while in seminary. Both view and approach that work from different perspectives. Those differences may be traced, in part, to alternative assumptions at work in the pedagogies of their seminaries about how to move students from initial encounters with the knowledge and skills of the profession to the knowledge in practice that comes with increasing professional proficiency.

ENDNOTES

1. In *Good Work*, the authors use the term *alignment* to describe the relationship of the "culture," "domains," and "fields" in professional education and work. "Culture" is analogous to our understanding of the "ethos and traditions" of a given school or professional institution; "domains" includes the skills and codes embedded in "social practices" that we consider in teaching practice; and "field" constitutes the social roles of educators and learners in a given institutional environment.

2. Trinity Lutheran Seminary inherited the more classical education tradition from Evangelical Lutheran Seminary and the more contextual education tradition from Hamma Theological Seminary.

3. Tillich's modern formulation of theological "correlation," which runs through much of his writing (and explicitly in *Systematic Theology*, volume 1) is built on the poles of human-divine interaction (that is, human questions, revelation's answers), which is largely bipolar and oriented toward some synthesis of the two. When adapted to field education pedagogies, a method of correlation sets up a relationship between two domains, which in practice may not be as complex or teleological as in Tillich's discussion.

PART FOUR

SEMINARY EDUCATOR TEACHING PRACTICES

MANY OF THE SEMINARY GRADUATES participating in this study look back on their education with appreciation for the way it prepared them for professional practice. "Seminary was a wonderful foundation which enabled me to face the real world of parish ministry" wrote one. Another said that "I truly feel like I was being trained for ministry." And still another wrote that "I received a solid education that provided the groundwork for practical application in the rabbinate." For these members of the clergy their education has facilitated their professional practice. In these two final chapters, we return to the question about the relationship of professional education and practice that they experienced in their seminary experience—and that prompted this study: How does a seminary education cultivate a pastoral, rabbinic, or priestly imagination that integrates knowledge and skill with religious commitment and moral integrity for professional practice? In addressing this question, we focus attention in Chapter Eleven on the inclination toward the integration of knowledge, skill, moral integrity, and religious commitment in the teaching practices of seminary educators we observed. We found in that inclination a variety of pedagogical patterns, each emphasizing in distinctive ways the interdependence of the pedagogies of interpretation, formation, contextualization, and performance as well as a mutuality of the cognitive, practical, and normative apprenticeships that make up a professional education. We explore the dynamic of integration by looking closely at the teaching practices of two seminary educators.

In Chapter Twelve, we consider a series of questions that emerged through the study that figure significantly in any consideration of the relationship of the education of clergy to their future professional practice. We close with an invitation to conversation prompted by these questions—questions for which there are no quick answers but that are central to the continuing challenge of preparing students for the roles and responsibilities of religious leadership in a constantly changing world.

11

TEACHING TOWARD INTEGRATION: CULTIVATING THE PASTORAL, PRIESTLY, OR RABBINIC IMAGINATION

THROUGHOUT THIS STUDY, we met seminary educators who anticipated the possibility that through their teaching their students might discover a way of thinking about, relating to, and engaging the work of clergy practice. "I hope," wrote one, "[that my] students will come to see themselves as practical theologians engaging critically, constructively, and lovingly the practice of ministry." Those three terms—*critically, constructively,* and *lovingly*—suggest a pedagogical imagination that somehow links knowledge, skill, and student investment in clergy practice in the interactions of teaching and learning. Another seminary educator describes this integrative expectation more explicitly: "I hope my students will see their Judaism as a praxis that is nourished by Torah study and prayer rather than as a body of data or a repertoire of teachings for them to apply to other people. I hope they learn to keep a conversation going between the tradition, its texts and values, and the world they live in, the new problems it presents and the new wonders it reveals to us. Their job is to live out that conversation with integrity and to help others learn to do the same."

Another clergy educator shared a similar hope, desiring in students an experience of "ministerial formation that integrates theological vision and wise pastoral practice with a whole sense of Christian identity and vocation." Still another hoped "that students will come to see that loving God with the mind is not an alternative to loving God with the heart, but is essential to the final integrity of the latter." Changes such as these that seminary educators seek in students not only emphasize the integration of knowledge, skills, and the development of clergy identity, but also suggest the pastoral, priestly, or rabbinic imaginations they hope to be cultivating.

Seminary educators, we discovered, have a deep commitment to the notion of integration in student learning. When responding to survey questions and during interviews, they consistently identified integration as a highly desired outcome of their teaching. When we probed for their meaning of the term, we often heard "pulling it all together." We discovered rather quickly, however, that what they meant by "it" varied widely.

Sometimes it referred to some confluence of knowledge and skills from readings, presentations, and discussions in an integrative assignment, such as a research paper, case analysis, or sermon. Some seminary educators described this kind of integration as *theological thinking*. Sometimes it meant building on foundational knowledge and basic skills to develop increasingly complex and sophisticated understandings and competencies with a subject or task. This *vertical integration* is often structured into the curriculum to move students from introductory to advanced courses. Some looked for the ability to draw on knowledge and skills learned from a course in one field to advance the range and depth of one's knowledge and skills in another course in a different field. This cross-disciplinary learning could be called *horizontal integration*.

At the heart of clergy education is a still more complex integrative challenge—one that embraces, to some extent, all of these expectations. This integrative challenge emphasizes linking, in student learning, the knowledge, skills, and priestly, rabbinic, or pastoral identity typically identified with the educational tasks of the cognitive, practical, and normative apprenticeships. In this chapter, we explore how clergy educators meet this challenge. We begin with descriptions of the teaching practices of two seminary educators: Donn Morgan, the president of the Church Divinity School of the Pacific, who teaches an introductory course in Old Testament, and Rabbi Burton Visotzky, who teaches a course on the uses of classical rabbinical texts in preaching at Jewish Theological Seminary. Deeply reflective about their teaching, both quite intentionally draw on the resources of their religious and academic traditions for knowledge, skills, habits, and dispositions to foster an emerging clergy identity.

We use these descriptions as background for a discussion of the inclination toward integration evident in the interactions of seminary teachers and students. In particular, we look at teaching practices that contribute to the integration of knowledge, skills, moral integrity, and religious commitment in the cultivation of student pastoral, priestly, or rabbinic imaginations. The inclination toward integration is evident in

o The intentions of seminary educators for student learning

- Teaching practices that engage students in the mutuality of cognitive, skill, and identity formation apprenticeships through the strategic interplay of pedagogies of interpretation, formation, contextualization, and performance

- Modes of practical reasoning in professional judgments for negotiating norms of academic and religious traditions and contexts of clergy practice

- A community of practice that supports and reinforces the integration of learning

Inclination toward integration permeates the teaching practices of Morgan and Visotzky. They do not teach to prepare students *for* clergy practice, as many seminary educators have done in the past (and many still do in the present). Rather, in their teaching, like that of other seminary educators we observed, the familiar epistemology of theory to practice seems to be giving way to an epistemological perspective that emphasizes classroom praxis, or teaching toward participatory practice—what Lave has called "teaching, as learning, in practice" (1996, p. 149).

An Integrative Teaching Practice

Donn Morgan, Church Divinity School of the Pacific

We visited a session of Morgan's course in Old Testament in early December, near the end of the semester. Given the press of his administrative responsibilities, he told us, "my teaching has to turn me on." It soon became obvious to us that it certainly does.

He said that during the past thirty years he has varied his approach to the course four times. The most recent version grew out of his growing scholarly interest in "the processes of formation or education or wisdom in ancient Israel" and his realization that all his students had one thing in common: "when they leave here," they will all "be involved in teaching." Even "those who aren't ordained," he observed, "have still been seminarians and will thus be perceived as 'experts' in theology, Bible, etc., and will have some teaching role, whether formal or informal." The focus on preparing students for the performance practice of teaching has proven to be exciting for Morgan because its "beauty . . . is that one doesn't have to be an expert in advanced criticism in order to teach." But those who teach, he added, need "enough content" and an appropriate "framework for inquiry" both to teach and to keep on learning.

During the course, he uses a pedagogy of interpretation to introduce students to a framework for exploring the content of the Old Testament—forming, at the same time, their dispositions and habits for the practice of teaching. This framework emerges from the interaction of two questions: "In what ways is this text 'user-friendly' or 'unfriendly'? In what ways are you 'Bible-friendly' or 'unfriendly'?" The effect of these two questions, he has discovered, is to give students the "space to consider various ways to think about the hermeneutical issues involved in reading a particular text while forcing them to examine the presuppositions" they bring to that reading.

When we asked Morgan to illustrate his use of these two questions, he described a discussion from a class session the previous week, in which students were reading 1 Kings 9:1–9, depicting a dream of King Solomon. The text, Morgan noted, "evokes people's predictable outrage at such a punitive, vindictive God. . . . They don't like it." In the discussion that followed, however, students discovered that these motifs can be surprisingly significant in and for their original contexts. Morgan's pedagogical framework, in other words, heightens student consciousness to differences between the contexts of the Bible and their own contexts. By repeating this exercise over the course of the semester, the students begin to become "friends" with many seemingly "unfriendly texts."

Morgan's two questions establish a framework for building a practice of Bible reading and study for teaching. In each class session he engages students in an exercise to explore aspects of "user-unfriendliness" *and* "user-friendliness" to be found in a biblical text that challenges modern sensibilities. Over the course of the semester, Morgan introduces them to several "critical methods" for reading biblical texts, through which they might develop deeper understanding and acquire pedagogical resources for engaging others with difficult texts like the one from 1 Kings. In doing so, he is not as interested that they develop the ability to "write explicit definitions of source criticism" (for instance) as that they become increasingly proficient in being able to identify the "characteristics in a text that raise questions" that different theories of interpretation might answer. In planning for the course, Morgan correlated the texts and methods he had chosen to establish a structure to engage students with increasingly difficult texts as they progressed through the semester.

When we visited the class, Morgan was teaching some twenty students in a long, shallow classroom. The class was about equally divided among men and women; most students were white, and two had Asian backgrounds. They ranged in age from their twenties to their late fifties or early sixties and represented a variety of schools in the Graduate Theological Union. Although Morgan was clearly the primary teacher, he shared the leadership of the class with a doctoral student who was his teaching assistant.

Morgan opened the class session with a prayer written by William Sloane Coffin Sr., requesting that we listen to faithful voices from the past, receive the spirit of God in the present, and work for a better future. He had told us earlier that although his prayers had often been spontaneous when he began teaching, he had increasingly used collects (a short prayer appropriate to the occasion)—some of which he had written and others that he had gathered over the years, but all chosen for their connection to themes of that day's class session.

The first order of business following the prayer was a discussion of the third and final content exam of the course, due that day: a three-page paper tracing one of ten Old Testament passages cited in the New Testament that seemingly point toward Christ's birth and are often used as grounding for Christian Advent season themes. The exam and the discussion about it led to conversation about the use of Old Testament texts for the liturgical season of Advent. The conversation about Advent also established the worshipping congregation as the contextual perspective for engaging the pedagogical issues the students would encounter through their reading of the texts Morgan had chosen for that day's class discussion.

Morgan asked a student to read Ezekiel 2:9–3:11. In this passage, the prophet is commissioned to eat a papyrus scroll filled with words of woe to be delivered to the people of Israel. This reading set the stage for the four movements we observed in Morgan's teaching practice: a close reading of a biblical text, an examination of its context, an exploration of its pedagogical possibilities, and a discussion of interpretive issues and questions related to the text and its use in the church. The order of these four movements, Morgan told us, varies from one class session to the next.

Morgan introduced the first as he moved to the white board while asking members of the class to identify aspects of the text that strike them as "friendly." In a fashion we had also observed in his colleague Lyman's class, students responded quickly and freely, and the white board was soon filled with comments about the friendly aspects of the text: pleasure in the text's vivid sensory details; the image of deep, physical ingesting of the Word as a form of God's equipping Ezekiel for ministry; and the notion that "God's ongoing initiative in speaking to people is evidence of great love for them." Morgan then invited them to add "unfriendly" dimensions of the text. Student comments continued to fill up the board: "the stubbornness of the people," the "weirdness" of eating a scroll, the futility of Ezekiel's mission portrayed in the text. Many comments prompted extended discussion over the meaning of words, the apparently negative view of human nature conveyed in the text, the portrayal of Ezekiel—as one both set over against the people of Israel and as stubborn as they are in resisting the words of the Lord.

At this point, with the white board filled, Morgan suggested the class "go through these responses to see whether it's we or the text that is actually unfriendly." They worked through the comments on the board as he underlined responses students identified as "our problem" and placed dashes by responses in which they located the problem "in" the text. The exercise prompted debate at several points. Morgan concluded this segment of the class session with several summary comments, noting, among other things, that "most of the things noted as unfriendly in the text" turn out to be "problems we bring to the text"; that we "have negative reactions" to things the "original recipients" in their context "presumably found comforting or hopeful." He also observed that most of the "things we considered friendly [such as the reassurance of God's ongoing presence] are almost entirely in the text." This led into a conversation about how ancient texts conveying judgment are almost always perceived by people today as unfriendly and how this becomes an issue for clergy as teachers introducing these texts to people in their congregations.

At this point, Morgan shifted the focus of the class session to the second movement in his pedagogy. He suggested the class "step back" from the text for a collective "Bible content quiz" or brainstorming exercise. He said he had three areas in which he "wants them to demonstrate all they know." After writing student responses to his first question, "What do you know about the exile?" on the whiteboard, Morgan observed that "monumental historical/cultural upheavals in the lives of people have characterized the very essence of Judaism and later, of Christianity to the present day." For Jews, the exile was a radical turning point in their history. Any understanding of Ezekiel, consequently, requires understanding something about the exile of the Jews in Babylon.

The next two questions had to do with the relationship of Ezekiel to another of their readings, this time from 2 Isaiah, that section of the Old Testament book of Isaiah beginning with chapter 40.[1] Morgan guided the discussion, eliciting student input about each prophet with specific questions regarding emphases in their writings, in the places where they were written, in the uses of both texts by Jews and Christians. He concluded this discussion by distributing a sheet of instructions to the members of the class to guide their discussion in small groups (of three or four, for about twenty minutes) on the similarities and differences in the messages of the two texts. After a break, they would convene to "talk about how we live in biblical community with both Ezekiel and 2 Isaiah and how we use their visions to speak to our contemporary issues." He gave an example to illustrate the task that awaits them. In that morning's *New York Times,* he had seen an article by Thomas Friedman about the need for religious communities to embrace pluralism, to expand their narrow visions. In light of that challenge, Morgan asked, how are "we then to put Ezekiel and 2 Isaiah in dialogue? How do we live with them both today?"

After the break, Morgan's graduate assistant, Joe Marchal, introduced the third movement in the class session by asking the small groups to share major insights from their discussion. He followed Morgan's example and wrote students' lists of similarities and differences between Ezekiel and 2 Isaiah on the board. While he looked over their responses he then asked them to brainstorm ways they might convey the messages of these prophets in their ministries. Their suggestions were quite specific, ranging from creating a drama of good cop/bad cop, to developing a study of God images in each text, to contrasting images of the strict father in Ezekiel and the comforting mother in Isaiah. When Morgan asked, "What about the kids?" a student suggested they might have children role-play contrasts between the two prophets. Through this discussion, students continued to express difficulty with Ezekiel's message, finding it less accessible or comforting to Christian ears than 2 Isaiah.

Morgan then introduced the fourth movement of the class session, beginning with an observation that the historical contexts of the two prophets are different. "Ezekiel is preexilic *and* exilic, while 2 Isaiah is entirely exilic." The differences in their experience are quite significant. "Imagine you are at a church meeting or convention and you have Ezekiel and 2 Isaiah there in person," each arguing for visions of restoration in the church today as diverse as these actual prophetic texts are from one another. After contrasting their two visions, he asked, "Which side do you take?" He warned, "Remember, you are deeply invested in this institution, and it has to move forward. Whose vision should we back?"

The silence that followed was a long one. A couple of students finally expressed their surprise that in this situation Ezekiel seemed more practical and compelling. Then Morgan began to trace how these two prophets' visions had in fact been picked up in later Jewish and eventually Christian tradition. And this discussion led into a lecture about the changing shape and function of prophetic literature. "The prophet," he emphasized, "is a messenger of the Word [of both judgment and promise] which is seen as powerfully relevant to the present context. Invariably, some immediate action is called for, some return to the old, in light of the new [in this case exile]." From this perspective, Morgan noted, the prophetic word applies over and over again—even to the present day.

In the course of his lecture, Morgan described two ways of reading biblical texts. "*Biblical critics*" read "in order to tease out various sources, layers of redaction," so that the original Isaiah, for example, appears to foretell historical events that took place only later, the whole book compiled out of generations of oral accumulation yet attributed back to a single author. In contrast, "*biblical readers*" take the entire text at face value, and thus the "prophet's present-oriented Word has a highly eschatological effect." Biblical readers in later generations consequently often feel as if God is speaking through the prophet of the past to their present.

Morgan continued from this point to argue that the pluralism Friedman was seeking is actually built into the biblical text. Just as a given prophetic text "works" by pointing forward into God's future, so, too, through the authority of the two prophets' inclusion in the canon, the movement from preexilic judgment in Ezekiel to the exilic message of forgiveness and return in 2 Isaiah represents a similar movement "forward." The very different answers of Ezekiel and 2 Isaiah are held "together in the canon" and we can "learn from them" how to embody the sort of active religious pluralism in which "different answers can find space in ongoing dialogue." He concluded with the observation that in future classes they will encounter still different versions of these tensions in the book of Job and then in Daniel and apocalyptic writings in which "history is rewritten and revisioned yet again."

An Integrative Teaching Practice

Burton Visotzky, Jewish Theological Seminary

On the other coast, at Jewish Theological Seminary, we observed a course in using midrashic texts in preaching, which illustrates another quest to facilitate the integration of student knowledge, skill, and identity in clergy practice. This was Visotzky's first semester teaching the course. A professor in the department of Talmud and rabbinics, his own academic training and prior teaching had centered primarily on midrashic texts as well as Talmud. Unlike Morgan's class, in which most students were in their first semester of seminary, in Visotzky's class most of the twenty-one students were in their fourth year of rabbinic studies. This meant that unlike Morgan, Visotzky could assume advanced technical skills in the study of sacred texts. Through this course, he told us, he seeks to prepare students to "take their place in the long rabbinic tradition," to participate in this "human tradition of teaching," to "contribute to the oral Torah."

In its focus on the midrashic texts, the course differed from preaching courses we had observed elsewhere. In its structure, however, it seemed, at first, to be similar. During the first hour, the class discussed a selected midrash on a biblical text (involving pedagogies of interpretation). The class spent the second hour hearing and reviewing student preaching (engaging students in pedagogies of performance).

The class session we observed began with a general discussion on the genre of midrash. Visotzky then introduced the midrash for the day, on Genesis 29:25, in which Jacob wakes up "to discover he has married the wrong wife." Visotzky had chosen a midrashic text deriving from Italy around the year 1139 C.E. to accompany the upcoming Sabbath's Torah portion from the synagogue lectionary. He told us that because he wanted students to "use the classical tradition to speak their message today," he typically chooses difficult midrashim like this one, so students will be forced to struggle from inside the tradition with sexist, homophobic, and otherwise distinctly unmodern texts. Through their struggle with these texts, he hoped, the students would develop the capacity both "to own the tradition and to counter it with another part of the tradition—to see that these are struggles *within* Judaism."

The class spent the rest of the hour closely and collaboratively examining "how Leah pulled off this deception," by progressively reading and translating portions of the text as catalysts to discussion. They focused attention on words in the text, relationships (such as that between Leah and her sister Rachel, and between Jacob and his sons), and the secrecy and codes embedded in those relationships. The discussion extended to implications for rabbis as readers and interpreters of biblical secrets and to the students' own encounters with the secrets embedded in the structures and relationships of people in congregations.

During the second hour, several students preached and received comments from their peers. Every week, each student prepares and then posts a seven-hundred-and-fifty-word *d'var Torah* (literally "word of Torah," or homily) on a class Web site that Visotzky maintains. He designed the experience to provide an early taste of the rabbi's unceasing weekly rhythm of preparing and preaching. The length is limited so that Visotzky will not "drown in paper" while reading and responding individually to each student (he writes a one- to three-paragraph commentary about each sermon). After reading their submissions each week, he selects two to four sermons and asks their authors to come prepared to preach them in class.

On the day we observed the class, Visotzky had asked three students to preach. Each candidly spoke in their sermons about their struggles with the text and with the personal and contextual issues it raised for them. Discussion followed two of the sermons. Visotzky timed the presentation of the third sermon to conclude with the end of the class hour. Since the preacher had engaged in a personal and intense examination of the struggle with God in the text, Visotzky wanted it to linger in the students' memories as they left the classroom.

For Visotzky, the invitation to self-disclosure in both written and oral forms requires a "safe environment" in which students are "free to experiment and fail"—to risk sharing their engagement with difficult texts without always having to discuss it further. The issue at stake is not simply pedagogical: it has to do with the "ethics of preaching" and taking seriously "questions of power, authority, and responsibility." Consequently, Visotzky monitors the dynamics of the class closely. He had asked the students for their permission, for example, to invite us to observe the session. The Web site is open only to students in the class—although at the end of the semester, after students have had a chance to edit or delete their sermons, Visotzky intended to make the site public.

In the otherwise highly competitive academic environment of the seminary, Visotzky also "insists on gentle critique" and will in fact "shut students down rather than let them move" in an excessively critical direction. His weekly written comments contribute to this affirmative critique. He meets with each student for thirty to sixty minutes at the midpoint of the semester to review the files of *d'vei Torah* each is creating and to discuss their general progress, experience, and struggles as they move through the course. These formal interactions are followed up by phone calls—often prompted by some assignment or interaction in class—or informal luncheon conversations with students he senses need more guidance. Through these personal interactions, he has become for a number of students their rebbe.

When we met later to talk about the class session, we discovered another extensive and parallel layer of interaction between teacher and student that occurs online and is not something we had experienced in other preaching classes. Visotzky showed us the online syllabus that establishes the structure and expectations as well as the resources to be used during the course. It included hypertext links to Web sites addressing Jewish biblical or midrashic interpretation and homiletics; the books he had assigned; and the midrashic texts the class would be studying. He showed us the midrashic text for the day in the syllabus, which pops up in PDF format in Hebrew, ready for students to print out.

He then showed us the screen into which students may write and edit their sermons prior to submitting them to the class, as well as the sermons submitted for the class session we observed. Although he could edit their submissions, he rarely does, except occasionally for grammar. After reading their sermons he sends his comments back to them by e-mail. Many respond to his comments by rewriting the sermon, deleting the old one, and posting the new one in its place. Students can also read one another's *d'vrei Torah* or collection of sermons on the Web site. By the end of the semester, they have an extensive file of sermons on each week's Torah portion for the months they have been meeting: a rich resource to draw on in their movement into the rabbinate.

The structure of the course is demanding for both instructor and student. In this regard, Visotzky believes it prepares students for challenges they will experience as rabbis. Although students in the seminary frequently take incompletes in their courses and turn in assignments late, no student had missed a deadline. "This is just like rabbinical life, where, of course, there are no excuses. You're up there in that pulpit week after week, no matter what other funerals, weddings, crises, etc. come along." In other words, the course does more than prepare students for the discrete tasks of the rabbinate; students are incrementally and systematically "moving into the speaking role" of the rabbi. He pushes students, for instance, to consider carefully, "What is the persona you are creating here as you begin to move into speaking as 'the rabbi'? How is this persona different from *you*?" These questions raise important issues of professional identity, boundaries, authenticity, and self-disclosure as students move toward rabbinic practice.

Teaching to Cultivate a Pastoral, Priestly, or Rabbinic Imagination

The seminary educators who participated in this study were identified by their deans only as experienced teachers reflective about their practice and respected for their teaching by their colleagues. We provided no explicit criteria for choosing participants on the basis of *best* teaching practices. Yet, as we bring this discussion of seminary educators' teaching practices to a close, we have become intrigued by the remarkable implicit consensus among those deans, across the spectrum of Jewish and Christian seminaries, about the kind of teaching reflective teachers do. They seem to share some shared notion of *preferred,* if not *best,* teaching practices. In our observation, these preferred practices consistently linked religious tradition with clergy practice and emphasized rigor in thinking, generosity of spirit, expansiveness of attention, disciplined habits of mind, contextually grounded dispositions, and commitments to the larger educational mission of the school. They emphasized, in one way or another, the mutuality of cognitive, skill, and professional identity formation in and through their teaching.

That emphasis provides the impetus to an integrating pedagogy. In the pages that follow, we draw on the teaching practices of Morgan, Visotzky, and other seminary educators we interviewed and observed to explore some of the features of that integrating pedagogy in seminary education. We have identified those features as impulses toward the integration of cognitive, skill, and identity formation in fostering the pastoral, priestly, or rabbinic imaginations of their students.

Integrating Intentions

When Morgan and Visotzky describe their intentions for student learning in their courses, they describe an integrative pedagogy for cultivating the professional imaginations of their students. Those intentions emerged, as they did for many seminary educators we interviewed, as they envisioned their students working at the intersection of their disciplinary studies and future professional practice—an exercise of the pedagogical imagination. This vision of their students in professional practice led these seminary educators to attend to issues of professional identity formation while engaging their students in disciplinary and professional practice knowledge and skills.

Morgan's intentions for student learning shifted as he became increasingly interested in the "processes of education" contributing to the formation of Israel and as he realized, at about the same time, that all his students would be teaching—they, too, would be involved in the formation of contemporary religious and academic communities. Similarly, as a long-time teacher of Talmud and Midrash now teaching a course on preaching, Visotzky approached the course with the intention of preparing students to "take their place in the long rabbinic tradition" of teaching and to thereby make their own contributions to "oral Torah." Through their teaching, both Morgan and Visotzky envisioned or imagined the possibility of developing in students a habitus or imaginative capacity for deepening their engagement with disciplinary knowledge and skills interactively with the knowledge and skills associated with clergy practices of teaching and preaching.

Seminary educators talk about the integrative dynamics in their intentions for student learning in a variety of ways. These variations may be traced in part to the seminary educators' participation in different seminary education traditions. Morgan, for example, structured his introductory course to engage students at the intersection of disciplinary and professional "knowing in action" to facilitate the critical capacities of students for what many seminary educators call *theological thinking*. This capacity has also been identified as the most valued goal for student learning by respondents to the 2003 survey of U.S. and Canadian seminary educators conducted by Auburn Theological Seminary's Center for the Study of Theological Education. In the session we observed, Morgan engaged students in this exercise when he asked them to ponder how we today are to "live in biblical community" with the contrary messages of "both Ezekiel and 2 Isaiah," then expanded the exercise to include attention to their future roles as teachers by asking how they are to "use" the visions of these prophets "to speak to our contemporary issues."

Questions like these have their roots in Timothy Dwight's vision of a learned clergy who bring to their ministries a rigorous engagement with both old and new knowledge. From this perspective, theological thinking should be second nature. It should involve the ability to conceptualize—to describe and analyze events and circumstances in theological categories without relying on or confusing them with categories from psychology or other of the social sciences. This is what Morgan's first question asks of students—to articulate a response from inside the resources of the traditions of theology. Practice in theological thinking should also lead to an increasing sense of proficiency that comes with being self-critical when assessing whether or not a diagnosis of a situation is theologically appropriate—which for Morgan is a necessary step in using one's knowledge in teaching.

For Visotzky, at Jewish Theological Seminary, a comparable practice is rooted in the notion of study that dominated the pedagogical imagination of Solomon Schechter. Following his lead, contemporary practices of *study* in much of Jewish rabbinic education require modern linguistic tools and textual knowledge to foster students' growing ability to participate intelligently and vigorously in the dialogical practices of the rabbis through the ages—practices we illustrated when describing Lehman's course on the Talmud (Chapter Three). The quest at the heart of *study* is also directed toward meaning, but the emphasis is not on finding the most appropriate interpretive response possible. Rather, it involves acquiring the knowledge and skills to enter the rabbinic dialogue across the ages, to struggle with multiple perspectives in that dialogue in one's very different present context—always realizing that the struggle integral to the dialogue will continue.

We observed similar examples of the influence of other traditions of seminary education in the intentions of seminary educators for the pastoral, priestly, or rabbinic imaginations of students throughout the study. We saw at St. John's Seminary, for example, that for Benson the imaginative capacity of theological thinking could be described as the appropriation of the teachings of the church—by which he meant having enough familiarity with those teachings to make pastoral judgments congruent with their intent in the varying situations and circumstances of priestly activity. His expectations for the theological thinking of priests seem to link Bishop Ireland's vision of a liberally educated and missional priest—who could be both apologist and activist in the life of the church—with a priestly character marked by devotion to the sacramental presence of Christ.

In the pedagogical use of narrative that we observed in the teaching of Sanders at Howard and of Pauw and Williamson at Louisville, we saw a linking of Bishop Payne's legacy of social and racial emancipation with Dwight's legacy of a learned clergy. A similar confluence of American seminary education traditions is evident in the teaching of Butler at Fuller, who honors both the integrity of popular piety valued in evangelical seminar traditions and the constructive and transformative engagement with biblical texts in Dwight's vision of a learned clergy. The confluence of traditions may also be seen in most contemporary seminaries, in their appropriation of practices of spiritual formation historically rooted in Catholic seminary education and of field education pedagogies that may be traced back to Emma Dryer's religious training school.

Integrating Practices

When seminary educators envision their students' futures as clergy, they focus on core clergy practices: for example, fostering motivation for the knowledge and skill involved in text study for teaching, as we saw in Morgan's class, or the integration of textual knowledge and expertise for preaching that we saw in Visotzky's. These educators do not assume that the cognitive apprenticeship is confined to the traditional "academic" subjects of the seminary curriculum. They do not limit the practice apprenticeship to "practical" courses or field education. They do not leave the apprenticeship of identity formation to programs of spiritual or human formation, clinical or field settings, or denominational candidacy processes for ordination.

Morgan and Visotzky, albeit in different ways, teach into the mutuality of the cognitive, skill, and professional identity apprenticeships by emphasizing the interdependence of the pedagogies of interpretation, formation, contextualization, and performance in constructing and conducting their classes. Both introduce students to sacred texts through pedagogies of interpretation and contextualization that not only engage them in dialogue with the meaning of those texts but also clarify the contextual influences on the texts and their interpretations down through the centuries. Both engage in pedagogies of formation so students may experience themselves as teachers or preachers engaging and mediating ancient messages in contemporary settings. Both draw students into pedagogies of performance—Morgan in a preliminary way, as students articulate emerging understandings and envision pedagogical exercises to convey those understandings to others; Visotzky in the writing and preaching of *d'vrei Torah*.

The strategic shape of Morgan's teaching practice, for instance, draws students into the mutuality of the three apprenticeships. It begins with the cognitive practice of reading biblical texts—with an expanding repertoire of new skills for exploring their sense of the "user-friendliness" and "user-unfriendliness" of a text they are examining in relation to a critical assessment of whether their own reading is "Bible friendly" or "unfriendly." Proficiency in this kind of reading does not come easily. It requires an introduction to "critical methods" for making those judgments. This first movement, in other words, already engages students in pedagogies of formation (deepening self-awareness in their relationship to the text) and pedagogies of interpretation (acquiring skills in critical reading).

A second movement in Morgan's teaching strategy involves introducing students to the context of the text and, to some extent, to the contexts of subsequent readings, highlighting the influence of their own contexts to understand why they find certain texts friendly or unfriendly. Pedagogies of contextualization, in other words, deepen possibilities of identification with—and meaning from—the texts they are reading. A third movement begins when Marchal, Morgan's teaching assistant, asks students to think about how they would teach the text they are studying. The task involves a shift of consciousness from apprentice Bible student to novice teacher (through a pedagogy of formation) and requires them to envision using their knowledge and skills to engage others as teachers (a preliminary step in pedagogies of performance). A fourth movement can pick up on issues or tasks that have been raised along the way. In this session, the fourth movement consisted primarily of pedagogies of interpretation to explore questions related to a deeper understanding of the text. These movements have no established order—an indication that they are so embedded in Morgan's pedagogical imagination that he can move them around and link them in many different ways.

The strategic structure of Visotzky's teaching practice is as visible and complex. The rhythm of the interaction of teaching and learning begins as students, drawing on knowledge and skills from prior classes, study a midrashic text (chosen by Visotzky to complement the week's Torah portion) on which to write and post a *d'var Torah* for the class to read. The class session begins with a discussion of the chosen text, with attention to the struggles students have had as they worked through the text in preparing and writing their sermons. Pedagogies of interpretation become the means through which Visotzky nurtures the preaching voice of students. Pedagogies of performance take precedence as students preach, but Visotzky shapes the subsequent discussion to support the development of the student as a participant in the ongoing conversation of the rabbis— that is, as preacher. This emphasis on rabbinic formation is reinforced through comments Visotzky makes on sermons and in the way he uses e-mail to follow up with students on personal and academic issues that are raised in class.

The impulse toward the integration of the cognitive, practical, and normative apprenticeships, in other words, is embedded in the pedagogical imaginations of Visotzky and Morgan and is given form in their teaching practices. Both model the integration they seek in their students—during each class session, in the construction of the syllabi and tasks of class assignments, in their leadership of worship or other seminary gatherings, and in encounters in the hallway or by e-mail.

The impulse toward integration is reinforced by the strategic repetition of the movements in their pedagogies each time they meet. Through that repetition, students are gathered into the complexities and nuances of the professors' teaching practices. They participate in those practices with increasing confidence in their own competence to make personal connections with the knowledge and skills associated with their studies and the habits and dispositions they are developing as future preachers and teachers, rabbis and priests. That confidence is tested and reinforced as Morgan and Visotzky coach students through each class period and in their feedback on assignments—Morgan most explicitly during this class session in his feedback to student comments, Visotzky especially through his running e-mail commentary.

Despite the imaginative structures of these educators' classes, the excitement of learning in both Morgan's and Visotzky's classes emerges from the students' growing confidence in their own competence to make reflective judgments about sacred texts as teachers and preachers. Their competence grows out of their increasing familiarity with the knowledge and skills integral to the practice, with their acceptance of its standards of excellence in their actions, and with their ability to play with its possibilities in new situations and for different circumstances.

Integrating Practical Reasoning

In a study of professional practice, Chris Argyris and Donald Schön (1974) noted that critical moments in professional practical reasoning require congruence in action if they are to be effective. They contrasted the "espoused theories" often learned in professional education with the "theories-in-use" that clients experience in the ways they carry out their professional practice. Their research suggests that practical reasoning involves "judgment-in-action"—a third impulse toward integration in the teaching practices of seminary educators.

In Morgan's class, the pedagogical impetus to this moment of judgment-in-action may happen as students begin to think about the implications in a text for teaching. In Visotzky's class that moment might occur in the course of making decisions as they write a *d'var Torah* and again at the point of posting it for the class to read. Argyris and Schön's insight builds on Dewey's observation that any action or question, when explored, prompts new questions or problems that, when examined, prompt new questions. That happened in Morgan's class when his imagined scenario of the two prophets participating in a church convention posed new questions for the text. It happened in Visotzky's class when students chose to rewrite sermons they had posted based on his comments, or when a peer's feedback opened challenge or insight to the preacher. Through moments such as these, students find themselves involved in a way of thinking that begins in practice and is shaped by practice.

The process of learning this way of thinking takes time. As students develop an increasing facility for participation in the dialogue with religious tradition and context of clergy practice to make judgments in action for teaching or preaching, they participate in the discovery of new information. They refine old skills. They revisit old assumptions. They examine new perceptions of themselves and their roles as clergy. And they begin to pull together the strands of their education in anticipation of their future roles and responsibilities.

In Chapters Eight and Ten, we introduced discussions of the role of practical reasoning in the cultivation of the pastoral, priestly, or rabbinic imagination. It is also pertinent to our exploration of the impulses toward the integration of learning in seminary educator teaching practices. We have noted that modes of practical reasoning begin, in practice, with a question or presenting problem that calls for reflection. Whoever is engaged in the activity of practical reasoning brings to the activity their accumulated knowledge, skills, sense of personhood, religious commitments, and professional identity. The question pulls them into—or attracts their participation in—the dialogue between the contextuality of the presenting question and the contextuality of the resources to engage it. The dialogue may test new cognitive, relational, or technical skills—or hone and refine old ones—while engaging the multidimensionality of the presenting question. It may also lead to new perceptions of self and relationships to others, God, and vocation that reveal new questions, reengaging the dialogue with new resources. In the expanding and deepening repetition of this dialogical interaction, the mutuality of the knowledge, skills, and identities of those involved are intensified.

Modes of practical reasoning in Jewish and Christian communities have a distinctive shape. That shape is generally influenced by the encounter of norms, both in the context of the presenting question or problem and associated with the resources for addressing that question or problem. In the activity of practical reasoning, people bring to that question commitments, knowledge, and skills from prior engagements with their religious traditions and the context of the question or problem. Consequently, for seminary educators, the interactions of practical reasoning have boundaries.

By comparing Morgan and Visotzky's classes, we see something of the influence of those boundaries. Morgan recast his introductory course explicitly to engage students, as future teachers of Old Testament, in the interplay between the religious tradition of an Anglican seminary in an ecumenical consortium of seminaries and the professional practice the students envision for themselves in Anglican and other religious traditions. Morgan's pedagogical decision established a framework for engaging students in the dialogical practice of practical reasoning we have been describing. He introduced the practice by asking them to consider "How one is to teach this difficult biblical text?" Morgan structures student encounters with that question by inviting them to participate in and help facilitate the dialogical interaction of religious tradition associated with the text and its use, especially in those dimensions of Christian religious tradition that his students most identify with the contemporary church and world in which they might teach it. He supplies critical tools to explore the extent to which a text is "user friendly" or "user unfriendly" in this dialogical interaction and whether they, as readers and critics, are "Bible friendly" or "Bible unfriendly."

As students move through the various levels of this dialogue, opinions shift, meanings are altered, new questions arise. As soon as they *begin* to develop some comfort with the task, Morgan asks them to ponder their engagement with the text, no longer as student, but as teacher. His questions are strategic, but they require students to begin to envision themselves making professional judgments about the use of authoritative texts in their religious tradition or traditions in imagined and real contexts. Then, in this session, he complicated the exercise by expanding the original "presenting question" to include the challenge of thinking about teaching Ezekiel along with another, more familiar and seemingly more "friendly" text. Now the exercise involved a comparative dimension not only between the texts as resources from religious tradition but also in the differences in their reception in Christian communities past and present with their own understanding and experience of both texts. Morgan had taken them to a new level of dialogue, requiring more knowledge and greater skill—and, indeed, a greater sense of awareness of themselves as readers and interpreters of biblical texts within their religious traditions. Now that they were approaching the end of the semester of this introductory course in Old Testament, this exercise of practical reasoning may well have marked for them their progress in the practice of thinking about difficult texts for teaching—from novices to advanced beginners.

In Visotzky's class, the students are not novices in the study of texts. They bring to this class the experience of many classes in Talmud and Bible. They have a more expansive knowledge of Conservative Judaism in the still more expansive world of Jewish religious tradition. So the presenting question that prompts the pedagogical activity in this class takes the form of what can be preached from the juxtaposition of given texts in that tradition. The challenge is similar to Morgan's in that Visotzky also assigns difficult texts so students will discover, as they prepare to preach, that they participate in a community that has long struggled with them. The challenge is different in that the dialogue between the texts of religious tradition and the contexts of the preacher and congregation centers on a *d'var Torah* in preparing to preach and on the re-presentation of that dialogue in the activity of preaching.

As we have noted earlier, the notion of time in the study of sacred texts in Jewish seminaries is different from that in most Christian seminaries. All voices on a page of the Talmud speak as contemporaries. Whereas Morgan teaches students to discover themselves as heirs and, therefore, agents of a living biblical tradition, Visotzky teaches students to engage rabbis from many different eras and places whose midrashim illumine the biblical text under scrutiny. So the practice is dialogical: first between the preacher and the texts, leading to the writing and presenting of a sermon, and again in conversation with teacher and peers.

The impulse toward integration in practicing modes of practical reasoning in the teaching practices of Morgan and Visotzky can be seen in three actions. First, they have organized the class so that as students think about teaching and preaching they are engaged in the dialogue of religious tradition and religious practice. Second, they structure the class explicitly to practice the way of thinking they seek to cultivate. Morgan and Visotzky engage students in this practice each week—in and outside of class. To borrow a sports metaphor, they scrimmage every time they meet, with the expectation that when they are teaching or preaching in the future those processes will have become second nature. Third, as they scrimmage each week, Morgan and Visotzky coach them through the performance of the practice of practical reasoning at work in thinking about teaching and preparing to preach. Their coaching centers on developing in their students increasing facility with the modes of thinking and practice they are cultivating—to move them beyond the stages of novice and advanced beginner into perspectives and abilities that indicate competency and even proficiency in the practical reasoning that links, in educating for clergy practice, the apprenticeships of knowledge, skill, and identity formation.

Practicing Integration in Community

A fourth inclination toward the integration of learning in fostering student pastoral, priestly, or rabbinic imaginations is located in what Wenger has called the community of the practice—in this case the communities associated with the teaching practices of seminary educators. Wenger notes that a community of practice is a "knowledge-based social structure" consisting of a "group of people who share a concern, a set of problems, or a passion about a topic, and who deepen their knowledge and expertise" through their interactions with each other "on an ongoing basis" (2002, p. 4). His description fits many classes, field education reflection groups, or chapel programs, as well as the interest or action groups to be found in many seminary communities—especially those engaged in pedagogies of practical reasoning.

One of the most powerful forces contributing to the processes of integration in cultivating a pastoral, priestly, or rabbinic imagination in clergy practice occurs in these interactions of "learning together." Morgan and Visotzky, for example, structured their classes to enhance the contributions of each student to their collective experience. Visotzky did so by requiring weekly student contributions to a sophisticated online process of interaction, as well as through expectations of ongoing reading, class participation, and the shared creation of safe communal space. Students in Morgan's class were also expected to be familiar with the texts to be discussed, and his mode of analysis of these texts depended on their participation and contributions. The focus on the collective thinking of the group was punctuated by mini-lectures given by both teachers and by the sermons of students in Visotzky's class. These moments of "input" facilitated and reinforced the predominantly relational patterns of teaching and learning in the class. They provided information to extend and expand group discussion or to provide a coherent summation of that discussion—often in dialogue with resources still unfamiliar to most students. These collaborative and relational patterns in the classroom (as well as in field education, chapel programs, and other settings) serve to carry along, challenge, and reinforce individual student learning—in other words, to facilitate the impulse toward integrating new and altered bodies of knowledge and new and refined skills with new and more disciplined dispositions and habits of thought and action.

We observed many variations in the communal patterns of seminaries that facilitate the integration of student learning. Trinity Lutheran Seminary and St. John's Seminary, as we described in Chapter Ten, established comprehensive formal procedures to track and link student experience across chapel, field, and classroom as they moved sequentially and developmentally through the course of study. The Howard University School of Divinity faculty, in contrast, designed a series of required courses to function as integrative centers around the kinds of questions students often ask as they move from the first to the second to their final year in seminary. The first course provides a relatively informal small-group setting to explore the seminary's vision of the church in ministry in and through students' experience with the curriculum. The second course provides another small-group setting to focus attention on the dialogue (and sometimes conflict) between the faith they bring to their studies and the knowledge they are acquiring in classes. The final course provides still another small-group setting to explore the transitions they are making from the knowledge and practices of the seminary community to the expectations of congregations, linking the life of faith to the wisdom and practices of black Christian religious traditions. In settings like these the impetus to integration seems to be active all the time.

Lave and Wenger make an important distinction about the ways in which teaching facilitates integrative learning. They observe that people give much educational effort to notions of "learning as internalization." From this perspective, knowledge and skills are internalized "whether 'discovered,' 'transmitted' from others, or 'experienced in interaction' with others" (1991, p. 47). The dynamics of teaching and learning are predominantly transactional from the knowing of the teacher to the knowing of the student.

Lave and Wenger contrast this notion of learning with a view of "learning as increasing participation in communities of practice." Learning from this perspective emphasizes "the relational interdependency of agent [that is, students and teachers] and world, activity, meaning, cognition, learning, and knowing. It emphasizes the inherently socially negotiated character of meaning and the interested, concerned character of the thought and action of persons-in-activity" (1991, p. 50). Teachers from this perspective do more than transmit knowledge and skill or create environments for learning; they welcome students as newcomers or apprentices into the community of practice. They model participation in the community and coach them out of the naïveté, ignorance, and awkwardness of their participation as novices and toward the knowledge, skill, and facility associated with expertise in the practice.

The first notion, of "learning as internalization," which many seminary educators would describe as the "integrative learning" they seek in the courses they teach, is the goal of instruction. It predominates in schools where theory-to-practice epistemologies dominate the pedagogical practices of faculty or where the pedagogical relationships of faculty and students are often distant and formal, and in some places—even in seminary education—where students are viewed as consumers of knowledge.[2]

The second notion, of "learning as increasing participation in communities of practice," socially mediates the particular world view, values, dispositions, habits, and activities that constitute a given class or a particular seminary as a community of practice. This learning occurs in the mutuality of pedagogical judgments facilitating cognitive, skill, and identity formation. When Visotzky establishes a pedagogical environment to facilitate the participation of his students in ongoing oral Torah, for example, the focus of his attention is on student ability to enter that social practice. Morgan did not use similar language, but he has also organized a pedagogical environment to emphasize conversation and collaboration in developing knowledge, skills, habits, and dispositions integral to becoming contemporary agents of biblical tradition as teachers.

In seminary education, the community of practice is larger than the classroom. The impulse toward integration in a seminary educator's teaching practice is typically supported and intensified by shared values and practices in the life of the school—often articulated in the mission statement and reflected in the interactions of the community. Walter Taylor, who teaches New Testament at Trinity Lutheran Seminary, highlighted this feature of seminary education when he contrasted the ways he teaches his introductory course in New Testament and his senior seminar. The curricular intention of introductory courses in the seminary is to introduce students to the vocabulary (language, concepts, tools of analysis) needed to participate in the discourse of the seminary as a theological community. He chooses, for the most part, pedagogies to transmit this information to students and to assess the extent to which they give evidence of increasing familiarity and facility in its use. In his senior seminar, however, which involves students in the dialogue of rigorous textual analysis and critique, with reflections on their previous year's internship experience in ministry, the pedagogy is predominantly collaborative and conversational. He assumes students enter the conversation not only with expertise developed in prior courses, but also as colleagues with questions and insights from their year as interns in congregations. Although in the class session that we observed he maintained a tight grip on the flow of the conversation, participation was confident and lively and roles fluid and flexible.

Taylor is sensitive to the way his teaching reinforces the trajectory of learning of the students in the seminary. He and his colleagues meet regularly to discuss course syllabi. He hears students in integration groups discuss their experience in other classes and in field education. His teaching practices are rooted in the mission of the seminary and are supported and reinforced by the general pedagogical culture of the seminary. At Trinity, the alignment of mission, culture, and teaching practices establishes a powerful impetus toward the integration of the breadth and depth of a student's educational experience.

A similar situation exists at Church Divinity School, where Morgan teaches. The faculty is small and, like Morgan, most have been teaching there a long time. When we visited classes we observed among the senior members of the faculty similar teaching strategies. When Morgan collected and wrote information from student reading on the white board as the catalyst to an exercise of analysis, for example, we recalled seeing a similar pedagogical strategy in Lyman's introductory class. In their first semester at Church Divinity School, many students have two opportunities to refine this way of retrieving and analyzing information from texts. At the same time, the involvement of all master of divinity students on a regular rotation of supervised leadership in chapel over the course of their three years, supplemented by the academic study of worship and liturgical practices, distinctively shapes the pedagogical culture in which every other educational activity takes place. Morgan can assume, consequently, that students in his introductory course in Old Testament are being introduced to the lectionary use of Scripture. They are developing habits and dispositions related to the role and place of Scripture in liturgy. He can introduce questions about the use of lectionary readings in Advent, for example, because students are also introduced to the role of Scripture in the liturgical calendar and to the challenge of working with biblical texts in liturgical settings.

Visotzky views the location of the course of preaching in the Jewish Theological Seminary educational experience somewhat differently. He assumes students bring from other classes in the seminary knowledge, attitudes, and skills related to the study of sacred texts that he can build on as he engages them in a course on preaching. At the same time he seeks to create in this class an environment for student learning that provides an alternative to the school's highly competitive and academic pedagogical culture. He therefore emphasizes that in this class it is safe to explore and experiment; as in clinical pastoral education, confidentiality is valued; and students are his colleagues in this enterprise. In this constructive "misalignment" of the course with the competitive dimensions of the pedagogical culture of the school, students have the sense they are participating in a special learning community—one that especially takes their future roles as rabbis seriously. For some, at least, this involves some changes of behavior—getting assignments in on schedule, changing habits of critique to facilitate Visotzky's expectations for risk and experimentation in safe space, and struggling with difficult texts appreciatively. This strategic decision, he has discovered, often leads to heightened student responsibility. It also intensifies the integrative dynamics of making sense of difficult texts not only for oneself but, through sermons, for the other members of the class.

Pedagogical Imagination–Clergy Imagination

As they teach day in and day out, Morgan and Visotzky invite students into their own practices of integrating knowledge, skill, moral integrity, and religious commitment as they engage the subject of their teaching. Embedded in their pedagogical imaginations are trajectories of possibility for the future clergy practice of their students. The relationships of teachers to the subjects of their teaching and to the students they teach, in the context of their mutual engagement with the deepest meanings and practices of their religious traditions, are central to the cultivation of a pastoral, priestly, or rabbinic imagination. This is something many seminary educators recognize. "I have a passion for the subject matter," one seminary educator told us, "and I always learn new things from my students, most of whom rather quickly develop a passion of their own. It is marvelous to work with them in this regard."

Graduates looking back on their seminary education also emphasized the importance of the passion of a teacher's involvement in the engagement of students with the subject of their teaching in their learning. They talked about this influence in a variety of ways. One seminary graduate, describing a teacher in a course that had been particularly influential, wrote: "I witnessed this brilliant woman articulating the teachings of our church yet stretching and reaching with us for insight into the incomprehensible mystery of God. It was a powerful witness for me of the humility needed to stand before God as theologian." Another graduate noted that "The most significant part of this class was the kinds of conversation the class fostered. Both the readings and the students were very diverse and we had several important and difficult discussions on difference, diversity and community. [The professor] did very well in inviting people into these challenging conversations and modeling how to talk to one another. This was a hopeful model to me. I witnessed students (including myself) enter into conversation for the first time with someone who was different from them in some or several respects, not to simply spout a position but to hear others out and to wrestle with what they were hearing and how it challenged their understandings of God, faith, and community."

In a similar vein, another student wrote that "the professor not only believes in what he teaches, or as he says, what he preaches each day in the classroom, but he has staked his life on the truth of what he passes on to us from the heritage of Christ and the Catholic Church. His passion is infectious." Another noted that an influential professor "knew that this course would be intense for many students who had not previously studied mysticism and kabbalah in a serious way. He was careful to respect that and yet consistently pushed us to engage with the material and realize the powerful ideas it held and offered." Each of these former students viewed these teachers as models of possibility for their own lives and work.

Each of these teachers had encouraged and supported—indeed, had helped to coach—their students into communities of religious practice. Many in the survey we conducted used the language of "love" to describe the depths of their commitments to the encounter of students with the fields or disciplines they teach. Said one: "I LOVE the students and their interaction; I like being with them when they discover WHY history is exciting and critical to their lives and ministries"; another told us, "I love teaching. There is no career or vocation for me which would be more satisfying; the basic reason?—the fire of the students." A teacher of Talmud told us "I love the diversity of opinions, which generates still greater diversity in student reactions."

One more comment may capture something of the spirit in the pedagogical imaginations that we observed in the teaching practices of seminary educators who are cultivating the imaginative capacities of their students for their own professional lives. "I am a very good teacher," this seminary educator wrote at the conclusion of the survey instrument. "I care passionately about teaching, the students, the churches they will serve and the gospel they will proclaim. I find the excitement of having a student grasp a difficult concept or master an important skill among the most gratifying experiences in my life." The excitement for us as researchers was to discover seminary educators like these in every school in the study.

ENDNOTES

1. Scholars have long observed a break in the subject matter of the book in the Bible identified with the prophet Isaiah. Those chapters up to 39 reflect very different historical conditions from those in chapter 40 and following. Scholars typically have identified that section of the book beginning with chapter 40 as 2 Isaiah. From very early days in the Christian movement, parts of 2 Isaiah have been associated with the birth and ministry of Jesus and are therefore quite familiar to most Christian seminary students.

2. In their critique, Lave and Wenger miss the point that pedagogies of internalization have often also been influential in cultivating communities of practice, but they have been most effective when exercised in relatively homogenous contexts in which they reinforced or supplemented the contributions of many other educational activities contributing to the education of the members of a community.

12

AN INVITATION
TO CONVERSATION

NEGOTIATING THE RELATIONSHIP of religious tradition and modernity in pedagogical and curricular decisions is one of the most persistent challenges seminary educators face. In Chapters Seven and Eight, we briefly traced the story of those negotiations over the past two hundred years. Several seminary educators we interviewed explicitly addressed that challenge through their teaching. Magid's decision to introduce Conservative Jewish students to Orthodox critiques of the modernity that Conservative Judaism has embraced is one example. Similarly, Nairn engaged students in the analysis of medical ethics cases, with careful attention to correlating respect for religious tradition with modern tools of analysis to identify the facts of the case.

Many seminary educators in the study do not explicitly set up for their students an encounter between modernity and religious tradition, but their intentions for student learning clearly reveal the influence of each in their teaching. One seminary educator emphasizes both, for example, in wanting students to "ground their spirituality in the liturgy of the church" *and* to "develop competency in basic interpretive tools" to use in their lives and when they teach others. Another begins with religious tradition by providing students with a foundational survey of early church history so that later they can engage in modern practices of "Christian critical theological discourse." At the Church Divinity School of the Pacific, students carefully trained in the traditions of liturgical leadership move on to classes in pastoral care and theology using the most recent of research methods. Similar encounters between modernity and tradition are deeply rooted in the dynamics of teaching and learning in seminary education.

Perhaps the most provocative of recent articulations of the challenge raised in the encounter between tradition and modernity has been Kelsey's exploration of the dual commitment in Protestant theological education to the values of *paideia* and *wissenschaft*—commitments to learning in community and the rational objectivity of inquiry that have their parallels in Catholic and Jewish seminary education as well (1992, pp. 63–100; 1993). To our own study, however, we brought a different perspective.

At first we articulated it in rather simple terms. We knew that we wanted to build on prior studies that had explored the innovations and persisting traditions in seminary education, but we also wanted to explore similarities and differences across those traditions. We knew we did not want to conduct a study that would reduce teaching to "what seminary educators do" in a manner similar to Ken Bain's thoughtful examination of the teaching strategies and methods of college and university teachers (2004). This would have blinded us to the influence of religious tradition on seminary educator teaching practices. Within the time, budget, and personnel constraints imposed by the grants funding the project, we wanted to find a way to explore the relationship between seminary educators' intentions for their teaching and the conduct of their classes, and the relationship between classroom teaching and the communal pedagogies of the institution. This interest shaped our research agenda.

In our extended conversations with teachers, administrators, and students from across the spectrum of Jewish and Christian seminaries, this interest focused us on how, in the interactions of teaching and learning, they negotiate the relationship of religious tradition and modernity. The interviews heightened our attention to the paucity of formal, focused, and extended conversation among seminary educators about the relationship of modernity and religious tradition that is embedded in their assumptions about many issues—students as learners, the location of the authority for what and how they teach, their own authority and role in the classroom, the character of the seminary as a community of teaching and learning, and the assessment of student learning. Seminary educators do talk about these issues, we discovered, but most often informally with friends and departmental colleagues or when involved in developing or assessing some program.

As a catalyst to faculty conversation—first among the colleagues of a faculty, then in wider circles of seminary educators—we propose a series of explorations. Several issues emerge from the interplay of religious tradition and modernity in the teaching mission of the seminary. These issues are not new—at least not in the schools we visited—but they have not typically been the subject of sustained conversation in the faculties with which we are familiar. These issues presented in this final chapter, and the study questions and workshop suggestions in the study book that accompanies this report, provide a structure for sustained conversation.

We identified four issues, which we will first pose as brief questions. Throughout the chapter, we examine these questions with insights gleaned from the data. The four questions:

o How shall we speak of "God"?

o What images of clergy practice do we hold up?

o How do our teaching practices cultivate clergy imaginations?

o How do the elements in our education of clergy fit together?

How Shall Teachers and Students Speak of "God"?

In the introduction to this volume, William Sullivan argues that what distinguishes the clergy profession is the attention it gives to "interpreting God" or the "God-language" in the clergy's religious traditions. The task is not easy in the contemporary world. What could religious traditions from cultures and with world views impossibly far from our own have to say that would speak to the contemporary task of interpreting God or making sense of God-language? How can one assume to interpret God, much less speak of God's presence and action—as many, of course, do—in a fragmented, religiously chaotic, postmodern world? For many the issue is even more fundamental: Who or what is God? What does the symbol God mean?

In a provocative study of beliefs and attitudes about identity, faith, and God voiced by a range of contemporary Americans of various religious stripes, Douglas Porpora demonstrates that answers to this question are not obvious (2001, p. 20). Since 93 percent of Americans claim to believe in God, what is meant should be self-evident. Yet most of Porpora's interviewees—religious and nonreligious, and from a range of cultural, social class, and educational backgrounds—were unable to articulate who or what God is for them. The significance of this incapacity goes beyond mere theological fuzziness. Porpora makes a strong case for the importance of interpreting God when he argues that lack of clarity about either God or some ultimate coherence to reality diminishes the ability of people to articulate a sense of identity, vocation, or moral purpose in life.[1]

This suggests that questions about God or ultimate meaning have everything to do with the capacity of persons and communities to foster and contribute to existentially coherent human life or to the greater common good in the face of the fear, greed, chaos, uncertainty, and suffering of human existence. Interpreting God and God-language, in other words, matters. Two implications follow for seminary educators cultivating the pastoral, priestly, or rabbinic imagination of students for clergy practice. They must constructively facilitate student struggles with notions of God and God-language during their seminary years. And they must help prepare them to speak of, mediate, or interpret God and God-language as preachers, teachers, caregivers, liturgists, evangelists, or administrators for and with people in whatever situation or condition they meet them.

So who or what does the term *God* mean for seminary educators as they teach? If interpreting God is the distinguishing feature of the clergy profession, it would follow that answers to this question are an important feature of a seminary education. Unlike Porpora's sampling, however, participants in our study—seminary faculty, students, and alumni and alumnae—are professionally articulate on the subject of God. Although we did not ask them to describe their theological beliefs or to answer questions about God, the survey instrument we developed provided various opportunities for respondents to convey their assumptions about God, God-language, or ultimate meaning or reality as they reflected on their vocations, their teaching and learning, and the values and practices of the seminary community. We discovered in these comments at least five different, although often interconnected, ways of speaking of God. In the pages that follow, we explore those ways and trace how each provides resources for reflecting on a central dimension of human experience in clergy practice.

First, and perhaps most broadly, faculty respondents spoke of God as generally *invisible* from worldly notice or human perception, which (or Whom) clergy *mediate through their leadership or embody and make visible* for congregants or the world. The ancient human experience of the remoteness, absence, or nonexistence of God, intensified by the rational objectivity of our contemporary scientific age, is reflected in the expectations of some faculty respondents that the work of clergy involves being "agents of God," "ambassadors of God," "mediators of God," a "bridge to the Holy." Clergy, in other words, have a special calling to reveal, make real, mediate, or come to terms with this otherwise inaccessible God. The interpretive task of clergy is to *represent* (to re-present; to make tangibly, verbally, physically, bodily present) through rituals, practices, and traditions a God to people who have lost a sense of mystery in their frantic, competitive, technological world, who have lost touch with their own personal significance or purpose in life, or who call out in suffering in the face of apparent cosmic silence.

This cluster of imagery shows up in seminary educator descriptions of their own sense of vocation. Asked to describe a self-image as a teacher, a Candler professor wrote, "A living mediator of the life-giving Christian tradition: . . . a spring of cold, clear water; an ever-renewing bunch of grapes of Christ the true vine." Similarly, a student at Hebrew Union College wrote of a professor, "He conveyed the realness of the Divine."

These images point implicitly to a notion of God (or a dimension of God) otherwise inaccessible, remote, or impersonal—the Transcendent—who is brought close or re-presented in religious practices and in particular human roles or persons. In this first sort of God-language we do not get a clear picture of who exactly this God that is being represented *is*, except of divine Otherness and the need for some kind of mediation to humanity.

A second use of God-language among faculty is quite different. Here faculty respondents use actual *images* to describe God. Over thousands of years of tradition, a vast repertoire of these images of the divine has emerged from the social and poetic imaginations of countless generations of prayers, scholars, preachers, and exegetes. Ranging from natural imagery (for example, God as life, light, fire, wind, dove, lioness, wellspring, rock, cloud of unknowing, lamb, bread); to human roles (shepherd, king, nursing mother, father, warrior, law-giver, judge, lover, spouse, vinedresser, child, advocate); to theological images (creator, wisdom, "I AM," redeemer, savior, holy one, spirit, mystery, paradox); to attributes (omnipotent, merciful, just, wrathful, vulnerable, faithful and full of steadfast kindness, incarnate, crucified and risen, protector of orphans). The language of God rooted in these and other images used through the centuries illustrates both the astonishing range of ways in which people in Jewish and Christian traditions have attempted to convey some sense of who or what they have experienced or understand God to be and also the inability of any single image to contain or express adequately that experience or understanding.

This second way of speaking of God suggests several pedagogical tasks for seminary educators, ranging from the analysis of the forms of divine self-revelation conveyed through these images, to the exploration of these images in religious tradition (including those submerged or forgotten over time), to the identification of images potentially revelatory for the new contexts and situations of religious traditions. A central problem often encountered in this use of God-language is some form of idolatry—as when, over time, God is increasingly identified with one or another image, name, or attribute. As one example, for some faculty respondents identifying

God with the image of the human male is problematic because this has often been used to reinforce the authority and power of (usually white) men and fails to mirror adequately the divine image in which women, people of other races or cultures, or those of differing social circumstances are created.

This second use of God-language thus often has a critical edge based on the recognition that God images can have powerful political or hierarchical implications. Sensitivity to this issue is reflected in the goals of another Candler professor for a course in which students were expected to "recognize the variety of images of Christ present in World Christianity; be familiar with and evaluate the various images in terms of their contextual relevance and christological appropriateness; formulate criteria for appreciating and assessing the various images of Christ." A Catholic Theological Union graduate, describing the influence of a teacher who may have had similar goals, noted that this person's teaching not only helped "us learn how to swim (or at least tread water) in the great ocean of God," but also "shattered my childish images of God—and opened my mind and heart to the mystery of the Creator."

For many professors and students, the primary dimension of language about God circles around images or metaphors for *human relationships with God*. The Catholic Theological Union graduate just quoted hints at this way of speaking about God in the metaphor of "one's heart opened . . . to the mystery of the Creator." This third use of God-language among seminary educators was typically couched in expressions of hope that students might experience authentic personal intimacy with the divine Other. The language here becomes quite different. The God implied here tends to be personal, relational, friendly, or intimate—indeed, the God-language is often quite anthropomorphic. These terms for God are often accompanied by a notion of growth in that relationship not necessarily present in the first two uses of God-language. Thus the human condition that this third use of God-language reflects tends to be psychic, emotional, or developmental, as seen in terms such as *human malaise, loneliness, alienation,* or *immaturity.*

This emphasis on encouraging students' growing relationship with God is evident in the comments of several seminary educators about their teaching—often with their own relationship with God as a primary resource. Wrote one educator: "Students [in my class] were asked to turn in weekly reflection papers on their encounters with God. This was in preparation for preaching. I believe they don't have much to say if they can't listen so this was an exercise for promoting listening to God."

Another cites a question addressed to students: "How do the prophetic writings contribute to your evolving relationship with God and understanding of the experience of the Jewish people?" And still another professor describes drawing her own God-relationship right into the process of teaching itself: "I am formed by faithful attendance at community Eucharist and chapel services. I experience my bond in Christ with my students most strongly there, and it is out of that experience of communion that I find my teaching nourished.

A fourth approach to God-language may be the most characteristic of the seminary as an academic enterprise. Here the references are to views of God embedded in traditions of dialogue, interpretation, and practice—and, therefore, the *ultimate object of study*. The focus of attention is to trace, rigorously and systematically, the ways in which biblical authors or medieval philosophers or seventeenth-century mystics or twentieth-century Latinas—to name a few examples—conceive of God, and how these understandings build on or contribute to (or in turn challenge or deconstruct or reanimate or deviate from) those of the tradition they inhabit. For example, a goal for a course in Hebrew scriptures at Trinity Lutheran Seminary reads: "to understand the nature of the crisis of the Babylonian exile and how that crisis gave rise to radically new understandings of God." At Louisville Presbyterian Theological Seminary, a different course goal aims "That students become equipped to . . . reflect theologically on the way God engages humankind (God's 'pathos' as defined by Abraham Heschel)." A professor at Hebrew Union College uses the striking image of "dialogue with 'the mind of God'" to describe theological study as "a spiritual benefit of studying the Jewish tradition." Thus, in this use of the language of God, we see the divine as a Mystery which, although still transcendent and ultimately unknowable, is nevertheless thinkable to curious human minds in an ongoing critical and constructive debate across centuries, cultures, and traditions.

The human condition reflected in this use of God-language might initially seem more abstract than the first three we have described, but it can be just as existential. An alumna from Associated Mennonite Biblical Seminary notes, with appreciation, that rigorous attention to theological notions can be liberating. In response to being asked for an image of a favorite professor's teaching, she writes: "*Open window* would probably come closest. How I understand God, God in relationship to humanity, how I perceive and relate to God became much broader. [Professor X] and the classes I took from him set my spirit free to explore, think, feel God in a much more complete (and scarier!) way. . . . [This gave me a] wider concept of God, seeing the vulnerability of God but also the limitlessness." Studying God, in this instance, has led her to think of God in some of the other ways we have been describing as well.

Finally, we note a fifth way that those involved in clergy education speak of God: as an *active force at work for good in the world*. In contrast to several of the earlier views—in which God could appear implicitly as a more or less static object of contemplation or study—in this view, divine initiative and energy are at the forefront. Faculty speak primarily of God as desiring love, justice, compassion, reconciliation, and peace, and of the human response as being engaged in or participating in the fulfillment of that desire. This use of God-language emphasizes God as deeply involved in the world, permeating and sustaining creation; raising up servants and leaders for compassion and vision and justice; ceaselessly laboring for righteousness and the restoration of all things, not only in "religious" contexts but in the neighborhood and community, the nation and world, and the broad sweep of history and, indeed, of the entire cosmos. This is a God passionately concerned with the suffering and need of all creatures, all people, and actively at work to love and cherish and restore all things.

The human condition reflected in this understanding of God centers on issues of poverty, injustice, oppression, fear, and hatred—all conditions that oppose God's desire for abundant fullness of life. In some religious circles God's desire for cosmic restoration is seen to take place only outside history or at the end of time, often in apocalyptic visions of how "the end" will take place when God finally triumphs over all forces of evil. In other circles the emphasis is more powerfully on God's *present* desire for resistance to evil here and now, the pouring out of divine mercy and healing, reconciliation and *shalom,* to all who cry out in distress. Yet although often highly "this-worldly," this fifth aspect of God-language is clearly eschatological: that is, it describes a vision of God as the One who longs for and is ultimately bringing about a world—and human hearts, souls, and bodies—healed, redeemed, and at peace.

In this view, clergy "participate" in this divine initiative of love in the world, as "God's partners on earth" in the words of a professor at Jewish Theological Seminary. Two professors at Garrett-Evangelical have parallel images of the clergy vocation responsive to this view of God: "that they become spiritual leaders, transformative agents of the reign of God," and "affirm . . . all creation's belonging in God."

Some faculty use similar images to ground visions of their own vocation as well. For instance, a professor at Yale speaks of herself "as a dance teacher, trying to help students figure out how to use certain muscles with control and grace so that they might be able to help others experience the beauty of faith, community, and the flourishing of creation." This is God-language that takes seriously the violence, suffering, and pain of the world, not so much as an insoluble problem, but as the site or the focus of the activity of God. Such a stance is evident in the words of a Catholic Theological Union graduate who writes of his seminary experience: "[I learned] a fundamental appreciation of God alive in all people." It is also reflected in another comment from an Associated Mennonite graduate who described how her seminary education prepared her to respond as she did in ministry to the September 11, 2001, crisis. In her view, her years in seminary provided her with: "(1) An overarching belief and teaching position that Christ is with us in all things, in all experiences. (2) A belief and teaching that Jesus brought a message of peace and reconciliation. (3) A far-reaching understanding that Christ's love (and therefore OUR love) exceeds nationalism—it includes love of the different, the enemy, the last, the least." This response and others like it in our alumni and alumnae survey illustrate that when called on to interpret God, they use God-language in many ways to speak to the flourishing of human lives, religious communities, even the threatened and precious fabric of global well-being.

Seminary educators take seriously the vocation of clergy to "mediate divine presence" through the practices of their religious communities. We experienced lively conversations about God in each of the schools participating in this study. They occurred in classes, in field education reflection groups, and in chapel. What seemed to be missing, however, was some formal attention to the different ways in which faculty speak together of God as they reflect on how their teaching practices participate in and prepare leaders for the religious communities of living religious traditions.

What Images of Clergy Practice Do We Hold Up?

In this study, we have been impressed by the shared commitment among seminary educators to the development of contemporary clergy as stewards of human meaning, identity, and action. Contrary to what secularization theorists might assume, we did not encounter a single seminary or tradition of seminary education that approached the education of clergy as a privatized quest or as a "separate sphere" of knowing and doing at a remove from modern, public life. Instead, clergy educators and their graduates pursue encompassing visions of meaning and purpose for the communities of their religious traditions, which intersect with a wide range of public issues, including science and technology; education; literature and the arts; popular culture and the media; social issues of race, class, and gender; the ethics of sexuality, life, and death; and political personalities and platforms. Although twentieth-century studies of the clergy often assumed the marginalization of religion in modern society, often as a catalyst to reinvigorating the public voice and roles of clergy, we have reached a different conclusion.

Religion is reexerting itself as a major public force in contemporary U.S. society, in part because of its ability to provide comprehensive narratives of meaning, identity, and action. Clergy are at the center of this meaning-making enterprise for most religious communities as they construct "symbolic worlds" within which human meaning and identity are created (Bellah, 1970, pp. 89–96).[2] It is precisely these comprehensive frameworks of meaning, identity, and action that the technical rationality and market culture of U.S. society have failed to provide many of its citizens. We observed seminary educators taking seriously the task of preparing clergy for this meaning-making enterprise at the juncture of their religious communities and public life, but we did not see as much evidence that it has been formative in policy and program discussions. So, once again, we encourage a wider conversation about the implications of the ways in which the various members of a faculty contribute to the seminary's preparation of its graduates as agents of meaning, identity, and action in religious communities and public life.

We found three ingredients in the education of clergy that make these comprehensive frameworks of meaning, identity, and action in clergy practice possible: (1) the primary role of *canonical texts* in the education enterprise, (2) the development of *social practices* of meaning-making, and (3) the formation of a *habitus,* or embodied worldview, with corresponding forms of character, or *paideia,* among its members.

First and foremost is the critical and devotional attention given to *canonical texts* in clergy education. Although each tradition's definition of sacred canon varies—from the Bible and Talmud, for Jews; to the Old and New Testaments of the Christian Bible, for Protestants; to the Christian Bible plus Apocrypha, for Catholics—these *scriptures* are a generative source of narrative and legal frameworks of meaning and purpose. With a traditional canon at the heart of clergy education, normative knowledge is built into the teaching and learning process from the start, but in a richly interpretive and adaptive way that might surprise those who think literalism is the norm. For example, the Jewish tradition emphasizes both halakhah (law) and aggadah (story) in the use of sacred texts, which keeps the interplay between ethical action and narrative meaning very close in religious practice. Many Protestants place the vast literature of the Bible within a teachable framework of doctrinal summaries, called confessions. Others emphasize liturgical frameworks that establish a rhythmic pattern for linking spiritual practices to the routines of life. Catholics emphasize the place of Scripture in the history of the church's interpretation and theology, or *tradition,* and develop catechisms that reflect dominant interpretations. The canon that a community privileges and the way it construes that canon in making meaning lies at the heart of its identity and patterns of action.

Educators whose teaching practices have been described in this study have capitalized on a variety of interpretive strategies within and beyond their own seminary education traditions. Benson, of St. John's, for example, uses Socratic recitation to equip students in making judgments about the whole of the Catholic tradition, that they might "appropriate" that tradition faithfully in moral dilemmas. He wants students to become competent in interpreting "what the church says" about moral issues, but in richly interpretive and situationally responsive ways. Lehman, of Jewish Theological Seminary, on the other hand, develops interpretive skills that mirror the literature of the Talmud itself. She coaches students in tracing the "strands" of rabbinic dialogue and identifying the various voices found in a Talmudic text. The very practice of reading rabbinic commentary, then, begins a dialogue about the dialogue within the text, before moving to an investigation of historical and contemporary implications.

Other educators we talked to include steps of interpreting sacred and historical texts that are remarkably similar, reflecting modern hermeneutical theory—itself a product of nineteenth-century clergy education.[3] Lyman, of Church Divinity School of the Pacific, teaches a threefold practice (reading a text "for what it says" on its own, in relation to its context, and finally for its contemporary meaning) involving students in an interpretive movement from "text" to "historical context" to "contemporary meaning" found in others as well. Bergant, at Catholic Theological Union, speaks of historical context as the "world behind the text," the text itself as "the world within the text," and issues of contemporary appropriation as "the world in front of the text." She then offers a different "order" of these three interpretive moments in reading biblical texts to place "the world in front of the text" at the beginning and endpoint of the interpretive process. In this pedagogical decision, Bergant requires readers of biblical texts to take seriously how their own experience and world view influence their interpretations of the texts they are reading.

The rich interpretive practices we observed in their classes and others in each seminary we visited stress the complexity of treating religious texts as sources of meaning, identity, and action for the present. In whatever order they may occur, the textual moments in the interpretive process are meant to bracket the student's assumptions and projections of their own world, so they might receive the otherness and uniqueness of the "world within the text." The historical moment creates further distance from the "world behind the text" and the present in a disciplined way, so the student can learn to speak for the distinctive concerns of that time and place. The moment of "contemporary meaning," however, culminates in interpretation through personal engagement—so the student, and some day his or her community, can find their world enriched and enlivened by the stories, images, and values of the text.

Many seminary educators share, albeit in different ways, Bergant's view that different communities and cultures will bring their own issues and interests to that act of appropriation and meaning-making. In short, they assume that sacred or traditional texts require more than a philological or historical sophistication: they require that interpretation bring the implications of that text to the present, in a way that shapes the meaning, identity, and action of contemporary lives and communities.

Second, clergy are educated in *social practices* of meaning-making that transmit and reconstruct the traditions of their faith, in the context of community life. Each of the religious traditions we studied has practices of meaning-making that clergy carry from their education to their settings of professional practice. For Catholic and some Protestant seminaries, liturgies in the daily rhythm of seminary life are powerful vehicles for nurturing the corporate memory of some clergy as they seek to help communities of faith claim and reinvigorate their collective identity. For some students in Jewish seminaries, the practice of *havrutah,* or partner-debate, establishes a context for ongoing dialogue around sacred texts. Evangelical practices of Bible study and group prayer shape the social pieties that many clergy bring to youth groups, congregational studies, and retreats. In each of these instances, clergy are educated not so much as specialists but as *engaged participants* in these practices to a degree that authorizes them to carry them to others throughout their ministry. *Communal pedagogies* of worship, prayer, and observance create an ethos of committed participation in which students and faculty alike are invited (or sometimes required) to share.

Key to *social practices* of meaning, then, is the ability of clergy to draw their communities into *deep participation* in the stories, rites, and practices of observance of their religious traditions. Clergy are educated as *participant-leaders* who share the commitments and passions of the practicing community, but also serve as models and guides to the community's full engagement. We saw, for example, how Fragomeni helps students focus on their leadership role in the liturgy by examining their use of gesture, voice, eye contact, and physical presence to convey the rubrics in ways that are inviting and meaningful. Such intentional presiding at the Eucharist, for example, guides and inspires parishioners to participate fully in the symbols, rhythms, and narratives of the rite. Tull, on the other hand, guides student groups into a close reading of the Hebrew scriptures, with an eye toward decoding and interpreting the text for historical meaning as well as pastoral and homiletical use. Such textual practices not only carry forward to the pastor's study, in preparation for the weekly sermon, but also translate well to congregational bible study and education, in which the pastor can serve as an historical and language resource to a close, textual study of the English Bible. Scholarly competence and skill is oriented toward the leadership role of clergy in the social practices of meaning in the community of faith. Thus the community's *deep participation* through social practices of its tradition generates a host of symbols, characters, plots, and values that shape the community's own identity.

What results from social practices of meaning is a *living memory* of the faith or tradition, one that is oriented toward a *vision or horizon* of how the world can be. Although the social location of an interpretive community has a profound effect on the way a faith community shapes its memory of the tradition, the *horizon of interpretation* the community constructs out of its setting is an even more profound influence. Sanders's intentional use of texts can be seen as a strategy for creating distinct layers of memory in her students' ethical decision making: examples range from Biblical memory (in the use of Hayes's text) to Christian memory (through Niebuhr's text) to the black civil rights memory (in Marsh's text). The horizon of "black liberation/womanist" she brings to her teaching is a culmination of this memory trajectory, as it provides an interpretive telos for gathering up these layers of memory into the present and future.

In contrast, Magid raises the critical questions of modernity for Conservative rabbinical students through the eyes of their neighbors and critics—the ultra-Orthodox. By turning the tables, Magid invites students to examine their own commitments to modernity and its companion—Zionism—through the eyes of its sharpest critics in the Jewish community. This critical and passionate reexamination of an assumed rapprochement with modernity among many Conservative Jews requires that they reposition their sense of the tradition, and their understandings of the Talmud, in relation to crucial questions of Jewish civilization and identity today. In both cases, clergy students are challenged to shape a horizon of interpretation for their own ministries and communities, as a way of gathering the memory of the tradition into a living encounter with an urgent set of issues and decisions for community life. This interplay of tradition and context gives rise to a new *vision* of the faith for the coming age.

Third, clergy are educated to employ the symbols, narratives, and observances of their tradition toward the formation of a habitus or a collective vision of how to live in the world, and its corresponding forms of personal character or *paideia*. Catholics have a long tradition of monastic vocations, for example, that grows out of distinct *charisms* and visions of the founders of each religious community. Protestants, on the other hand, affirm the personal *calling* of each Christian, born out of a vision of God's providential plan for each member of the community. The Jewish tradition of *gemiluth chasadim* or social work, which is incumbent upon its members, arises from a vision of caring for "catholic" Israel, wherever its members may be in the world. Each collective vision has corresponding forms of life or service that mark the character of the community's members. In the end, the greatest power of clergy practice may be in shaping the identities, dispositions, and forms of action of members of their religious communities according to these wider visions of how to live faithfully in the world.

Clergy educators share a concern to shape the *paideia* of their students to embody and reconstruct religious visions in new community settings. One faculty member of Jewish Theological Seminary, describing rabbis as *klei kodesh* or holy vessels, explains that they "are instruments for transmitting the sacredness of the Jewish tradition through contact with others, rather than 'holy people' set aside from others" (Lebeau, 1997, pp. 6–8). In a variety of ways, this theme runs through the teaching of many of the seminary educators we met. Magid's juxtaposition of Orthodox texts of religious commitment to the Conservative stance of objective inquiry poses two distinct visions of Jewish life. His question "How does one teach passion?" drives home the point that each religious vision generates a distinct way of life and set of commitments. A survey respondent emphasizes the importance of students identifying "with the tradition into which they are being called," as context and resource for using "their creative imaginations to bring fresh vigour to the work ahead of them." The Orthodox emphasis that Rossi coaches, "letting one's mind descend into one's heart" in prayer, raises the question of the student's own disposition toward his or her faith in the practice of prayer. In short, many clergy educators insist that clergy must place themselves squarely within the vision of life of their tradition and internalize aspects of that vision within their own character and person. Such authenticity of one's faith and practice, it seems, is essential if the clergyperson is to embody the vision in a way that models and inspires others to develop such self-placement in their own lives.

So to answer our original question, clergy students today are formed with patterns of *interpretation, social practice,* and *a way of life* that equips them to both embody and build the meaning and identity of communities according to sacred texts and traditions. Seen this way, seminary educators teach to prepare clergy to be *culture bearers* and *culture builders* of distinct religious visions.

How Do Our Teaching Practices Cultivate Clergy Imaginations?

We asked faculty survey respondents "Who or what in your institution supports your best efforts in teaching?" Many respondents identified the dean, the technology and resource center staff, and the students in their classes. Several identified a small number of colleagues, especially in their own fields. A significant number had participated in workshops on teaching sponsored by the Wabash Center for Teaching and Learning in Theology and Religion and by their professional societies. In some schools teaching has been the subject of faculty retreats and, in two or three schools in the study, of regularly scheduled workshops or consultations throughout the academic year. Even though teaching is a primary responsibility of seminary educators, few faculties are involved in sustained and generative conversations on teaching. As a community practice, however, sustained conversations on teaching may be one of the most effective ways for seminary educators to strengthen their effectiveness as teachers.

In the first chapter we briefly described our use of the term *practice,* building on the definition of Dykstra and Bass to connote "a sustained cooperative pattern of human activity" that addresses "some fundamental feature of human existence" (2002, p. 22). The term, however, is used in several ways. Doctors, lawyers, clergy, and professors are engaged in *professional practice*—the exercise of a distinctive complex of knowledge, skills, habits, and dispositions in some service to others. *Community practices* include shared patterns of activity that help maintain the identity and character of social groups. Hospitality, reconciliation, and eating together are examples. Some community practices may be described more specifically as *spiritual practices*—that is, a way of being in relation to God and one another constitutive of a religious tradition or community. Hence community practices of hospitality or reconciliation in Jewish and Christian communities, reflecting deeply rooted assumptions about the hospitality or reconciling nature of God, also reflect the internal goods of a spiritual practice.

A teaching practice is a community practice incorporating each new generation and any newcomers as members into increasingly proficient participation in its traditions, rituals, and practices and equipping members of the community for roles and responsibilities to ensure its continuing vitality and relevance. Because seminary educators teach to prepare the leadership of religious communities—to cultivate pastoral, priestly, or rabbinic imaginations in clergy action—this study has increasingly led us to think of their teaching practices as a spiritual practice. In the pages that follow, as a catalyst to faculty conversations about the character of their own practices of teaching, we trace the development of this thought.

The impetus to thinking about teaching as a practice may be traced back to the research team's decision to attempt to sort out ways of thinking about the relationship of theology, epistemology, and pedagogy. This attempt intensified as our attention was increasingly drawn to ways in which seminary educators deal with the relationship of piety, intellect, truth, and faith or observance in both classroom and communal teaching practices. When we asked how seminary educators *cultivate* (emphasizing pedagogy) a *pastoral, priestly, or rabbinic imagination* (emphasizing religious ways of knowing), we made a decision to focus on the relationship of theology, epistemology, and pedagogy as we sought to understand how seminary educators prepare students for clergy identity, roles, and responsibilities.

Seminary educators we interviewed and observed illuminated a variety of ways in which to view their relationship. When Butler said that through his teaching he hopes to stretch the faith of his students, he acknowledged that they share, at least to some extent (although at many different levels of understanding), truth claims articulated in the doctrinal statement that provides a theological umbrella for all Fuller faculty and students. When Wilson, at Yale Divinity School—who teaches some students who identify with Christian tradition and others who do not—wants students to discover the right method for engaging given biblical texts, he seems to limit notions of knowing to cognitive assessments of literary style, situation, and context; but then, when reminding us that the mission at Yale is to "love God," he emphasizes that finding the right method may have a spiritual as well as a cognitive role in student quests to know. When Benson, at St. John's Seminary, expects students in his classes to appropriate church teaching embedded in church tradition, he assumes that the knowing at the heart of Catholic faith originates in and is sustained by its truth. When Visotzky wants students to struggle with a midrashic text, he assumes they are learning that one can never fully know or understand the object of one's study and that the dynamics of knowing center on the never-ending struggle to ascertain meaning rather than on quests for discovering truth or faith in any definitive sense.

Understanding the relationship of theology, epistemology, and pedagogy in the teaching practices of seminary educators is, of course, not a new challenge. Almost two hundred years ago, Dwight proposed that in the new seminary at Andover the education of clergy should embrace both "intellect and piety." The stories of the various traditions of seminary education in America trace the course of debates, through the nineteenth and early twentieth century, over the relationship of intellect and piety, truth and faith or observance—debates among Catholic Americanists and traditionalists, among Protestant modernists and fundamentalists, and among Reform, Conservative, and Orthodox Jews.

It is a challenge that has intrigued scholars and been a concern for church and synagogue leaders who work most closely with candidates for the clergy. It is a challenge lived out daily, however, by seminary educators as they make decisions about what and how to teach. In their teaching we observed a mode of attention to the relationship of theology, epistemology, and pedagogy that differs from that typically found in scholarly treatises on theological education or in the curricular structures of seminaries.

We have described, in prior chapters, how seminary educators we interviewed and observed typically model and then coach students into ways of linking intellect, piety, truth, and faith or observance through their teaching. This insight drew us back to the discussions of MacIntyre, Dykstra and Bass, Fairfield, de Certeau, Wenger, and others about the formative dynamics in notions of practice generally and in the teaching practices of seminary educators specifically. As we have reflected on our observations of how clergy are educated, those discussions have led us to the following conclusions about teaching, first of all as a practice, and second as a spiritual practice—even in university divinity school settings in which students engage their teachers with a range of expectations about the relationship of academic and spiritual values.

Seminary educators reflective about their craft typically configure pedagogies of interpretation, formation, contextualization, and performance into strategies for student learning. We have called this strategic configuration of pedagogies a signature pedagogical framework. It shapes the teaching of seminary educators in several distinctive ways. It integrates the pedagogical functions of the cognitive, skill, and identity formation apprenticeships in their teaching. This means their teaching encompasses something more than the signature pedagogies that have historically been associated with each of these apprenticeships—as in, for example, limiting cognitive attention to information and theories in text-based courses or to communication and rhetorical skills in practice-oriented classes. It also means that through the strategic integration of pedagogies of interpretation, formation, contextualization, and performance, seminary educators engage students with what Shulman has called their deep structures. Those deep structures draw students into formal ways of thinking, doing, and being identified with the work of pastors, priests, or rabbis in religious communities and public life.

In the strategic integration of these pedagogies, intellect, piety, truth, and faith or observance do not function as alternative modes of knowing. Their relationship in the dynamics of teaching and learning has more of the character of a holograph, by which we mean that with slight shifts of emphasis, perspective, or task their relationship varies. In the teaching practices of Morgan and Visotzky, for example, the structure of the practice remained intact throughout the academic term, but with great dexterity they drew on pedagogies of interpretation, formation, contextualization, and performance as they perceived these were needed. Yet as students participated in the sustained patterns of their teaching, they were brought into particular ways of knowing, being, and doing associated with clergy practice.

Although the strategic forms of the teaching practices of seminary educators vary from teacher to teacher, discipline to discipline, and seminary tradition to seminary tradition, the features of the signature pedagogical framework that gives rise to seminary educator decisions about what and how to teach are not only widely shared by educators across the spectrum of Jewish and Christian seminaries, but also distinguish the teaching in seminaries from the teaching in law or medical schools. As a shared practice, the teaching that flows from this signature pedagogical framework may also be described as a practice of the community of clergy educators.

As a community practice, seminary educators' teaching cannot be reduced to "what they do when they teach." It is more than the application of technique or the tracing of the causal relationship between teacher intentions and student outcomes (Dykstra, 1991, pp. 39–40). Rather, students enter the community of the seminary educator's practice as apprentices through the educator's teaching practice. No matter what strategic configuration of the four pedagogies seminary educators may develop to engage students with the subject of their teaching, they model and then coach students to participate with increasing confidence and competence in the life of that community.

The community of seminary educator teaching practice has a long history. Throughout that history it has been distinguished from other communities of teaching practice by its engagement in the quest to explore, mediate, and interpret God. It should not have been surprising, then, to discover that almost all faculty participants in the survey we conducted said their teaching had a spiritual or sacramental character. A university divinity school professor underscores the point: "Pedagogy is a deeply spiritual thing for me—midwifing students in one aspect of their spiritual journeys, encountering the Word in the Old Testament" and modeling "my adoration of God . . . in my passionate engagement with the Bible."

This seminary educator illustrates something of the depth in which the teaching practices in seminary education are grounded as they give form to the religious or spiritual values of the communities they are designed to maintain and renew. It is at this point that we come back to the theological, epistemological, and pedagogical challenge we encountered throughout this study of seminary educator teaching practices. The "internal goods" that seminary educators seek through the learning of their students are first, a deepening sense of identification with their religious tradition, and second, their confident and competent participation in the leadership of its religious communities.

As they participate as teachers in the various disciplinary sectors of those communities in the seminary context, they continue to encounter new situations and circumstances outside the practices of teaching and learning that give rise to new knowledge. Even as they model how to participate in the theological or biblical or pastoral care discourse of their particular seminary education communities and guilds, at the same time they are attentive to new possibilities or realities appearing on the horizon that give rise to new knowledge, new ways of living or being.

This may be especially true for educators for whom God functions as both the symbol and the reality of that horizon. In this regard, the object of the seminary educator's teaching invariably centers on some interplay of intellect, truth, faith, observance, and knowledge. Together, as members of a seminary faculty, they constitute the community of practice into which they seek to introduce their students.

In the best practices of seminary education the pastoral, priestly, or rabbinic imagination of students is cultivated as they are drawn into the community of the practices of thinking, being, and doing as clergy. When seminary educators model and then coach students into the community of thinking, being, and doing as clergy, they invite their participation in the practices that distinguish that community. We are reminded of

Thompson's observation: "I've come to realize . . . [that] no matter what the content [of your teaching] is, at some very deep level you are teaching yourself. That not only are you the lesson they see but that you cannot teach what you do not know." Thompson models the configuration of academic, skill, and identity formation she seeks in her students. She engages them in practicing the interplay of intellect and piety, truth and faith, and coaches through example, instruction, and examination their increasingly confident participation in practices of thinking, being, and doing that give rise to and shape their relationship. The point has been reinforced by the observations of students who answered our survey questions and met with us in focus groups. In the best teaching they remember, they caught a glimpse, through their professors and each other in the dynamics of teaching and learning, not only of the vitality of the subject of their study, but of living Torah, living Truth; not only knowledge about God but knowledge and love *of* God—indeed, at times the very reality and presence of God in their midst.

How Do the Elements in Our Education of Clergy Fit Together?

Earlier chapters have alluded to the institutional distinctiveness of the schools in this study. It was not a surprise that we encountered these differences; we selected schools to obtain a relative cross-section of the seminary population. But in addition to noting various cultures of teaching and learning and differing models of clergy formation, our study also yielded some qualities by which institutions could be described, compared, and contrasted. These include the qualities of *institutional self-consciousness about teaching, institutional cohesion,* and *curricular balance*—all subjects for faculty conversation. Each contributes to the ability of a school community to align its mission, ethos, and pedagogies in its educational efforts.

Institutional self-consciousness about teaching refers to a school community's self-reflexivity with regard to educational purposes and practices in general, and teaching in particular. From site visits and survey responses, we found some variation across schools with respect to the level of introspection and dialogue among school administrations and faculties around the goals, purposes, structure, and effectiveness of educational programs and teaching. Some seminaries seemed to be continuously reflective about what they were doing, so much so that a few teachers reported being overwhelmed by workshops and evaluations.[4] (Because we selected schools to study, in part, for the degree to which they seemed invested in improving their effectiveness in the training of future clergy, we were not surprised to encounter this level of self-reflection.) The impact of the Association of Theological Schools and regional accrediting agencies has been significant, in that self-evaluation and strategic planning are built into their accreditation processes.

In spite of this, we did hear from faculty whose institutions—for lack of either interest, time, personnel, or funding—seemed to have a very low level of commitment to the collective examination of their educational objectives and how they were being accomplished. Often this seemed to reflect the culture of the institution. For example, one professor commented that a focus on improving educational effectiveness at his institution was hampered by "a reward/promotion system that uses only academic criteria" and "an institutional culture which prizes *wissenschaft* above all else."

Our respect for the quality of self-consciousness comes not from our being wedded to a culture or ideology of reform, but rather from the appreciation we have gained for the institutions we encountered that placed at the forefront of their mission the needs of the world in which their ministers were to serve. We witnessed the powerful and transformative effects on students participating in educational programs that were underscored by a commitment to authentic and earnest engagement with the issues and struggles of congregations and the pressing needs of our times. It is this kind of self-reflection, regarding the efficacy of an institution's educational structures and programs in promoting a model of courageous and committed ministry, that we wish to applaud and encourage.

Another qualitative feature that drew our attention was that of *institutional cohesion*—the degree to which a school shows internal consistency and coherence in its programs. Institutions that train clergy are acutely aware of various accountabilities under which they operate. They develop and implement programs that must be attentive to denominational ordination processes and standards, to theological and doctrinal frameworks, to the hierarchies and policies of religious and church bodies, to their own institutional history and ethos, to disciplinary and academic standards of higher education, to their understanding of divine will, and to the people and contexts that define the purpose of their students' future ministry. In each of the schools we visited, it was apparent that balancing these accountabilities in the framework of a purposefully focused program was a challenge, but one that, overall, we found them to be meeting quite successfully.

Several of the seminaries we visited exhibited a particularly strong sense of cohesion, a palpable sense of purpose with regard to the end-to-end preparation of students for the ministerial role. Cohesion is arguably easier to develop in more denominationally homogenous settings, in which the range of variables is smaller. On the other hand, even at an institution as large and diverse as Fuller, we witnessed a coherence of ministerial focus that students, faculty, and administration could articulate with relative clarity. But suggesting that schools work toward cohesion does not imply a promotion of homogeneity. We are aware of the potential for ultracohesion, wherein rigidity supplants the concept of a purposeful focus that we are discussing here.[5] Cohesion refers to the manner in which the school can be seen to implement an educational program that clearly attends to the ethos of the school and in which various courses, resources, and programs can be seen to reinforce or build upon one another. Although institutional cohesion in and of itself is no guarantee that its students will be optimally prepared for ministry, students do self-select for a given school on the basis of their perceptions of the ministerial emphases promoted by the institution. To this end, coherence in philosophy and practice appeared to provide students and alumni with a valuable integrative framework both for their educational experiences and for future ministerial practice.

A third institutional quality that arose in our analysis was that of *curricular balance,* in particular between classroom and in-situ learning. Almost without exception, alumni and alumnae in our survey reported that they had received an excellent theological education at their seminaries. From the earlier discussion about the historical legacies of clergy education, it is clear that certain philosophical emphases and models of clergy continue to persist in the seminary-academe. Nearly all students identified coursework, in general, as a key formative influence on their growth as future ministers. Additionally, over three-fourths of the same alumni and alumnae cited in-situ learning—in the form of field education, internships, unsupervised ministry experience, or clinical pastoral education—as having been key to their professional formation as well. Several used the word *tools* to refer to the body of skills, knowledge, and experience they gained in seminary. They appreciated the opportunities that seminary provided for them to acquire the theological, textual, and social understandings and skills they viewed as germane to the clergy role.

But when we asked alumni and alumnae if they had encountered any particular postgraduation challenges for which they did not feel adequately prepared, more than 80 percent responded in the affirmative. Seminaries have long wrestled with the issue of what should be learned in school and what can or should be learned on the job. One alumnus spoke pragmatically about the scope of seminary education: "Of course there are things that are identified along the way for which one might say 'I wished I had learned about that in seminary!' But there's no way 'every-thing' can be taught. I feel that a good foundation was laid within the aca-demic setting to provide some tools for the context of ministry. I do value my experiences during internship and [clinical pastoral education] because so much that is necessary can't be book learned. These were both very valuable and practical experiences that allowed for some 'on-the-job train-ing' in advance of my first call."

But clearly many students, although fully appreciative of their seminary experiences, did feel underprepared for the leadership and management roles into which they were quickly cast after graduation. It was not sur-prising that often-cited concerns surrounded administration, management, and finance. Some were quick to also say that they did not expect this kind of training in seminary. A notable number of alumni called out in-sufficient preparation for pastoral care and handling the difficult and painful situations for which people sought ministers for counsel, such as the clergyperson who wrote, "My seminary only required one course in pastoral counseling, and I wish I had taken more classes in this area. Looking back, knowing what I know now, I would have taken more ini-tiative to learn from my field instructor/supervisors."

Another applauded the theological training she received in seminary but noted that, "I . . . never learned how to do a baptism or a wedding—I had to just make it up as I went along. [My school] is very academic and head in the clouds—the theology I learned there is great but stratospheric compared to what people in the pews can handle or what is relevant for ministry."

The concept of *curricular balance* is one way to talk about curricular emphasis and the relative breadth and depth of various aspects of clergy preparation programs. Our study of the nature of teaching and learning in both the classroom, communal, and in-situ ministry contexts helped us to theorize beyond the dichotomy of theory (classroom) versus practice (field education), toward viewing *all forms of seminary learning as inher-ently involved in the cultivation of clergy practice,* achieved through three inter-related apprenticeships. In this light, it became apparent that some clergy education programs were heavily skewed toward certain aspects of clergy practice and apprenticeship and less so toward others. Clearly, sociohistorical and structural influences have contributed to the rein-forcement of this circumstance. However, in light of the responses we re-ceived from alumni at these eighteen seminaries who spoke of the serious challenges facing working clergy today, it seems that this kind of curric-ular stiltedness is neither desirable nor justifiable.

Reflections on the Clergy Education Study

Throughout this study of the education of clergy, we were often asked if there had been any surprises—whether we had learned anything we had not expected to learn. For a long time, we did not quite know how to answer that question, but now, as we look back, several discoveries have indeed been surprises.

Generally, seminary educators do not isolate the educational tasks traditionally identified with the cognitive, practical, and normative apprenticeships in professional education. In some seminaries the interdependence of these three apprenticeships is built into the fabric of a student's total curricular experience. In every seminary we observed, seminary educators engage students in the mutuality of the three apprenticeships through teaching practices consisting of pedagogies of interpretation, formation, contextualization, and performance. In this regard, seminary education provides a model for other forms of professional education.

Apprentice patterns of teaching and learning dominate the teacher-student interactions among seminary educators reflective about their practice. Although seminary educators employ many different teaching styles across the disciplines of the seminary curriculum, they both model and coach students into ways of thinking, being, and doing integral to their visions of clergy identity and practice. They sustain the telos of the seminary enterprise as a graduate professional school preparing clergy for professional practice as they model and coach students in practices connecting academic and practical knowledge; they use insight and resourcefulness in forming in their students a pastoral, priestly, or rabbinic imagination and guiding them in its necessary practices.

In their teaching, seminary educators emphasize the importance of the third apprenticeship, the one concerned with the formation of professional identity. This emphasis is found in the attention given to the normative dimensions of religious traditions in educating the leadership of religious communities; in specially designed programs of spiritual and human formation; in the commitment of seminary educators to the integration of academic and practical learning in classes, clinical pastoral education, and field education; and in the judgments faculty in many seminaries make regarding the fitness of students as candidates for professional practice. This may well be one of the most distinctive features of seminary education—and one of its most distinctive contributions to discussions of professional and liberal education.

Seminary educators engage students in a community of teaching and learning practice. In ways that may be a model for professional education generally, in classrooms and other educational settings they explicitly seek to foster learning communities, to shape the collaborative patterns of apprenticeship into particular ways of knowing, doing, and being. In many schools these learning communities are expanded to include field education, chapel, and other programs of community life and student governance. When aligned with the mission and culture of the school, they contribute significantly to the integration and cohesion of student learning.

The tasks involved in sustaining the seminary as a community of teaching and learning practice may be among the most persistent challenges facing contemporary seminary educators. The increasing fragmentation of academic disciplines, the diversity of student backgrounds and preparation, and the attempts in every seminary to meet, through a common academic program, multiple academic goals—all these factors have intensified the challenge in recent years. New technologies that provide opportunities for distance learning and virtual communities only make the challenge more complex.

As we approached the end of the study, we began hearing another question that has become increasingly intriguing and troubling: "Is good teaching enough?" Can good teaching alone cultivate the imaginations of students for clergy practice? One of the most pleasant surprises of the study was the realization that good teaching abounds in seminary education. We came away from each site visit enthused, even inspired, by the rigor and vitality of the teaching we had observed. (Indeed, one of our regrets is that limits of space and time prevented us from including full descriptions of the teaching practices of the rest of the more than forty seminary educators we interviewed and observed.) As we have pondered comments from students and seminary graduates and as we have reviewed the experience of our site visits, however, the answer to this question, we must finally admit, is "no." Good teaching alone is not enough; more than this is needed. Good teaching can flourish only as long as it is sustained by a community that encourages and supports good teaching practice.

Shulman has made the point: "Teacher collegiality and collaboration are not important merely for the improvement of morale and teacher satisfaction. . . . they are absolutely necessary if teaching is to be of the highest order and thus compatible with the standards of excellence demanded by the recent reforms [in education]. Collegiality and collaboration are also needed to ensure that teachers benefit from their experiences and continue to grow during their careers" (2004, p. 311). He concludes these comments by noting "few accomplishments are as hellishly difficult as learning from experience" (p. 311). We would add, "especially when alone or in isolation." The conversation in the faculty that facilitates col-legiality creates the conditions for the reflexivity conducive to growth as teachers. Sustained and focused conversation among colleagues contributes an important "something more" to the cultivation of good teaching.

At the start of this chapter, we considered four brief questions. In clos-ing this volume, we offer them again, but slightly amplified, to help fos-ter the collegiality that sustains and renews the seminary as a community of teaching and learning practices. We offer them now as catalysts to con-versations among colleagues, for such conversations seem to be particu-larly important to strengthening the teaching practices of seminary educators who are committed to cultivating the imaginations of their stu-dents for the professional responsibilities they will be assuming as rabbis, priests, or pastors.

- o Because seminary educators understand the vocation of clergy involves mediating, embodying, and/or interpreting God, how are we to speak of God in and through our classroom and communal teaching practices?

- o Because seminary educators also assume that their graduates will be engaged in the leadership of religious communities that have something to offer the public, what images of their practices at the intersection of religious tradition and public life inform their decisions about what and how to teach?

- o Because seminary educators are committed to cultivating an imagination that integrates knowledge, skill, moral integrity, and religious commitment in clergy practice, what is the relationship of the pedagogies of interpretation, formation, contextualization, and performance in their classroom and communal teaching practices?

- o Because institutional self-consciousness, cohesion, and curricular balance facilitates the interdependence of the cognitive, practical, and normative apprenticeships in the education of clergy, how do the mission and culture of the school influence the shape of classroom and communal teaching practices?

ENDNOTES

1. Porpora's discussion of Americans' widespread inability to articulate anything of substance regarding the God in whom they claim to believe runs throughout the entire book, but Chapter Three (2001, pp. 95–126) provides a succinct summary.

2. This view of symbolic worlds is indebted to Bellah's understanding of "symbolic realism" (1970).

3. Modern hermeneutical theories of Gadamer, Heidegger, and Ricoeur may be traced back to the influences of Husserl, Dilthey, and finally Schleiermacher—himself a clergy educator at the University of Berlin.

4. The educational field's commitment to reform, along with its mixed blessings, may be spilling over into seminaries, as seen in one professor's wry comment that the "pressure to chase trendy themes" is occurring "at the expense of taking theology seriously." Another professor made the following illuminating comment: "I am not a 'process person': I do not see that everyone has to put in a comment and engage in endless dialogue. I am perfectly happy to see some decisions made by a competent sub-group, and not to require all faculty members to deal with everything. The paper glut borders on being a nightmare."

5. One faculty member, for example, shared a concern that an institutional emphasis on strong confessional boundaries created an atmosphere hostile to academic freedom.

APPENDIX
THE CLERGY EDUCATION STUDY:
RESEARCH DESIGN AND METHODOLOGY

THIS STUDY, funded by the Lilly Endowment, Inc., and Atlantic Philanthropies, is one of several related projects of The Carnegie Foundation for the Advancement of Teaching that are directed to the study of the professions. The comparative dimensions of this larger study helped establish several boundaries for the study of clergy education. It would be focused on institutions with accreditation from the Association of Theological Schools or the U.S. regional college and university accrediting associations. This criterion alone significantly narrowed the scope of the study, as clergy are educated in many diverse ways across the many religious traditions—in unaccredited seminaries, monasteries, and congregations, and by apprenticeship. Because most Buddhist, Hindu, Muslim, and Orthodox Jewish religious leaders receive their training outside the university system, this criterion also focused the study on the education of Conservative and Reform Jewish and Catholic, Christian Orthodox, and a significant proportion of Protestant Christian clergy. Although these accredited institutions typically offer a range of academic programs for ordained and nonordained religious leadership, this study focused attention only on (1) those receiving the master of divinity degree in seminaries educating clergy for Christian denominations and (2) the graduates of rabbinic programs in accredited institutions for Jewish denominations. Our criteria also focused the study on the education of those preparing for ordination in institutions in the United States.

With nearly three hundred seminaries accredited by the Association of Theological Schools or by one of the associations accrediting universities and colleges in the United States, the principal methodological decision we faced was how to capture a relatively accurate picture of seminary education within the constraints of time and personnel. We had to clearly define the scope of the project to ensure its manageability and eventual success. The research interests of the Carnegie Foundation in teaching helped us to focus our attention on the *teaching practices* of clergy educators. As we began the study, we saw teaching practices as comprising the manner in which teachers—individually, collaboratively, and as members of a faculty—reflect on, prepare, and implement activities for student learning. Limiting the scope in this way allowed for a more effective use of research resources to collect data on the perspectives and activities of teachers in the classroom and other educational settings, yet still bring in the perspectives of students, administrators, and others important to clergy education.

Methodology

The methodology for this study may best be described as an *appreciative inquiry.* Appreciative inquiry (Cooperrider and Srivastva, 1987; Cooperrider and Whitney, 1999) is a research framework and methodology oriented toward fostering organizational change by looking for what is already working in an enterprise and amplifying these aspects—as opposed to focusing on problems and attempting to fix them. The operative assumption underlying appreciative inquiry is that research questions send powerful messages that both affect who or what is being studied and determine the nature of the findings and conclusions emerging from the study. Although we did not employ the full methodology developed by Cooperrider and Srivastva, following it in spirit helped us maintain the focus of our research task.

The catalyst to the study originated in the overarching question prompting each of the studies in the Carnegie Foundation Preparation for the Professions Program: *How do professional schools prepare their students for their professional roles and responsibilities?* This question focused our attention on Jewish and Christian seminaries and the pedagogical practices of their faculty members in both classrooms and, more generally, the life of the seminary community. We limited our approach to this research task with a more specific question: *How do seminary educators foster among their students a pastoral, priestly, or rabbinic imagination that integrates knowledge and skill, moral integrity, and religious commitment in the roles, relationships, and responsibilities they will be assuming in clergy practice?* Reframing the more general question in this way focused our attention on how seminary educators engage students in appropriating the wisdom and practices of their religious traditions for leading contemporary religious communities. This question established the framework for the specific questions guiding the development of our research protocols and strategies:

○ What classroom and communal pedagogies do seminary educators employ as they seek to foster in their students a pastoral, priestly, or rabbinic imagination?

○ How do the various historic traditions of clergy education perpetuated in seminaries' missions and institutional cultures influence the
classroom and communal pedagogies and students' experience?

○ Does clergy education have a "signature" classroom pedagogy,
distinctive to it among the professions?

○ How does clergy education emphasize and integrate the cognitive, practical, and normative apprenticeships of professional
education?

We followed the precedent of prior projects in the Preparation for the
Professions Program of The Carnegie Foundation for the Advancement
of Teaching by exploring these questions in a sample of institutions of
higher education. The goal of the data collection and analysis process was
to find exemplars of good pedagogy ("good" in whatever idiosyncratic
ways that term may be defined). The following paragraphs outline the different tasks in the research process.

Literature Review

We conducted an extensive literature review of historical and contemporary contexts and conversations within seminary education. Key aspects
of this literature review included researching and developing synopses of
all prior major studies of clergy education in the United States; culling literature from areas including, but not limited to, cognition and learning,
theological or seminary education, professional education, teaching practices, and spiritual formation for resonant ideas, theories, and concepts;
and charting the evolution of various educational models and denominational strains of clergy preparation. In addition, to inform our prospective questions, analyses, and interpretations, we worked to identify the
operative tensions and implicit assumptions within which contemporary
seminary education functions.

Site Selection

The project design involved identifying a sample of twenty-one seminaries
to work with us in this inquiry. We asked expert informants to nominate
seminaries for this sample. In selecting this sample, we looked for

○ Representation of the diversity to be found in graduate-level
seminary education, with attention to the following categories:

Conservative and Reform Judaism

Christian Orthodox

Mainline Protestants (Anglican, Lutheran, Wesleyan, Reformed, and Free)

Evangelical Protestants (denominational, nondenominational, and peace church traditions)

Roman Catholic (religious and diocesan)

University-based, free-standing, and consortium affiliated schools

Geographical balance

o Institutions with a primary commitment to the training of clergy

o Institutions engaged in a "lively conversation around teaching"

Of the twenty-one schools we contacted, only three declined to participate; in each instance, the decision had to do with changes of administrative leaders or commitment to other comprehensive projects. The final sample comprised the following eighteen institutions (asterisks identify eight seminaries where we conducted site visits by the full research team, one seminary visited by one member of the research team, and one where we made a pilot visit only):

Associated Mennonite Biblical Seminary

Candler School of Theology, Emory University

Catholic Theological Union*

Church Divinity School of the Pacific*

Eden Theological Seminary

Fuller Theological Seminary*

Garrett-Evangelical Theological Seminary

Hebrew Union College

Howard University School of Divinity*

Jewish Theological Seminary*

Louisville Presbyterian Theological Seminary*

North Park Theological Seminary

Saint John's Seminary (Camarillo, CA)*

St. John's University School of Theology and Seminary

Saint Vladimir's Orthodox Seminary*

Southwestern Baptist Theological Seminary

Trinity Lutheran Seminary*

Yale University Divinity School*

Time and resource constraints precluded our making site visits to all eighteen of these institutions. We originally intended to collect from all eighteen schools archival materials and course syllabi, and to conduct a series of syllabus interviews on each campus by phone with professors. However, as we became aware of the level of logistics involved in scheduling, conducting, and transcribing a minimum of eighty one-hour phone interviews (with four professors per institution)—as well as the logistics, planning, and execution of eight multiday site visits—we realized our design had become too ambitious. We then entertained the possibility of conducting a survey.

Survey Design and Implementation

The survey component of our study was appended to our project plan at the end of the first year of the study, for the reasons mentioned above. The survey was focused on faculty reflections about their teaching practices and, in particular, how they talked about the relationship between their goals for teaching and their classroom practices. With the realization that collecting data only from faculty would be inadequate, we extended the survey to include alumni and alumnae (five or six years after graduation) and students (in their last year of study) of these institutions—asking them, in a kind of mirror-image fashion, to reflect on particularly noteworthy *learning* experiences both in the classroom and more generally in the life of the seminary community. (The survey instruments are available at www.carnegiefoundation.org/PPP/clergy study/).

After assessing the feasibility of a Web-based survey and verifying that all study schools had Internet connectivity, we decided to implement one. We again sampled faculty, students, and alumni at each of the institutions that agreed to participate. We contacted the chief academic officers, requesting that each school recruit survey participants and affirm their participation. We requested the names and e-mail addresses of eight persons from each constituency—faculty, alumni and alumnae, and students—to ensure a relatively equal representation across the schools. We asked that faculty participants represent a cross-section of disciplines in the curriculum, ages, faculty rank, gender, and race; be reflective about their teaching; and be respected by their colleagues as effective teachers. We requested graduating seniors and graduates with five or six years' experience who could be reflective about their experience in seminary.

Our goal in conducting these surveys was not to produce statistically significant trends or patterns (as our sampling methods may indicate), but rather to gain a substantive introduction to what was perceived to be high-quality teaching and learning taking place at these institutions. We hoped this data from the eighteen schools would substantially augment the understanding of good teaching practices in seminary education that we might obtain through our site visits. Our questionnaires consisted of approximately sixty questions, with a mixture of question types, including multiple choice, ranking, and essay or "free text" responses. In addition to demographic data, we asked faculty, students, and alumni and alumnae a series of questions pertaining to a course of their choosing. For faculty, this course was to be one that they particularly enjoyed teaching and that was designed primarily for ministry preparation; for students, alumni, and alumnae, the course was to be one "particularly important in your formation for ministry." The survey also asked more general questions about their perspectives on teaching (faculty) or learning (students) in the seminary.

The survey was beta tested on a small group of seminary students. The on-line surveys were then deployed and response data were collected over a period of two months. Response rates were quite high, likely due to the fact that volunteers had consented to participate before their schools forwarded their contact information to us.

Site Visits

The coordination and conducting of site visits constituted the entire second year of the study. Site visit teams—composed of four researchers, including members of the clergy education study team as well as other members of the Carnegie Foundation staff—spent three days at each of eight campuses. A preliminary pilot site visit was conducted at a ninth campus, and a member of the research team visited a Christian Orthodox seminary for two days after we had determined that the seminary education tradition it represented was distinctive enough to require more direct observation. Before each visit, archival material and syllabi were collected from the school and previsit interviews were conducted by phone with four professors who were recommended and available for class observation (we requested that one be teaching in the field of scripture or Talmud, another in some field of practical theology or rabbinics, and the other two selected from other disciplines). In every instance school administrative staff members were exceptionally helpful in scheduling meetings with key

staff and aiding the coordination of focus group participation. A complete
site visit typically included the following:

- o Orientation and overview meetings with administrator(s)
- o Campus tour
- o Classroom observations
- o Post–class observation interviews and focus group conversation
  with faculty
- o Student focus groups
- o Faculty focus groups
- o Interviews or focus groups with key personnel, per recommendation by the school
- o Observation of and participation in school activities (for example,
  prayer services, worship services, campus celebrations)
- o Informal conversations with students and other members of the
  seminary community

Protocols were employed for syllabus interviews, classroom observations, and post–class observation interviews, and to facilitate focus group
conversations. Many questions in these protocols for interviews and focus
groups had been generated from the initial review of questionnaire data.
Interviews and focus groups were conducted with written consent. We
used tape recorders extensively and took field notes throughout each visit.
Subsequent to each site visit, interviews and focus group sessions were
transcribed and site visit team members each generated summaries of their
impressions of the institution with respect to the nature of the enterprise
of teaching and learning,

Participation in a National Survey of Seminary Faculty

One additional source of data for this study was our participation in the
2003 survey of half of all faculty members in accredited seminaries in the
United States and Canada, conducted by the Center for the Study of Theological Education at Auburn Theological Seminary (Wheeler, Miller, and
Schuth, 2005). This wide-ranging survey generated profiles of theological
faculty in a number of areas, including employment trends, workload, job
satisfaction, salary, and demographic characteristics. The Center invited
our project to submit several questions, pertaining specifically to teaching, that would be appropriate for a larger sample of faculty than that in

our study. The resulting data from these questions, as well as the full results from the Auburn survey, enhanced our broader understanding of faculty views and concerns.

Data Analysis

As might be expected, each site visit produced copious amounts of data: dozens of recordings of class sessions, interviews, and focus group sessions, and field notes. All this information presented us with a particularly challenging analytical task. Our handling of it is detailed in the paragraphs that follow.

Case Study Development

Because we chose to focus our study most intensively on practices of teaching and learning, we found a useful analytical strategy in the development of case studies. The team members developed these around a number of teachers we encountered across the different schools, then distributed the studies for group review and discussion. The development of these case studies was valuable for several reasons. First, they helped illuminate what was distinctive and uniquely important about what seminary educators do (which we hope we have addressed in the body of this text). Second, developing these case studies of teachers allowed us to begin to make explicit the working philosophies, assumptions, and frameworks that might be implicit in the teaching practices we observed. And finally, they served as a site of integration and reflection about the multiple factors that may influence what teachers do in their classrooms and what schools do in programs of worship and field education, and for consideration of how denominational orientation, institutional setting, teacher, and student together make up any given experience of teaching and learning. The results of this exercise of documenting these "pedagogically rich" settings for learning would eventually evolve into the backbone of this volume.

Analysis of Survey Data

We analyzed the survey data by computing basic quantitative measures of response data and coding responses to selected questions. We would discover, during this period, that the response formats of some of our questions were more complicated than they needed to be, thus inhibiting the interpretive process. But at the same time we had to resist placing too much weight on the quantitative results that in this case were derived from a selective, nonrepresentative sample of the faculty, alumni, and students of an equally selective sample of seminary institutions. We worked to maintain a consciousness, in the analysis process, of the primary purpose of the survey instrument—namely, providing insights to possible key issues in seminary education along with advance notice of what we might be observing during our site visits. From this standpoint, although the quantitative comparisons provided interesting starting points for discussion, the narrative responses in the survey results proved to be of arguably greater value in that the respondents' voices pushed us to nuance our conceptual analyses and also to hold ourselves accountable to the realities reflected therein.

Interim Reporting and Dissemination of Findings

While the study was under way, the project director and project team had the opportunity to present preliminary findings in various venues: meetings with Carnegie Foundation colleagues, faculty workshops sponsored by educational institutions, the annual meetings of the Association of Professors and Researchers of Religious Education, the 2004 annual meeting of the Association of Theological Schools, meetings with the advisory committee for the project, and meetings cosponsored by our funders. These occasions proved invaluable to the project as catalysts for the articulation of our evolving conceptualizations and for eliciting much-needed feedback from advisors, educators, and practitioners. Additionally, at the end of the three-year study, we invited representatives from all participating schools to the Carnegie Foundation for a two-day event in which we presented overviews of the study findings along with summary reports for each of the eighteen schools. This meeting, too, helped us to further refine our focus with respect to our conceptual framework.

BIBLIOGRAPHY

Abbs, P. *Against the Flow: Education, the Arts, and Postmodern Culture.*
New York: RoutledgeFalmer, 2003.

Ackermann, D. M., and Bons-Storm, R. (eds). *Liberating Faith Practices:*
Feminist Theologies in Context. Leuven, Belgium: Peeters, 1998.

Ahlstrom, S. *A Religious History of the American People.* New Haven, Conn.:
Yale University Press, 1976.

Alexander, H. A. "Wissenschaft and Its Discontents: Rabbinic Education in
an Age of Disbelief." *Religious Education,* 1997, 92(2), 254–269.

Alinsky, S. D. *Rules for Radicals: A Practical Primer for Realistic Radicals.*
New York: Random House, 1971.

Appadurai, A. *Modernity at Large: Cultural Dimensions of Globalization.*
Minneapolis: University of Minnesota Press, 1996.

Argyris, C., and Schön, D. *Theory in Practice: Increasing Professional*
Effectiveness. San Francisco: Jossey-Bass, 1974.

Association of Theological Schools of the United States and Canada. *Fact Book*
on Theological Education, 2002–2003. Pittsburgh, Penn.: Association of
Theological Schools, 2003.

Atkinson, L. "Trusting Your Own Judgement (Or Allowing Yourself to Eat
the Pudding)." In T. Atkinson and G. Claxton (eds.), *The Intuitive*
Practitioner: On the Value of Not Always Knowing What One Is Doing.
Buckingham, UK: Open University Press, 2000.

Atkinson, T., and Claxton, G. (eds.). *The Intuitive Practitioner: On the Value*
of Not Always Knowing What One Is Doing. Buckingham, UK: Open
University Press, 2000.

Ayers, W. *Teaching Toward Freedom: Moral Commitment and Ethical Action*
in the Classroom. Boston: Beacon Press, 2004.

Bain, K. *What the Best College Teachers Do.* Cambridge, Mass.: Harvard
University Press, 2004.

Balmer, R. *Mine Eyes Have Seen the Glory: A Journey into the Evangelical*
Subculture of America. New York: Oxford University Press, 1989.

Banks, R. *Reenvisioning Theological Education: Exploring a Missional*
Alternative to Current Models. Grand Rapids, Mich.: Eerdmans, 1999.

Banner, J. M. Jr., and Cannon, H. C. *The Elements of Teaching.* New Haven, Conn.: Yale University Press, 1997.

Bartlett, D. L. *Between the Bible and the Church: New Methods for Biblical Preaching.* Nashville, Tenn.: Abingdon Press, 1999.

Baum, W. W. "The State of U.S. Free-Standing Seminaries." *Origins,* 1986, *16*(15), 315–325.

Bass, D. C. (ed.). *Practicing Our Faith: A Way of Life for a Searching People.* San Francisco: Jossey-Bass, 1998.

Behan, W. P. "An Introductory Survey of the Lay Training School Field." *Religious Education,* 1916, *11,* 47–52.

Bell, C. *Ritual Theory, Ritual Practice.* Oxford: Oxford University Press, 1992.

Bellah, R. *Beyond Belief: Essays on Religion in a Post-Traditional World.* New York: Harper and Row, 1970.

Bellah, R. *The Broken Covenant: American Civil Religion in a Time of Trial.* New York: Seabury Press, 1975.

Benner, P. *From Novice to Expert: Excellence and Power in Clinical Nursing Practice.* Menlo Park, Calif.: Addison-Wesley, 1984.

Benner, P., Tanner, C. A., and Chesla, C. A. *Expertise in Nursing Practice: Caring, Clinical Judgment, and Ethics.* New York: Springer, 1996.

Bentwich, N. *Solomon Schechter: A Biography.* Philadelphia: The Jewish Publication Society of America, 1938.

Berkovits, E. "A Contemporary Rabbinical School for Orthodox Jewry." In J. Neusner (ed.), *The Rabbi and the Synagogue.* New York: Ktav Publishing House, 1975.

Bess, J. L. *Teaching Alone, Teaching Together: Transforming the Structure of Teams for Teaching.* San Francisco: Jossey-Bass, 2000.

Boal, A. *Games for Actors and Non-actors.* Translated by A. Jackson. London: Routledge, 1992.

Bond, H. M. *The Education of the Negro in the American Social Order.* New York: Octagon Books, 1966.

Bourdieu, P. *The Logic of Practice.* Stanford: Stanford University Press, 1990.

Bourdieu, P. *Practical Reason: On the Theory of Action.* Stanford, Calif.: Stanford University Press, 1998.

Bourdieu, P., and Passeron, J. *Reproduction in Education, Society, and Culture.* Translated by R. Nice. London: Sage Publications, 1990. (Originally published 1977).

Boyle, H. C. "Ideas for Action." *Civic Engagement News,* 11. [www1.umn.edu/civic/new/newsletterOct2004.html]. 2004.

Brekke, M., Schuller, D., and Strommen, M. "Readiness for Ministry: Report on the Research." *Theological Education,* 1976, *13*(1), 22–30.

Brereton, V. *Training God's Army: The American Bible School, 1880–1940.* Bloomington: Indiana University Press, 1990.

Brookfield, S. *Developing Critical Thinkers: Challenging Adults to Explore Alternative Ways of Thinking and Acting.* San Francisco: Jossey-Bass, 1987.

Brown, R. M. *Is Faith Obsolete?* Philadelphia: Westminster Press, 1974.

Brown, W. A., and, May, M. A. *The Education of American Ministers.* New York: Institute of Social and Religious Research, 1934.

Browning, D. S. (ed.). *Practical Theology.* San Francisco: HarperSanFrancisco, 1983.

Browning, D. S. "Globalization and the Task of Theological Education." *Theological Education,* 1986, *23*(Autumn), 43–59.

Browning, D. S. *A Fundamental Practical Theology: Descriptive and Strategic Proposals.* Minneapolis: Fortress Press, 1991.

Browning, D. S., Polk, D. P., and Evison, I. S. *The Education of the Practical Theologian: Responses to Joseph Hough and John Cobbs' Christian Identity and Theological Education.* Atlanta, Ga.: Scholars Press, 1989.

Bruner, J. S. *The Culture of Education.* Cambridge, Mass.: Harvard University Press, 1996.

Caillois, R. *Man, Play, and Games.* Translated by M. Barash. Urbana: University of Illinois Press, 2001.

Cannon, K. G., and others. *God's Fierce Whimsy: Christian Feminism and Theological Education.* New York: Pilgrim Press, 1985.

Carey, P. W., and Muller, E. C. *Theological Education in the Catholic Tradition: Contemporary Challenges.* New York: Crossroad, 1997.

Carey, P. W., Appleby, R. S., Byrne, P., and Campbell, D. *Transforming Parish Ministry: The Changing Roles of Catholic Clergy, Laity, and Women Religious.* New York: Crossroad, 1989.

Carpenter, J. A. *Revive Us Again: The Reawakening of American Fundamentalism.* New York: Oxford University Press, 1997.

Carroll, J. W. "Project Transition: An Assessment of ATS Programs and Services." *Theological Education,* 1981, *18*(1), 45–165.

Carroll, J. W. "The Professional Model of Ministry—Is It Worth Saving?" *Theological Education,* 1985, *21*(Spring), 7–48.

Carroll, J. W., and Wheeler, B. G. "Doctor of Ministry Program: History, Summary of Findings and Recommendation." *Theological Education,* 1987, *23*(Spring), 7–52.

Carroll, J. W., Wheeler, B. G., Aleshire, D. O., and Marler, P. L. *Being There: Culture and Formation in Two Theological Schools.* New York: Oxford University Press, 1997.

Catholic Church and National Conference of Catholic Bishops. *Program of Priestly Formation for the National Conference of Catholic Bishops [of the] United States of America.* Washington, D.C., 1971, 1976, 1993.

Cetuk, V. S. *What to Expect in Seminary: Theological Education as Spiritual Formation.* Nashville, Tenn.: Abingdon Press, 1998.

Cherry, C. *Nature and Religious Imagination: From Edwards to Bushnell.* Philadelphia: Fortress Press, 1980.

Cherry, C. *Hurrying Toward Zion: Universities, Divinity Schools, and American Protestantism.* Bloomington: Indiana University Press, 1995.

Chopp, R. "Practical Theology and Liberation." In L. S. Mudge and J. N. Poling (eds.), *Formation and Reflection: The Promise of Practical Theology.* Philadelphia: Fortress Press, 1987.

Chopp, R. *Saving Work: Feminist Practices of Theological Education.* Louisville, Ky.: Westminster/John Knox Press, 1995.

Claxton, G. "The Anatomy of Intuition." In T. Atkinson and G. Claxton (eds.), *The Intuitive Practitioner: On the Value of Not Always Knowing What One Is Doing.* Buckingham, UK: Open University Press, 2000.

Cohen, N. J. "The Changing Face of Rabbinic Education. *Sh'ma: A Journal of Jewish Responsibility,* 1997, 27(527), 3–5.

Colby, A., Ehrlich, T., Beaumont, E., and Stephens, J. *Educating Citizens: Preparing America's Undergraduates for Lives of Moral and Civic Responsibility.* San Francisco: Jossey-Bass, 2003.

Coll, R. *Supervision of Ministry Students.* Collegeville, Minn.: The Liturgical Press, 1992.

Cone, C. W. *The Identity Crisis in Black Theology.* Nashville, Tenn.: The African Methodist Episcopal Church, 1975.

Cone, J. *A Black Theology of Liberation.* Philadelphia: Lippincott, 1970.

Cooperrider, D. L., and Srivastva, S. "Appreciative Inquiry in Organizational Life." In W. Passmore and R. Woodman (eds.), *Research in Organizational Change and Development,* Vol. 1. Greenwich, Conn.: JAI Press, 1987.

Cooperrider, D. L., and Whitney, D. "Appreciative Inquiry." In P. Holman and T. Devane (eds.), *Collaborating for Change.* San Francisco: Berrett-Koehler, 1999.

Cornwall Collective. *Your Daughters Shall Prophesy: Feminist Alternatives in Theological Education.* New York: Pilgrim Press, 1980.

Cox, H. *The Secular City: Secularization and Urbanization in Theological Perspective* (rev. ed). New York: Macmillan, 1971.

Cunningham, C. E. *Timothy Dwight, 1752–1817: A Biography.* New York: Macmillan, 1942.

Curran, R. E., and Emmett, S. J. "Confronting the Social Question: American-Catholic Thought in the Socio-economic Order in the Nineteenth Century." In W. Portier (ed.), *The Inculturation of American Catholicism, 1820–1900: Selected Historical Essays*. New York: Garland Publishing, 1988.

Daniel, W. A. *The Education of Negro Ministers*. New York: George H. Doran, 1925.

Daniels, W. H. *D. L. Moody and His Work*. London: Hodder and Stoughton, 1875.

Daniels, W. H. *Moody: His Words, Work, and Workers*. New York: Nelson and Phillips, 1877.

Darder, A., Baltodano, M., and Torres, R. D. (eds.). *The Critical Pedagogy Reader*. New York: RoutledgeFalmer, 2003.

Day, R. E. *Bush Aglow: The Life Story of Dwight Lyman Moody, Commoner of Northfield*. Philadelphia: The Judson Press, 1936.

de Certeau, M. *The Practice of Everyday Life*. Berkeley: University of California Press, 1984.

Dobschuetz, B. "Emma Dryer and the Moody Church: The Role of Gender and Proto-fundamentalist Identity, 1864–1900." *Fides es Historia*, 2001, *33* (Summer/Fall), 41–52.

Dolan, J. P. *Transforming Parish Ministry: The Changing Roles of Catholic Clergy, Laity, and Women Religious*. New York: Crossroad, 1989.

Dolan, J. P. "American Catholicism and the Enlightenment Ethos." In W. Shea and P. Huff (eds.), *Knowledge and Belief in America: Enlightenment Traditions and Modern Thought*. Washington, D.C.: Woodrow Wilson Center Press and Cambridge University Press, 1995.

Dorsett, L. W. *A Passion for Souls: The Life of D. L. Moody*. Chicago: Moody Press, 1997.

Downey, M. *Understanding Christian Spirituality*. New York: Paulist Press, 1997.

Dreyer, E. A., and Burrows, M. S. (eds.). *Minding the Spirit: The Study of Christian Spirituality*. Baltimore and London: Johns Hopkins University Press, 2005.

Dykstra, C. R. *Vision and Character: A Christian Educator's Alternative to Kohlberg*. New York: Paulist Press, 1981.

Dykstra, C. R. "Reconceiving Practice." In E. Farley and B. Wheeler (eds.), *Shifting Boundaries: Contextual Approaches to the Structure of Theological Education*. Louisville, Ky.: Westminster/John Knox Press, 1991.

Dykstra, C. R. "The Pastoral Imagination," *Initiatives in Religion*, 2001, *9*(1).

Dykstra, C. R., and Bass, D. C. "Times of Yearning, Practices of Faith." In D. C. Bass (ed.), *Practicing Our Faith: A Way of Life for a Searching People*. San Francisco: Jossey-Bass, 1998.

Dykstra, C. R., and Bass, D. C. "A Theological Understanding of Christian Practices." In M. Volf and D. C. Bass (eds.), *Practicing Theology: Beliefs and Practices in Christian Life.* Grand Rapids, Mich.: Eerdmans, 2002.

Earey, M. *Worship as Drama.* Cambridge, UK: Grove Books Limited, 1997.

Edwards, R. "Normal Schools in the United States." In M. L. Borrowman (ed.), *Teacher Education in America: A Documentary History.* New York: Teachers College Press, 1965. (Originally published 1865.)

Egan, K. *The Educated Mind: How Cognitive Tools Shape Our Understanding.* Chicago: University of Chicago Press, 1997.

Eggleston, E. *The Transit of Civilization from England to America in the Seventeenth Century.* Reprint, Boston: Beacon Press, 1959. (Originally published 1900.)

Eisner, E. W. *The Educational Imagination: On the Design and Evaluation of School Programs.* (2nd ed.) New York: Macmillan, 1985.

Elenes, C. A. "Reclaiming the Borderlands: Chicana/o Identity, Difference, and Critical Pedagogy." In A. Darder, M. Baltodano, and R. D. Torres (eds.), *The Critical Pedagogy Reader.* New York: RoutledgeFalmer, 2003.

Eliot, T. S. "East Coker." In *Four Quartets.* London: Faber and Faber, 1944.

Ellenson, D., and Bycel, L. "A Seminary of Sacred Learning: The JTS Rabbinical Curriculum in Historical Perspective." In J. Wertheimer (ed.), *Tradition Renewed: A History of the Jewish Theological Seminary,* Vol. 1. New York: Jewish Theological Seminary, 1997.

Evans, A., Evans, R., and Roozen, D. A. *The Globalization of Theological Education.* Maryknoll, N.Y.: Orbis Books, 1993.

Fairfield, P. *Theorizing Praxis: Studies in Hermeneutical Pragmatism.* New York: Peter Lang, 2000.

Farley, E. "The Reform of Theological Education as a Theological Task." *Theological Education,* 1981, *17*(2), 93—117.

Farley, E. *Theologia: The Fragmentation and Unity of Theological Education.* Philadelphia: Fortress Press, 1983.

Farley, E. *The Fragility of Knowledge: Theological Education in the Church and the University.* Philadelphia: Fortress Press, 1988.

Farley, E. *Practicing Gospel: Unconventional Thoughts on the Church's Ministry.* Louisville, Ky.: Westminster/John Knox Press, 2003.

Fichter, J. H., and Fichter, S. J. *Religion as an Occupation: A Study in the Sociology of Professions.* Notre Dame, Ind.: University of Notre Dame Press, 1961.

Fielding, C. R., and others. *Education for Ministry.* Dayton, Ohio: American Association of Theological Schools, 1966.

Findlay, J. F., Jr. *Dwight L. Moody: American Evangelist, 1837–1899.* Chicago: University of Chicago Press, 1969.

Fiorenza, F. S. "Theory and Practice: Theological Education as a Reconstructive, Hermeneutical, and Practical Task." *Theological Education,* 1987, 23(Supplement), 113–141.

Fish, S. *Is There a Text in This Class? The Authority of Interpretive Communities.* Cambridge, Mass.: Harvard University Press, 1980.

Fitzmier, J. R. *New England's Moral Legislator: Timothy Dwight, 1752–1817.* Bloomington: Indiana University Press, 1998.

Foster, C. R. "The Pastor: Agent of Vision in the Education of a Community of Faith." In R. L. Browning (ed.), *The Pastor as Religious Educator.* Birmingham, Ala.: Religious Education Press, 1989.

Fowler, J. W. "Practical Theology and Theological Education." *Theology Today,* 1985, (42), 43–58.

Fox, S., Scheffler, I., and Marom, D. *Visions of Jewish Education.* Cambridge, UK: Cambridge University Press, 2003.

Fraser, J. W. *Schooling the Preachers: The Development of Protestant Theological Education in the United States 1740–1875.* New York: University Press of America, 1988.

Freire, P. *Pedagogy of Freedom: Ethics, Democracy, and Civic Courage.* Translated by P. Clark. Lanham, Md.: Rowman and Littlefield, 1998.

Fried, S. *The New Rabbi: A Congregation Searches for Its Leader.* New York: Bantam Books, 2002.

Furlong, J. "Intuition and the Crisis in Teacher Professionalism." In T. Atkinson and G. Claxton (eds.), *The Intuitive Practitioner: On the Value of Not Always Knowing What One Is Doing.* Buckingham, UK: Open University Press, 2000.

Gardner, H., Csikszentmihalyi, M., and Damon, W. *Good Work: When Excellence and Ethics Meet.* New York: Basic Books, 2001.

Gawande, A. *Complications: A Surgeon's Notes on an Imperfect Science.* New York: Picador/Henry Holt, 2002.

Getz, G. *MBI: The Story of the Moody Bible Institute.* Chicago: Moody Press, 1969.

Gibbons, Cardinal J. *The Ambassador for Christ.* Baltimore: John Murphy Co., 1896.

Gilpin, W. C. *A Preface to Theology.* Chicago: University of Chicago Press, 1996.

Gore, J. "What Can We Do for You? What Can 'We' Do for 'You'?" In A. Darder, M. Baltodano, and R. D. Torres (eds.), *The Critical Pedagogy Reader.* New York: RoutledgeFalmer, 2003.

Graham, E. L. *Transforming Practice: Pastoral Theology in an Age of Uncertainty.* London: Mowbray, 1996.

Green, A. (ed.). *World Spirituality Series.* Vol. 14: *Jewish Spirituality: From the Sixteenth Century Revival to the Present.* New York: Crossroad, 1997.

Greene, M. *The Teacher as Stranger: Educational Philosophy for the Modern Age.* Belmont, Calif.: Wadsworth, 1973.

Greene, M. *Landscapes of Learning.* New York: Teachers College Press, 1978.

Greene, M. *Releasing the Imagination: Essays on Education, the Arts, and Social Change.* San Francisco: Jossey-Bass, 1995.

Greene, M. "In Search of a Critical Pedagogy." In P. Leistyna, A. Woodrum, and S. A. Sherblom (eds.), *Breaking Free: The Transformative Power of a Critical Pedagogy.* Cambridge, Mass.: Harvard Educational Review, 1996.

Griffin, P. R. *Black Theology as the Foundation of Three Methodist Colleges: The Educational Views and Labors of Daniel Payne, Joseph Price, and Isaac Lane.* Lanham, Md.: University Press of America, 1984.

Groome, T. *Christian Religious Education: Sharing Our Story and Vision.* San Francisco: Harper and Row, 1980.

Gumperz, J. J. "Contextualization Revisited." In P. Auer and A. di Luzio (eds.), *The Contextualization of Language.* Amsterdam/Philadelphia: John Benjamins, 1992.

Gustafson, J. M. "Priorities in Theological Education." *Theological Education,* 1987, *23*(Supplement), 69–87.

Gustafson, J. M. "The Vocation of the Theological Educator." *Theological Education,* 1987, *23*(Supplement), 53-68.

Gustafson, J. M. "Reflections on the Literature on Theological Education Published between 1955 and 1985." *Theological Education,* 1988, *24*(Supplement 2).

Hall, C. E. *Head and Heart: The Story of the Clinical Pastoral Education Movement.* Decatur, Ga.: Journal of Pastoral Care Publications, 1992.

Hall, D. J. "Theological Education as Character Formation?" *Theological Education,* 1988, *24*(Supplement 1), 53–79.

Hall, D. J. *Thinking the Faith: Christian Theology in a North American Context.* Minneapolis: Fortress Press, 1991.

Hall, E. T. *The Silent Language.* Greenwich, Conn.: Fawcett, 1959.

Hampton Normal and Agricultural School. *Twenty-Two Years' Work of Hampton Normal and Agricultural Institute: Records of Negro and Indian Graduates and Ex-students.* Hampton, Va.: Hampton Normal School Press, 1893.

Handy, R. T. "Trends in American and Canadian Theological Education, 1880–1980: Some Comparisons." *Theological Education,* 1982, *18*(2), 175–218.

Handy, R. T. *A History of Union Theological Seminary in New York.* New York: Columbia University Press, 1987.

Hansen, D. T. *Exploring the Moral Heart of Teaching: Toward a Teacher's Creed.* New York: Teachers College Press, 2001.

Harper, C. *A Century of Public Teacher Education: The Story of State Teachers Colleges as They Evolved from the Normal Schools.* Washington, D.C.: Hugh Birch-Horace Mann Fund for the American Association of Teachers Colleges, 1939.

Harris, M. *Teaching and Religious Imagination: An Essay in the Theology of Teaching.* San Francisco: Harper & Row, 1987.

Hart, D. G., and Mohler, R. A. (eds.). *Theological Education in the Evangelical Tradition.* Grand Rapids, Mich.: Baker, 1996.

Hays, R. B. *The Moral Vision of the New Testament: Community, Cross, New Creation: A Contemporary Introduction to New Testament Ethics.* San Francisco: Harper San Francisco, 1996.

Helmreich, W. B. *The World of the Yeshiva: An Intimate Portrait of Orthodox Jewry.* New Haven, Conn.: Yale University Press, 1986.

Hemrick, E. F., and Hoge, D. R. *Seminarians in Theology: A National Profile.* Washington, D.C.: United States Catholic Conference, 1985.

Hemrick, E. F., and Hoge, D. R. *Seminary Life and Visions of the Priesthood: A National Survey of Seminarians.* Washington, D.C.: National Catholic Educational Association, Seminary Department, 1987.

Hemrick. E. F., and Walsh, J. J. *Seminarians in the Nineties: A National Study of Seminarians in Theology.* Washington, D.C.: National Catholic Educational Association, 1993.

Hemrick, E. F., and Wister, R. *Readiness for Theological Studies: A Study of Faculty Perceptions on the Readiness of Seminarians.* Washington, D.C.: National Catholic Educational Association, Seminary Department, 1993.

Hennessey, P. K. *A Concert of Charisms: Ordained Ministry in Religious Life.* New York: Paulist Press, 1997.

Hesselgrave, D. J., and Rommen, E. *Contextualization: Meanings, Methods, and Models.* Grand Rapids, Mich.: Baker, 1989.

Hiltner, S. *Preface to Pastoral Theology.* Nashville, Tenn.: Abingdon Press, 1958.

Hodgson, P. *God in History: Shapes of Freedom.* Nashville, Tenn.: Abingdon Press, 1989.

Hoffman, L. A. *The Journey Home: Discovering the Deep Spiritual Wisdom of Jewish Tradition.* Boston: Beacon Press, 2002.

Holder, A., and Dahill, L. "Teaching Christian Spirituality in Seminaries Today." *Christian Spirituality Bulletin,* 1999, 7(Fall/Winter), 9–12.

Holifield, E. B. *A History of Pastoral Care in America: From Salvation to Self-realization.* Nashville, Tenn.: Abingdon Press, 1983.

Holifield, E. B. *Theology in America: Christian Thought from the Age of the Puritans to the Civil War.* New Haven, Conn.: Yale University Press, 2003.

Holmes, U. T., III. *Ministry and Imagination.* New York: Seabury Press, 1981.

Holtz, B. "On the Training of Rabbis: Scholarship, Belief, and the Problem of Education." In N. B. Cardin and D. W. Silverman (eds.), *The Seminary at 100.* New York: Rabbinical Assembly and the Jewish Theological Seminary of America, 1987.

hooks, b. *Teaching to Transgress: Education as the Practice of Freedom.* New York: Routledge, 1994.

hooks, b. "Confronting Class in the Classroom." In A. Darder, M. Baltodano, and R. D. Torres (eds.), *The Critical Pedagogy Reader.* New York: RoutledgeFalmer, 2003.

Hopewell, J. F. "A Congregational Paradigm for Theological Education." *Theological Education,* 1984, *21*(Autumn), 60–70.

Hough, J. C., Jr. "Reform in Theological Education as a Political Task." *Theological Education,* 1981, *17*(Spring) 152–166.

Hough, J. C., Jr. "The Education of Practical Theologians." *Theological Education,* 1984, *20*(Spring), 55–84.

Hough, J. C., and Cobb, J. *Christian Identity and Theological Education.* Chico, Calif.: Scholars Press, 1985.

Hough, J. C., and Wheeler, B. G. (eds.). *Beyond Clericalism: The Congregation as a Focus for Theological Education.* Atlanta, Ga.: Scholars Press, 1988.

Huber, M., and Morreale, S. P. (eds.). *Disciplinary Styles in the Scholarship of Teaching and Learning: Exploring Common Ground.* Washington, D.C.: American Association for Higher Education and The Carnegie Foundation for the Advancement of Teaching, 2002.

Hudson, W. S. "The Ministry in the Puritan Age." In H. R. Niebuhr and D. D. Williams (eds.), *The Ministry in Historical Perspectives.* New York: Harper and Brothers, 1956.

Hudson, W. S. *Religion in America.* New York: Scribners, 1981.

Huizinga, J. *Homo Ludens: A Study of the Play Element in Culture.* Boston: Beacon Press, 1950. (Originally published 1938.)

Hunter, G. *Supervision and Education—Formation for Ministry.* Cambridge, Mass.: Episcopal Divinity School, 1982.

Hunter, J. D. *Evangelicalism: The Coming Generation.* Chicago: University of Chicago Press, 1987.

Hunter, J. D. *Culture Wars: The Struggle to Define America.* New York: Basic Books, 1990.

Inchausti, R. *Spitwad Sutras: Classroom Teaching as Sublime Vocation.* Westport, Conn.: Bergin and Garvey, 1993.

Kauffman, C. J. *Tradition and Transformation in Catholic Culture: The Priests of St. Sulpice in the United States from 1791 to the Present.* New York: Macmillan, 1988.

Kavanagh, A. *On Liturgical Theology: The Hale Memorial Lectures of Seabury-Western Theological Seminary, 1981.* Collegeville, Minn.: Liturgical Press, 1992.

Kelly, R. *Theological Education in America: A Study of One Hundred Sixty-one Theological Schools in the United States and Canada.* New York: George H. Doran Co., 1924.

Kelsey, D. H. "Reflections on Theological Education as Character Formation." *Theological Education,* 1988, 25(1), 62–75.

Kelsey, D. H. "Conjuring Future Faculties." *Theological Education,* 1991, 28(Autumn), 27–35.

Kelsey, D. H. *To Understand God Truly: What's Theological About a Theological School?* Louisville, Ky.: Westminster/John Knox Press, 1992.

Kelsey, D. H. *Between Athens and Berlin: The Theological Education Debate.* Grand Rapids, Mich.: Eerdmans, 1993.

Kelsey, D. H., and Wheeler, B. G. "Mind Reading: Notes on the Basic Issues Program. *Theological Education,* 1984, 20(Spring), 8–13.

Kelsey, D. H., and Wheeler, B. G. "New Ground: The Foundations and Future of the Theological Education Debate." In R. R. Williams (ed.), *Theology and the Interhuman.* Valley Forge, Pa.: Trinity Press International, 1995.

Killian, C. (ed.). *Daniel Payne, Sermons and Addresses: 1853–1891.* New York: Arno Press, 1972.

Kitigawa, J. M. (ed.). *Religious Studies, Theological Studies, and the University-Divinity School.* Atlanta: Scholars Press, 1992.

Kuklick, B. *Churchmen and Philosophers: From Jonathan Edwards to John Dewey.* New Haven, Conn.: Yale University Press, 1985.

Lannie, V. P. "Alienation in America: The Immigrant Catholic and Public Education in Pre–Civil War America." In W. Portier (ed.), *The Inculturation of American Catholicism, 1820–1900: Selected Historical Essays.* New York: Garland, 1988.

Larsen, E., and Shopshire, J. "A Profile of Contemporary Seminarians." *Theological Education,* 1988, 24(Spring), 10–136.

LaRue, C. J. *The Heart of Black Preaching.* Louisville, Ky.: Westminster/John Knox Press, 2000.

Lave, J. "Teaching, as Learning, in Practice." *Mind, Culture, and Activity,* 1996, 3(3), 149–164.

Lave, J., and Wenger, E. *Situated Learning: Legitimate Peripheral Participation.* Cambridge, UK: Cambridge University Press, 1991.

Lebeau, W. "Rabbinic Education for the 21st Century." *Sh'ma: A Journal of Jewish Responsibility,* 1997, 27(527), 6–8.

Lederhendler, E. "The Ongoing Dialogue: The Seminary and the Challenge of Israel." In J. Wertheimer (ed.), *Tradition Renewed: A History of the*

Jewish Theological Seminary, Vol. 2. New York: Jewish Theological Seminary, 1997.

Lee, J. M. *The Shape of Religious Instruction: A Social Science Approach.* Dayton, Ohio: Pflaum, 1971.

Lehman, M. "For the Love of Talmud: Reflections on the Study of Bava Metzia, Perek 2." *The Journal of Jewish Education,* 2002, 68(1), 87–104.

Lehman, M., and Kress, J. "The Babylonian Talmud in Cognitive Perspective: Reflections on the Nature of the Bavli and Its Pedagogical Importance." *Journal of Jewish Education,* 2003, 69(1), 58–78.

Leistyna, P., and Woodrum, A. "Context and Culture: What Is Critical Pedagogy?" In P. Leistyna, A. Woodrum, and S. Sherblom (eds.), *Breaking Free: The Transformative Power of Critical Pedagogy.* Cambridge, Mass.: Harvard Educational Review, 1996.

Lesher, W. E. *Theological Education: Index to the Five Issues on Globalization in Theological Education.* Pittsburgh, Pa.: Association of Theological Schools, 1994.

Liebman, C. S. "The Training of American Rabbis." In C. S. Liebman (ed.), *Aspects of Religious Behavior of American Jews.* New York: Ktav Publishing House, 1974.

Lincoln, C. E., and Mamiya, L. H. *The Black Church in the African-American Experience.* Durham, N.C.: Duke University Press, 1990.

Lindbeck, G. "Spiritual Formation and Theological Education." *Theological Education,* 1988, 24(Supplement 1), 10–32.

Lindbeck, G., Deutsch, K. W., and Glazer, N. *University Divinity Schools: A Report on Ecclesiastically Independent Theological Education.* New York: Rockefeller Foundation, 1976.

Lischer, R. *Open Secrets: A Spiritual Journey Through a Country Church.* New York: Doubleday, 2001.

Little, S. *To Set One's Heart: Belief and Teaching in the Church.* Atlanta: John Knox Press, 1983.

Lynn, R. W. "Notes Toward a History: Theological Encyclopedia and the Evolution of Protestant Seminary Curriculum, 1808–1868." *Theological Education,* 1981, 17(2), 118–144.

MacIntyre, A. C. *After Virtue: A Study in Moral Theory.* Notre Dame, Ind.: University of Notre Dame Press, 1984.

Magolda, M. B. *Knowing and Reasoning in College: Gender-related Patterns in Students' Intellectual Development.* San Francisco: Jossey-Bass, 1992.

Mamiya, L. H. "A Black Church Challenge and Perspective." In R. Petersen (ed.), *Christianity and Civil Society: Theological Education for Public Life.* Maryknoll, N.Y.: Orbis Books, 1995.

Marsden, G. *Reforming Fundamentalism: Fuller Seminary and the New Evangelicalism.* Grand Rapids, Mich.: Eerdmans, 1987.

Marsden, G. *The Soul of the American University: From Protestant Establishment to Established Nonbelief.* New York: Oxford, 1994.

Marsh, C. *God's Long Summer: Stories of Faith and Civil Rights.* Princeton, N.J.: Princeton University Press, 1999.

Martin, J. P. "Competence Model Education." *Theological Education,* 1977 *13*(3), 125–136.

Matthews, L. *Memoir of the Life and Character of Ebenezer Porter, D.D., Late President of the Theological Seminary, Andover.* Boston: Perkins and Marvin, 1837.

McCall, R. D. "Do This: The Liturgy as Enactment." Doctoral dissertation, Graduate Theological Union, University of California, Berkeley, 1998.

Meland, B. E. *Faith and Culture.* Carbondale: Southern Illinois University Press, 1972.

Meye, R. P. "Theological Education as Character Formation." *Theological Education,* 1988, 24(Supplement 1), 96–126.

Meyer, M. *Response to Modernity: A History of the Reform Movement in Judaism.* New York: Oxford, 1988.

Miller, G., and Lynn, R. "Christian Theological Education." In G. Miller and R. Lynn (eds.), *Encyclopedia of the American Religius Experience: Studies of Traditions and Movements,* Vol. 3. New York: Scribners, 1988.

Miller, G. T. *Piety and Intellect: The Aims and Purposes of Ante-Bellum Theological Education.* Atlanta, Ga.: Scholars Press, 1990.

Ministry in Context: The Third Mandate Programme of the Theological Education Fund (1970–77). Bromley, England: Theological Education Fund, 1972.

Mintz, A. "The Divided Fate of Hebrew and Hebrew Culture at the Seminary." In J. Wertheimer (ed.), *Tradition Renewed: A History of the Jewish Theological Seminary.* New York: Jewish Theological Seminary, 1997.

Moore, M. E. *Teaching from the Heart: Theology and Educational Method.* Minneapolis: Augsburg Fortress, 1991.

Moss, R. V. "Contexts for Theological Education in the Next Decade." *Theological Education,* 1968, *V*(1:3), 3–14.

Mouw, R. J. "Spiritual Identity and Churchly Praxis." *Theological Education,* 1987, *21*(Supplement), 88–112.

Moynihan, J. H. *The Life of Archbishop John Ireland.* New York: Harper and Brothers, 1953.

Mudge, L. S. "Thinking About the Church's Thinking: Toward a Theological Ethnography." *Theological Education,* 1984, *20*(Spring), 42–54.

Mudge, L. S., and Poling, J. N. (eds.). *Formation and Reflection: The Promise of Practical Theology.* Philadelphia: Fortress Press, 1987.

Neumark, H. *Breathing Space: A Spiritual Journey in the South Bronx.* Boston: Beacon Press, 2003.

Neusner, J. *Analysis and Argumentation in Rabbinic Judaism.* Lanham, Md.: University Press of America, 2003.

Niebuhr, H. R. *Christ and Culture.* San Francisco: Harper and Brothers, 2001. (Originally published 1951.)

Niebuhr, H. R., and Williams, D. D. *The Ministry in Historical Perspectives.* New York: HarperCollins, 1956.

Niebuhr, H. R., Williams, D. D., and Gustafson, J. M. *The Advancement of Theological Education.* New York: Harper, 1957.

Ochs, C. *Our Lives as Torah: God in Our Own Stories.* San Francisco: Jossey-Bass, 2001.

O'Connell, M. R. *John Ireland and the American Catholic Church.* St. Paul: Minnesota Historical Society Press, 1988.

O'Malley, J.S.J. "Diocesan and Religious Models of Priestly Formation: Historical Perspectives." In R. Wister (ed.), *Priests: Identity and Ministry.* Wilmington, Del.: Michael Glazier, 1990.

Osmer, R. R. "Teaching as Practical Theology." In J. Seymour and D. E. Miller (eds.), *Theological Approaches to Christian Education.* Nashville, Tenn.: Abingdon Press, 1990.

Osmer, R. R., and Schweitzer, F. L. (eds.). *Developing a Public Faith: New Directions in Practical Theology.* St. Louis, Mo.: Chalice Press, 2003.

Palmer, P. J. *The Courage to Teach: Exploring the Inner Landscape of a Teacher's Life.* San Francisco: Jossey-Bass, 1998.

Palmer, P. J., Wheeler, B. G., and Fowler, J. W. (eds.). *Caring for the Commonweal: Education for Religious and Public Life.* Macon, Ga.: Mercer University Press, 1990.

Parsons, T. "Professions." In D. Sills (ed.), *International Encyclopedia of the Social Sciences,* Vol. 12. New York: Macmillan-Free Press, 1968.

Parsons, T., and Platt, G. M. *The American University.* Cambridge, Mass.: Harvard University Press, 1973.

Payne, D. A. "The Christian Ministry: Its Moral and Intellectual Character." 1859. In C. Killian (ed.), *Sermons and Address, 1853–1891.* New York: Arno Press, 1972.

Payne, D. A. *Annual Report and Retrospection of the First Decade of Wilberforce University.* Cincinnati: B. W. Arnett, 1873.

Payne, D. A. "The History, Origin and Development of Wilberforce University." In D. Smith (ed.), *The Biography of Rev. David Smith of the A.M.E. Church.* Xenia, Ohio: Xenia Gazette Office, 1881.

Payne, D. A. *Recollections of Seventy Years.* Nashville, Tenn.: Publishing House of the A.M.E. Sunday School Union, 1888.

Payne, D. A. "Essay on the Education of Ministry." In C. Killian (ed.), *Daniel Payne, Sermons and Addresses, 1853–1891.* New York: Arno Press, 1972.

Percy, M. "Sweet Rapture: Subliminal Eroticism in Postmodern Charismatic Worship." In R. Hannaford and J. Jobling (ed.), *Theology and the Body: Gender, Text, and Ideology.* Leominster, UK: Gracewing/Canterbury Books, 1999.

Peshkin, A. *God's Choice: The Total World of a Fundamentalist Christian School.* Chicago: University of Chicago Press, 1986.

Philipson, D. *Hebrew Union College Jubilee Volume, 1875–1925.* Cincinnati: Hebrew Union College, 1925.

Poling, J. N., and Miller, D. E. *Foundations for a Practical Theology of Ministry.* Nashville, Tenn.: Abingdon Press, 1985.

Pollock, J. C. *Moody: A Biographical Portrait of the Pacesetter in Modern Mass Evangelism.* New York: Macmillan, 1963.

Porpora, D. V. *Landscapes of the Soul: The Loss of Moral Meaning in American Life.* Oxford, UK: Oxford University Press, 2001.

Potvin, R. H., and Suziedelis, A. *Seminarians of the Sixties: A National Survey.* Washington, D.C.: CARA, 1969.

Pyle, W. T., and Seals, M. A. *Experiencing Ministry Supervision: A Field-Based Approach.* Nashville, Tenn.: Broadman and Holman Publishers, 1995.

Rahner, K. *Foundations of Christian Faith: An Introduction to the Idea of Christianity.* New York: Seabury Press, 1978.

Raphael, M. L. *Profiles in American Judaism: The Reform, Conservative, Orthodox, and Reconstructionist Traditions in Historical Perspective.* San Francisco: Harper and Row, 1985.

Raphael, M. L. *Judaism in America.* New York: Columbia University Press, 2003.

Reher, M. "Pope Leo XII and Americanism." In W. Portier (ed.), *The Inculturation of American Catholicism, 1820–1900: Selected Historical Essays.* New York: Garland, 1988.

Rhodes, L. N., and Richardson, N. D. *Mending Severed Connections.* San Francisco: San Francisco Network Ministries, 1991.

Robertson, R. "Glocalization." In M. Featherstone, S. Lash, and R. Robertson (eds.), *Global Modernities.* London: Sage, 1995.

Ropers-Huilman, B. *Feminist Teaching in Theory and Practice: Situating Power and Knowledge in Poststructural Classrooms.* New York: Teachers College Press, 1998.

Rosov, W. "Practicing the Presence of God: Spiritual Formation in a Rabbinical School." Doctoral dissertation, School of Education, Stanford University, 2001.

Roth, J. *The Halakhic Process: A Systemic Analysis.* New York: Jewish Theological Seminary of America, 1986.

Sanders, C. *Ministry at the Margins: The Prophetic Mission of Women, Youth, and the Poor.* Downers Grove, Ill.: InterVarsity Press, 1997.

Sarna, J. "Two Traditions of Seminary Scholarship." In J. Wertheimer (ed.), *Tradition Renewed: A History of the Jewish Theological Seminary.* New York: Jewish Theological Seminary, 1997.

Schechner, R. *Performance Theory.* (Rev. ed.) New York: RoutledgeFalmer, 1988.

Schechter, S. *Seminary Addresses and Other Papers.* Cincinnati, Ohio: Ark Publishing Co, 1915.

Schechter, S. *Fragments of the Cairo Geniza.* Ann Arbor: Michigan University Press, 1927.

Schneiders, S. M. *Finding the Treasure: Locating Catholic Religious Life in a New Ecclesial and Cultural Context.* New York: Paulist Press, 2000.

Schneiders, S. M. "The Study of Christian Spirituality: Contours and Dynamics of a Discipline." In E. A. Dreyer and M. S. Burrows (eds.), *Minding the Spirit: The Study of Christian Spirituality.* Baltimore/London: Johns Hopkins University Press, 2005.

Schner, G. P. "Formation as a Unifying Concept of Theological Education." *Theological Education,* 1985, *21*(Spring), 94–113.

Schner, G. P. *Education for Ministry: Reform and Renewal in Theological Education.* Kansas City, Mo.: Sheed and Ward, 1993.

Schön, D. A. *Educating the Reflective Practitioner: Toward a New Design for Teaching and Learning in the Professions.* San Francisco: Jossey-Bass, 1987.

Schön, D. A. *The Reflective Practitioner: How Professionals Think in Action.* New York: Basic Books, 1983.

Schreiter, R. J. *Constructing Local Theologies.* Maryknoll, N.Y.: Orbis Books, 1985.

Schreiter, R. J. *The New Catholicity: Theology Between the Global and the Local.* Maryknoll, N.Y.: Orbis Books, 1997.

Schuller, D. S., Galloway, A. E., and O'Brien, M. K. *Readiness for Ministry.* Vandalia, Ohio: Association of Theological Schools in the United States and Canada, 1975.

Schuller, D. S., and others. *Readiness for Ministry.* Vandalia, Ohio: Association of Theological Schools in the United States and Canada, 1976.

Schultze, Q. J. *Habits of a High-Tech Heart: Living Virtuously in the Information Age.* Grand Rapids, Mich.: Baker Books, 2002.

Schuth, K. *Reason for Hope: The Futures of Roman Catholic Theologates.* Wilmington, Del.: Michael Glazier, 1989.

Schuth, K. *Seminaries, Theologates, and the Future of Church Ministry: An Analysis of Trends and Transitions.* Collegeville, Minn.: Liturgical Press, 1999.

Schwartz, S. R. "The Schechter Faculty: The Seminary and *Wissenchaft des Judentums* in America." In J. Wertheimer (ed.), *Tradition Renewed: A History of the Jewish Theological Seminary,* Vol. 1. New York: Jewish Theological Seminary of America, 1997.

Schwarzfuchs, S. *A Concise History of the Rabbinate.* Oxford: Blackwell, 1993.

Seymour, J., and Wehrheim, C. A. "Faith Seeking Understanding: Interpretation as a Task of Religious Education." In J. Seymour and D. Miller (eds.), *Contemporary Approaches to Christian Education.* Nashville, Tenn.: Abingdon Press, 1982.

Shor, I., and Freire, P. *A Pedagogy for Liberation: Dialogues on Transforming Education.* South Hadley, Mass.: Bergin and Garvey, 1987.

Shriver, D. W. "The Globalization of Theological Education: Setting the Task." *Theological Education,* 1986, 22(Spring), 7–18.

Shulman, L. S. *The Wisdom of Practice: Essays on Teaching, Learning, and Learning to Teach.* San Francisco: Jossey-Bass, 2004.

Shulman, L. S. "Searching for Signature Pedagogies: Teaching and Learning in the Professions." *Daedelus,* forthcoming.

Sloan, D. *Faith and Knowledge: Mainline Protestantism and American Higher Education.* Louisville, Ky.: Westminster/John Knox Press, 1994.

Stackhouse, M. L. "Contextualization and Theological Education." *Theological Education,* 1986, 23(Autumn), 67–82.

Stackhouse, M. L. *Apologia: Contextualization, Globalization, and Mission in Theological Education.* Grand Rapids, Mich.: Eerdmans, 1988.

Sterk, A. (ed.). *Religion, Scholarship, and Higher Education: Perspectives, Models, and Future Prospects.* Notre Dame, Ind.: University of Notre Dame Press, 2002.

Stone, H. W., and Duke, J. O. *How to Think Theologically.* Minneapolis: Fortress Press, 1996.

Stott, J.R.W. "Foreword." In R. T. Coote and J.R.W. Stott (eds.), *Down to Earth: Studies in Christianity and Culture: The Papers of the Lausanne Consultation on Gospel and Culture.* Grand Rapids, Mich.: Eerdmans, 1980.

Sullivan, W. M. *Work and Integrity: The Crisis and Promise of Professionalism in America.* San Francisco: Jossey-Bass, 2005.

Tanner, D., and Tanner, L. *Curriculum Development: Theory into Practice.* Englewood Cliffs, N.J.: Prentice-Hall, 1995.

Taylor, M. K. *Remembering Esperanza: A Cultural-Political Theology for North American Praxis.* Maryknoll, N.Y.: Orbis Books, 1990.

Thurman, H. *The Creative Encounter: An Interpretation of Religion and the Social Witness*. New York: HarperCollins, 1954.

Tomlinson, J. *Globalization and Culture*. Chicago: University of Chicago Press, 1999.

Tracy, D. *The Analogical Imagination: Christian Theology and the Culture of Pluralism*. New York: Crossroad, 1986.

Tracy, D. *Plurality and Ambiguity: Hermeneutics, Religion, Hope*. San Francisco: Harper San Francisco, 1987.

Tracy, D. "Can Virtue Be Taught? Education, Character and the Soul." *Theological Education*, 1988, 24(Supplement), 35–52.

Vella, J. K. *Learning to Listen, Learning to Teach: The Power of Dialogue in Educating Adults*. San Francisco: Jossey-Bass, 1994.

Volf, M., and Bass, D. C. (eds.). *Practicing Theology: Beliefs and Practices in Christian Life*. Grand Rapids, Mich.: Eerdmans, 2002.

Wangler, T. E. "John Ireland and the Origins of Liberal Catholicism in the United States." In W. Portier (ed.), *The Inculturation of American Catholicism, 1820–1900: Selected Historical Essays*. New York: Garland, 1988.

Warford, M. L. *Practical Wisdom: On Theological Teaching and Learning*. New York: Peter Lang, 2004.

Washington, B. T. *Tuskegee and Its People: Their Ideals and Achievements*. New York: D. Appleton and Company, 1905.

Welch, S. "An Ethic of Solidarity and Difference." In H. A. Giroux (ed.), *Postmodernism, Feminism, and Cultural Politics: Redrawing Educational Boundaries*. Albany, N.Y.: State University of New York Press, 1991.

Wells, D. *God in the Wasteland: The Reality of Truth in a World of Fading Dreams*. Grand Rapids, Mich.: Eerdmans, 1994.

Wenger, E. *Communities of Practice: Learning, Meaning, and Identity*. New York: Cambridge University Press, 1998.

Wenger, E., McDermott, R., and Snyder, W. M. *Cultivating Communities of Practice: A Guide to Managing Knowledge*. Boston: Harvard Business School Press, 2002.

Wenzke, A. S. *Timothy Dwight (1752–1817)*. Lewiston, N.Y.: Edwin Mellen Press, 1989.

Wertheimer, J. (ed.). *Tradition Renewed: A History of Jewish Theological Seminary*, Vols. 1 and 2. New York: Jewish Theological Seminary of America, 1997.

Wheeler, B. G. *Is There a Problem: Theological Students and Religious Leadership for the Future*. Auburn Studies 8. New York: Auburn Theological Seminary, 2001.

Wheeler, B. G., Miller, S. L. and Schuth, K. *Signs of the Times: Present and Future Theological Faculty.* Auburn Studies 10. New York: Auburn Theological Seminary, 2005.

White, E. "Puritan Preaching and the Authority of God. In *Preaching in American History: Selected Issues in the American Pulpit, 1630–1967.* Edited by D. Holland, Nashville, Tenn.: Abingdon Press, 1969.

White, J. M. *The Diocesan Seminary in the United States: A History from the 1780s to the Present.* Notre Dame, Ind.: University of Notre Dame Press, 1989.

Whitehead, J. D., and Whitehead, E. E. *Method in Ministry: Theological Reflection and Christian Ministry.* Kansas City, Mo.: Sheed & Ward, 1995.

Williams, D. D. *The Andover Liberals: A Study in American Theology.* New York: King's Crown Press, 1941.

Williams, R. *Retooling: A Historian Confronts Technological Change.* Cambridge, Mass.: MIT Press, 2002.

Wilmore, G. S. (ed.). "Black Pastors/White Professors: An Experiment in Dialogic Education." *Theological Education,* 1980, *16*(1)(Special Issue).

Wilson, R. "Unity and Diversity in the Book of Kings." In S. Olyan and R. C. Culley (eds.), *A Wise and Discerning Mind: Essays in Honor of Burke O. Long.* Providence, R.I.: Brown Judaic Studies, 2000.

Wood, C. M. *Vision and Discernment: An Orientation in Theological Study.* Decatur, Ga.: Scholars Press, 1985.

Woods, L. *History of the Andover Theological Seminary.* Boston: James R. Osgood and Company, 1885.

Ziegler, J. *ATS Through Two Decades: Reflections on Theological Education, 1960–1980.* Vandalia, Ohio: ATS, 1984.

Ziegler, J., and Deem, W. H. *Theological Education in the 1970s: A Report of the Resources Planning Commission.* Dayton, Ohio: American Association of Theological Schools, 1969.

Ziegler, J., and others. "Theological Education and Liberation Theology: A Symposium." *Theological Education,* 1979, *16*(1).

NAME INDEX

A

Abbs, P., 40, 64
Ackerman, D. M., 255
Addams, J., 201
Adler, R., 24, 26
Ahlstrom, S. A., 194, 197, 267
Aleshire, D. O., 188
Alexander, H. A., 65
Alinsky, S. D., 151, 155
Andrews, D., 169
Appadurai, A., 264, 271
Appleby, R. S., 253
Aquinas, Thomas, 98
Argyris, C., 38, 126, 345
Atkinson, T., 37, 66
Ayers, W., 37

B

Bain, K., 356
Baltodano, M., 155
Banks, R., 241
Banner, J. M., Jr., 37
Barnard, H., 202
Barth, K., 267
Bartlett, D., 76, 85–89, 91–92, 93, 94, 96, 97, 172, 183
Bass, D. C., 27, 29–30, 37, 90, 369
Baum, W. W., 256, 257
Baxter, R., 196
Beaumont, E., 16
Beecher, L., 194
Behan, W. P., 268
Bell, C., 38
Bellah, R., 261, 364, 381
Benner, P., 319

Benson, R., 81–85, 93, 95, 96, 97, 98, 183, 342, 365, 370
Bentwich, N., 225, 226, 227
Bergant, D., 41, 47, 49, 50, 53, 54, 56, 59–60, 61–62, 69, 98, 129, 183, 365, 366
Berkovits, E., 230
Bess, J. L., 37
Blodgett, B., 301–302, 309–310, 317, 320
Boal, A., 185
Bond, L., 15
Bons-Storm, R., 255
Bourdieu, P., 23, 38, 50, 151, 171
Boyle, H. C., 37
Brekke, M., 254
Brerton, V., 201, 205, 207, 239
Brookfield, S., 92–93
Brown, M., 209
Brown, R. M., 42
Brown, W. A., 253
Browning, D. S., 252, 261, 262
Bruner, J., 29, 38
Brunner, E., 267
Burrows, M. S., 259
Bushnell, H., 198
Butler, J., 41–42, 47, 49, 50, 51, 53, 54, 56, 61, 62, 63, 187, 342, 370
Bycel, L., 228, 229, 234, 254
Byrne, P., 253

C

Caillois, R., 186
Cairns,, 256
Caldwell, M., 218–219

SUBJECT INDEX

A

Academic uses of God-language, 361–362

Academy of Jewish Science, 225

Action: critical reflection and, 148–149; practical reasoning and congruent, 345

African Americans. *See also* Schools of emancipation: first seminaries for, 207–208; seminary studies for, 212–213, 241–243; studying historical dialogue of black women, 147–148

African Methodist Episcopal (AME) Church: origins of, 207; schools opened by, 242

Agency of contexts, 129–130

Alignment: creating with spiritual practices, 292–294; defining, 324

American Missionary Society, 208

Americanists, 243–244

Andover Theological Seminary, 194–197

Apprenticeships. *See also* Field education: cognitive, 25; field education and, 298; identity formation and student, 123–125; participating with teacher's practices as, 28–29, 30; practical, 5–6; professional identity and normative, 7–8, 378; training in liturgical performance, 159–161, 283–284; types of, 5

Aristotle, 23

Ashmun Institute, 207

Association of Theological Schools (ATS), 65

Athens and Berlin (Kelsey), 47

Atlantic Philanthropies, 383

Audience, student as, 170–173, 180

B

Being There (Carroll and others), 188

Belonging, 35–36

Ben Sira, 227

Benedictines, 232

Between the Bible and the Church (Barlett), 86

Bible schools. *See* Religious training schools

Biblical texts. *See also* Canonical texts: framework for exploring, 331–336; interpreting, 85–89, 364–365; preparing sermons from, 86–89; teaching practices for, 40–42, 59–60; teaching practices for reading, 40–42, 59–60; understanding religion through study of, 78; varying curricular approaches to, 50–51

Birth of a Nation, 70

Black clergy, 212–213, 242. *See also* African Americans; Schools of emancipation

C

Campus ministries, 252

Campus setting and teaching practices, 44–46

Canonical texts: framework for exploring, 331–336; heightening awareness of, 137; interpreting,